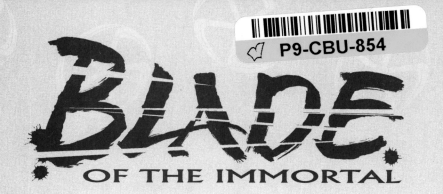

OF THE IMMORTAL

Secrets

publisher
Mike Richardson

series editors
Mike Hansen & Tim Ervin-Gore

collection editor
Chris Warner

collection designer
Debra Bailey

English-language version produced by Studio Proteus for Dark Horse Comics, Inc.

BLADE OF THE IMMORTAL VOL. 10: SECRETS
Blade of the Immortal © 2001, 2002 by Hiroaki Samura. All rights reserved. First published in Japan in 1998 by Kodansha Ltd., Tokyo. English translation rights arranged through Kodansha Ltd. This English-language edition © 2001, 2002 by Studio Proteus and Dark Horse Comics, Inc. All other material © 2002 by Dark Horse Comics, Inc. All rights reserved. No portion of this publication may be reproduced, in any form or by any means, without the express written permission of the copyright holders. Names, characters, places, and incidents featured in this publication either are the product of the author's imagination or are used fictitiously. Any resemblance to actual persons (living or dead), events, institutions, or locales, without satiric intent, is coincidental. Dark Horse Comics® and the Dark Horse logo are trademarks of Dark Horse Comics, Inc., registered in various categories and countries. All rights reserved.

This volume collects issues fifty-eight through sixty-five of the Dark Horse comic-book series, *Blade of the Immortal*.

Published by
Dark Horse Comics, Inc.
10956 SE Main Street
Milwaukie, OR 97222

www.darkhorse.com

To find a comics shop in your area, call the
Comic Shop Locator Service toll-free at 1-888-266-4226.

First edition: June 2002
ISBN: 1-56971-746-X

1 3 5 7 9 10 8 6 4 2

Printed in Canada

BLADE
OF THE IMMORTAL

art and story
HIROAKI SAMURA

translation
Dana Lewis & Toren Smith

lettering and retouch
Tomoko Saito

Secrets

DARK HORSE COMICS®

ABOUT THE TRANSLATION

The Swastika

The main character in *Blade of the Immortal*, Manji, has taken the "crux gammata" as both his name and his personal symbol. This symbol is also known as the *swastika*, a name derived from the Sanskrit *svastika* (meaning "welfare," from *su* — "well" + *asti* "he is"). As a symbol of prosperity and good fortune, the swastika was widely used throughout the ancient world (for example, appearing often on Mesopotamian coinage), including North and South America and has been used in Japan as a symbol of Buddhism since ancient times. To be precise, the symbol generally used by Japanese Buddhists is the *sauvastika*, which moves in a counterclockwise direction and is called the *manji* in Japanese. The arms of the *swastika*, which point in a clockwise direction, are generally considered a solar symbol. It was this version (the *hakenkreuz*) that was perverted by the Nazis. The *sauvastika* generally stands for night, and often for magical practices. It is important that readers understand that the swastika has ancient and honorable origins, and it is those that apply to this story, which takes place in the 18th century [ca. 1782–3]. *There is no anti-Semitic or pro-Nazi meaning behind the use of the symbol in this story. Those meanings did not exist until after 1910.*

The Artwork

The creator of *Blade of the Immortal* requested that we make an effort to avoid mirror-imaging his artwork. Normally, Westernized manga are first copied in a mirror-image in order to facilitate the left-to-right reading of the pages. However, Mr. Samura decided that he would rather see his pages reversed via the technique of cutting up the panels and re-pasting them in reverse order. While we feel that this often leads to problems in panel-to-panel continuity, we place primary importance on the wishes of the creator. Therefore, most of *Blade of the Immortal* has been produced using the "cut and paste" technique. There are, of course, some sequences where it was impossible to do this, and mirror-imaged panels or pages were used.

The Sound Effects & Dialogue

Since some of Mr. Samura's sound effects are integral parts of the illustrations, we decided to leave those in their original Japanese. We hope readers will view the unretouched sound effects as essential portions of Mr. Samura's extraordinary artwork. In addition, Mr. Samura's treatment of dialogue is quite different from that featured in typical samurai manga and is considered to be one of the features that has made *Blade* such a hit in Japan. Mr. Samura has mixed a variety of linguistic styles in this fantasy story, with some characters speaking in the mannered style of old Japan while others speak as if they were street-corner punks from a bad area of modern-day Tokyo. The anachronistic slang used by some of the characters in the English translation reflects the unusual mix of speech patterns from the original Japanese text.

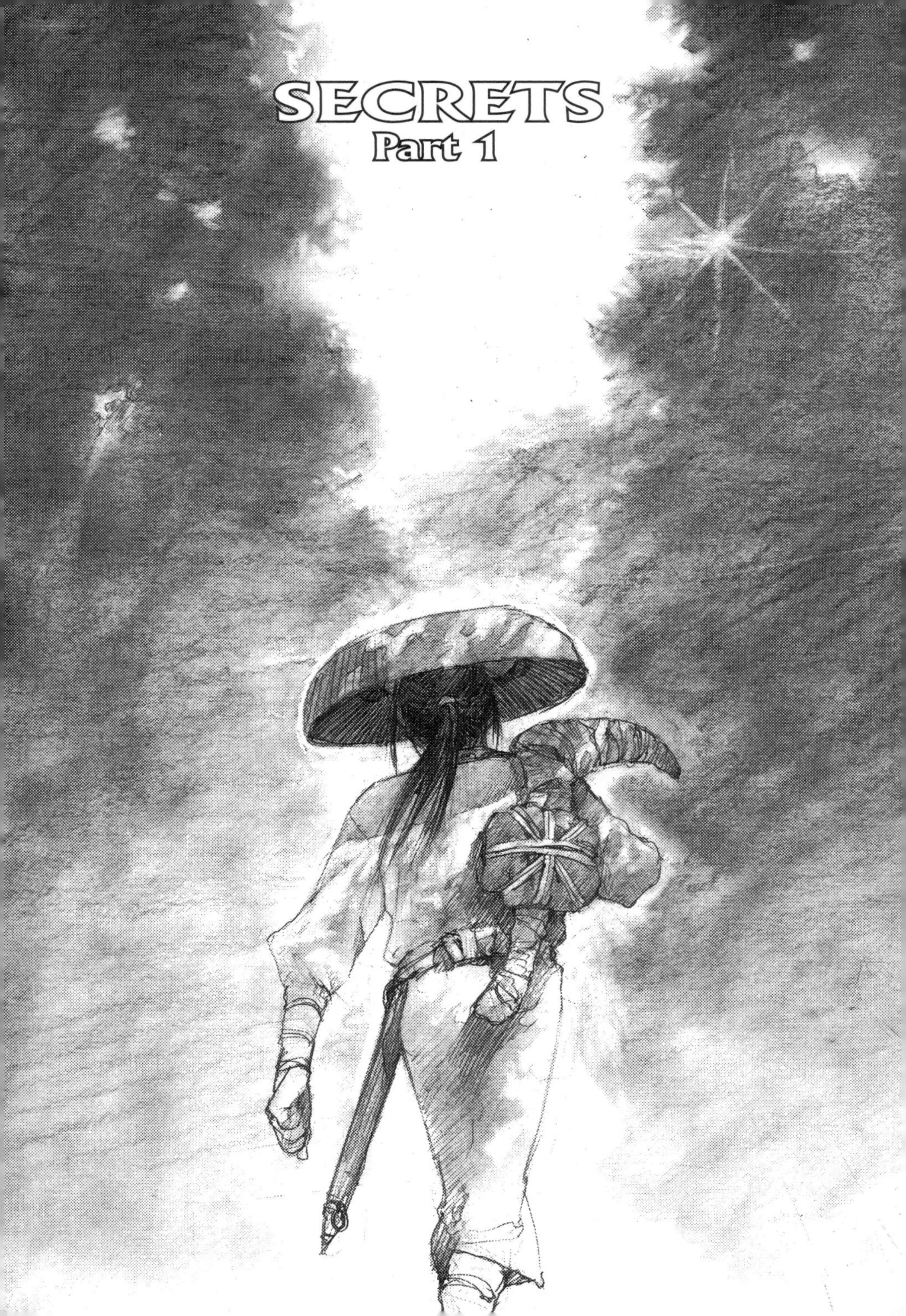
SECRETS
Part 1

KAGA

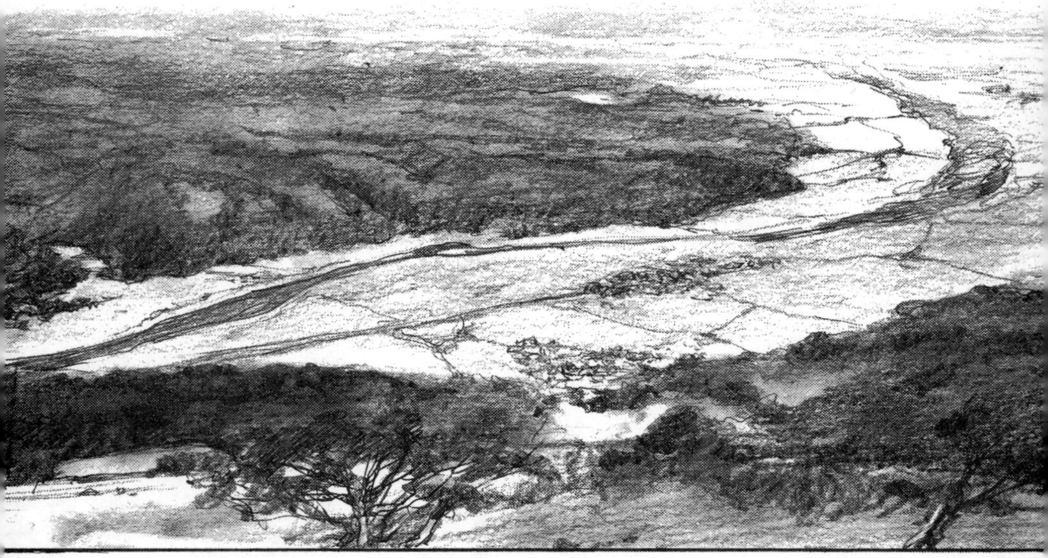

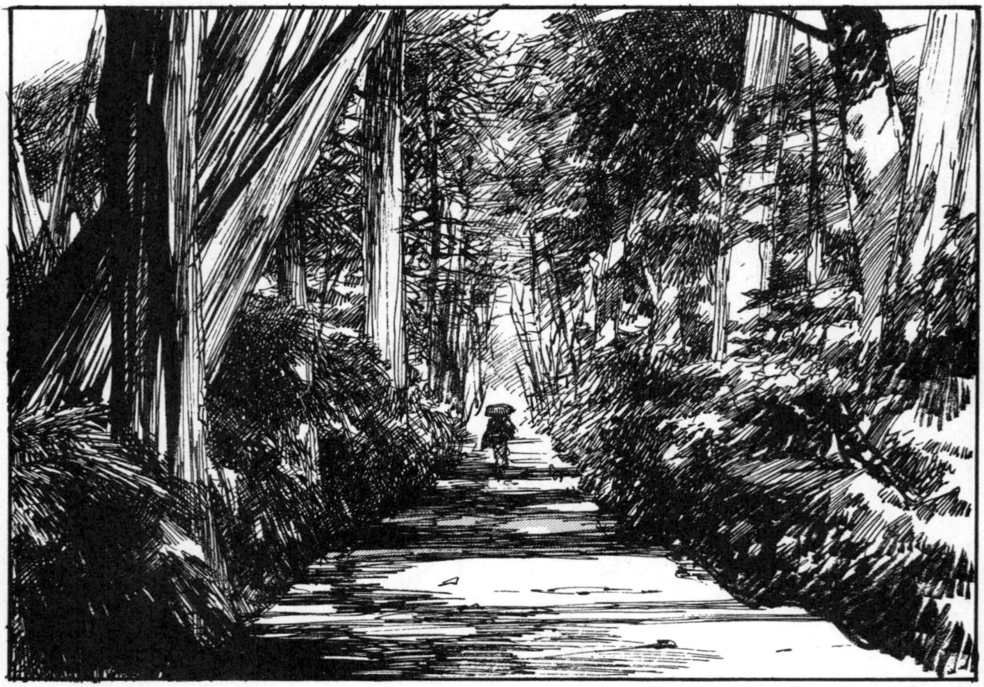

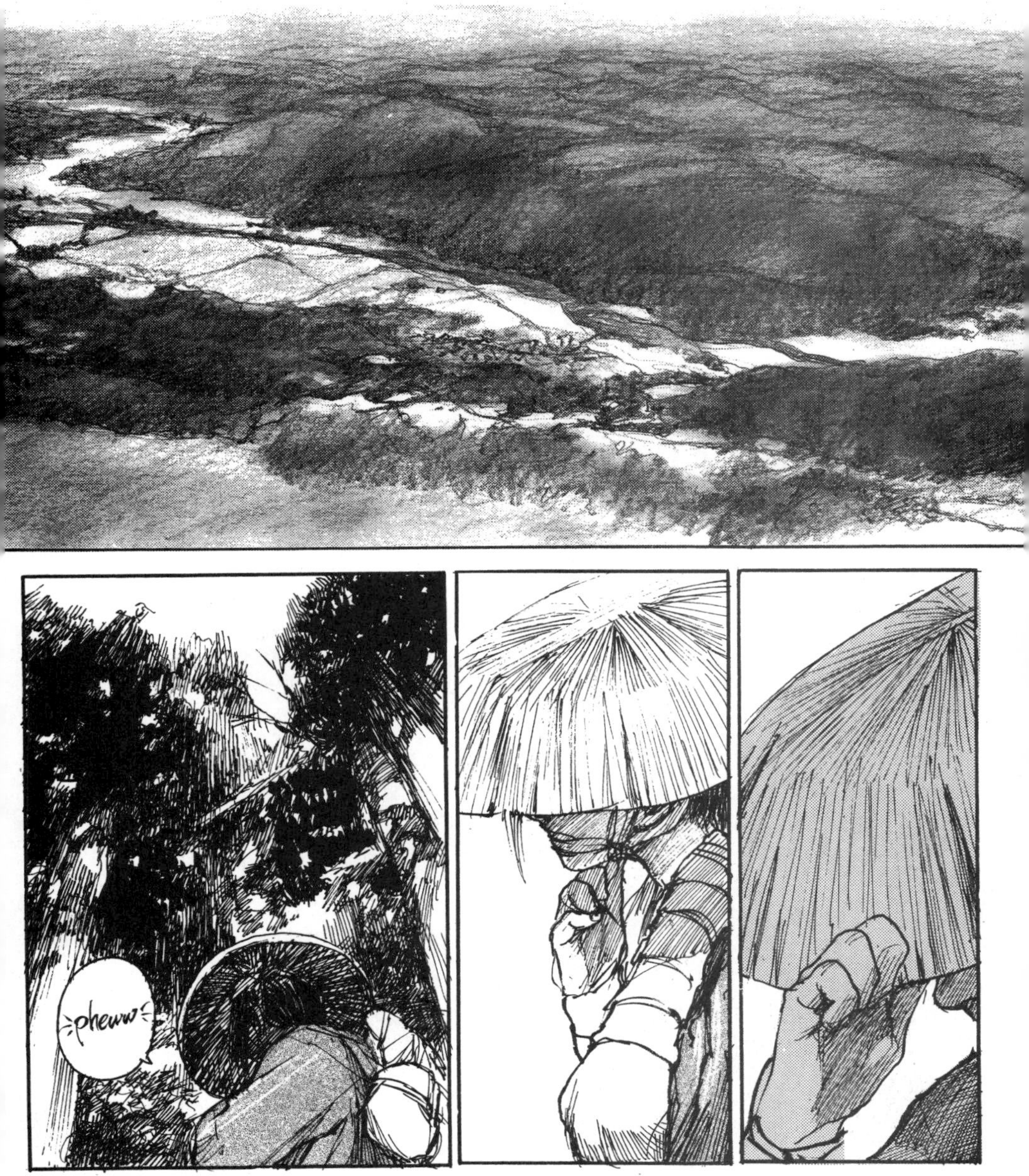
pheww

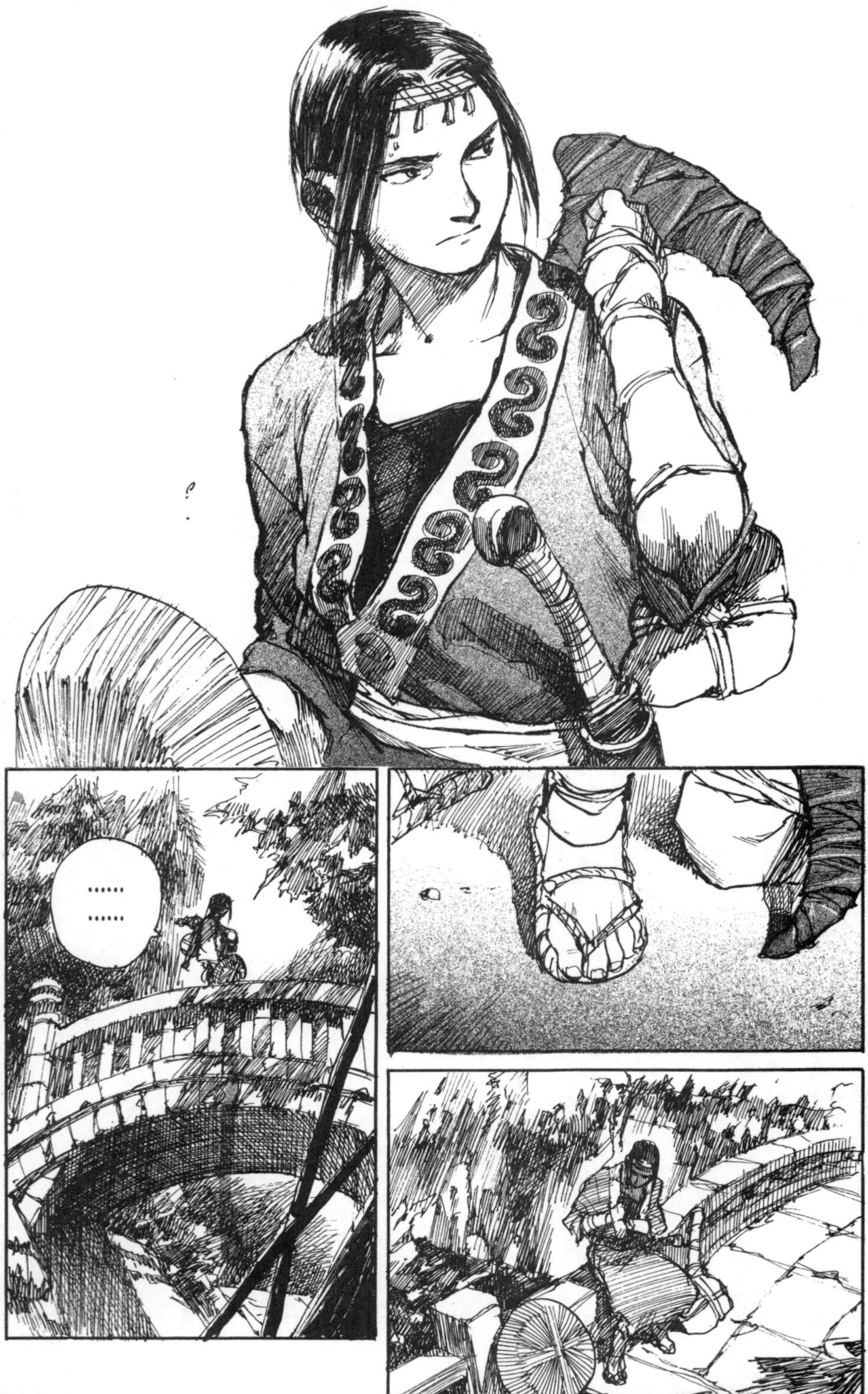
……
……

I SHOULD HAVE ASKED BACK AT THAT FARM-HOUSE...

HMM... THAT'S PROBABLY THE "PATH TO THE SHRINE."

!!

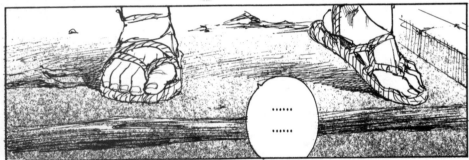

......

......

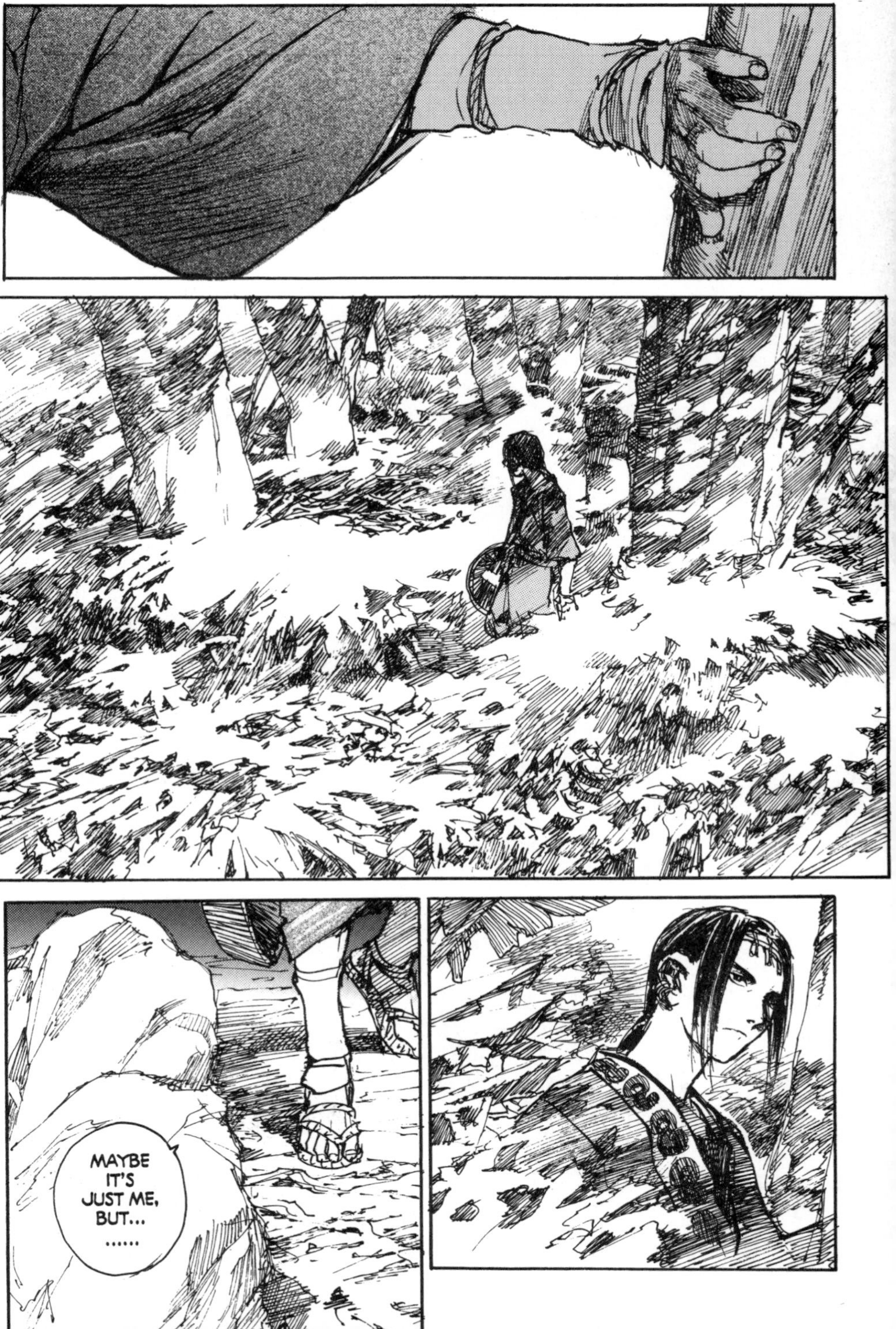
MAYBE IT'S JUST ME, BUT... ......

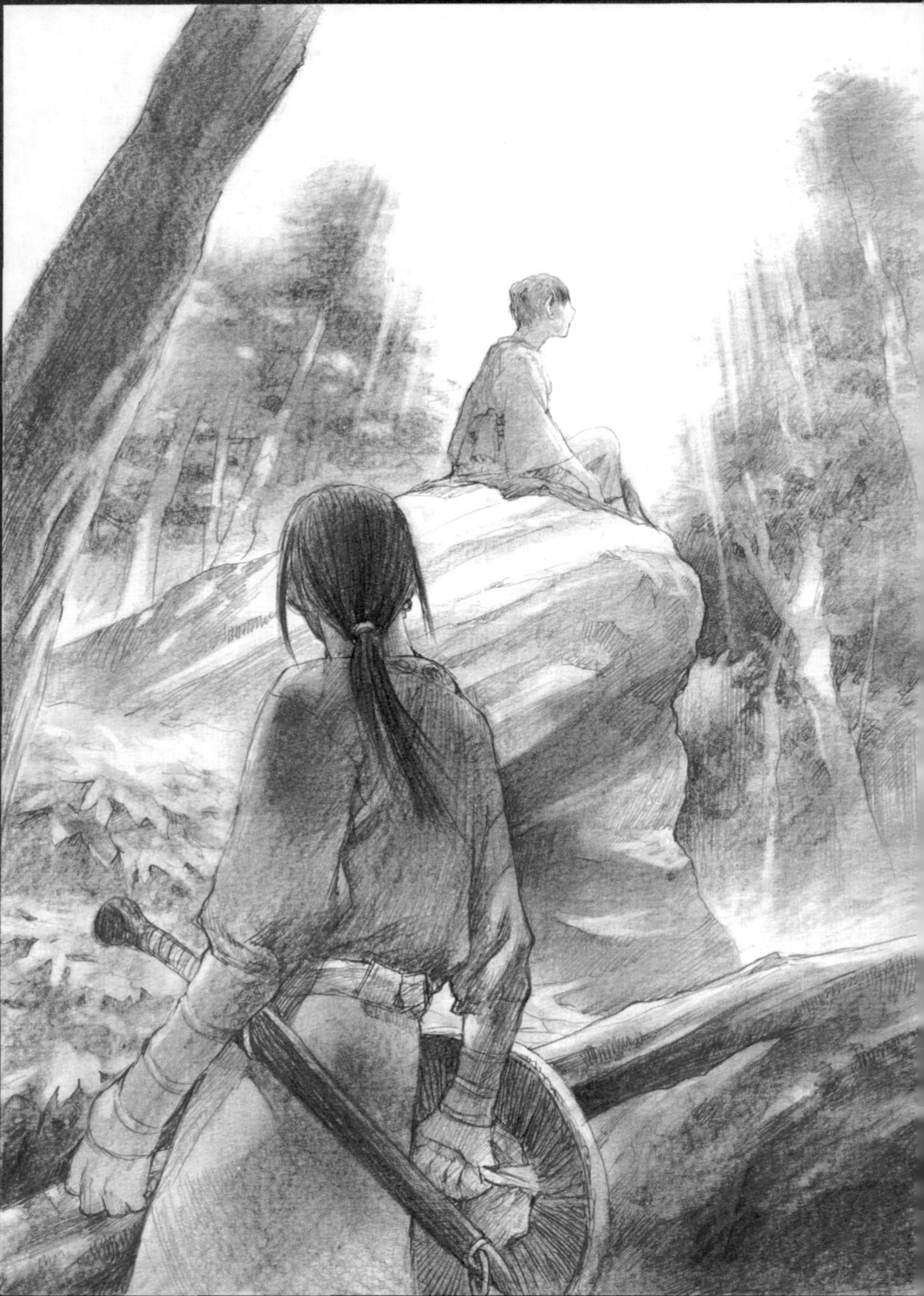

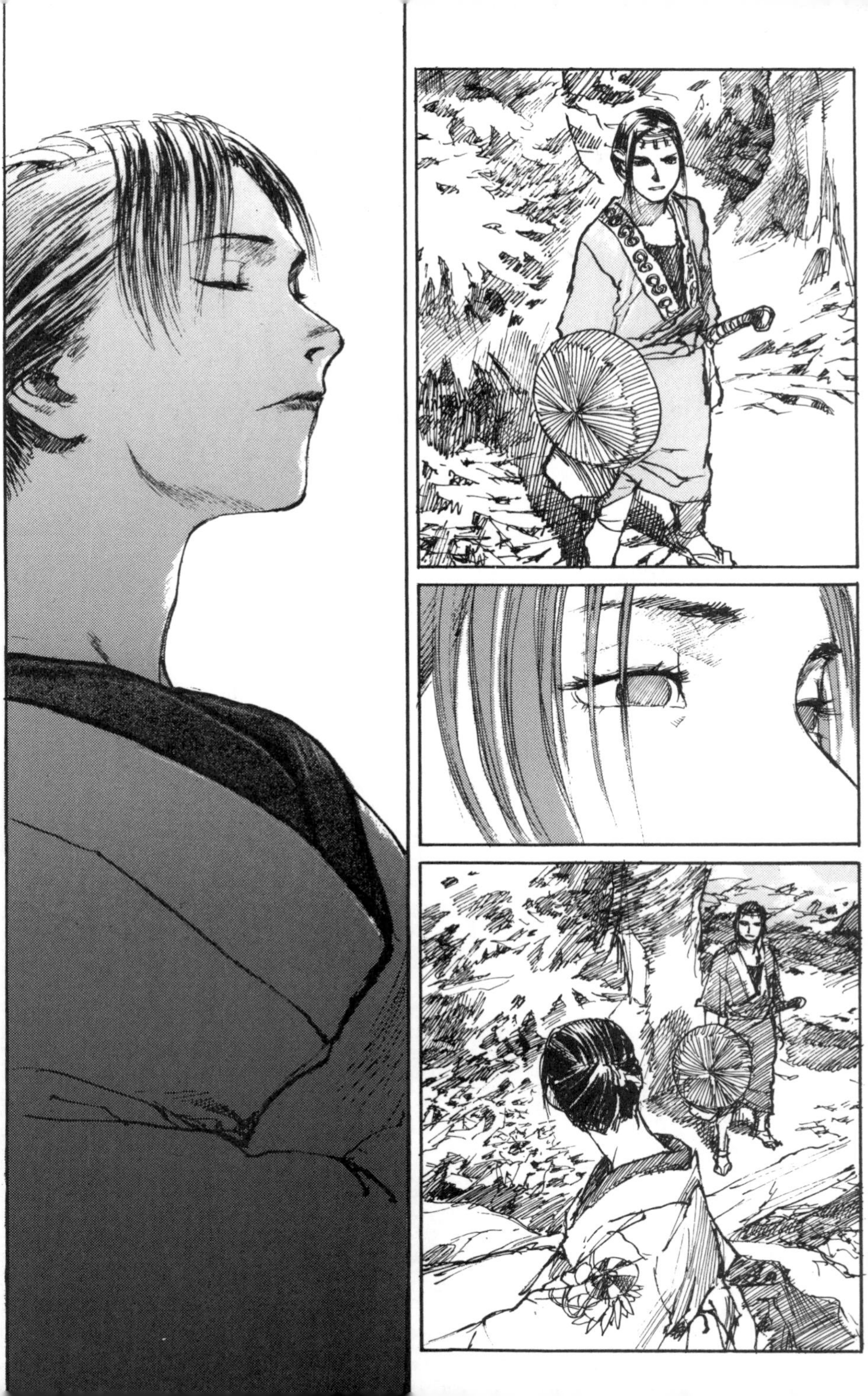

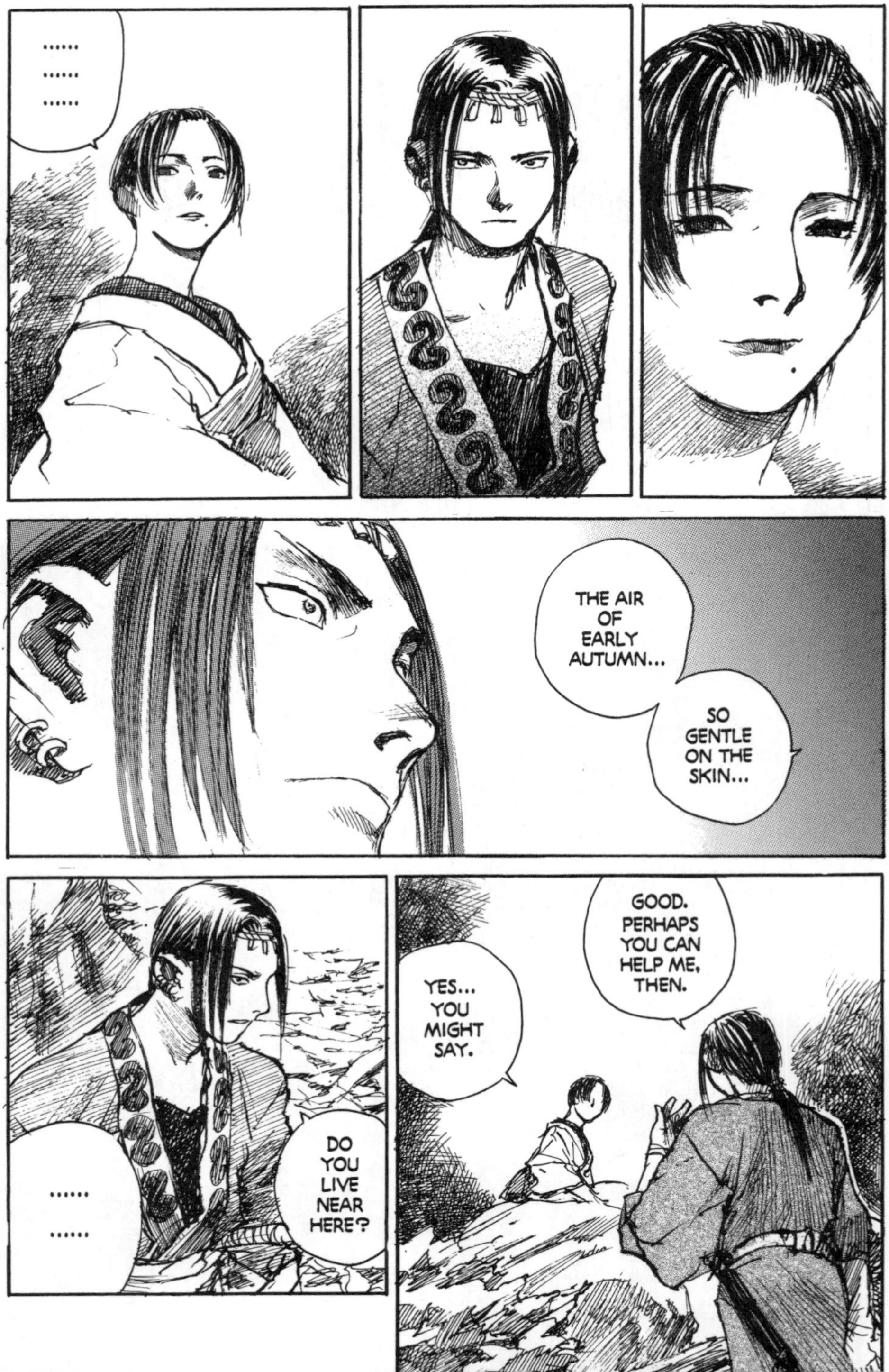
....
THE AIR OF EARLY AUTUMN...
SO GENTLE ON THE SKIN...
DO YOU LIVE NEAR HERE?
....
YES... YOU MIGHT SAY.
GOOD. PERHAPS YOU CAN HELP ME, THEN.

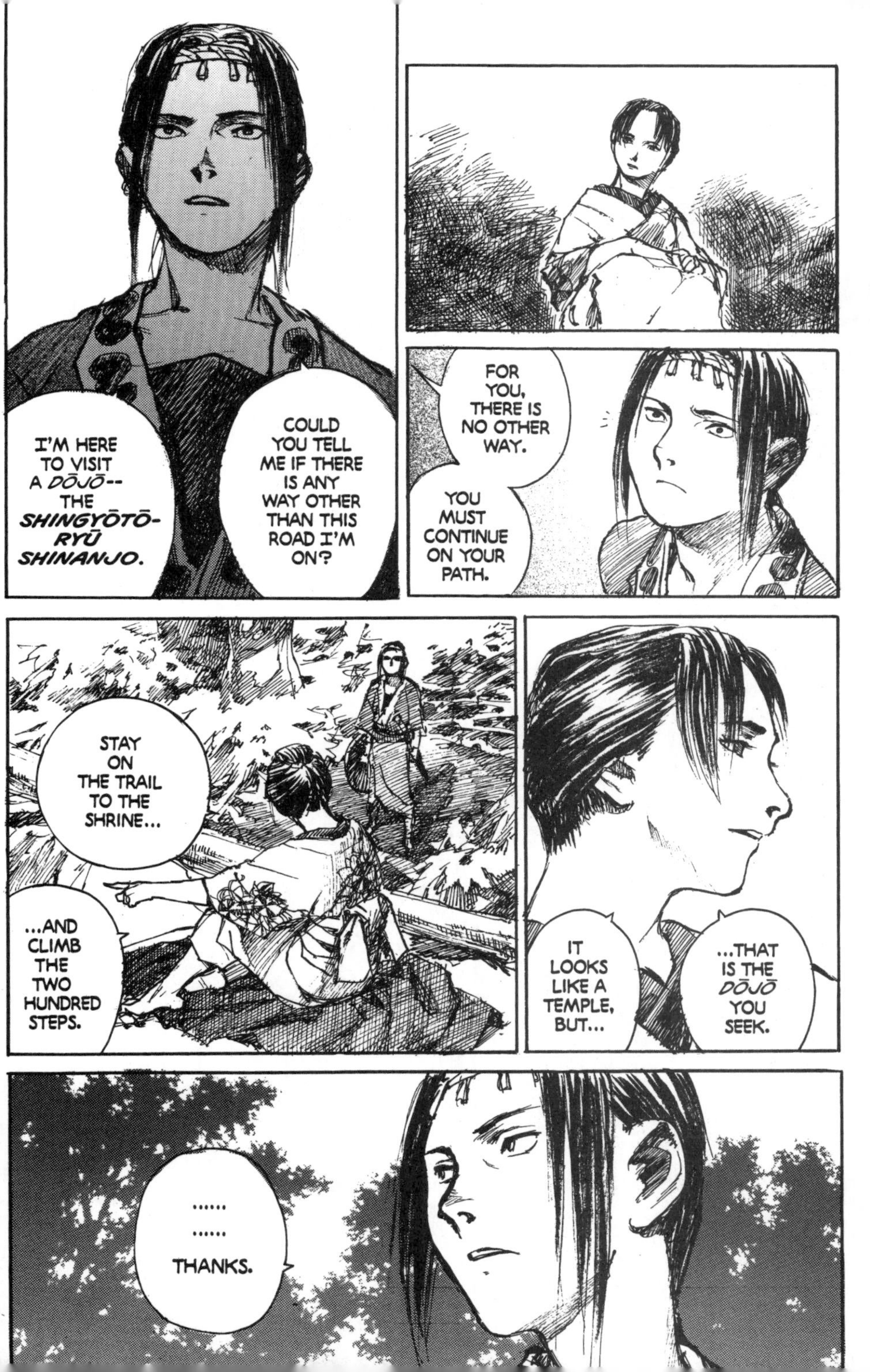
I'M HERE TO VISIT A *DŌJŌ*-- THE ***SHINGYŌTŌ-RYŪ SHINANJO.***
COULD YOU TELL ME IF THERE IS ANY WAY OTHER THAN THIS ROAD I'M ON?
FOR YOU, THERE IS NO OTHER WAY.
YOU MUST CONTINUE ON YOUR PATH.
STAY ON THE TRAIL TO THE SHRINE...
...AND CLIMB THE TWO HUNDRED STEPS.
IT LOOKS LIKE A TEMPLE, BUT...
...THAT IS THE *DŌJŌ* YOU SEEK.
......
......
THANKS.

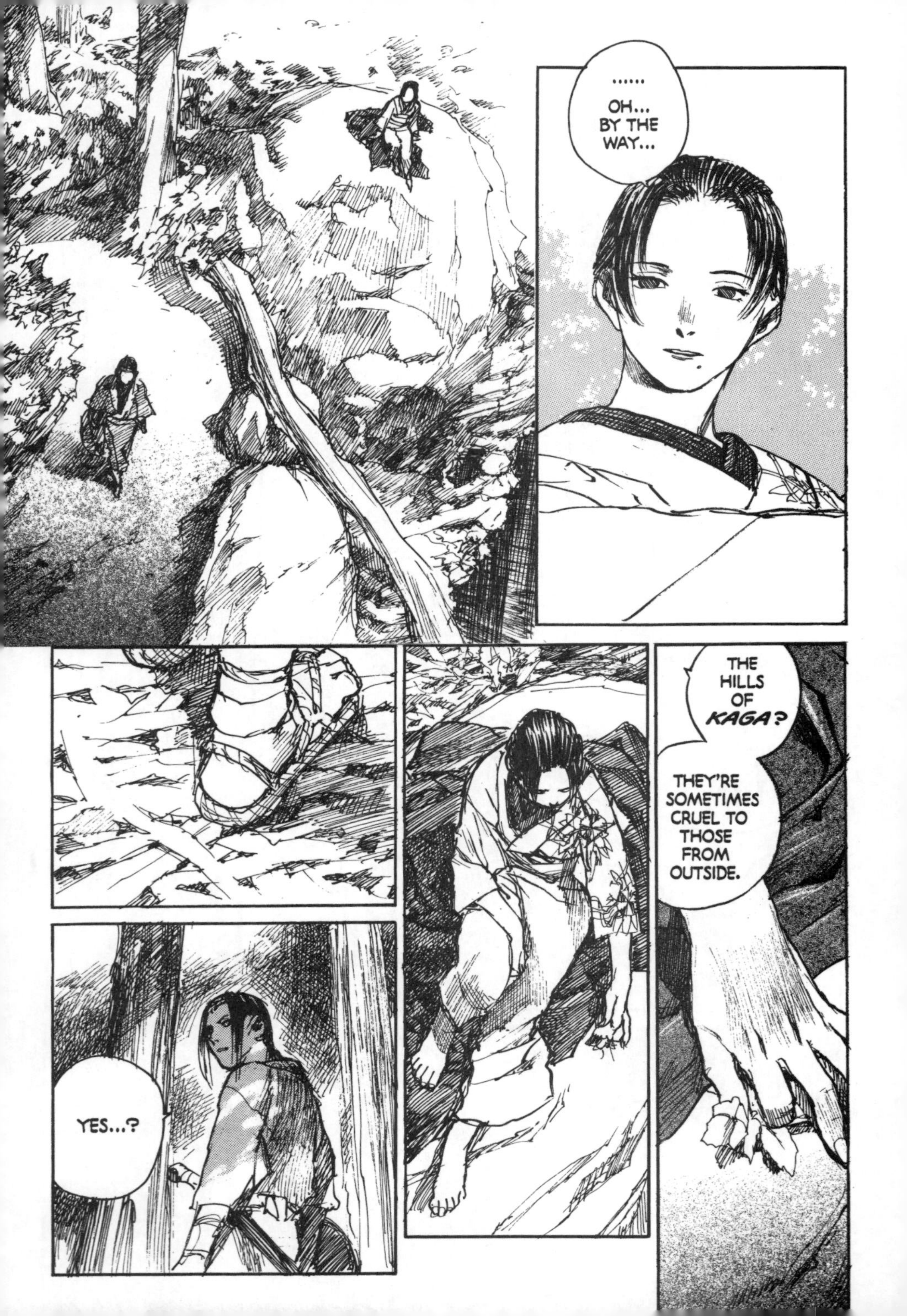
......
OH... BY THE WAY...
YES...?
THE HILLS OF *KAGA*?
THEY'RE SOMETIMES CRUEL TO THOSE FROM OUTSIDE.

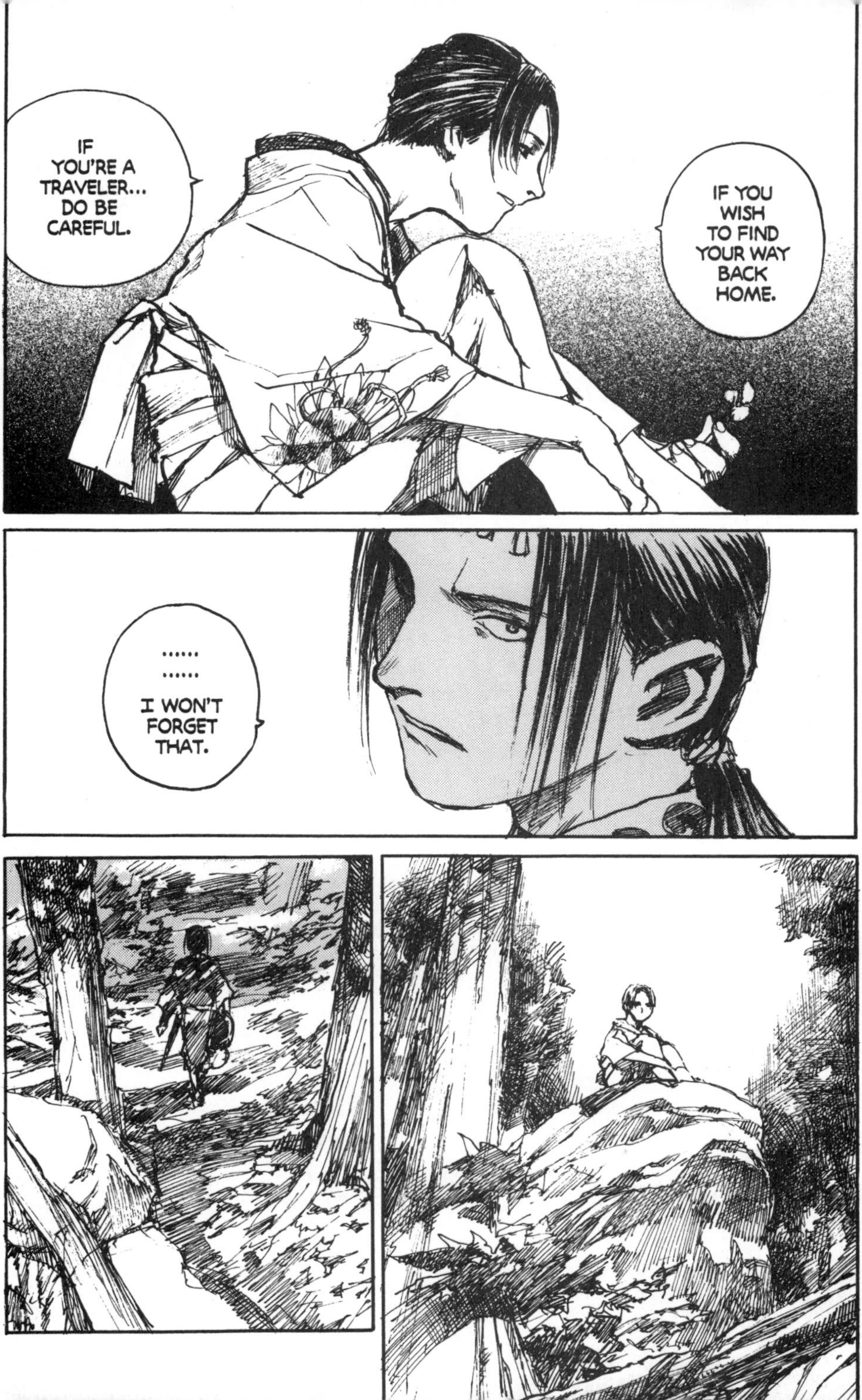
IF YOU'RE A TRAVELER... DO BE CAREFUL.
IF YOU WISH TO FIND YOUR WAY BACK HOME.
......
......
I WON'T FORGET THAT.

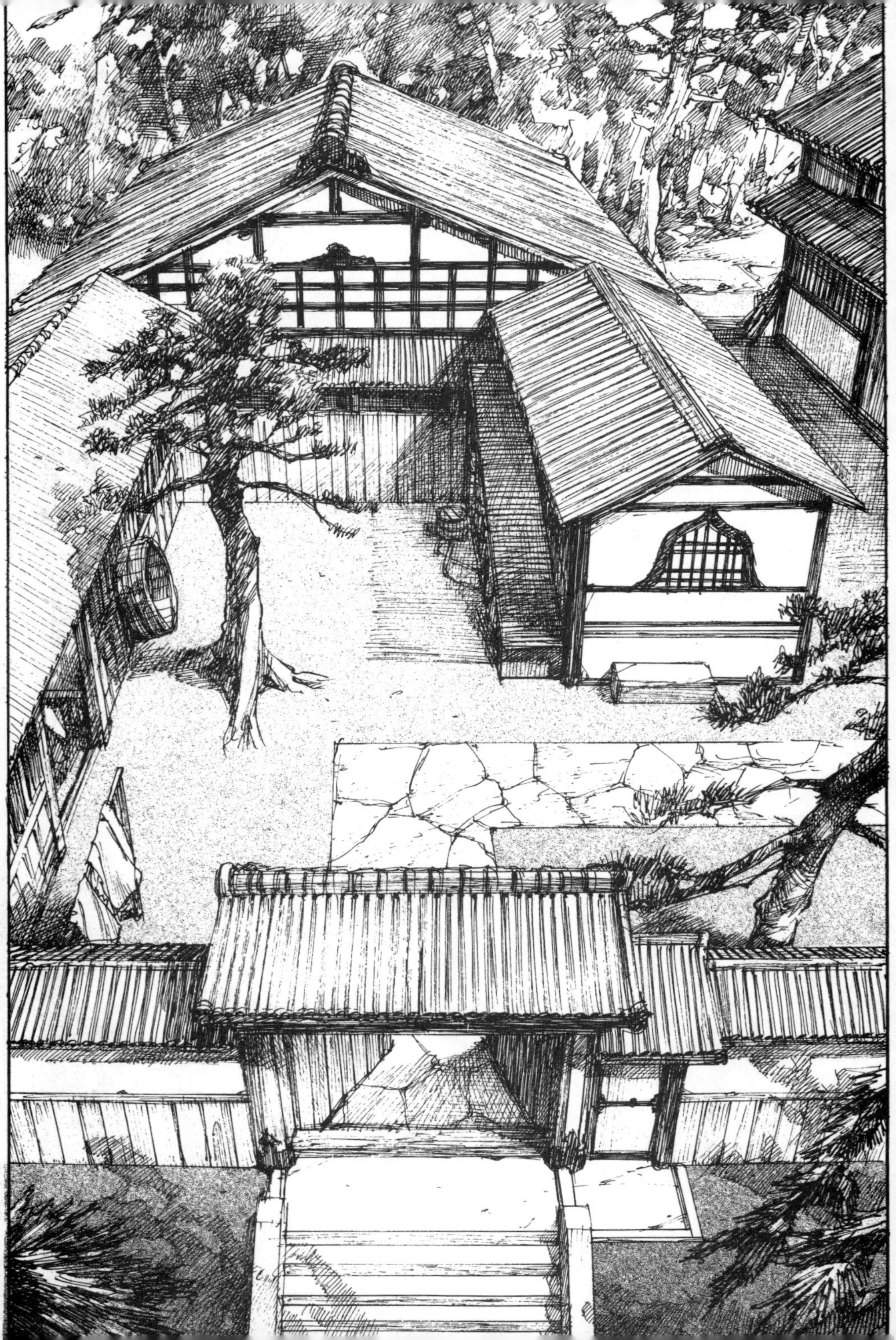

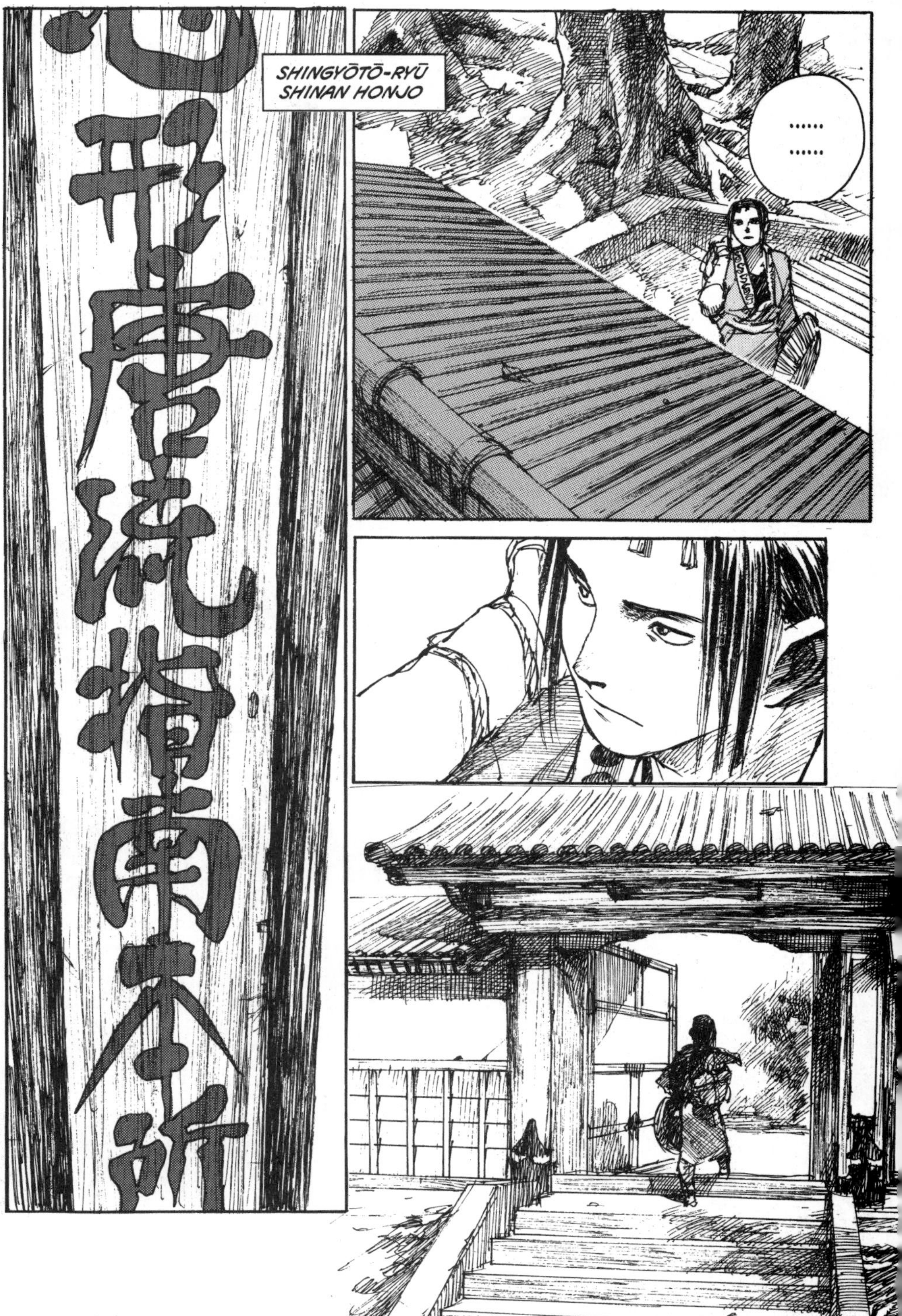
SHINGYŌTŌ-RYŪ SHINAN HONJO
......
......

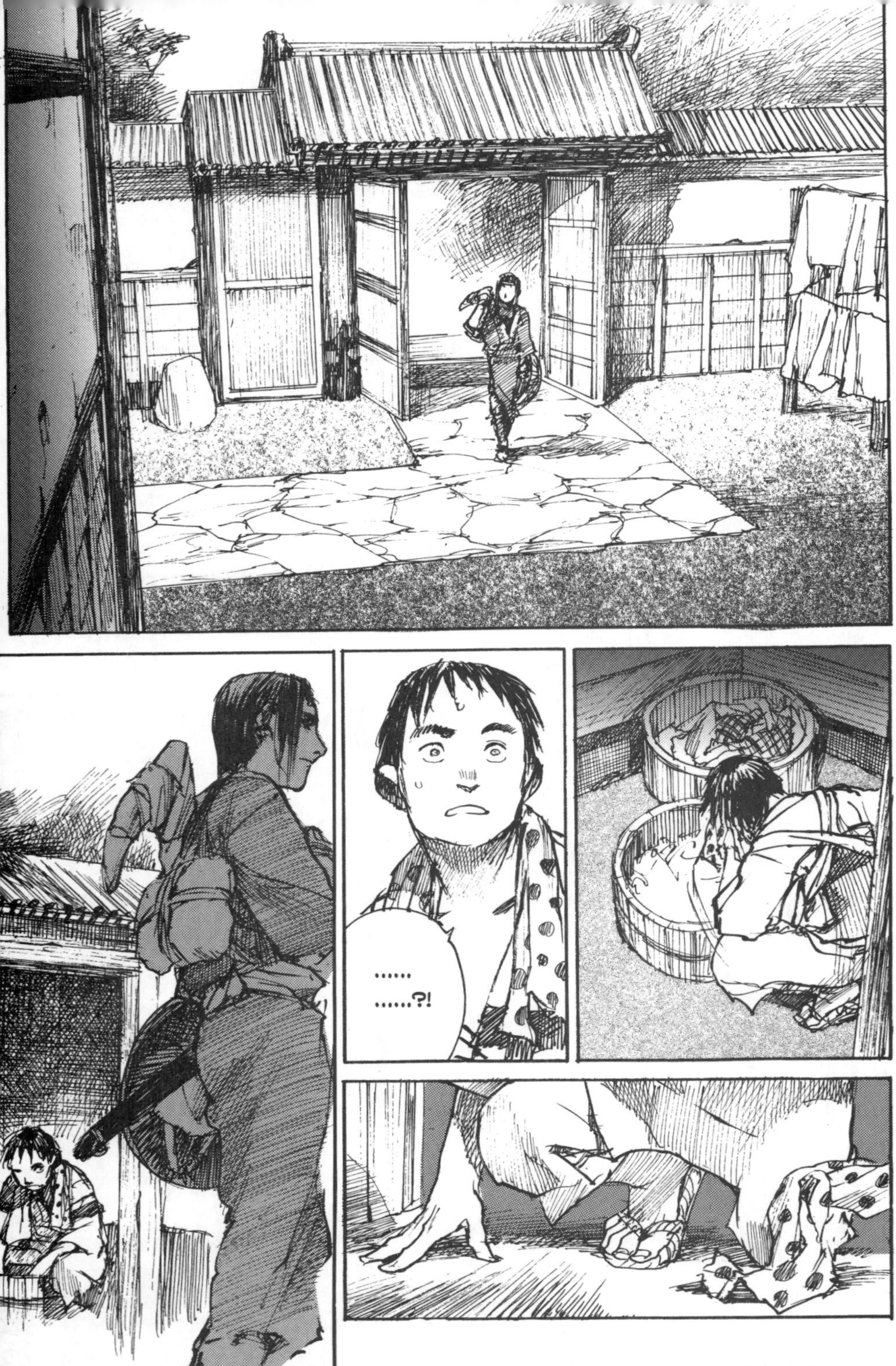
......
......?!

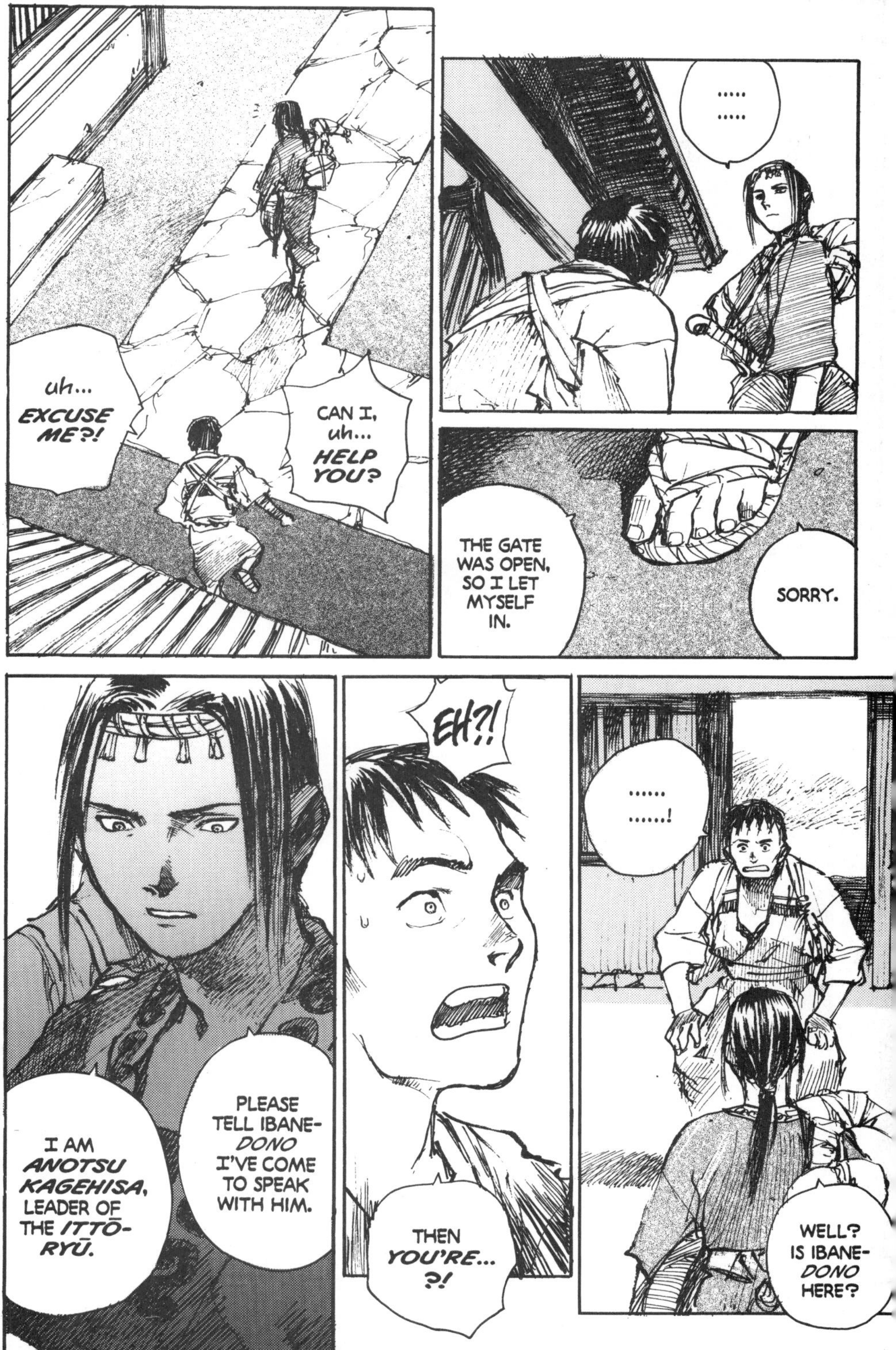
uh... EXCUSE ME?!
CAN I, uh... HELP YOU?
......
......
THE GATE WAS OPEN, SO I LET MYSELF IN.
SORRY.
I AM ANOTSU KAGEHISA, LEADER OF THE ITTŌ-RYŪ.
PLEASE TELL IBANE-DONO I'VE COME TO SPEAK WITH HIM.
EH?!
THEN YOU'RE...?!
......
......!
WELL? IS IBANE-DONO HERE?

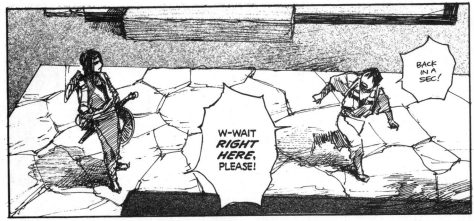

W-WAIT *RIGHT HERE,* PLEASE!

BACK IN A SEC!

~whew~

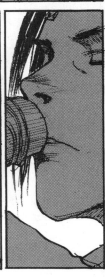

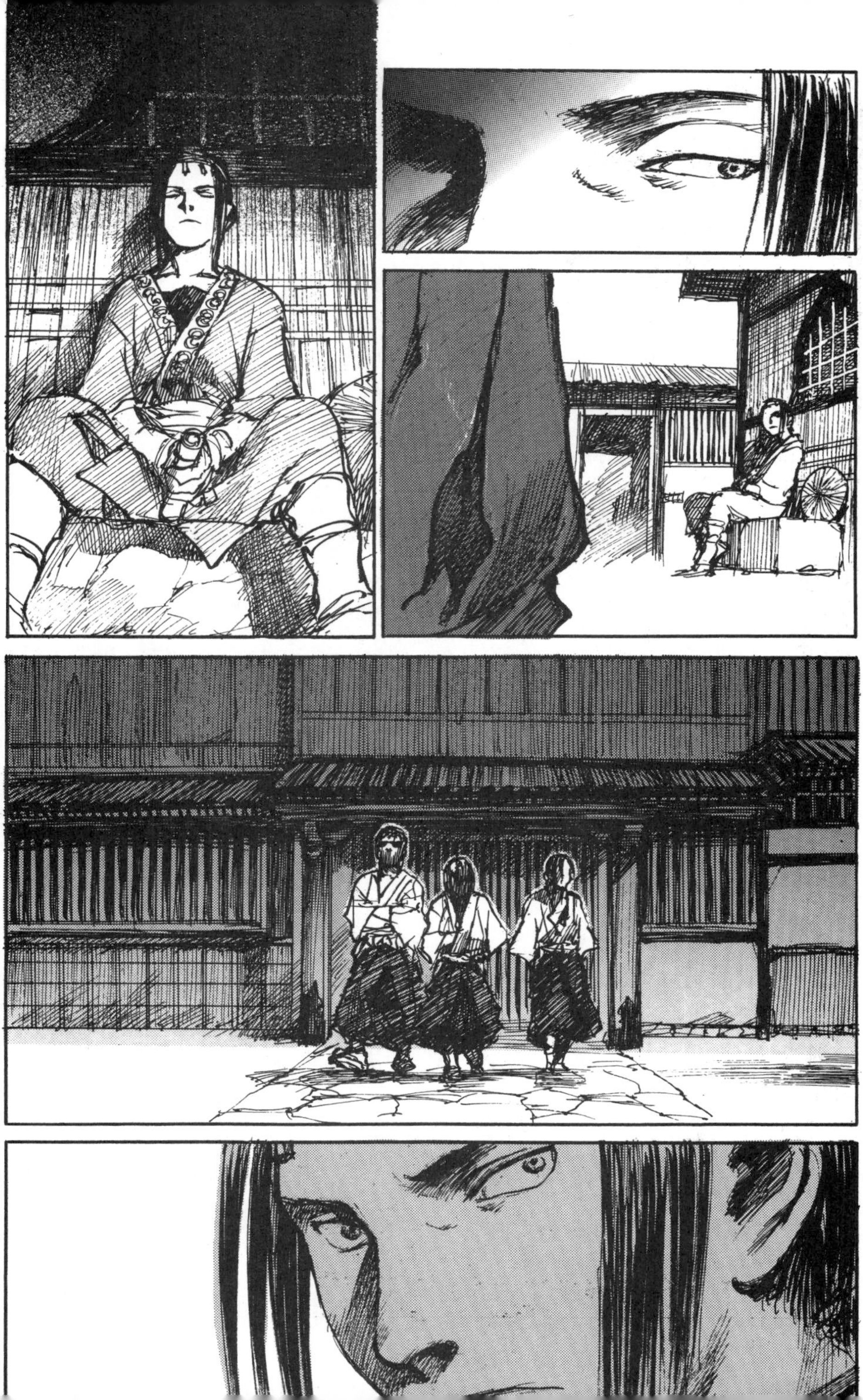

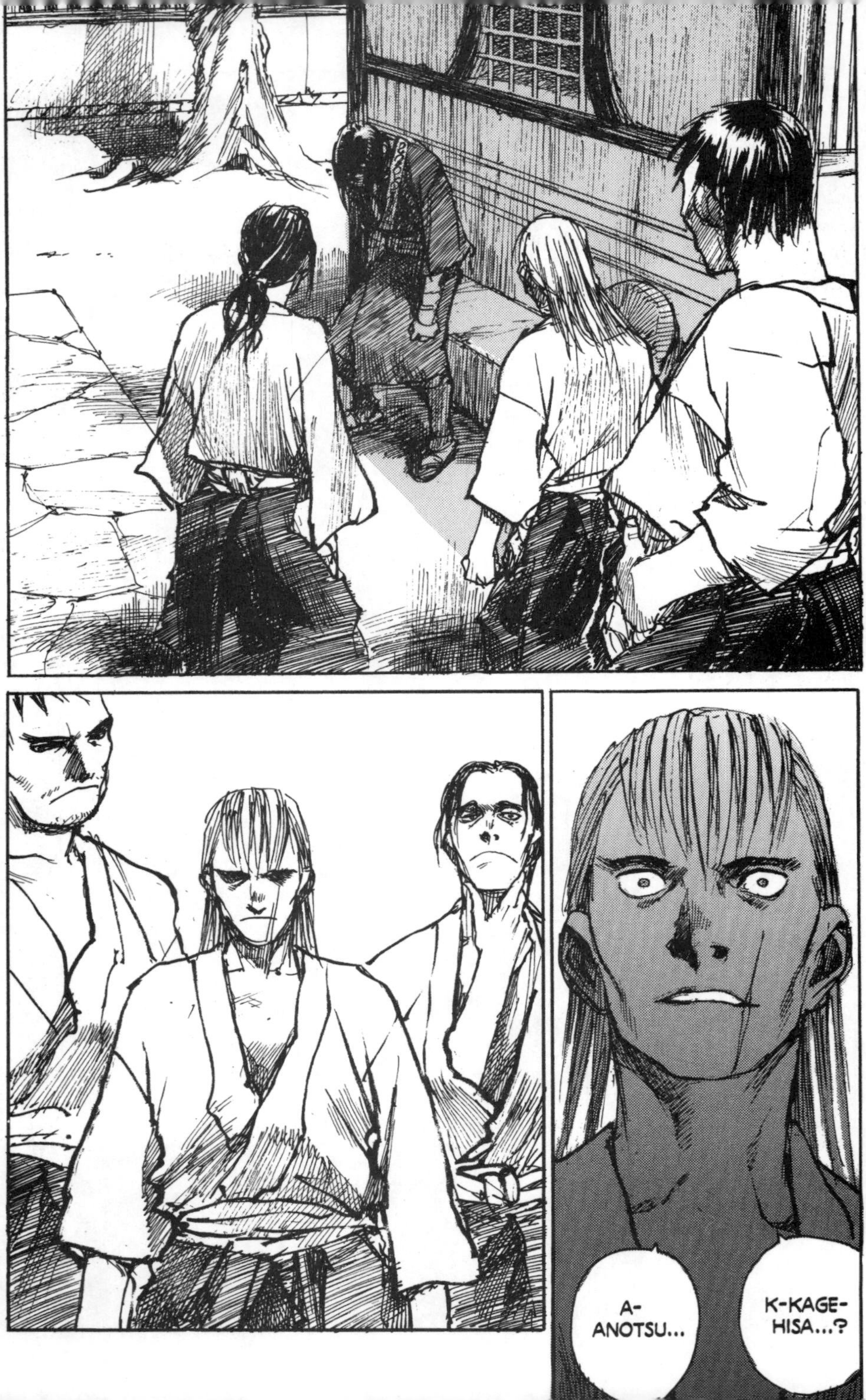
A-
ANOTSU...
K-KAGE-
HISA...?

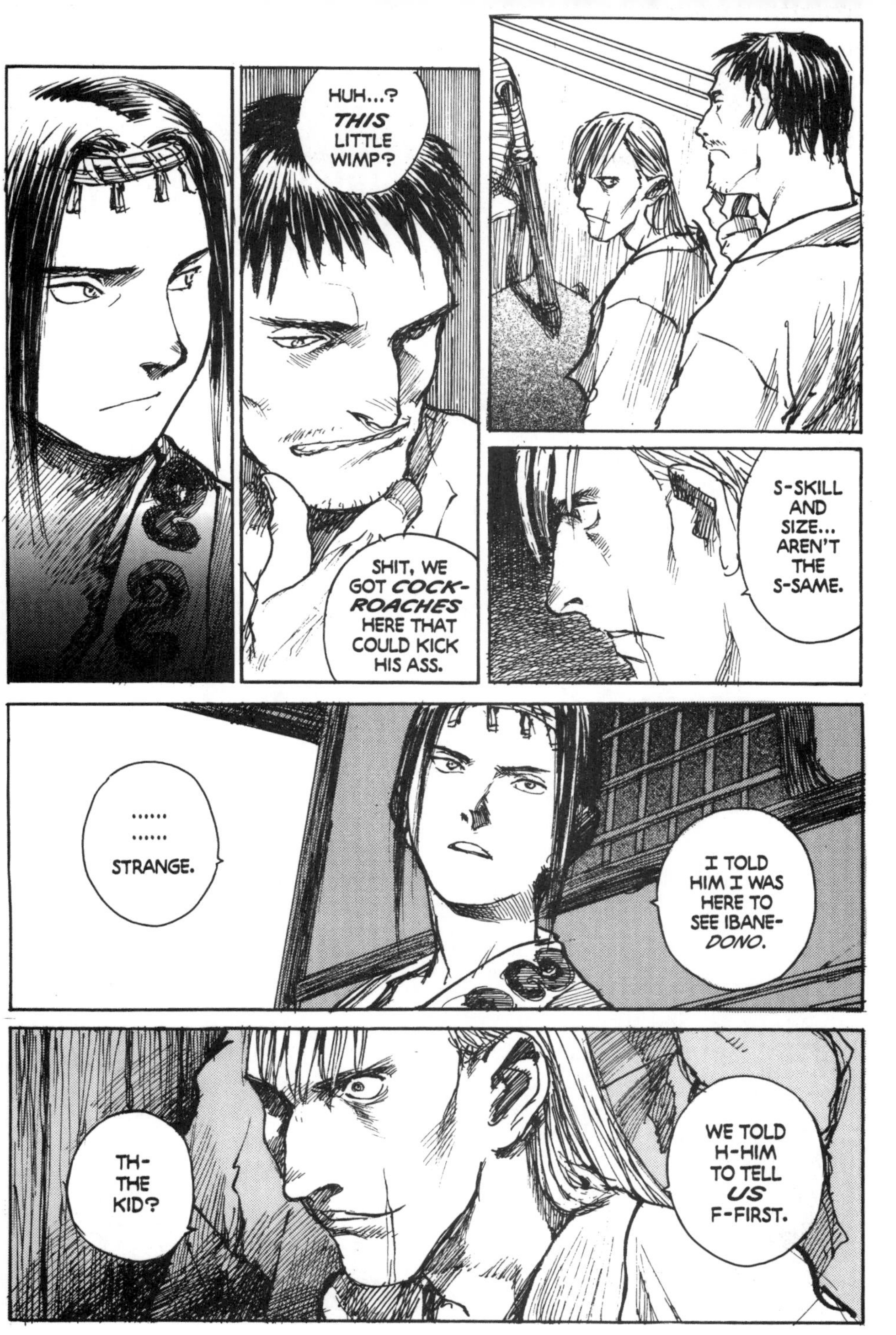
HUH...? *THIS* LITTLE WIMP?
SHIT, WE GOT *COCKROACHES* HERE THAT COULD KICK HIS ASS.
S-SKILL AND SIZE... AREN'T THE S-SAME.
.... STRANGE.
I TOLD HIM I WAS HERE TO SEE IBANE-*DONO*.
TH-THE KID?
WE TOLD H-HIM TO TELL *US* F-FIRST.

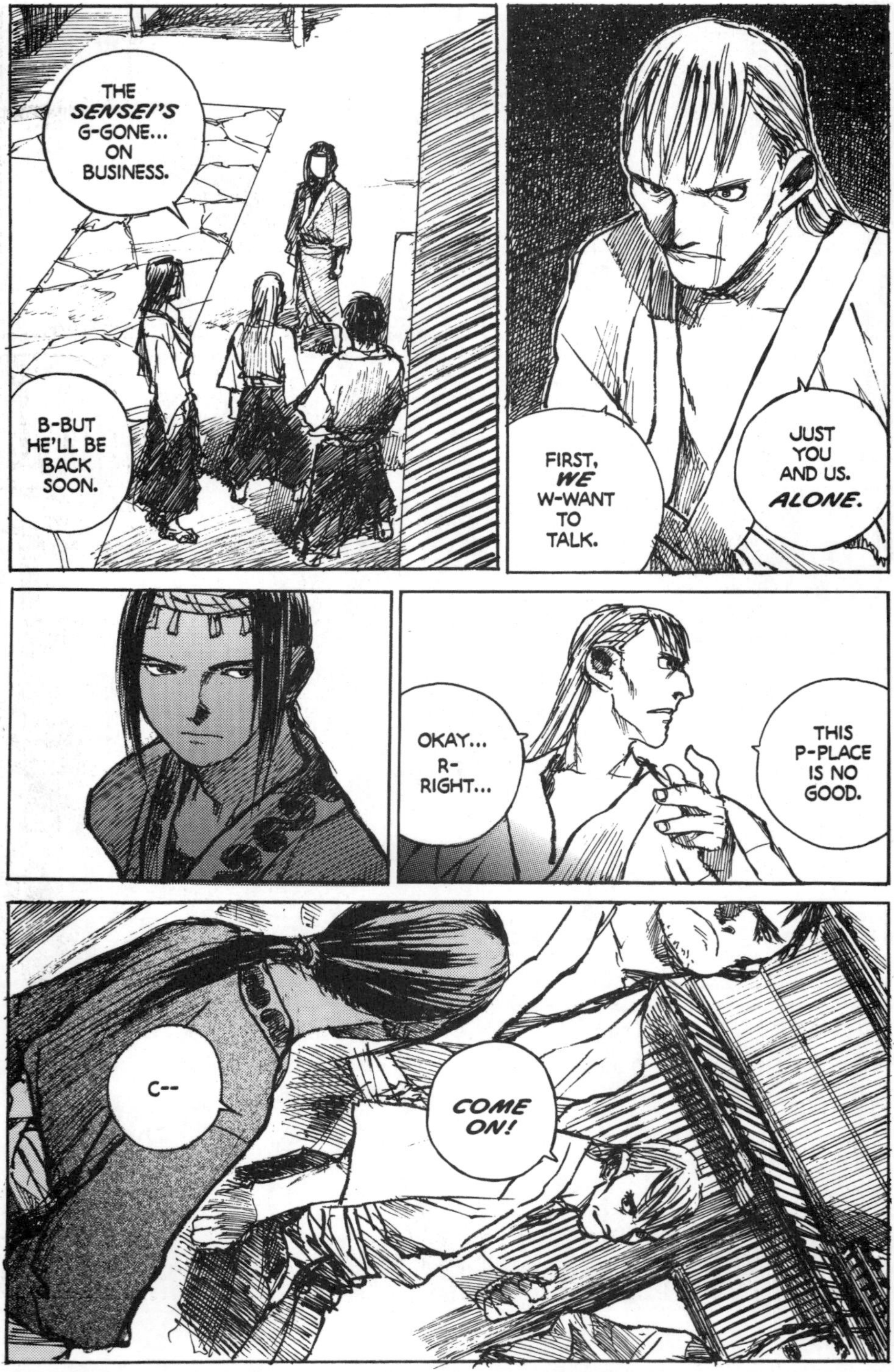
THE SENSEI'S G-GONE... ON BUSINESS.
B-BUT HE'LL BE BACK SOON.
JUST YOU AND US. ALONE.
FIRST, WE W-WANT TO TALK.
THIS P-PLACE IS NO GOOD.
OKAY... R-RIGHT...
C--
COME ON!

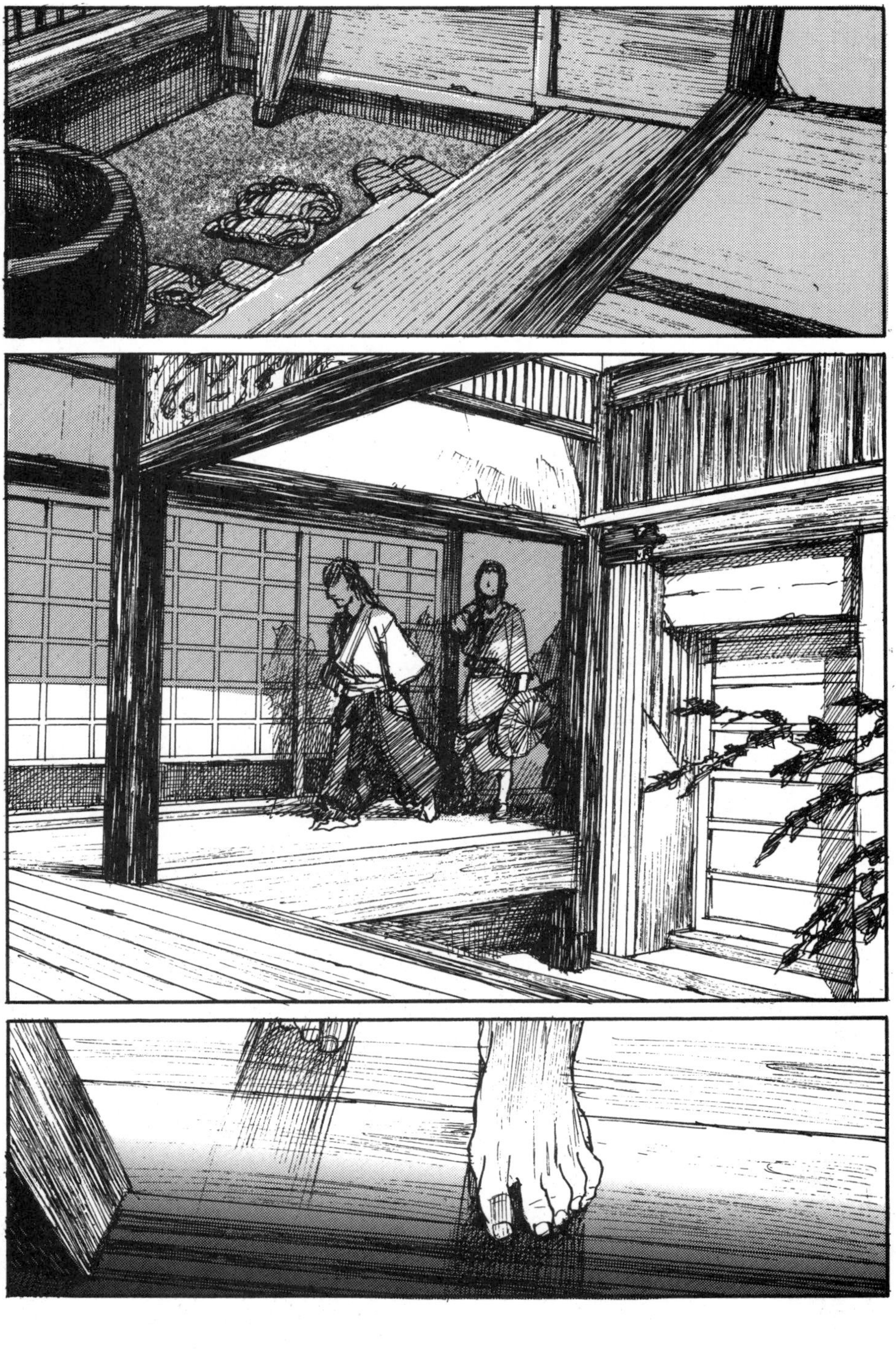

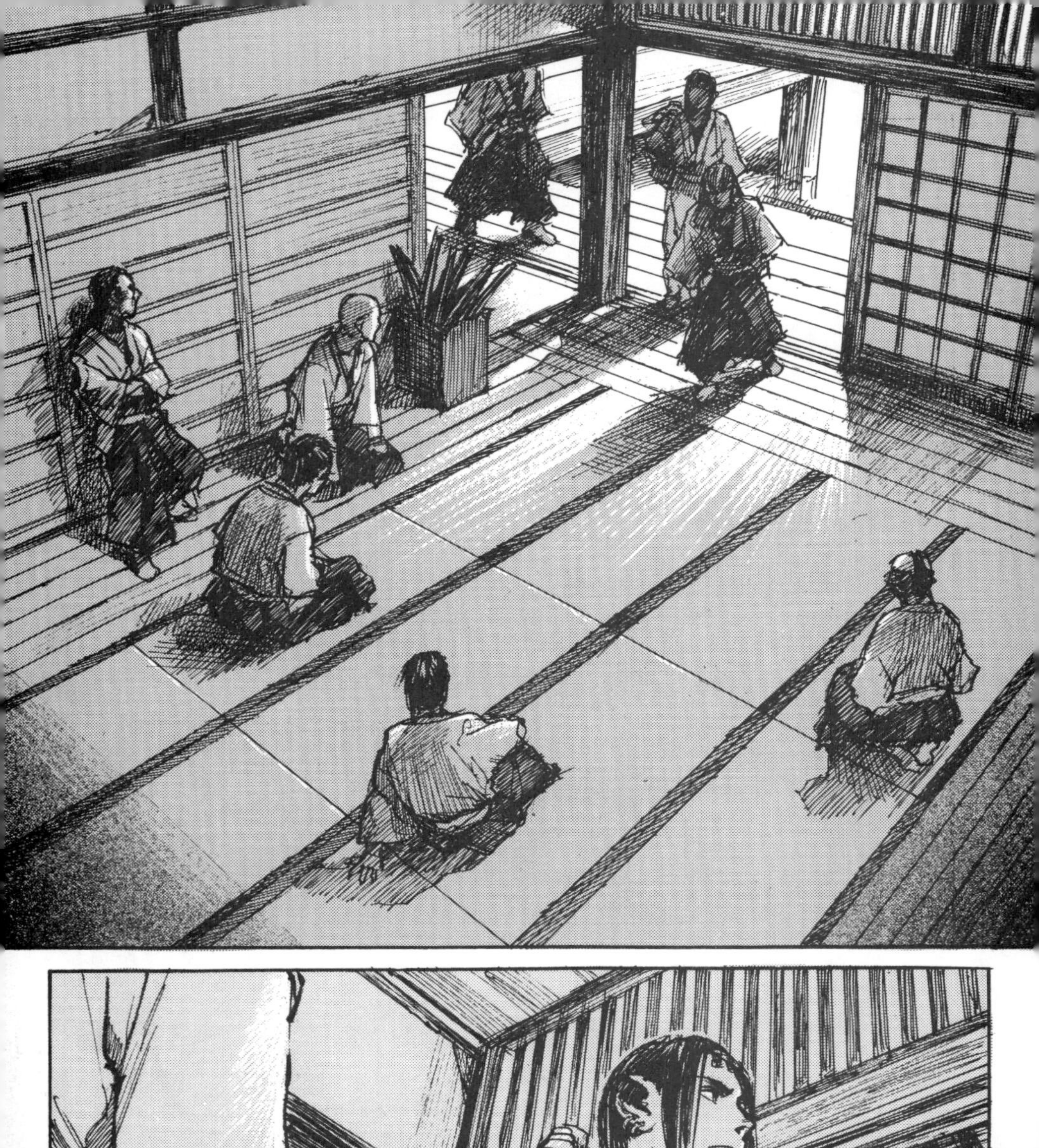
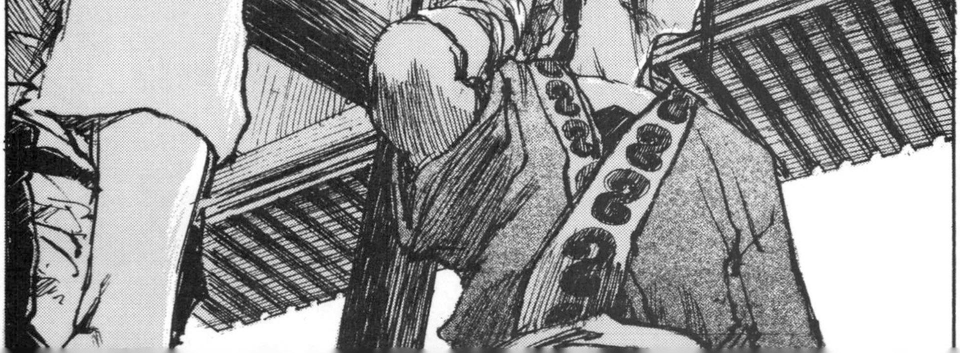

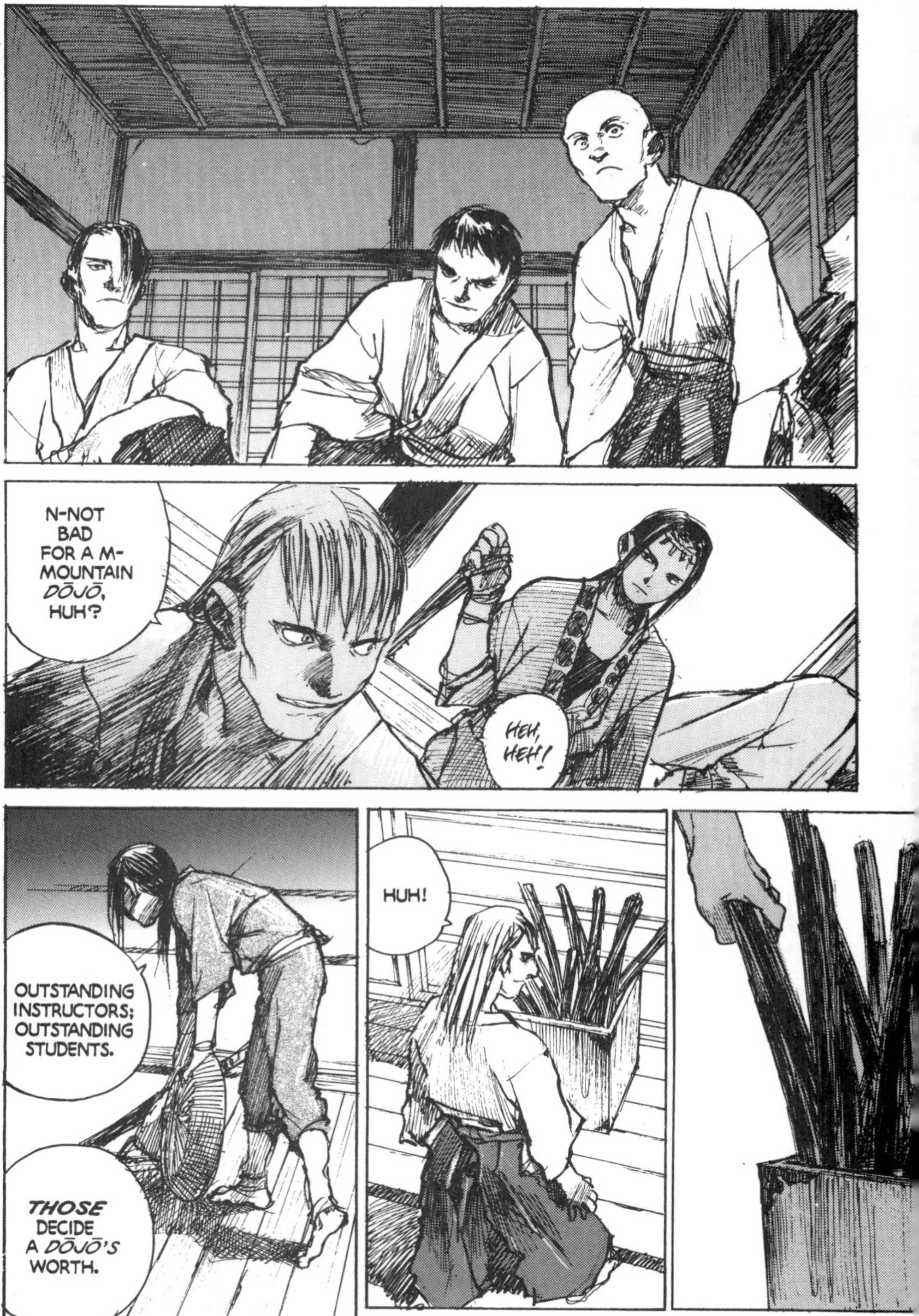
N-NOT BAD FOR A M-MOUNTAIN *DŌJŌ*, HUH?
HEH, HEH!
OUTSTANDING INSTRUCTORS; OUTSTANDING STUDENTS.
THOSE DECIDE A *DŌJŌ*'S WORTH.
HUH!

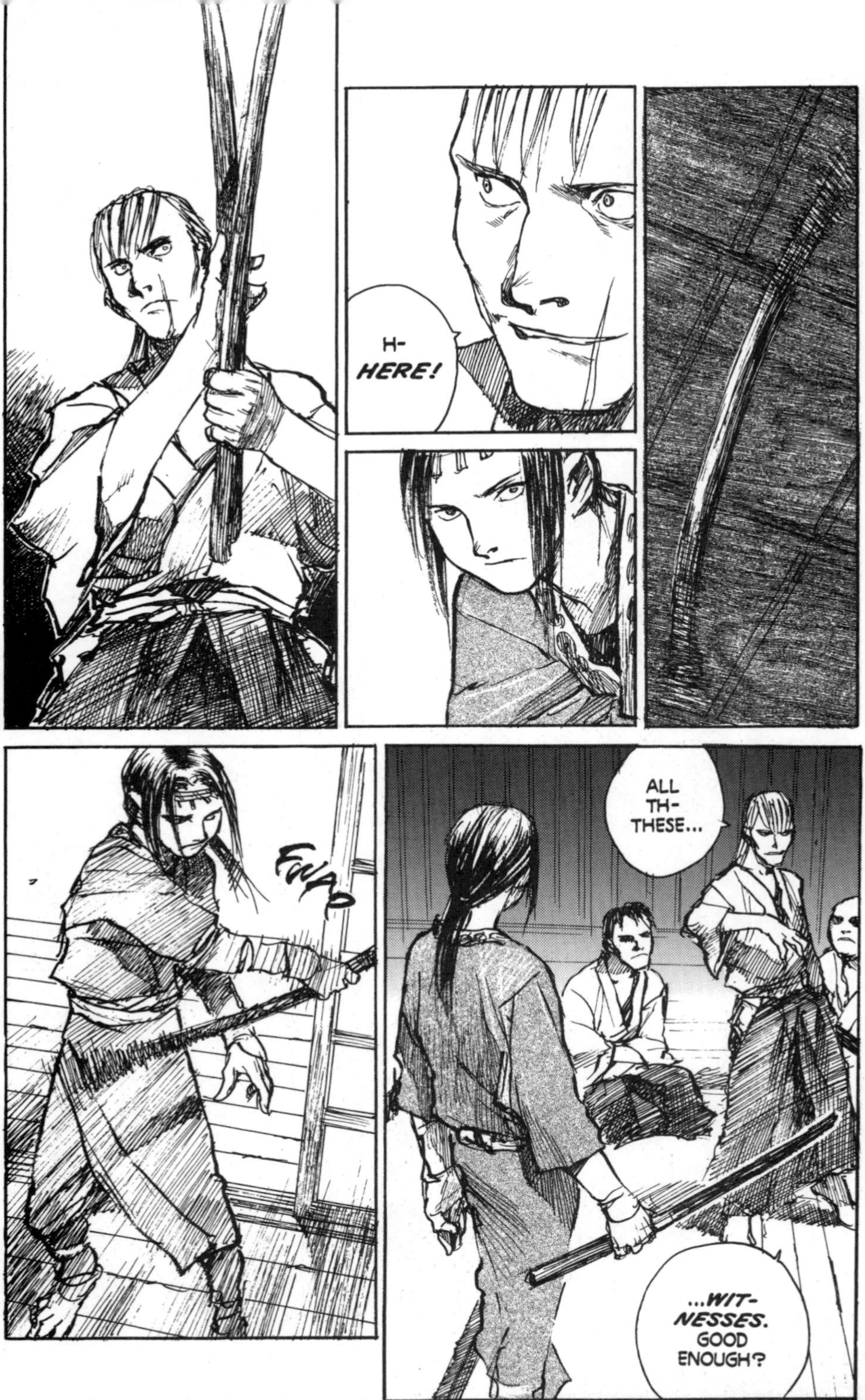
H- HERE!
FWAP
ALL TH- THESE...
...WIT- NESSES. GOOD ENOUGH?

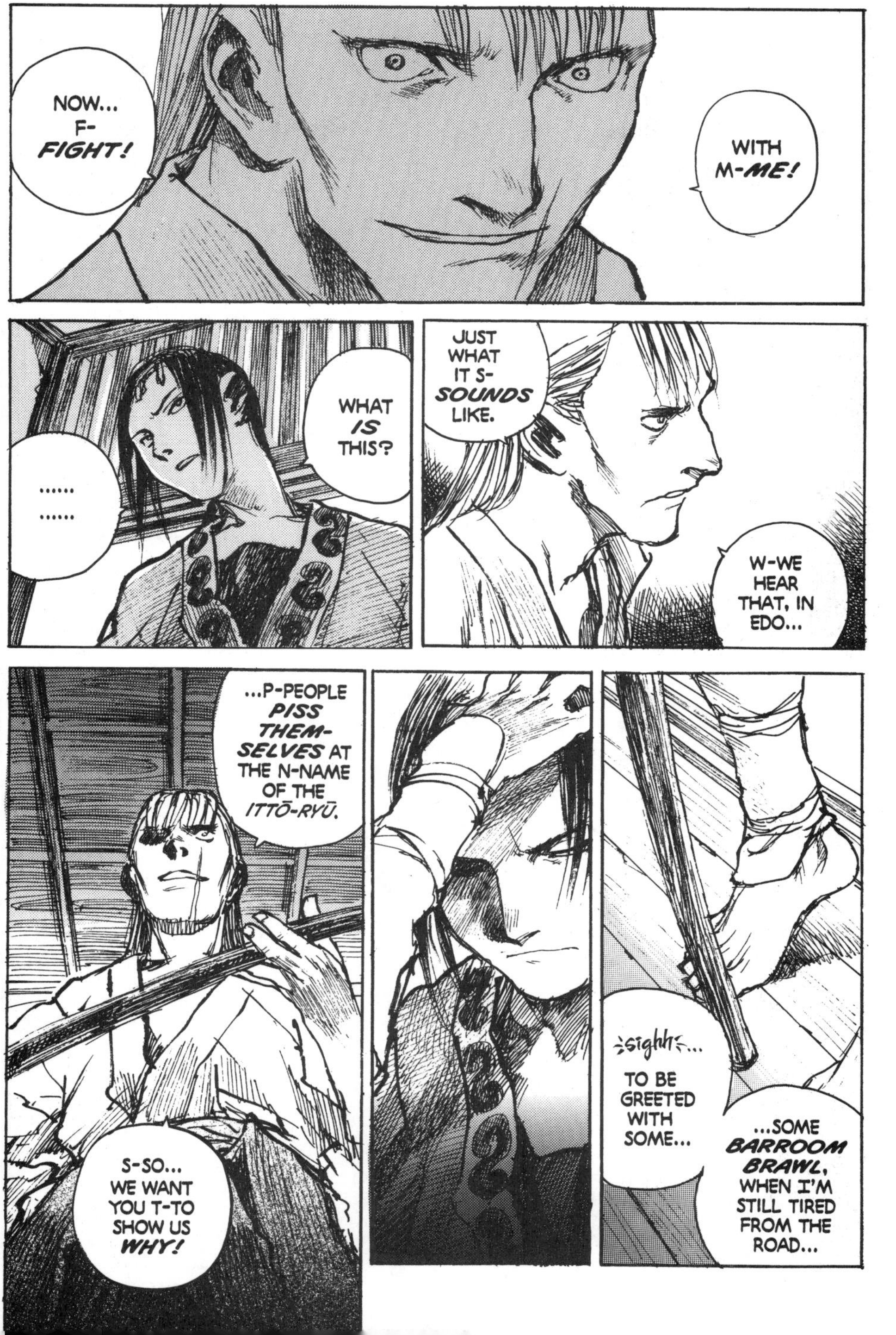
NOW... F-FIGHT!
WITH M-ME!
......
......
WHAT IS THIS?
JUST WHAT IT S-SOUNDS LIKE.
W-WE HEAR THAT, IN EDO...
...P-PEOPLE PISS THEM-SELVES AT THE N-NAME OF THE ITTŌ-RYŪ.
S-SO... WE WANT YOU T-TO SHOW US WHY!
sighh...
TO BE GREETED WITH SOME...
...SOME BARROOM BRAWL, WHEN I'M STILL TIRED FROM THE ROAD...

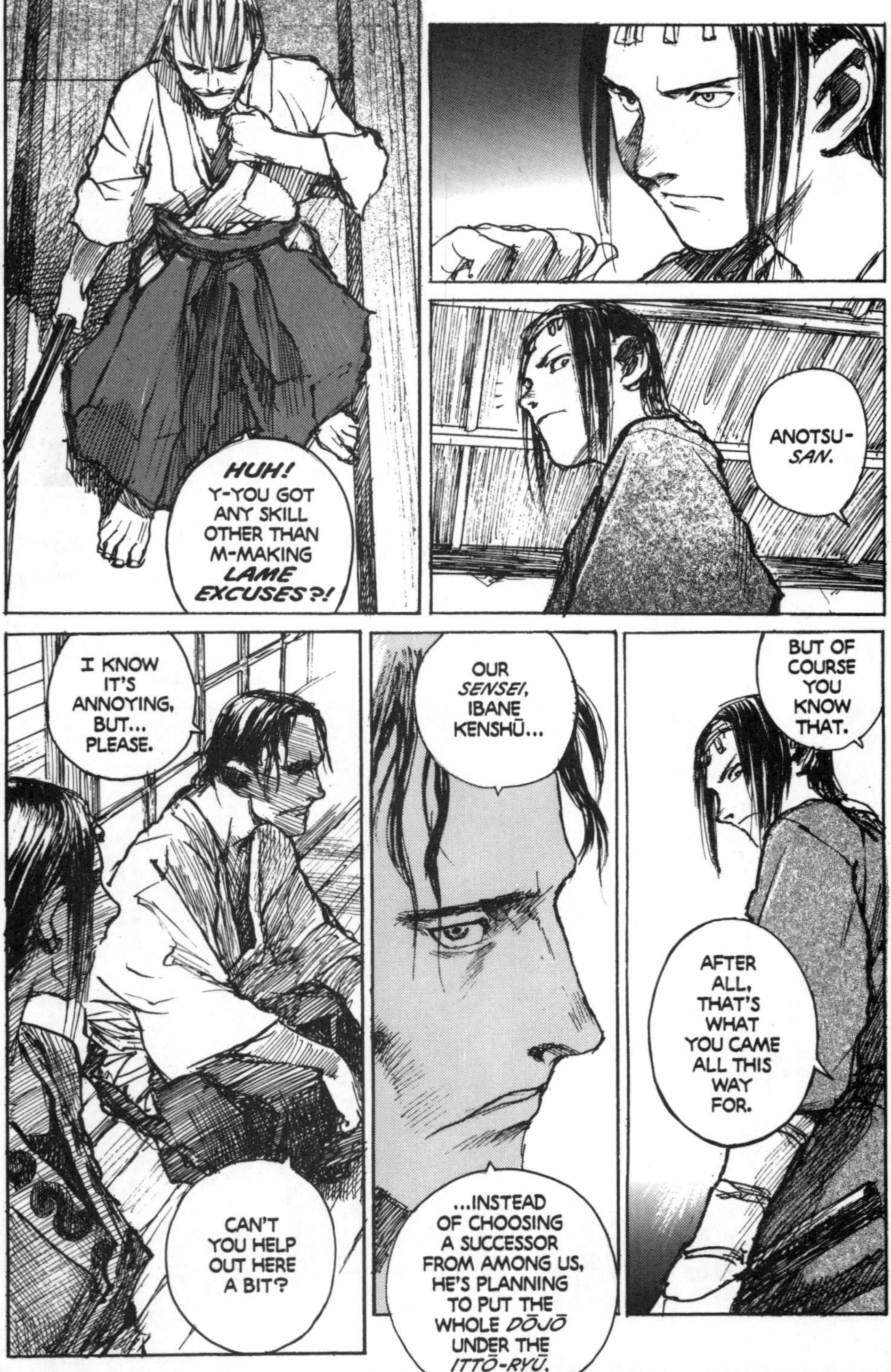

HUH! Y-YOU GOT ANY SKILL OTHER THAN M-MAKING LAME EXCUSES?!
ANOTSU-SAN.
I KNOW IT'S ANNOYING, BUT... PLEASE.
CAN'T YOU HELP OUT HERE A BIT?
OUR SENSEI, IBANE KENSHŪ...
...INSTEAD OF CHOOSING A SUCCESSOR FROM AMONG US, HE'S PLANNING TO PUT THE WHOLE DŌJŌ UNDER THE ITTŌ-RYŪ.
BUT OF COURSE YOU KNOW THAT.
AFTER ALL, THAT'S WHAT YOU CAME ALL THIS WAY FOR.

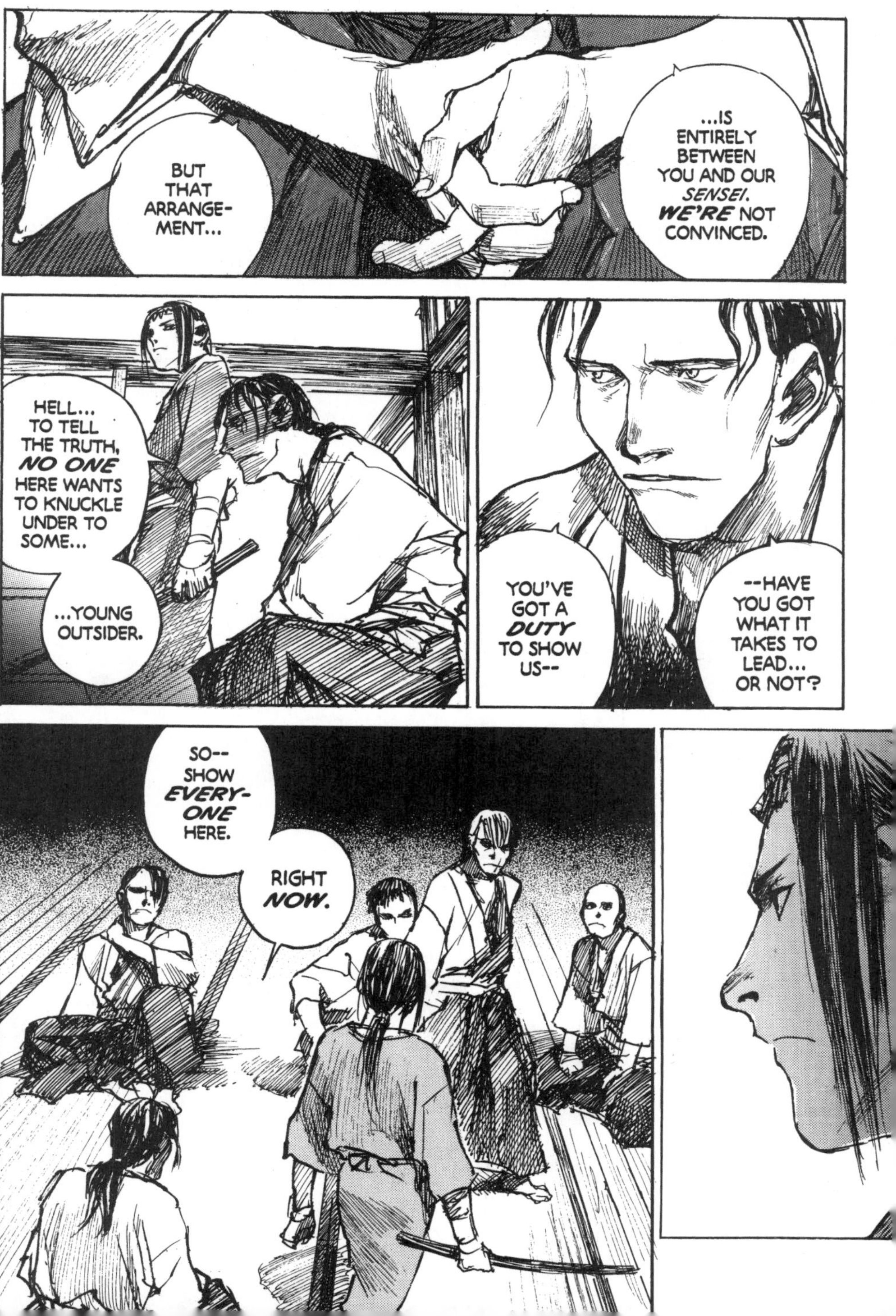
BUT THAT ARRANGE-MENT...
...IS ENTIRELY BETWEEN YOU AND OUR *SENSEI*. ***WE'RE*** NOT CONVINCED.
HELL... TO TELL THE TRUTH, ***NO ONE*** HERE WANTS TO KNUCKLE UNDER TO SOME...
...YOUNG OUTSIDER.
YOU'VE GOT A ***DUTY*** TO SHOW US--
--HAVE YOU GOT WHAT IT TAKES TO LEAD... OR NOT?
SO-- SHOW ***EVERY-ONE*** HERE.
RIGHT ***NOW.***

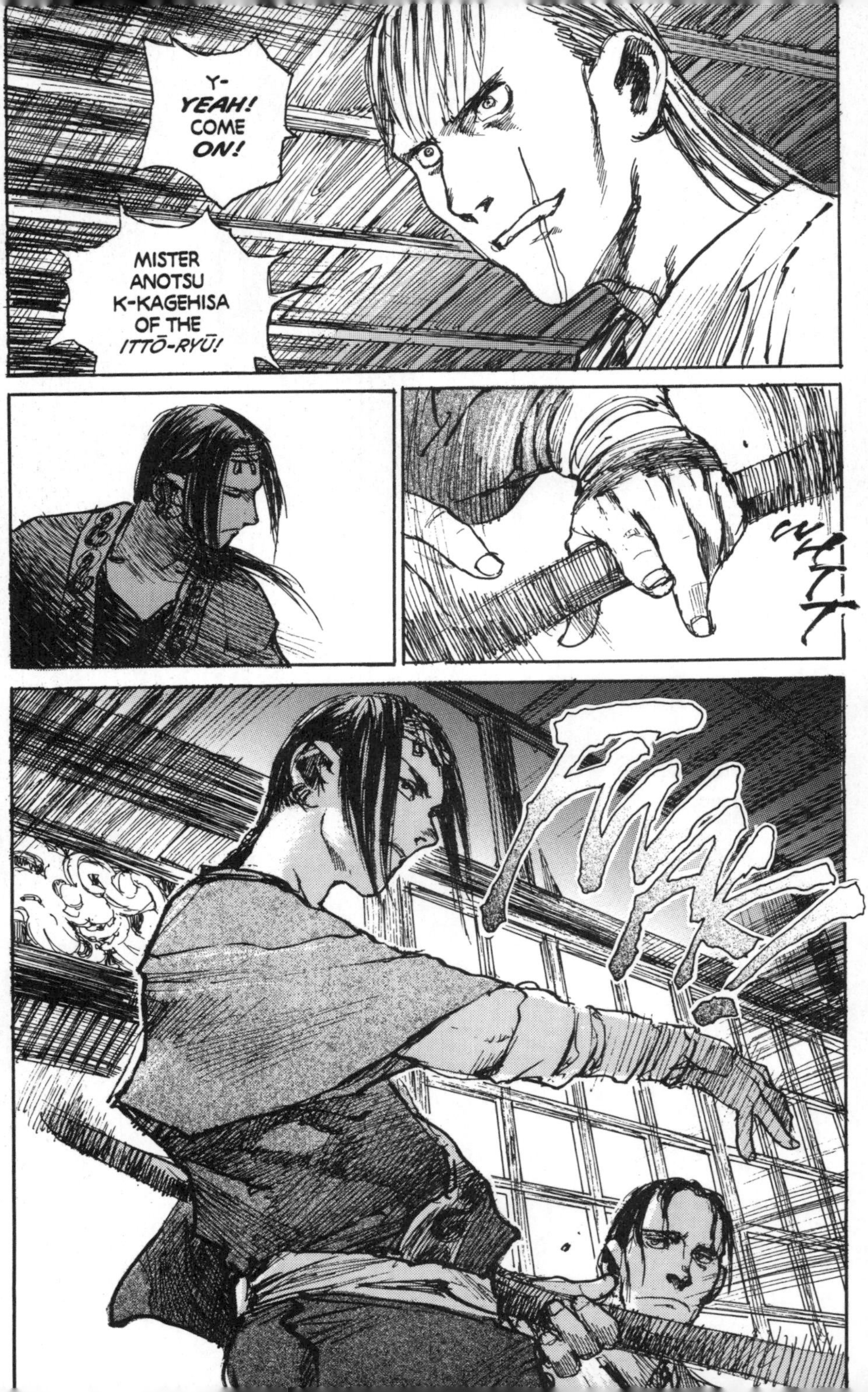
Y-
YEAH! COME ON!
MISTER ANOTSU K-KAGEHISA OF THE ITTŌ-RYŪ!
FWAK!

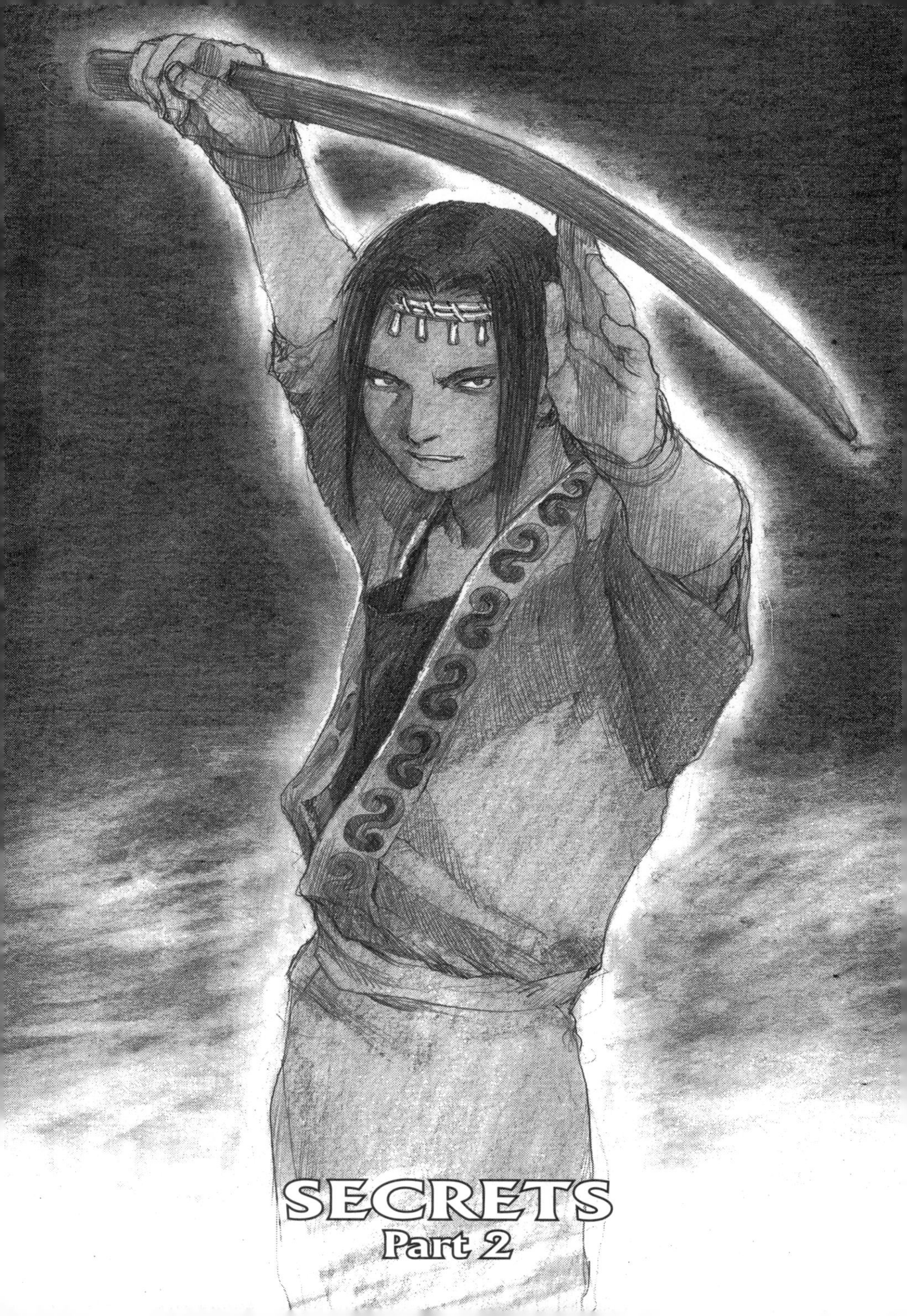

SECRETS
Part 2

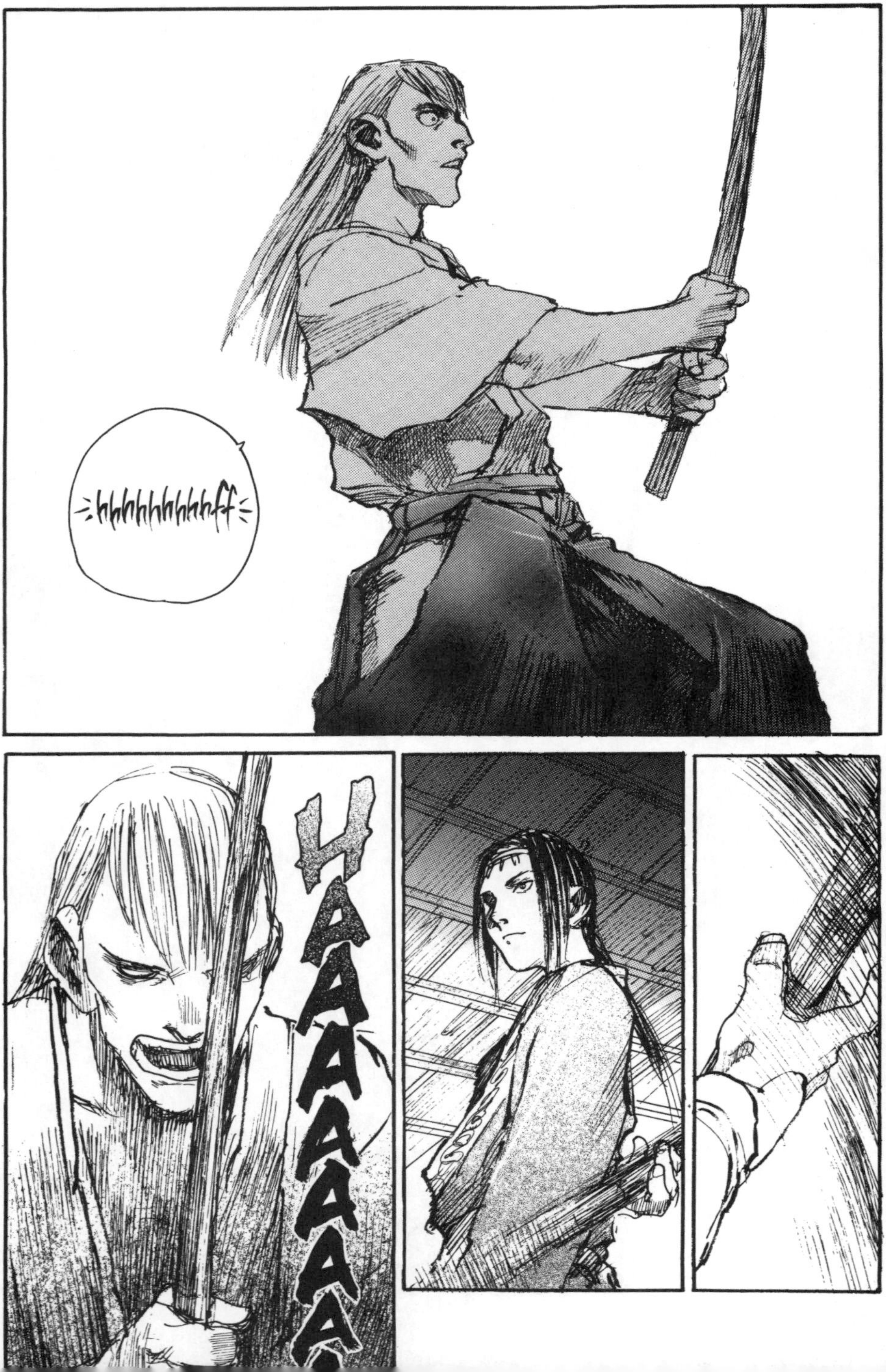
hhhhhhhhhff
HAAAAAAA

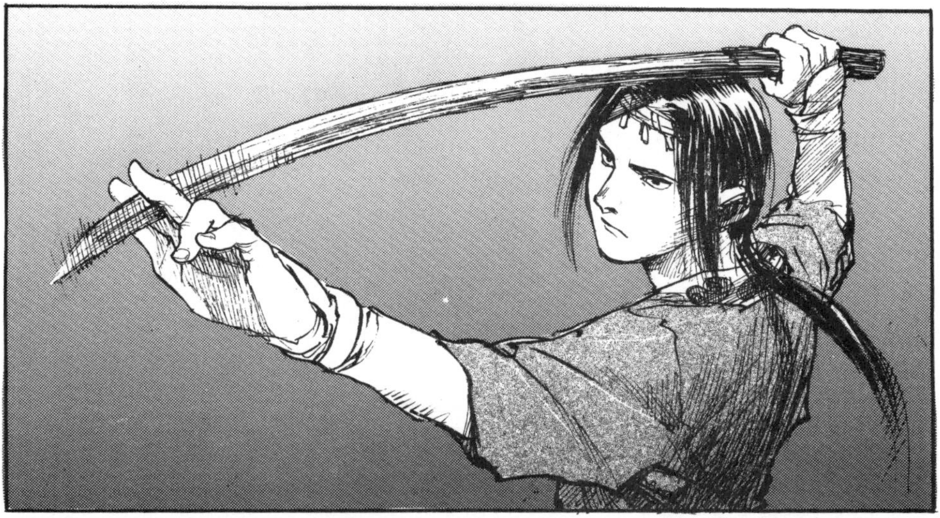
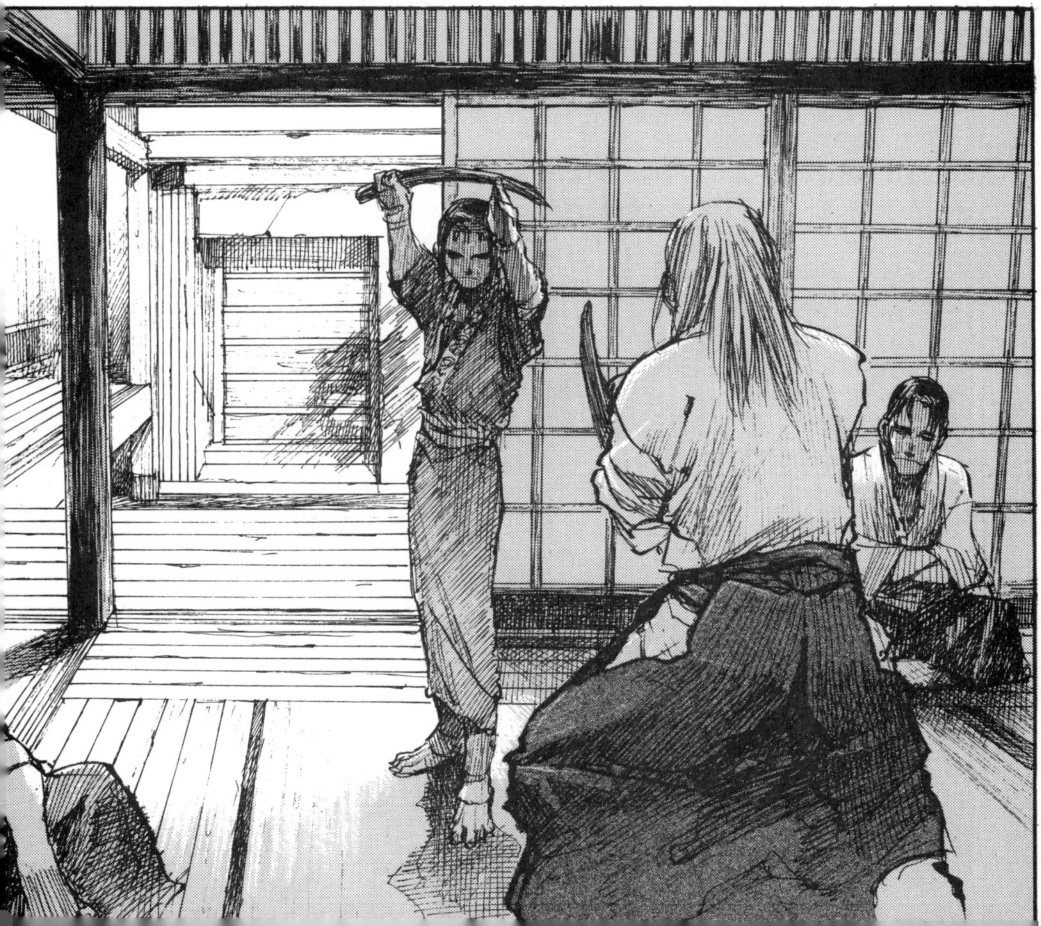

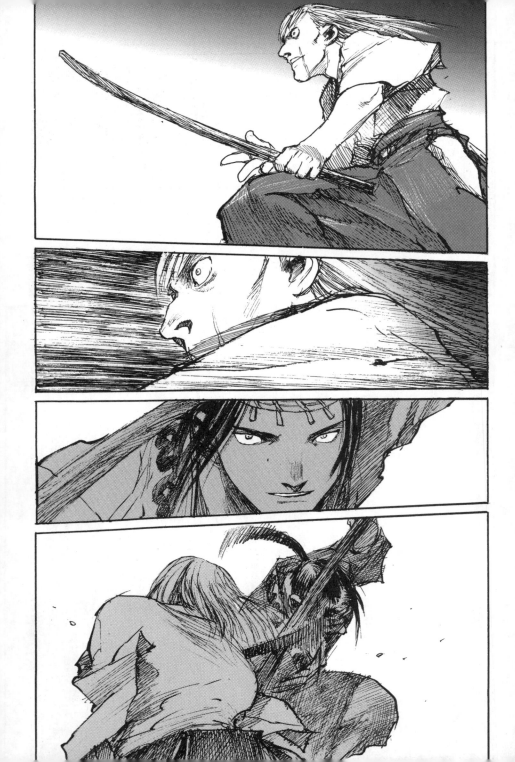

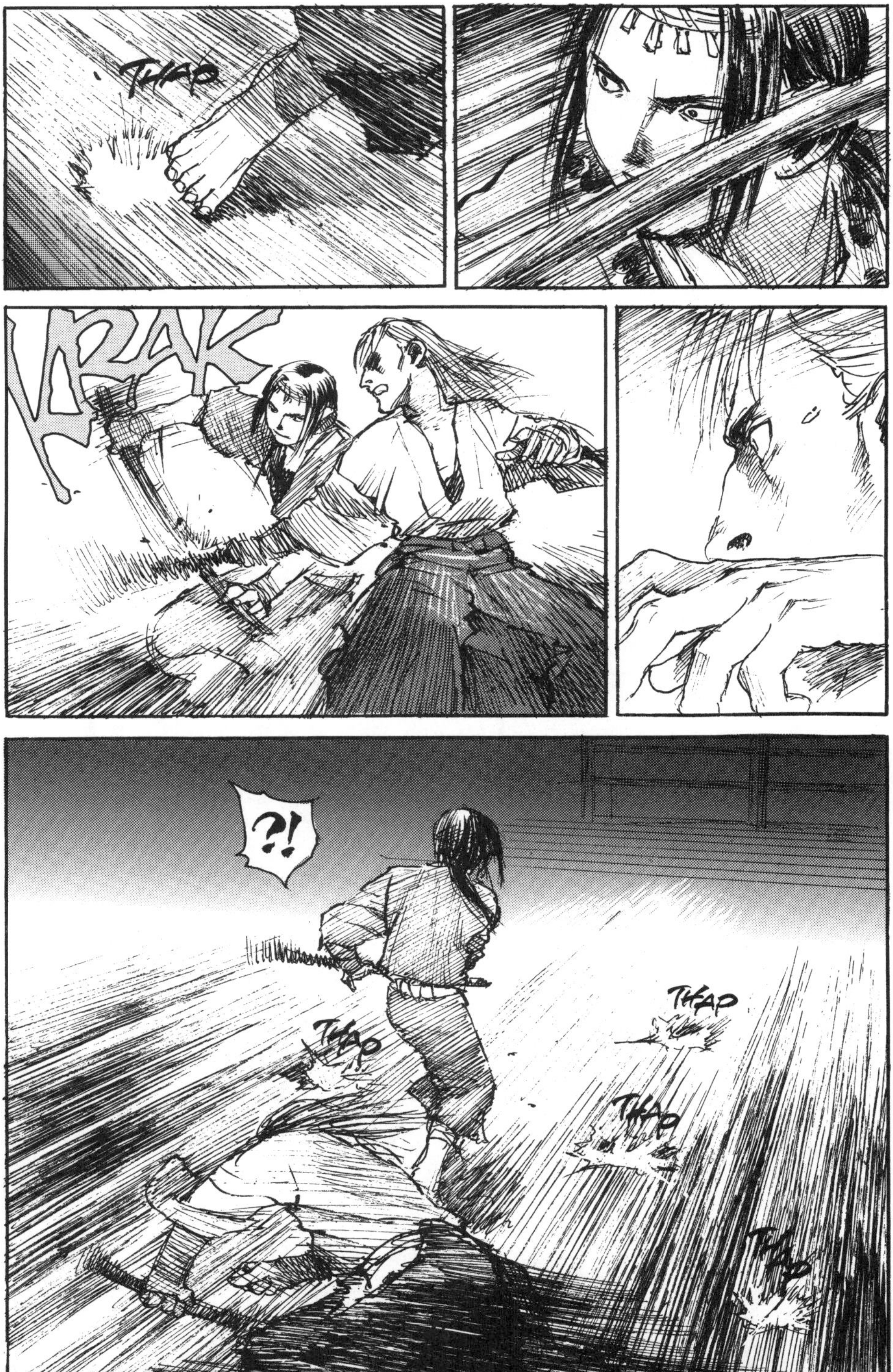
THAP
VRAK
?!
THAP
THAP
THAP
THAP

KRAK!

......
......
......!

?!
AH...?

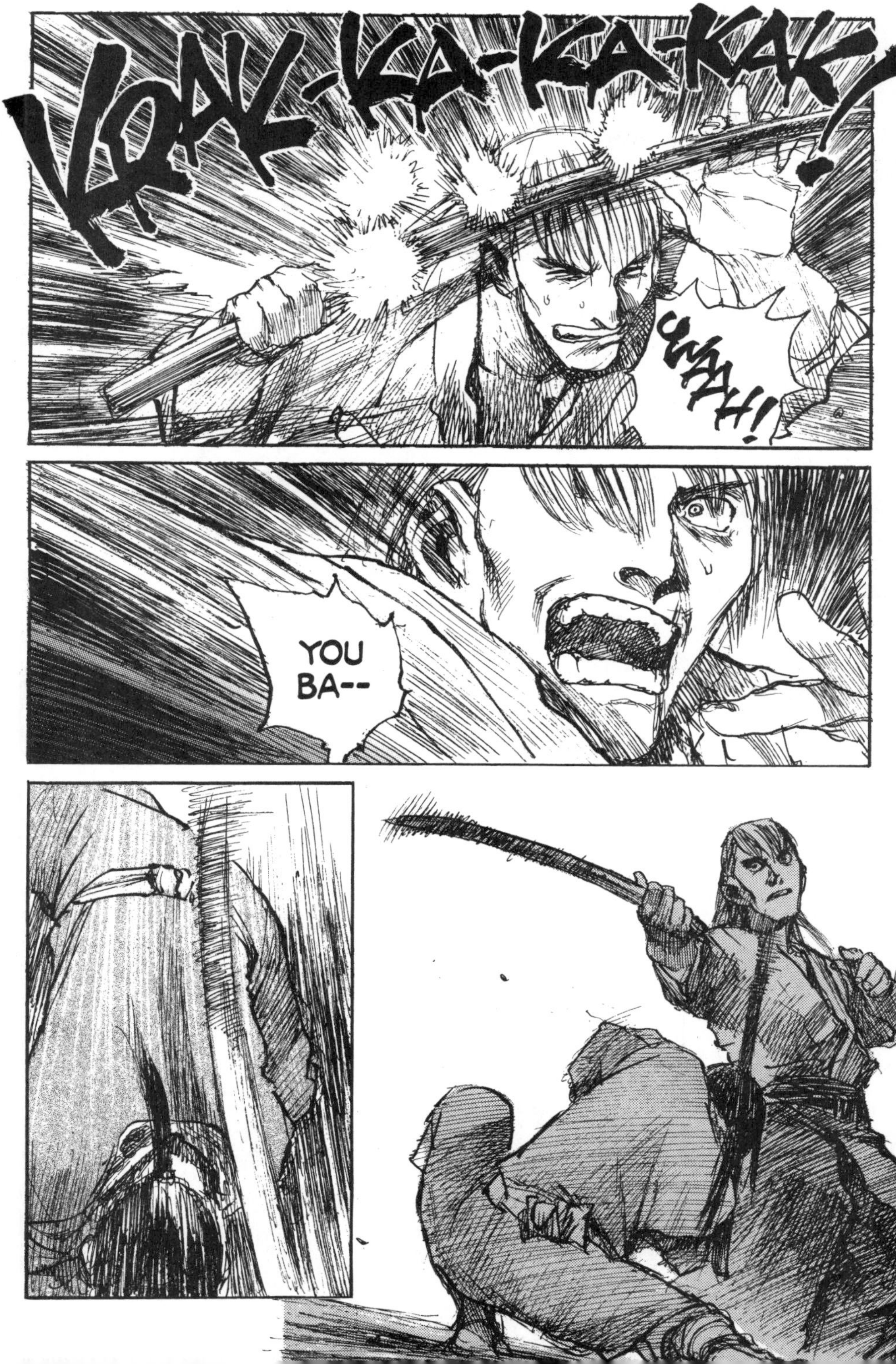
KOAK-KA-KA-KAK!
UWAH!!
YOU BA--

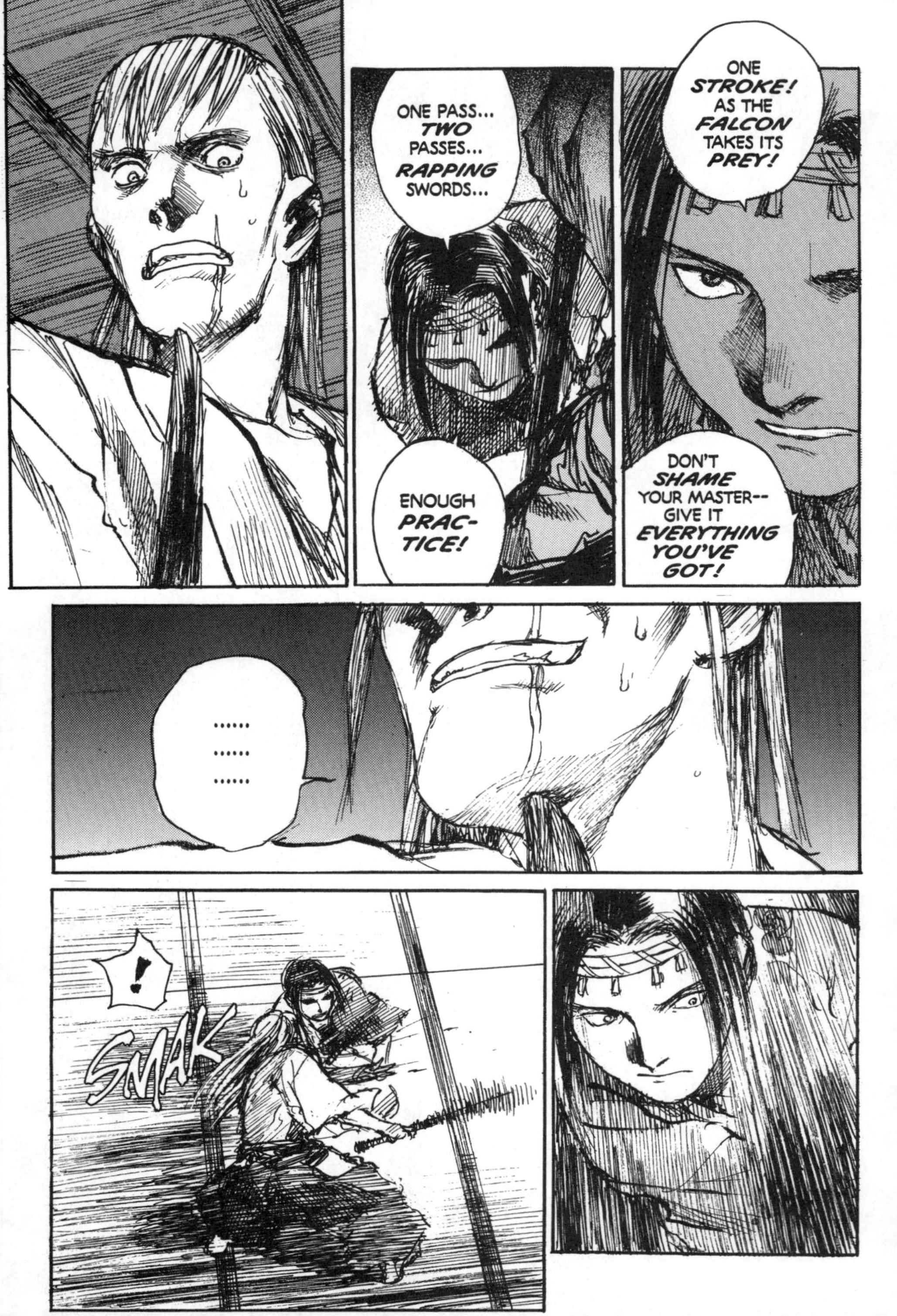
ONE PASS... TWO PASSES... RAPPING SWORDS...
ENOUGH PRAC-TICE!
ONE STROKE! AS THE FALCON TAKES ITS PREY!
DON'T SHAME YOUR MASTER-- GIVE IT EVERYTHING YOU'VE GOT!
......
......
......
!
SMAK

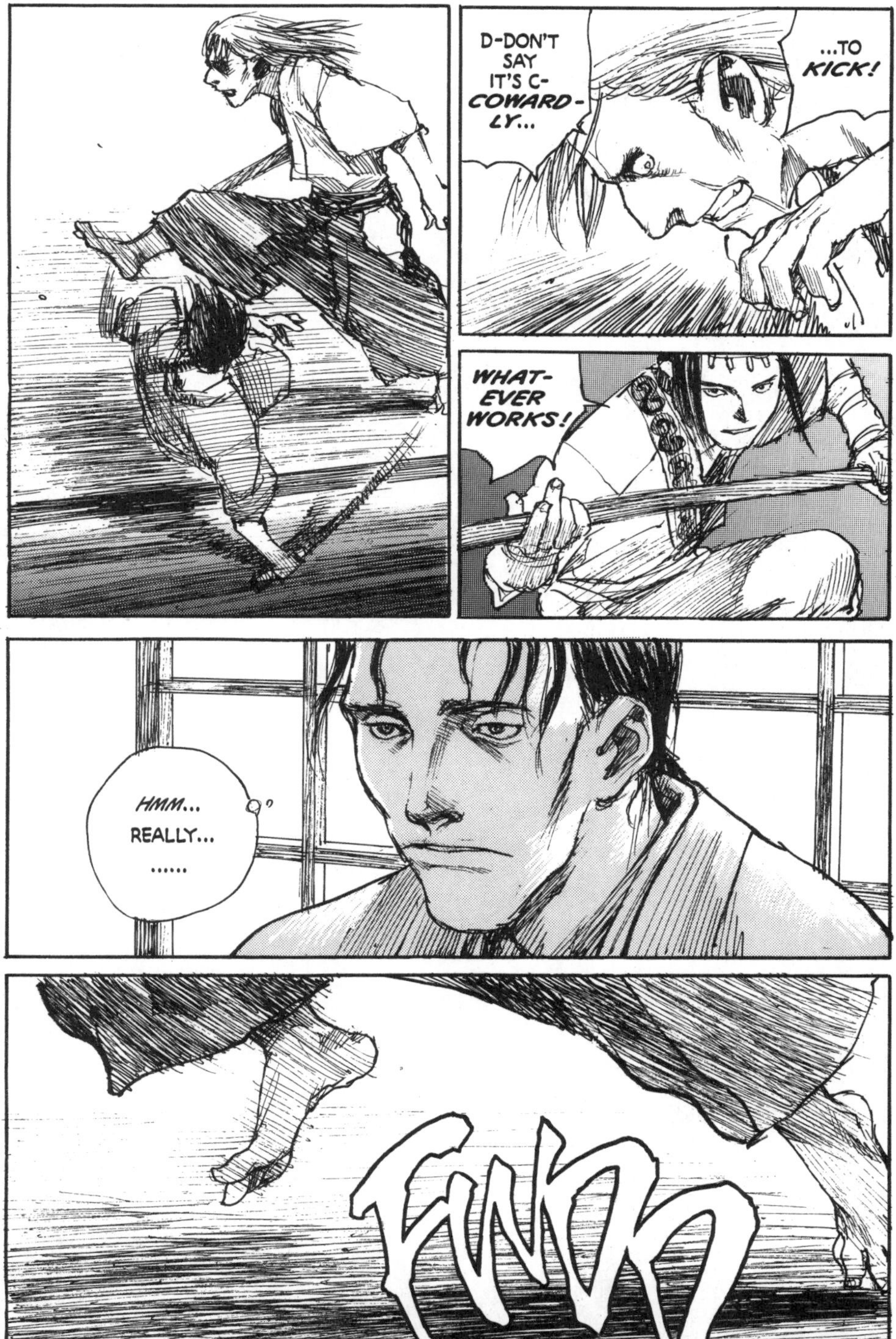
D-DON'T SAY IT'S C-COWARD-LY...
...TO KICK!
WHAT-EVER WORKS!
HMM... REALLY... ......

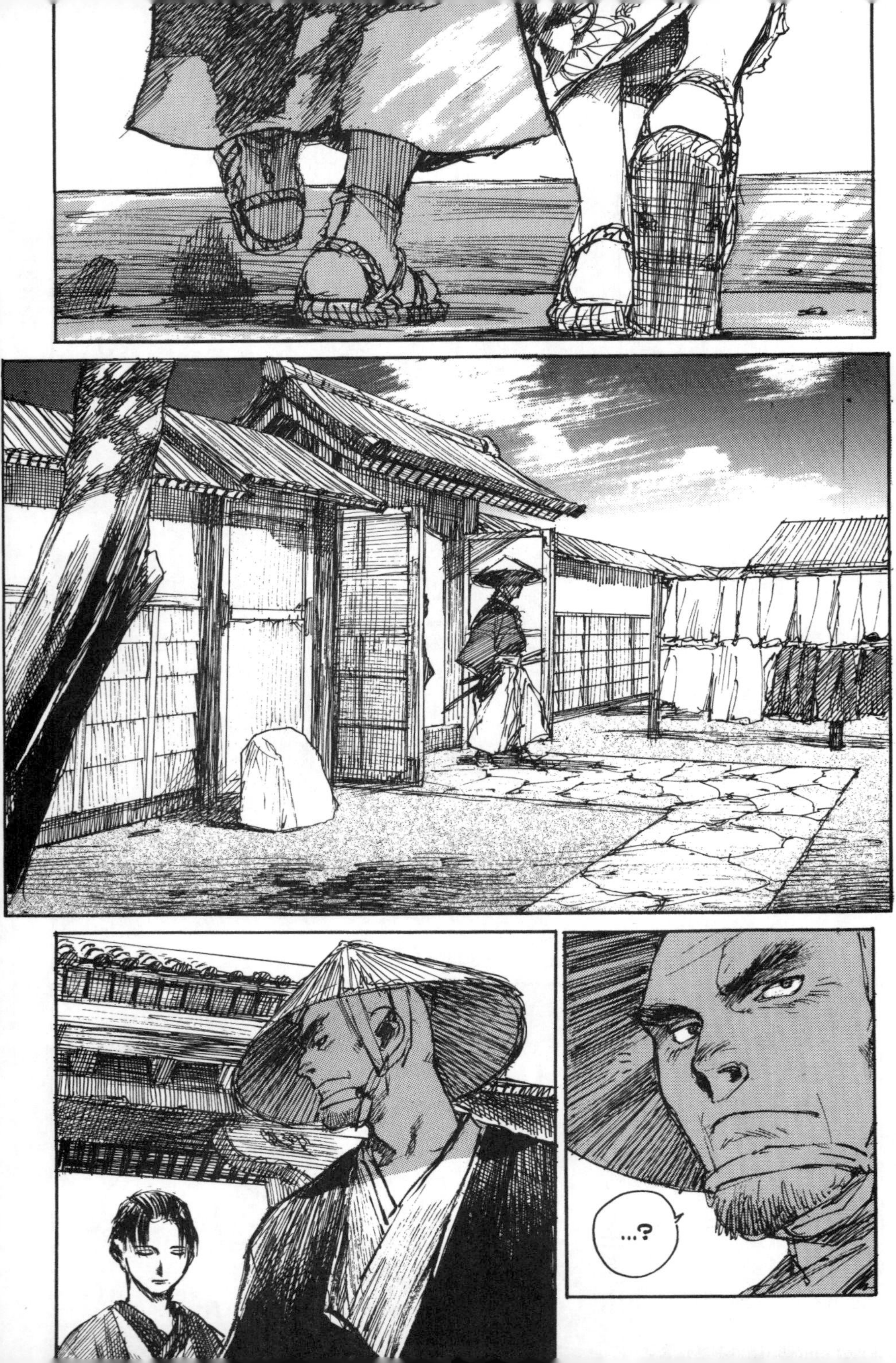
...?

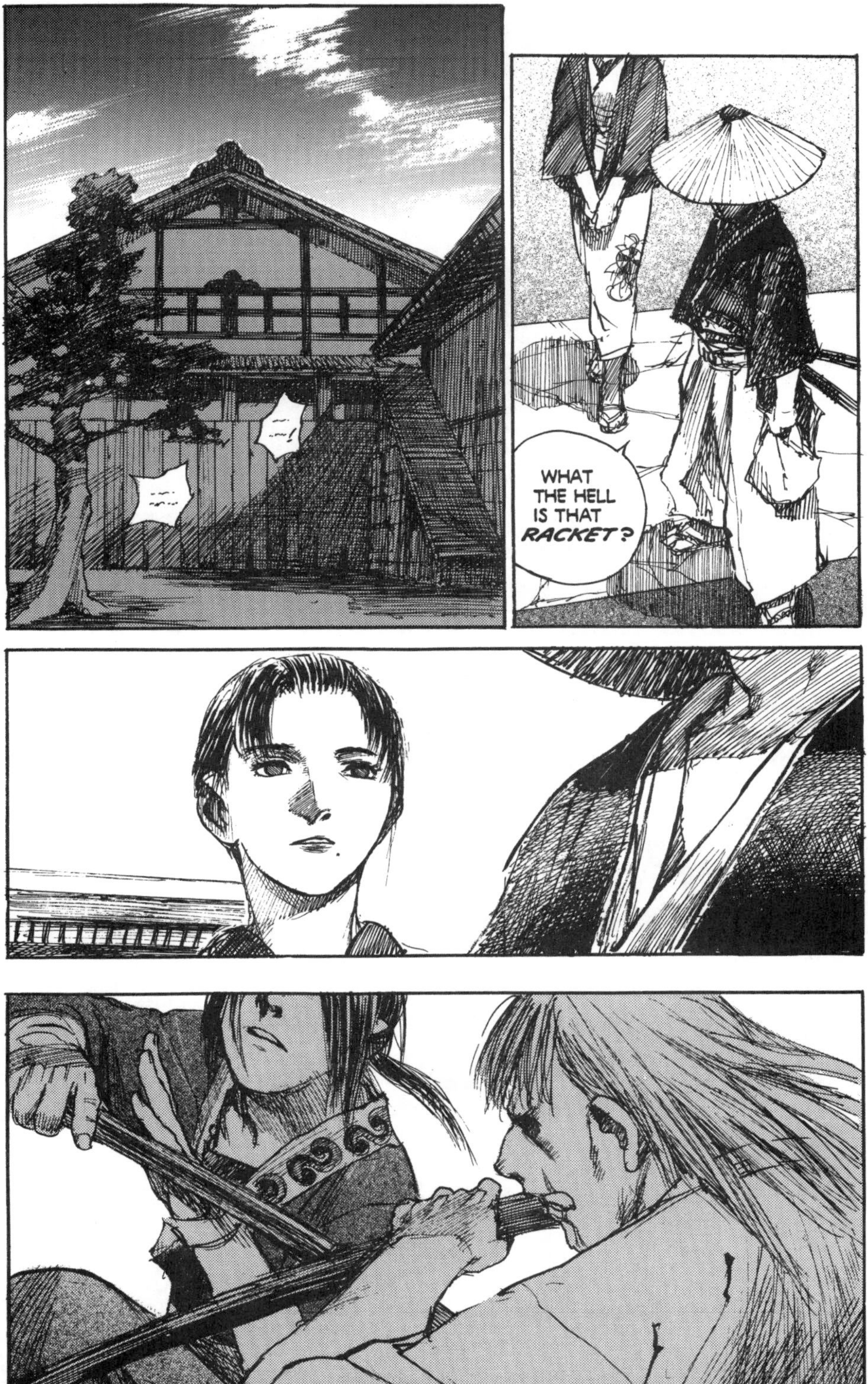
WHAT THE HELL IS THAT RACKET?

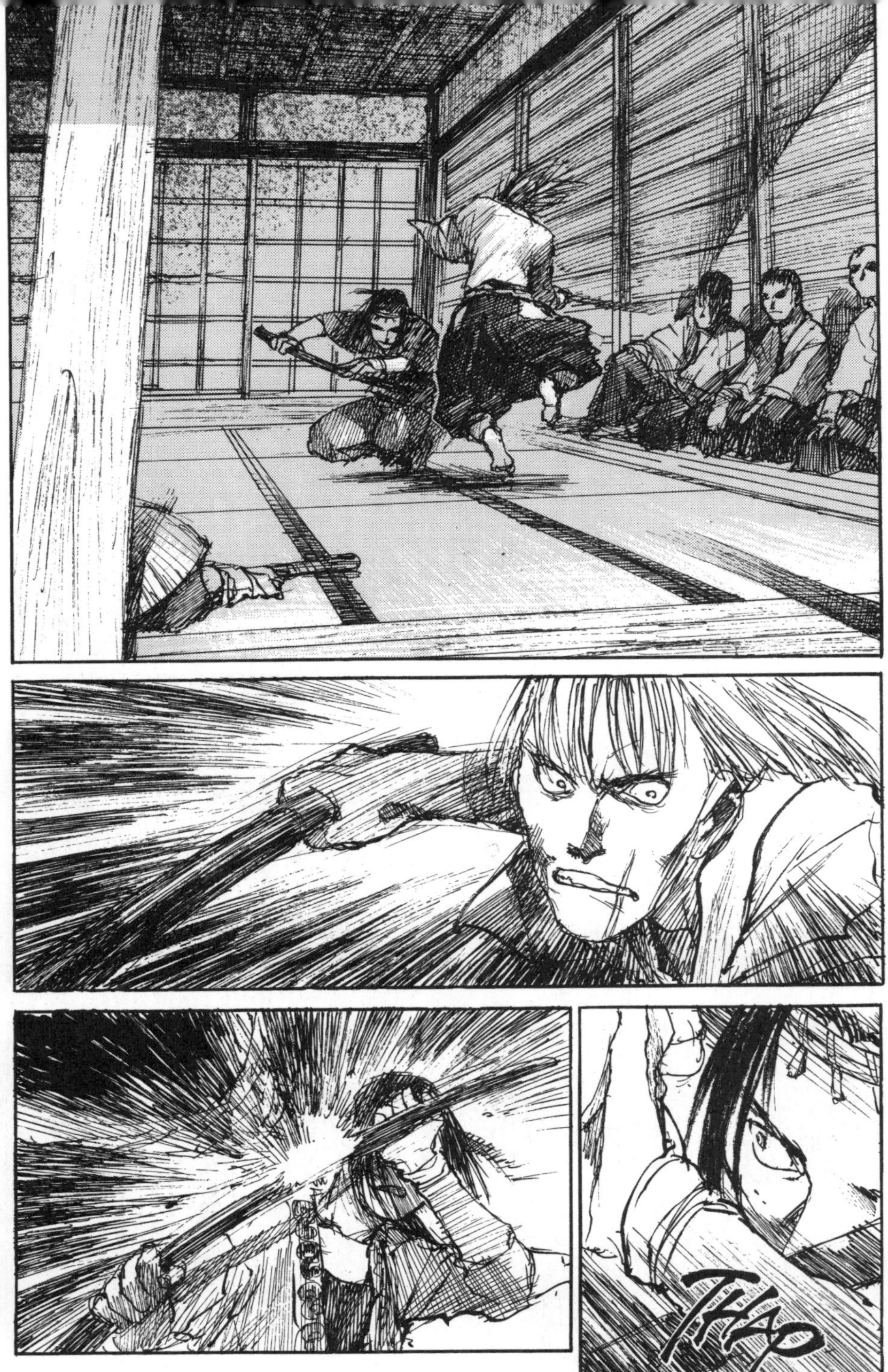
THAP

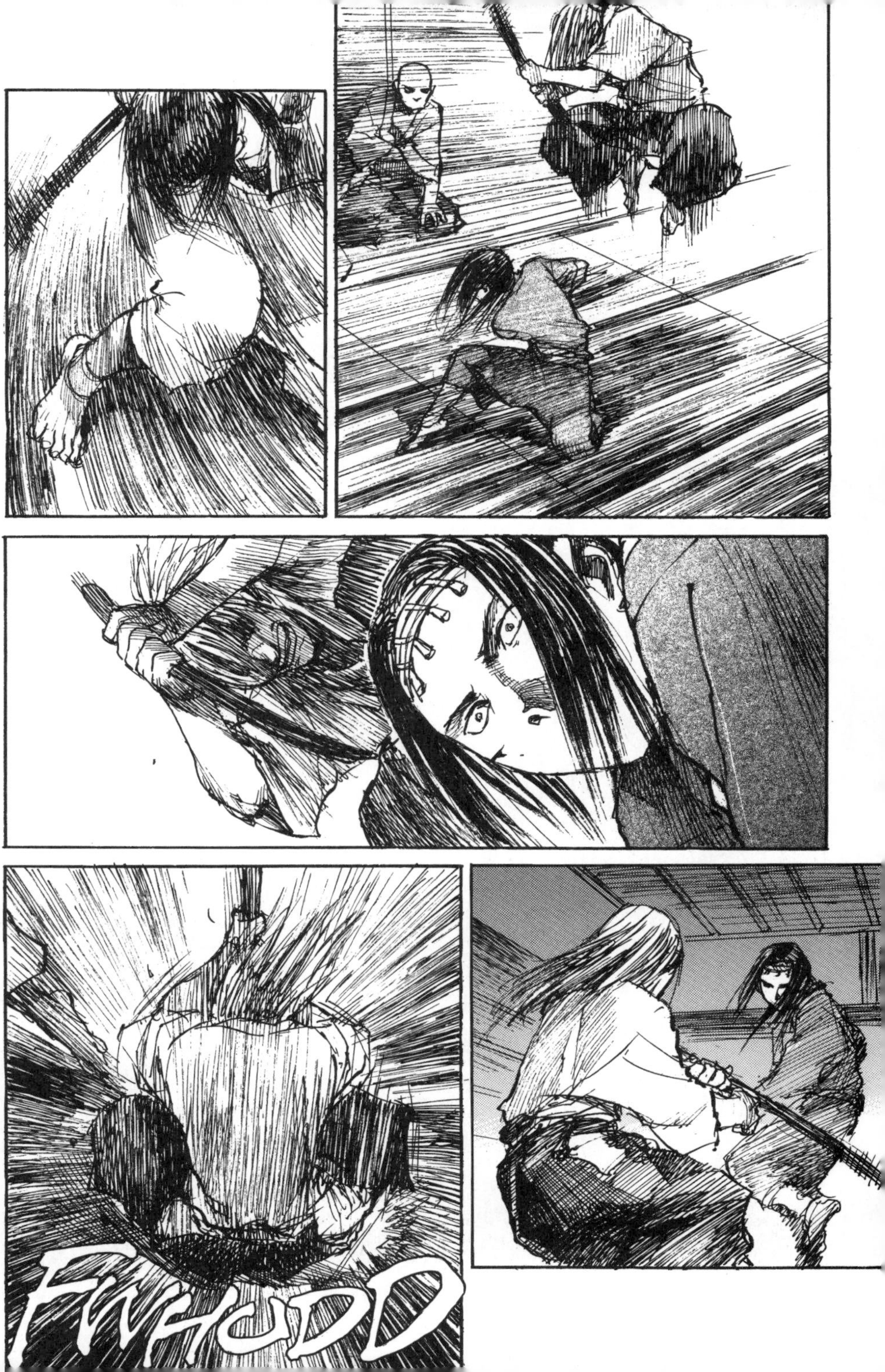
FWHUDD

HYAA!

WASSHT

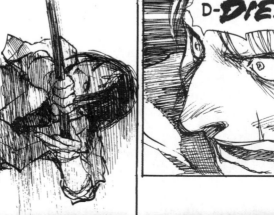

D-DIE...!

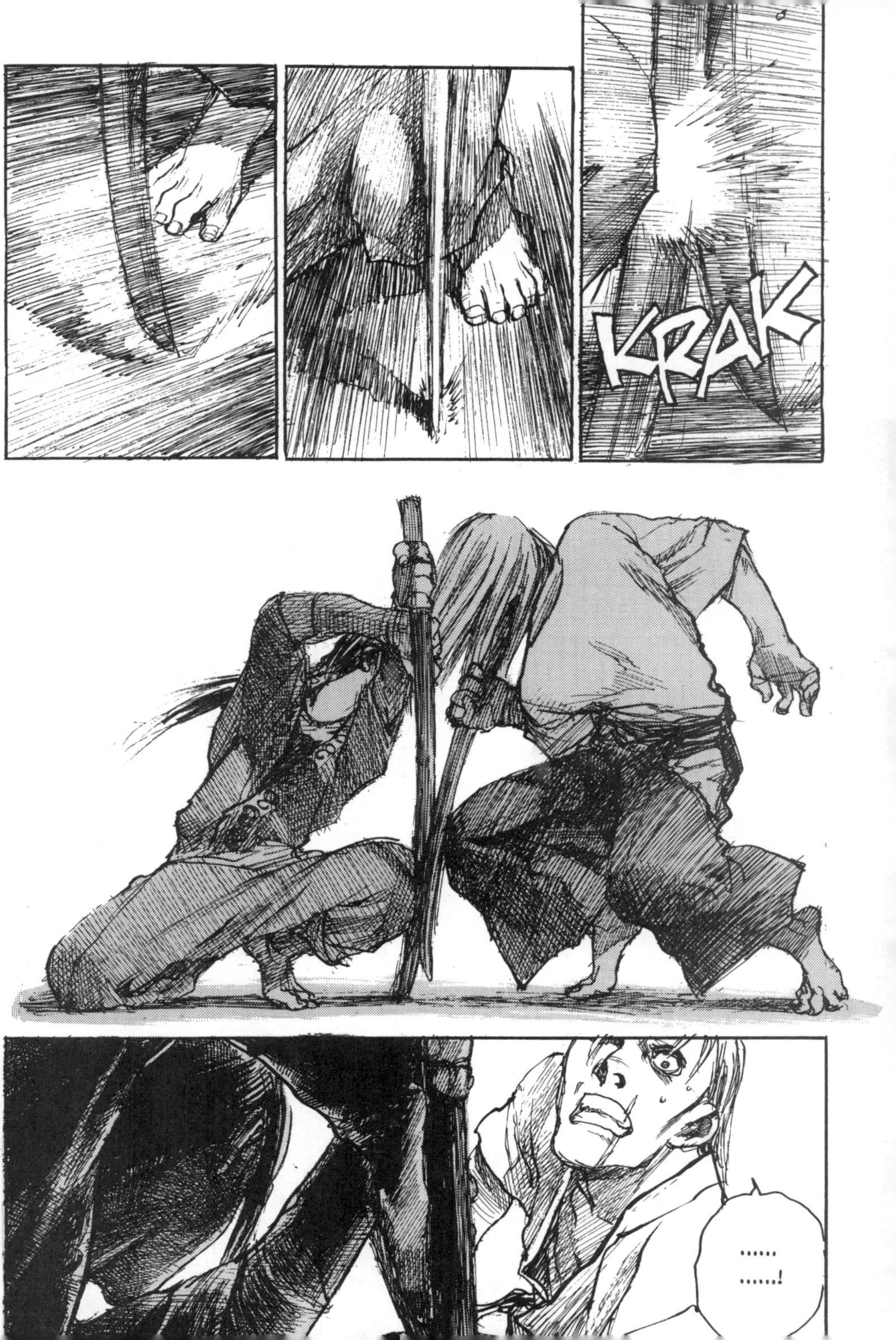
KRAK
......
......!

YOU'RE *FAST*-- I'M IMPRESSED. IF YOU CAN MOVE LIKE THAT, MAYBE YOU *DESERVE* TO CALL YOURSELF...

...ITTŌ-RYŪ!

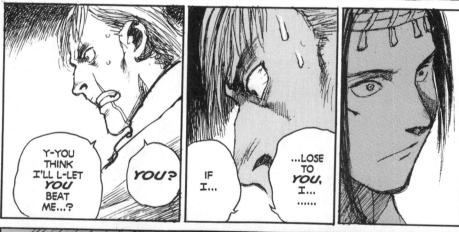

Y-YOU THINK I'LL L-LET *YOU* BEAT ME...?

YOU?

IF I...

...LOSE TO *YOU*, I... ......

RYAAH!

FRAK

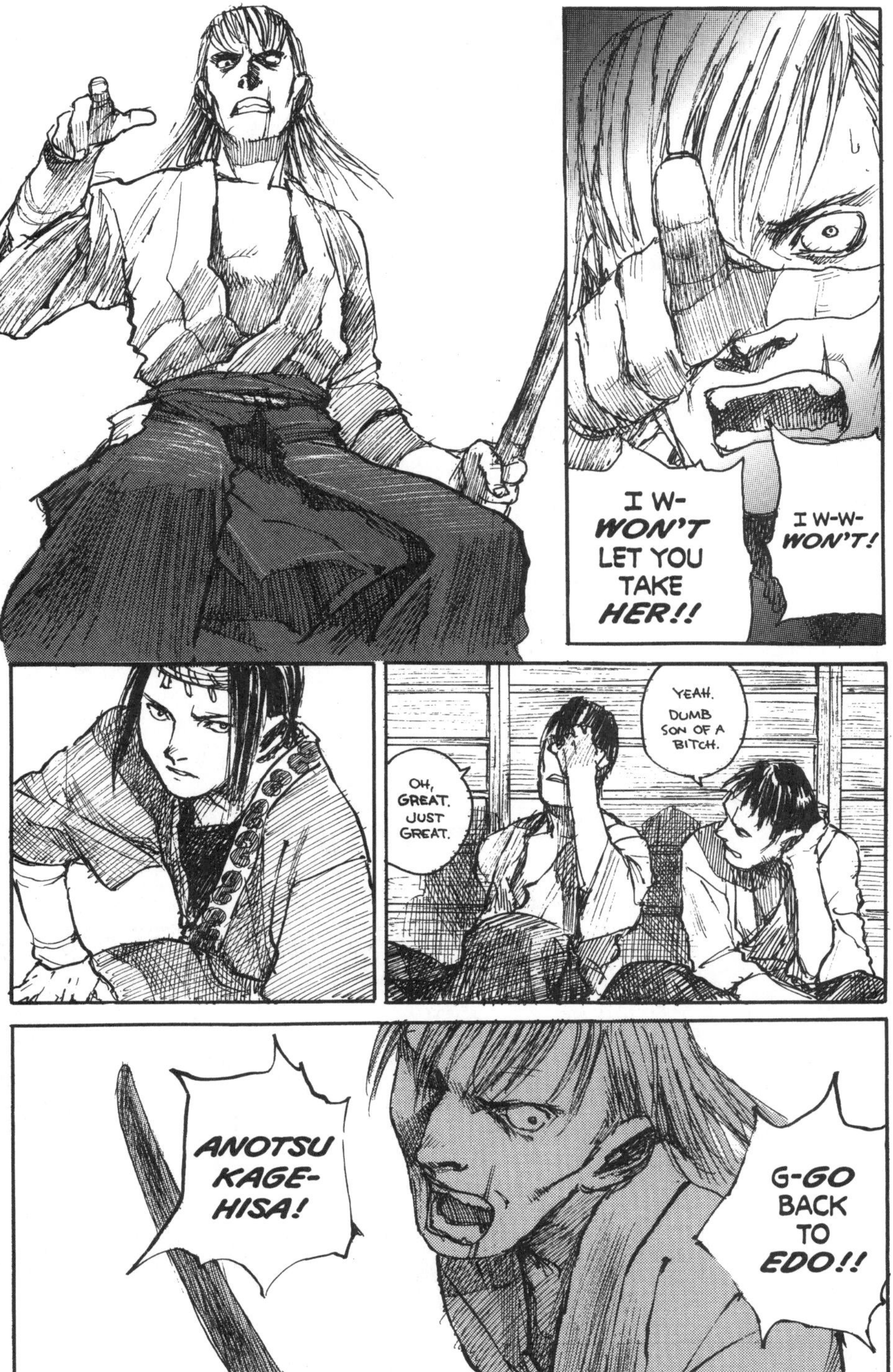
I W-WON'T LET YOU TAKE HER!!
I W-W-WON'T!
OH, GREAT. JUST GREAT.
YEAH. DUMB SON OF A BITCH.
ANOTSU KAGE-HISA!
G-GO BACK TO EDO!!

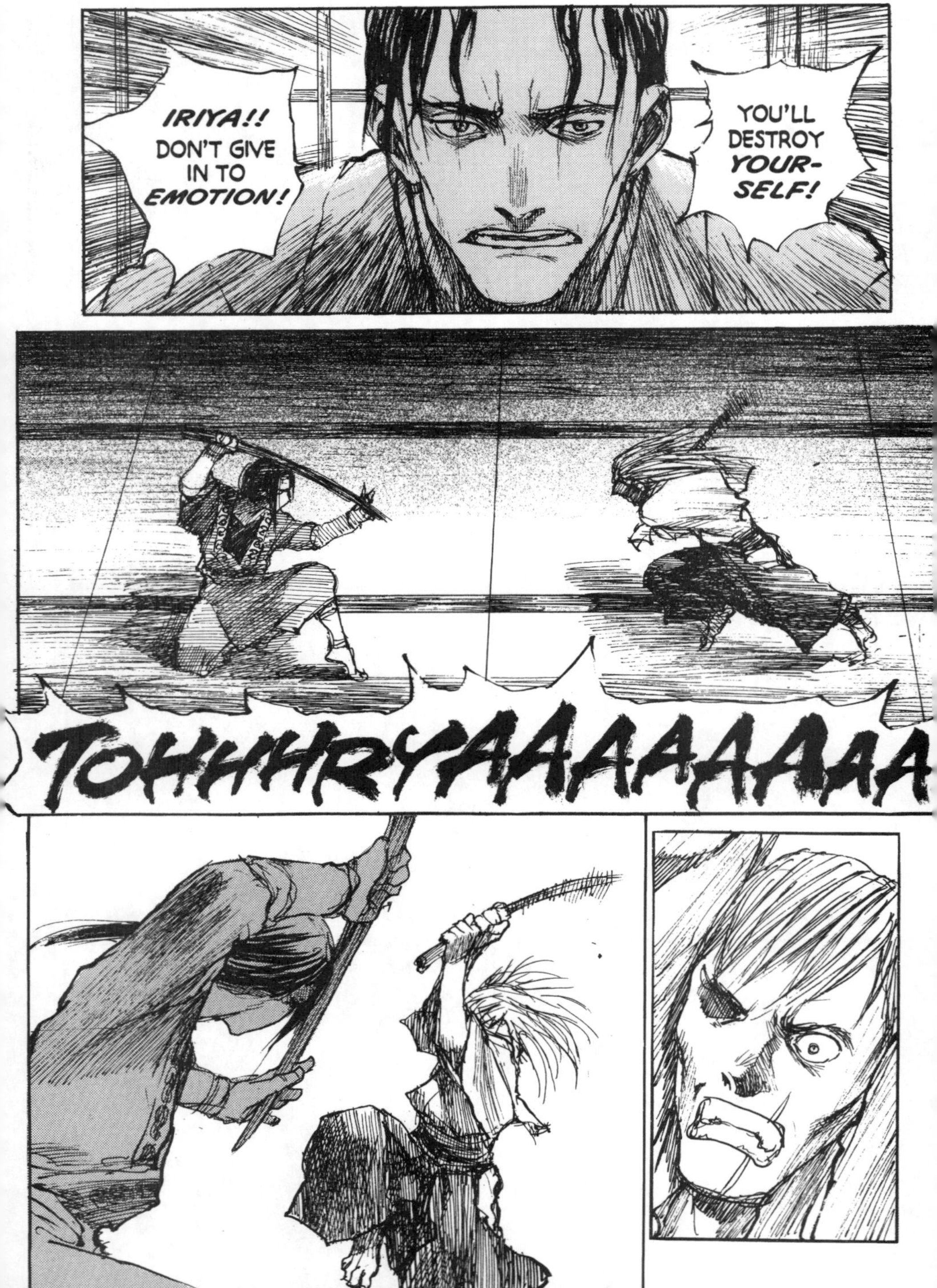
IRIYA!! DON'T GIVE IN TO EMOTION!
YOU'LL DESTROY YOURSELF!
TOHHHRYAAAAAAAAA

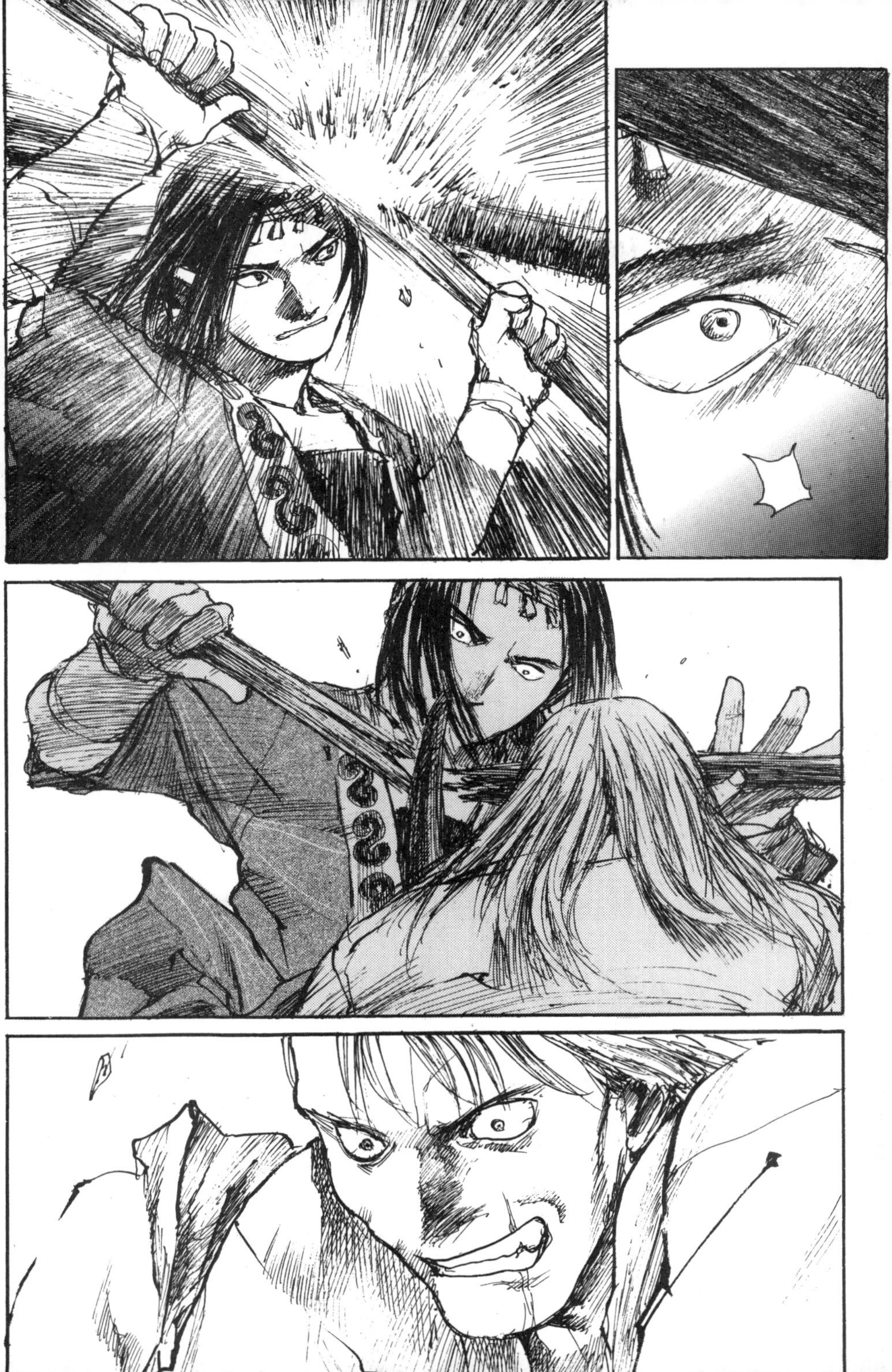

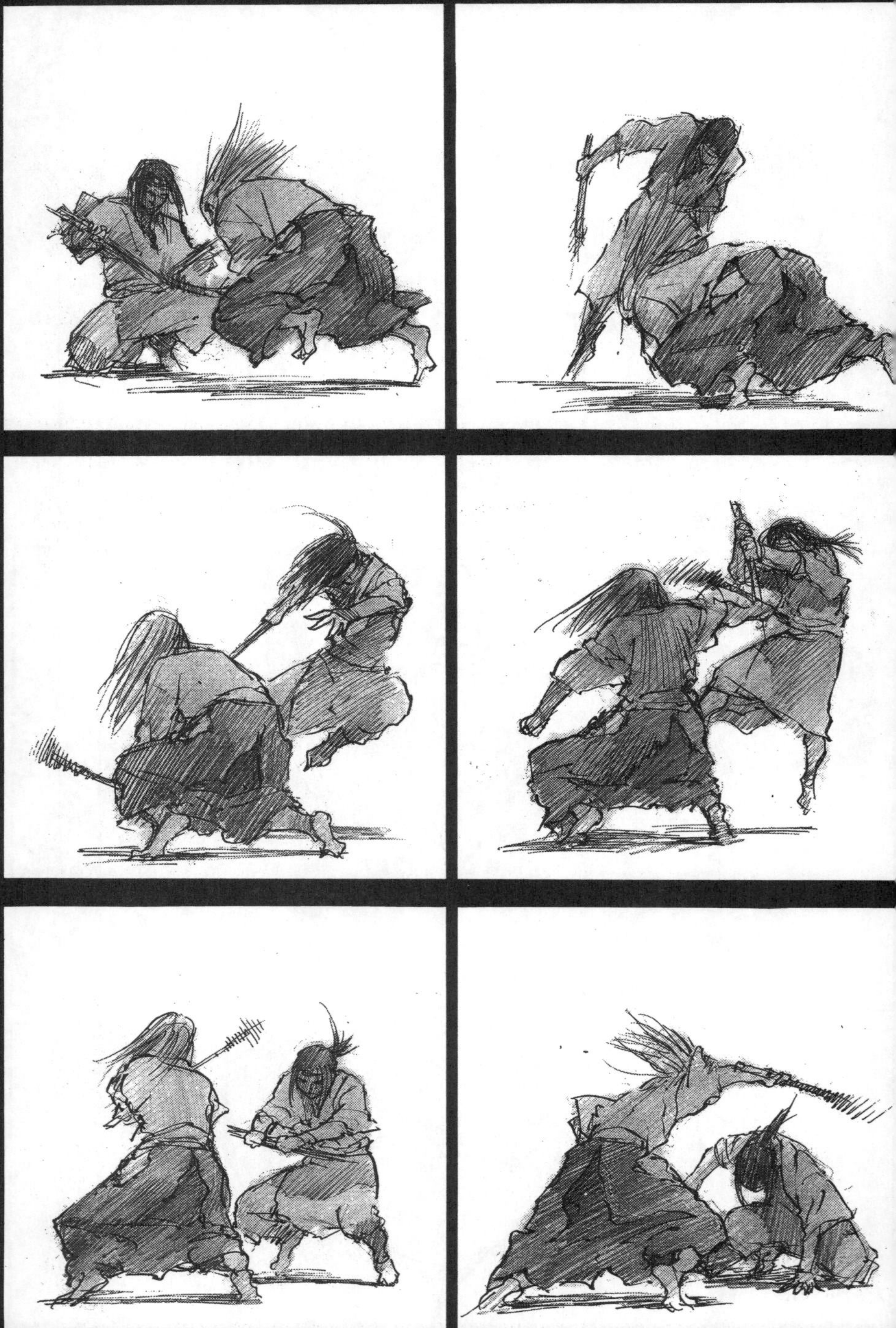

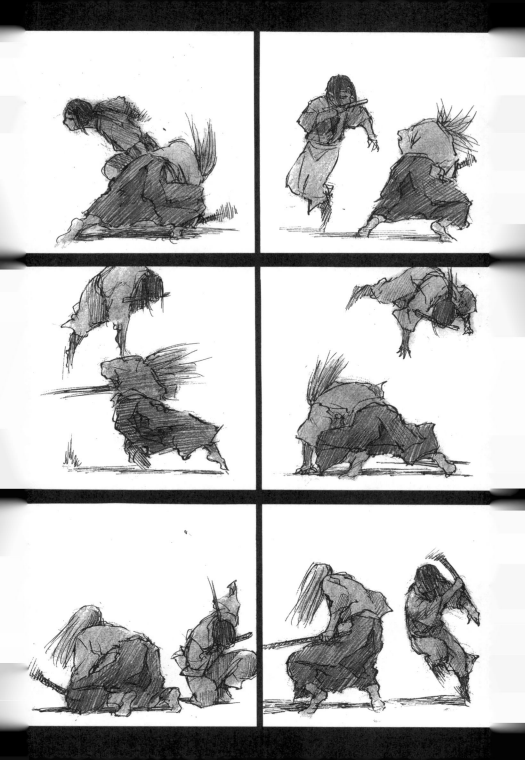

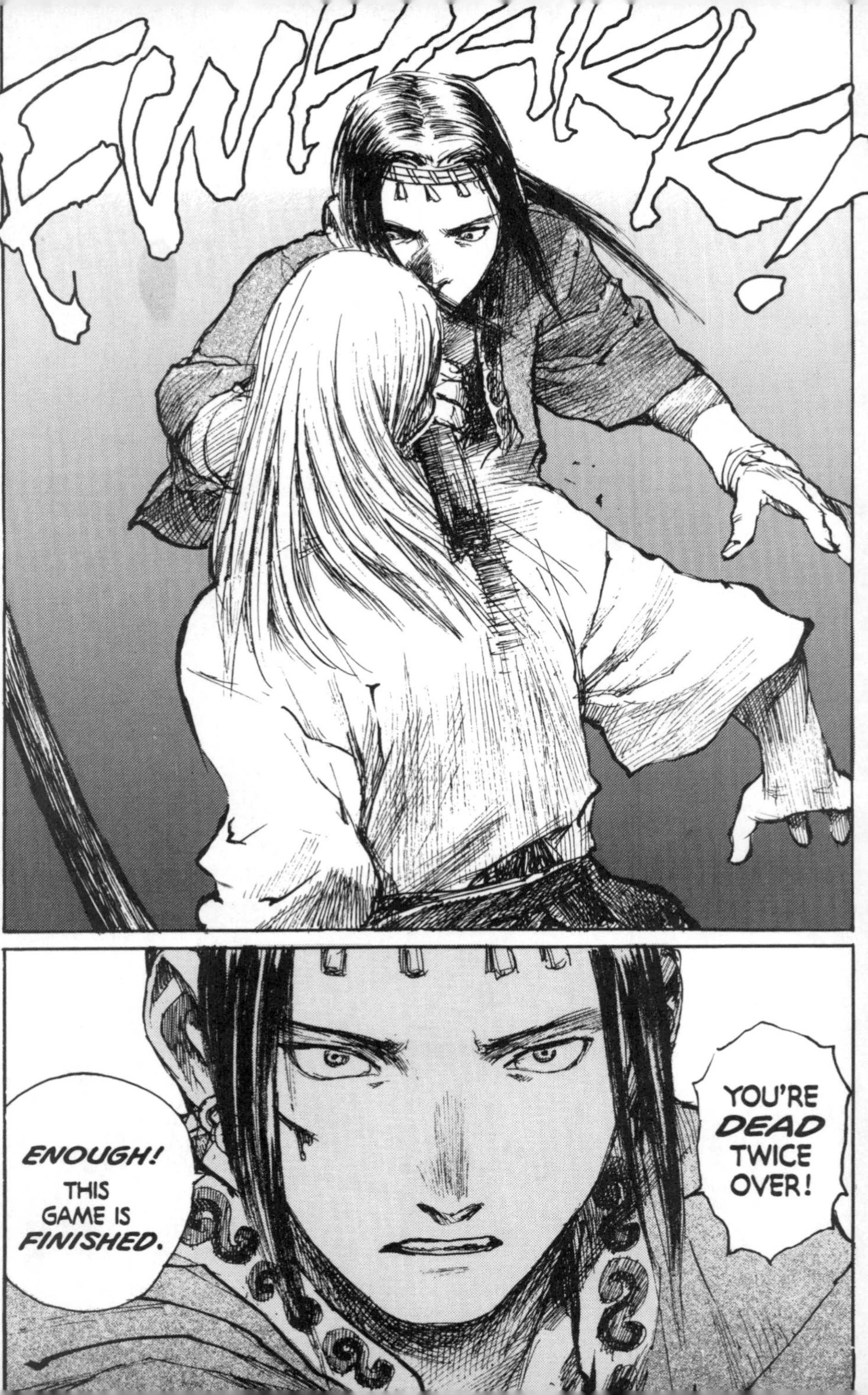
FWHAKK!
ENOUGH! THIS GAME IS FINISHED.
YOU'RE DEAD TWICE OVER!

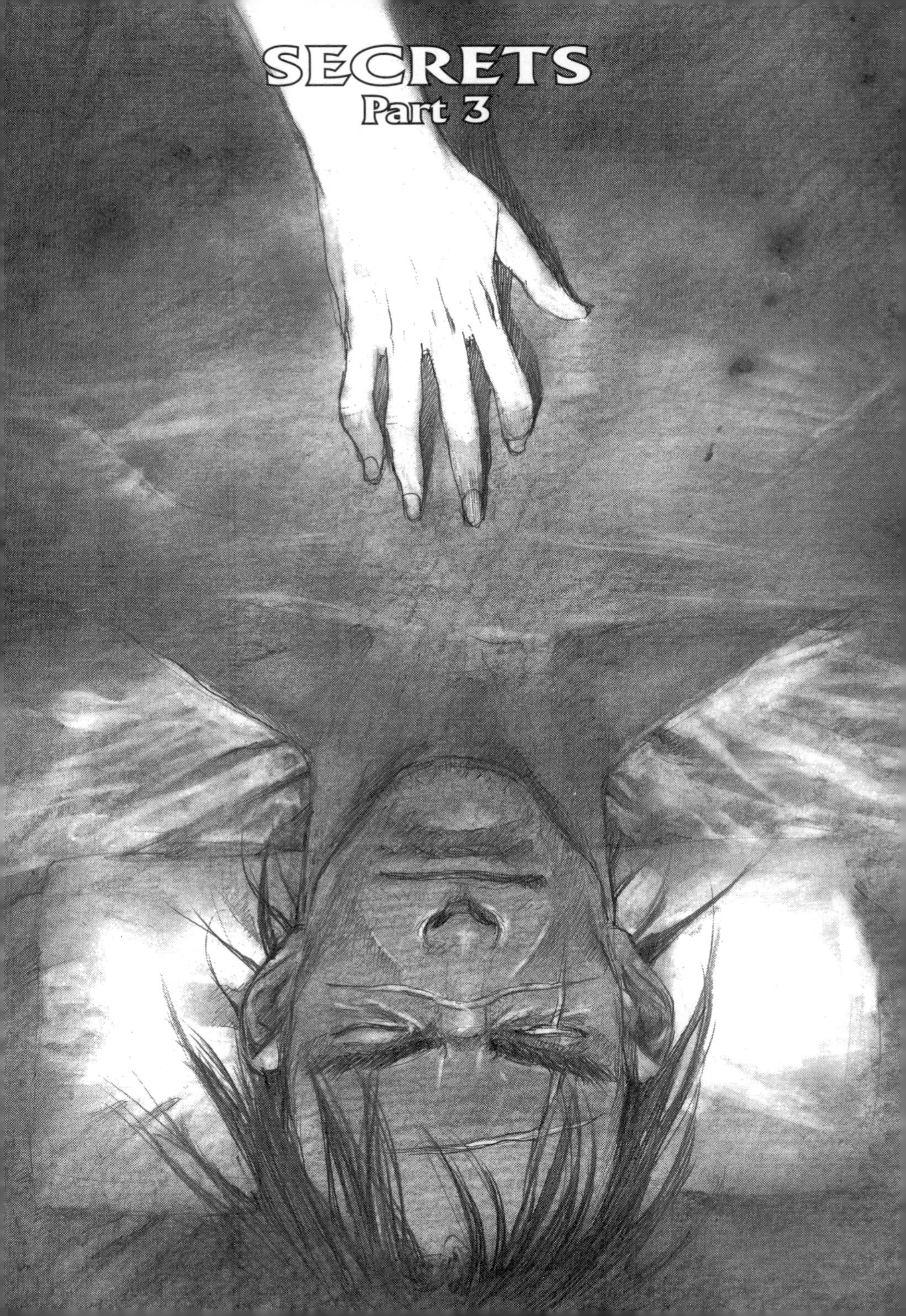
SECRETS
Part 3

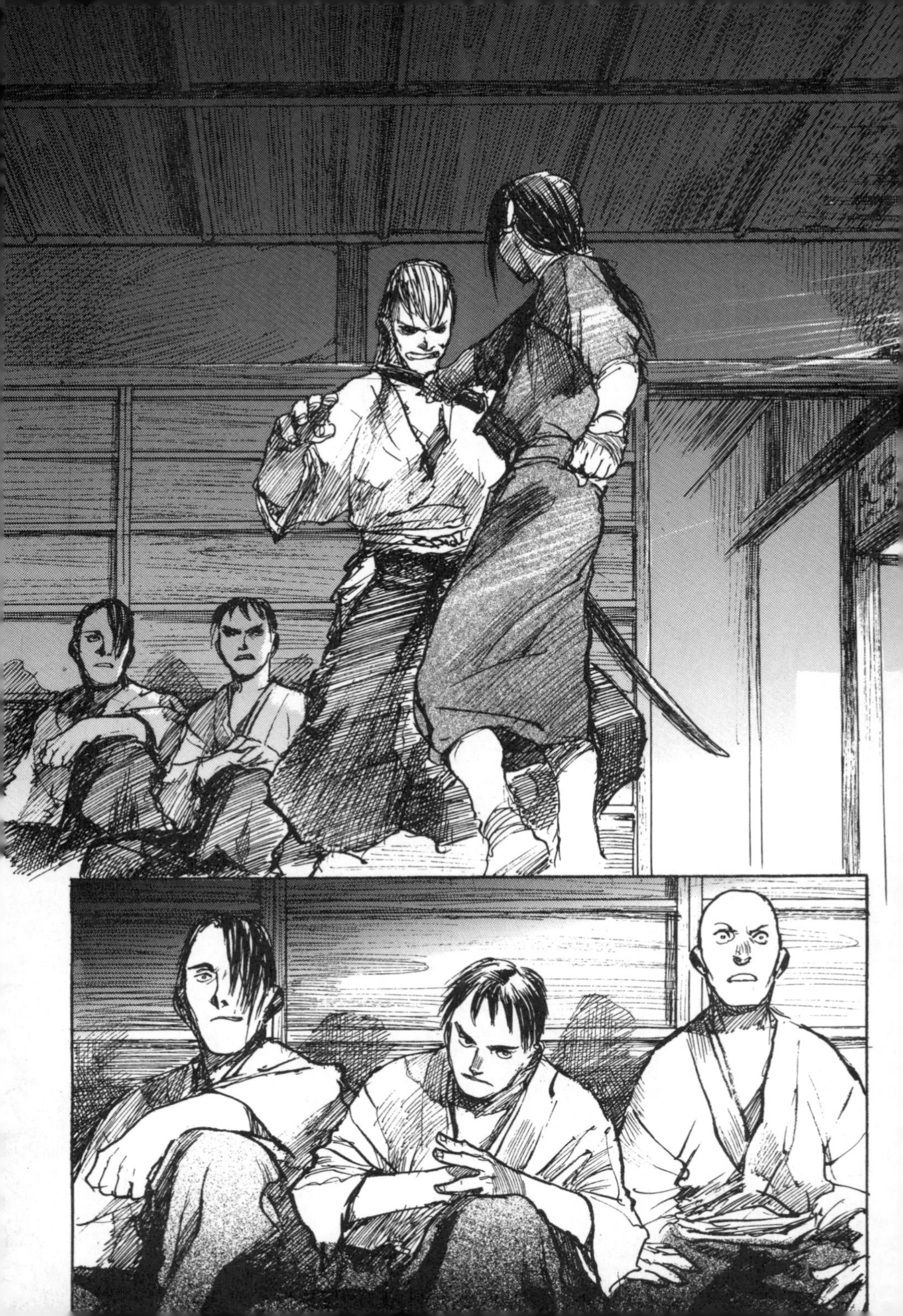

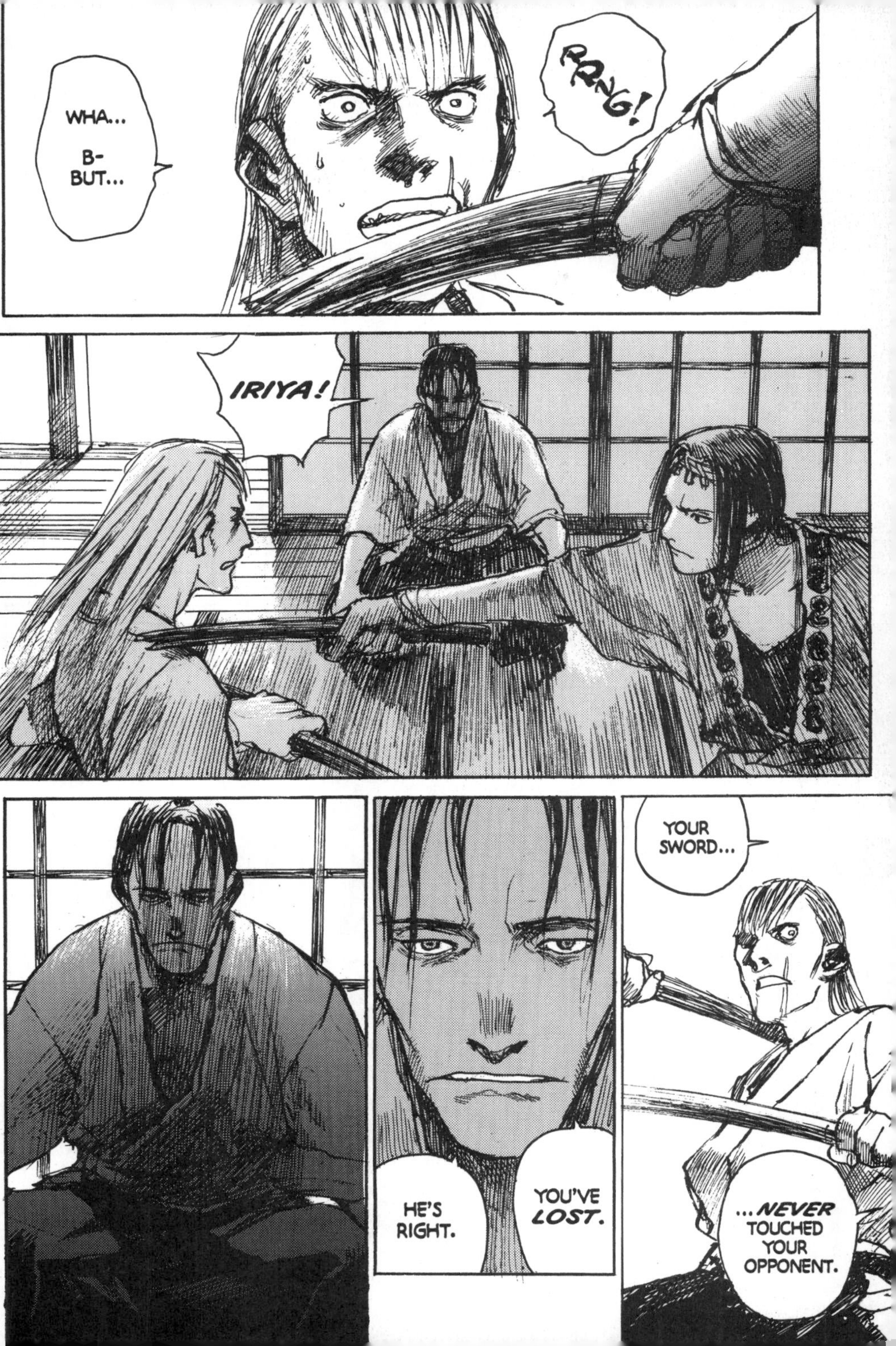
RRNG!
WHA... B- BUT...
IRIYA!
YOUR SWORD...
...NEVER TOUCHED YOUR OPPONENT.
YOU'VE LOST.
HE'S RIGHT.

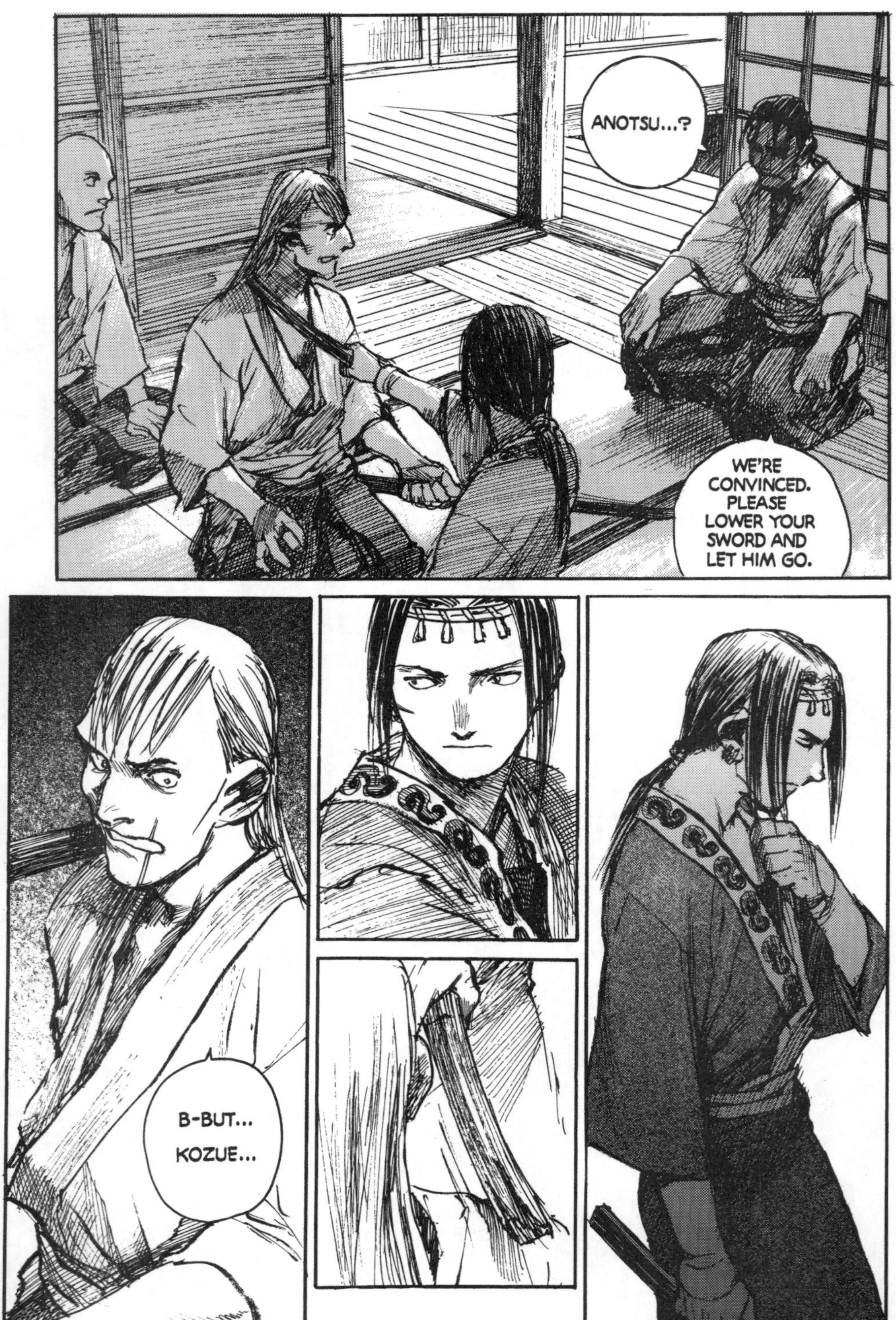
ANOTSU...?
WE'RE CONVINCED. PLEASE LOWER YOUR SWORD AND LET HIM GO.
B-BUT... KOZUE...

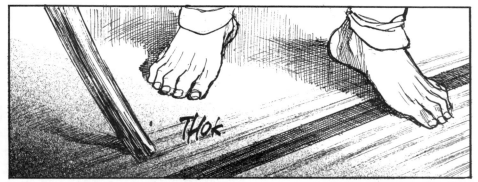

THOK

KOZUE! Y-YOU!

WH-WHAT *IS* THIS?! WHOSE *SIDE* ARE YOU *ON*?!

SHUT UP, IRIYA.

YOU SAID *SIZE* DOESN'T DETERMINE STRENGTH.

WELL, NOW YOU KNOW...

...THAT *AGE* DOESN'T, EITHER.

B-BUT I WAS--

AND ANOTHER THING.

NOT KNOWING WHEN TO *QUIT* IS MORE HUMILIATING THAN *LOSING*.

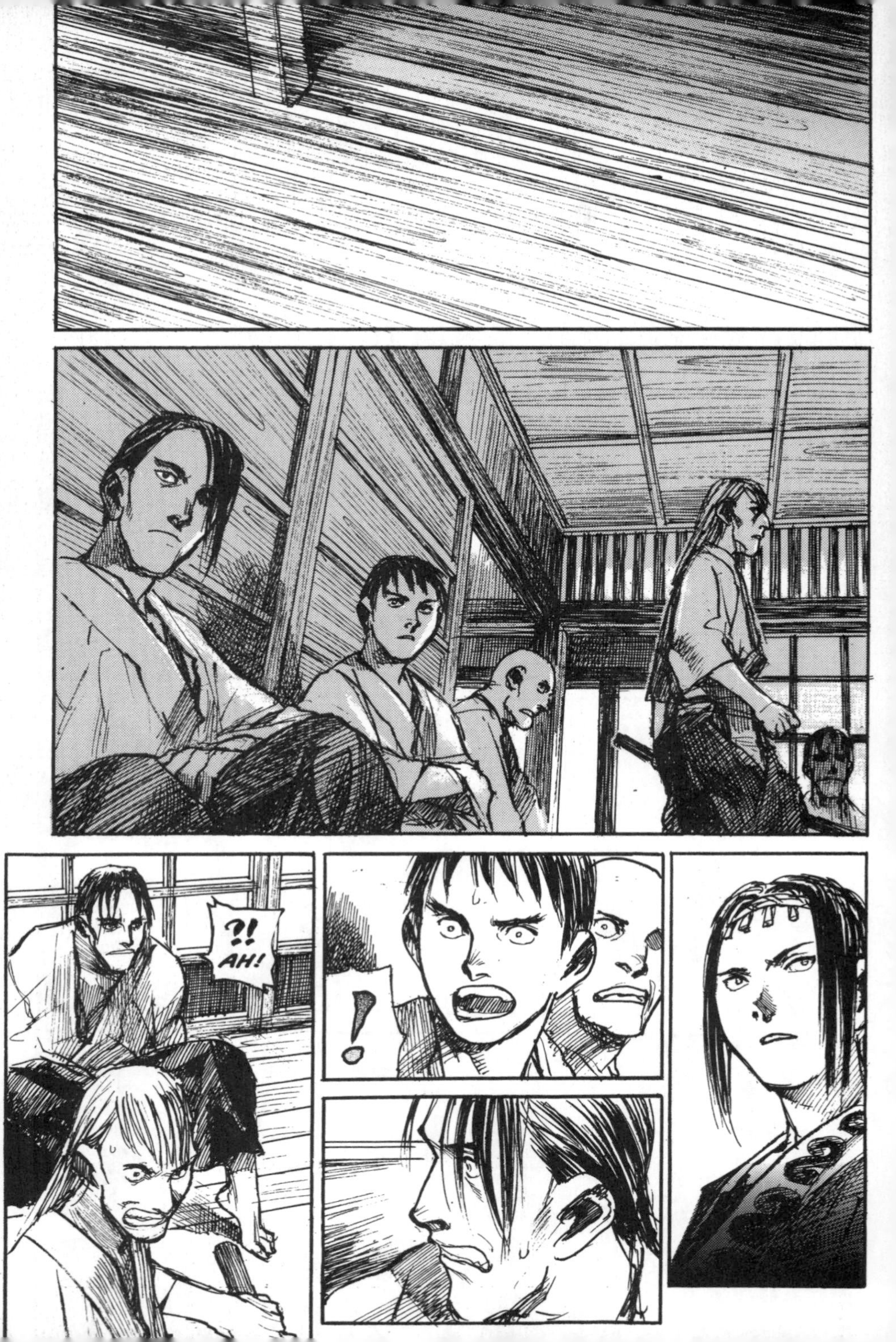
?!
AH!
!

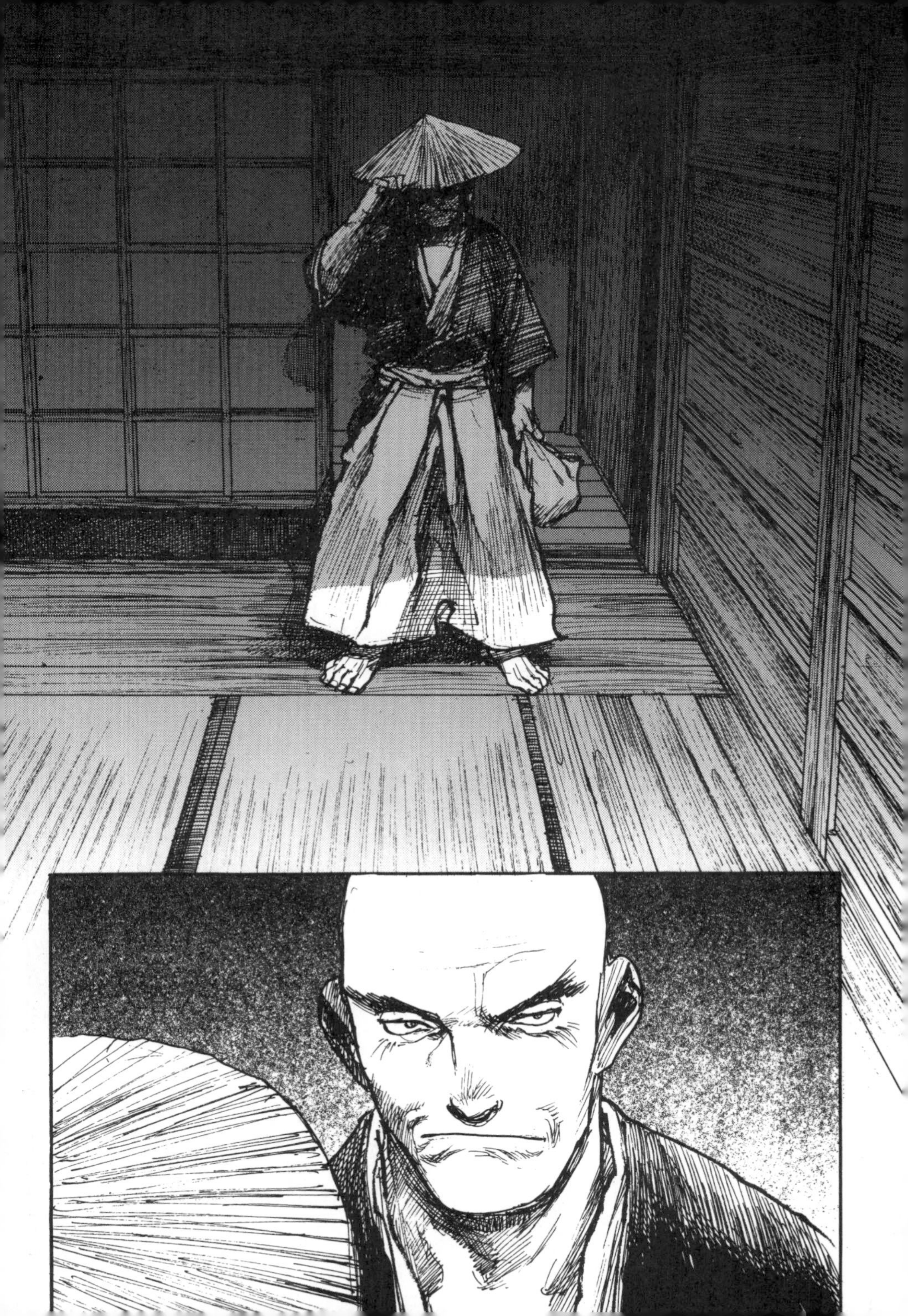

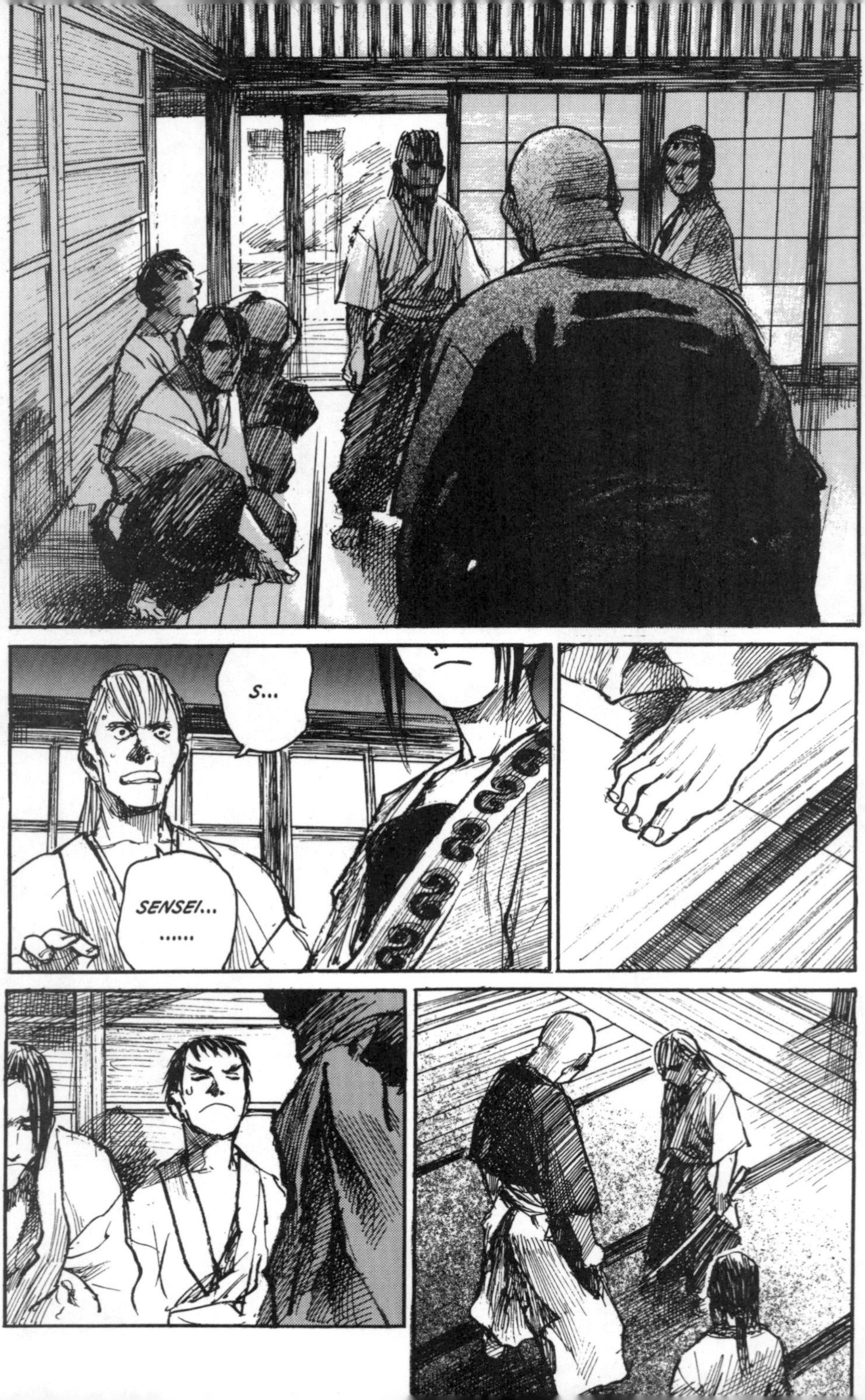
S...
SENSEI...
......

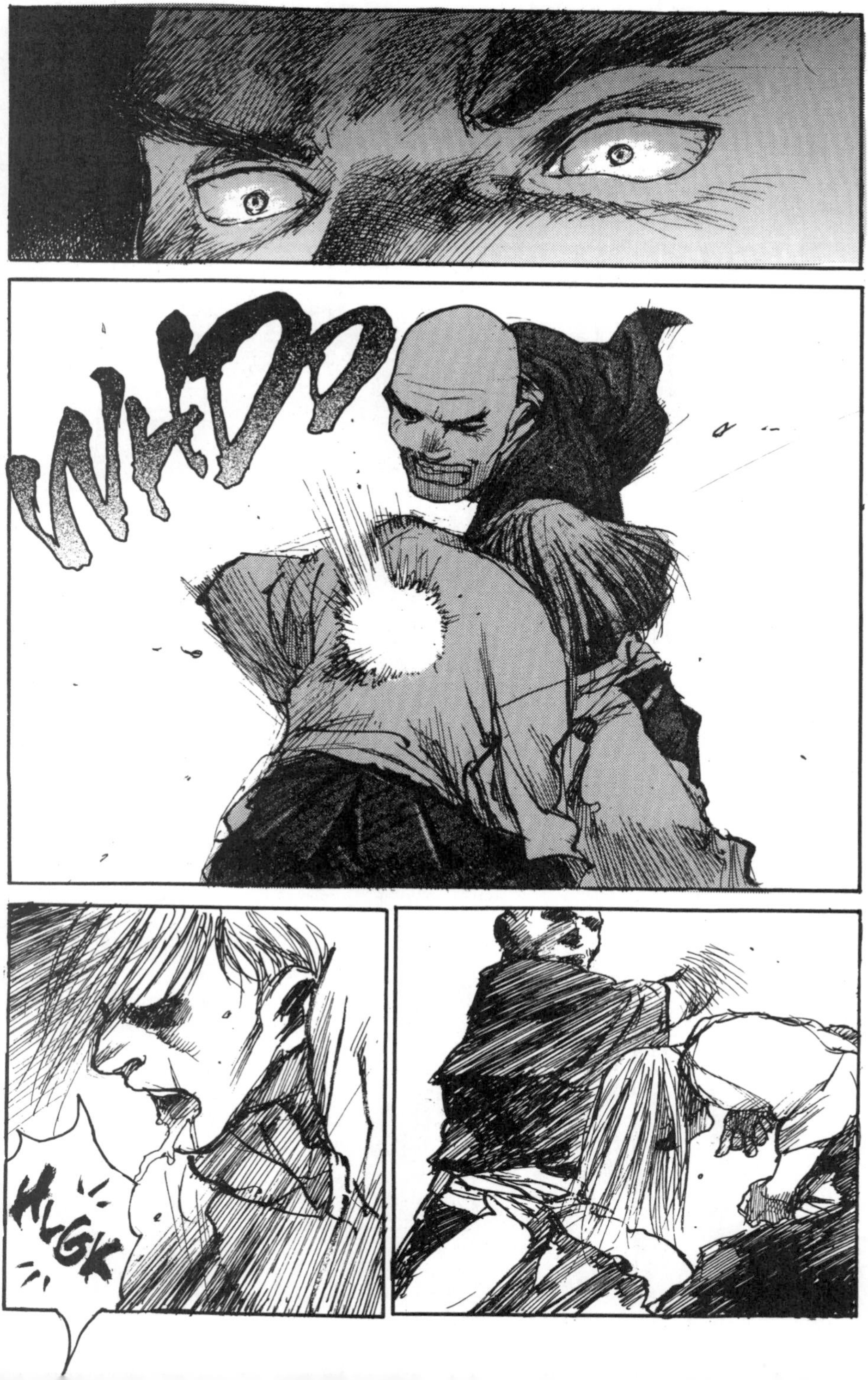
HUGK

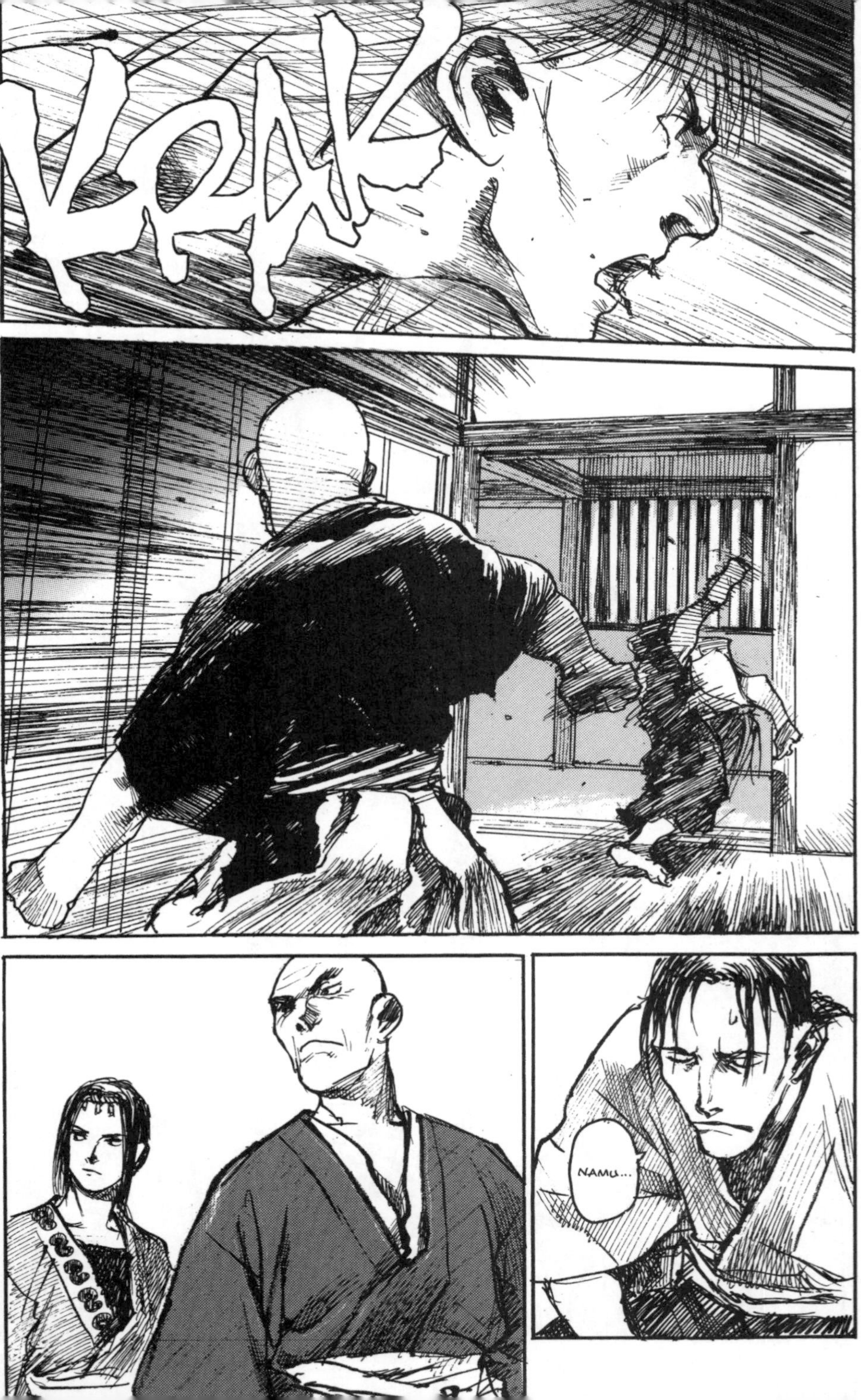
KRAK
NAMU...

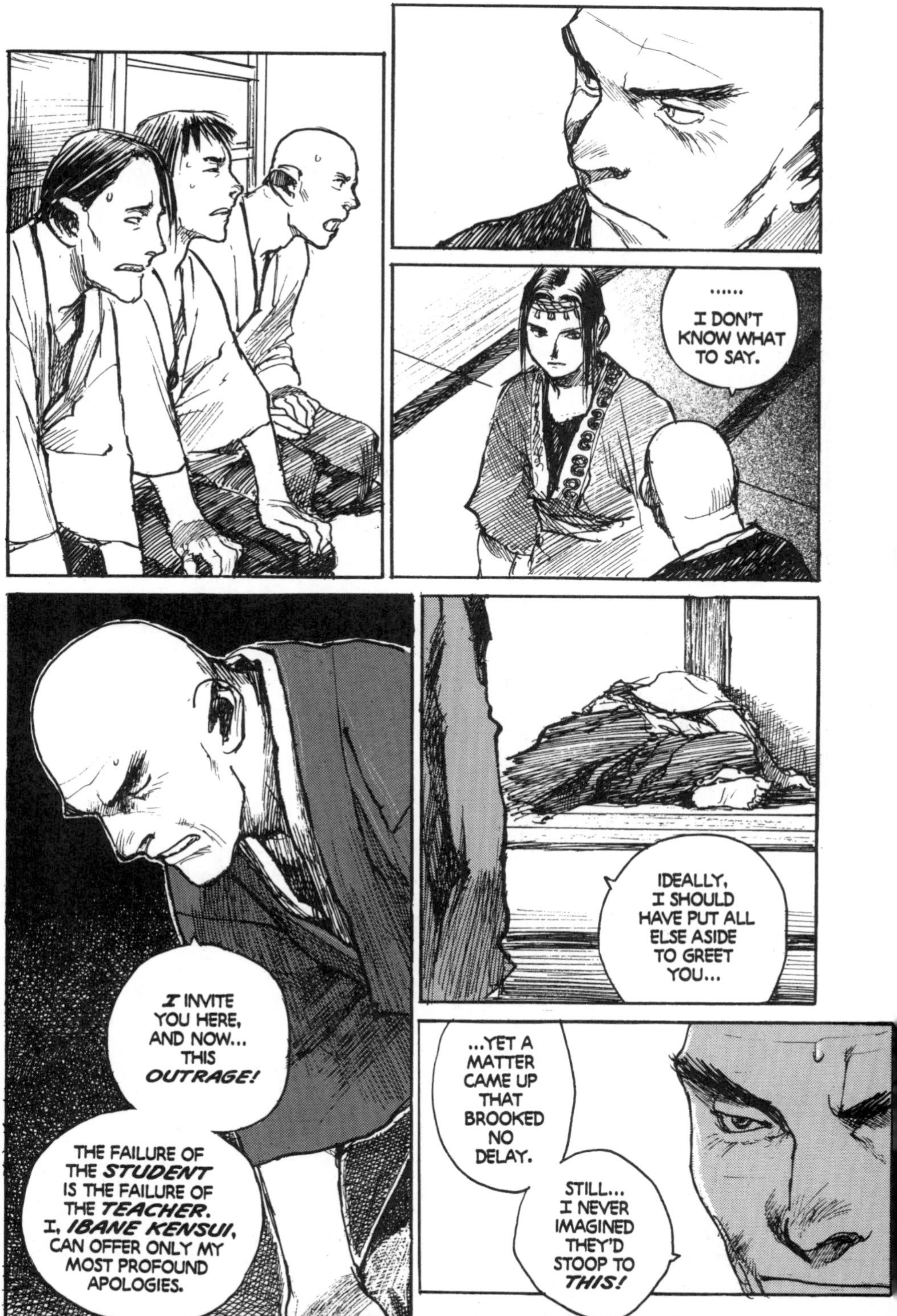
......
I DON'T KNOW WHAT TO SAY.
I INVITE YOU HERE, AND NOW... THIS OUTRAGE!
THE FAILURE OF THE STUDENT IS THE FAILURE OF THE TEACHER. I, IBANE KENSUI, CAN OFFER ONLY MY MOST PROFOUND APOLOGIES.
IDEALLY, I SHOULD HAVE PUT ALL ELSE ASIDE TO GREET YOU...
...YET A MATTER CAME UP THAT BROOKED NO DELAY.
STILL... I NEVER IMAGINED THEY'D STOOP TO THIS!

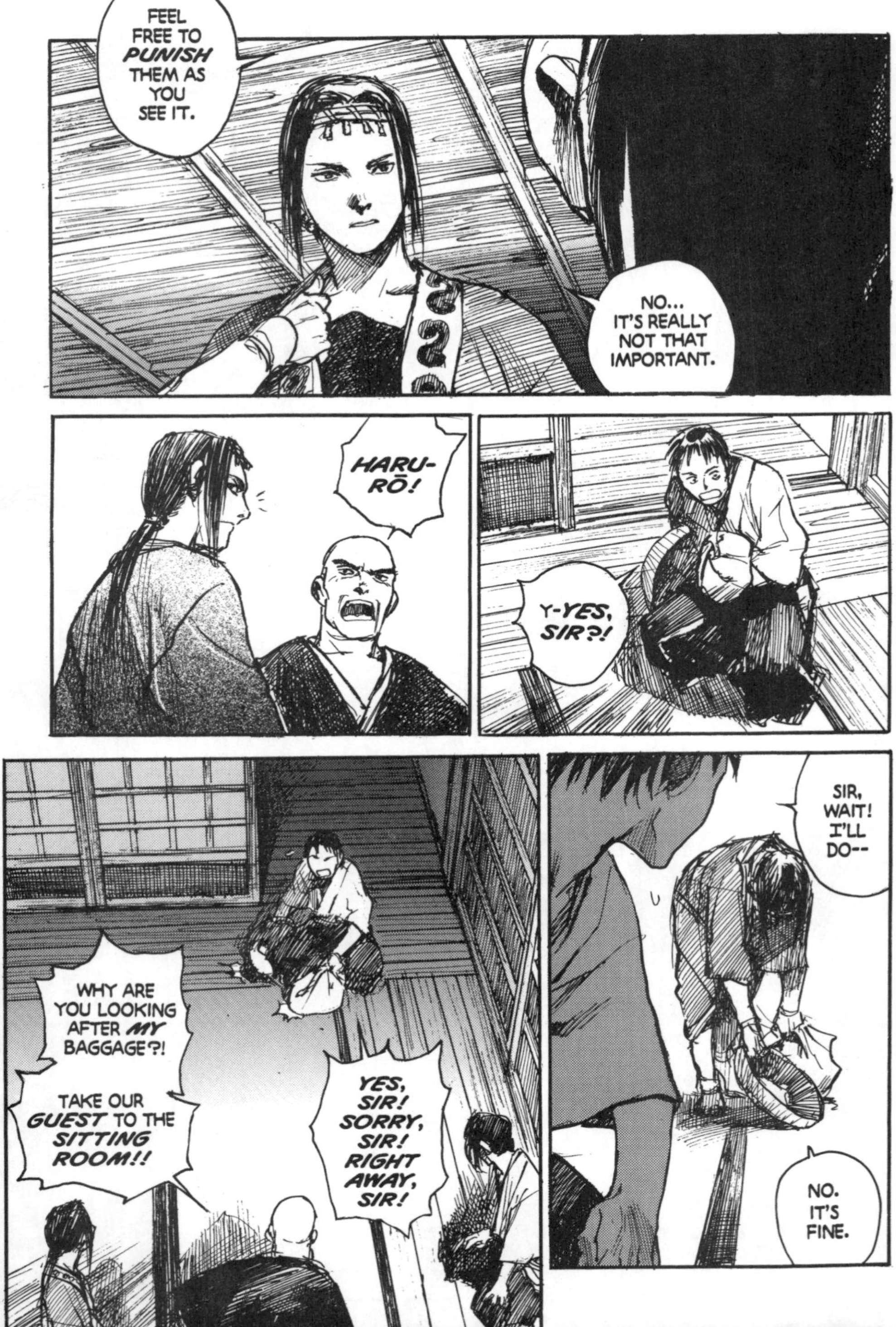
FEEL FREE TO PUNISH THEM AS YOU SEE IT.
NO... IT'S REALLY NOT THAT IMPORTANT.
HARU-RŌ!
Y-YES, SIR?!
WHY ARE YOU LOOKING AFTER MY BAGGAGE?!
TAKE OUR GUEST TO THE SITTING ROOM!!
YES, SIR! SORRY, SIR! RIGHT AWAY, SIR!
SIR, WAIT! I'LL DO--
NO. IT'S FINE.

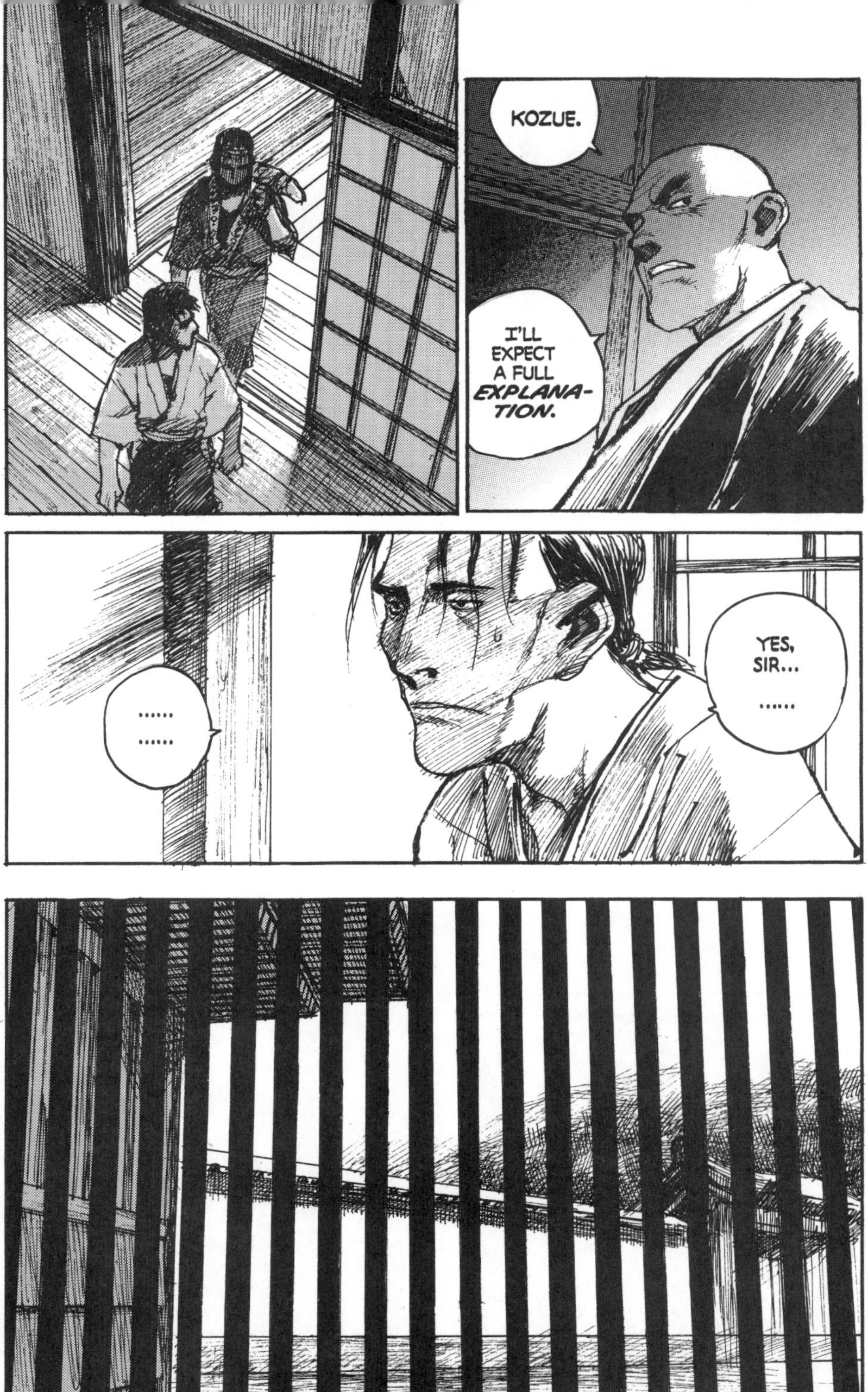
KOZUE.
I'LL EXPECT A FULL *EXPLANATION.*
......
......
YES, SIR...
......

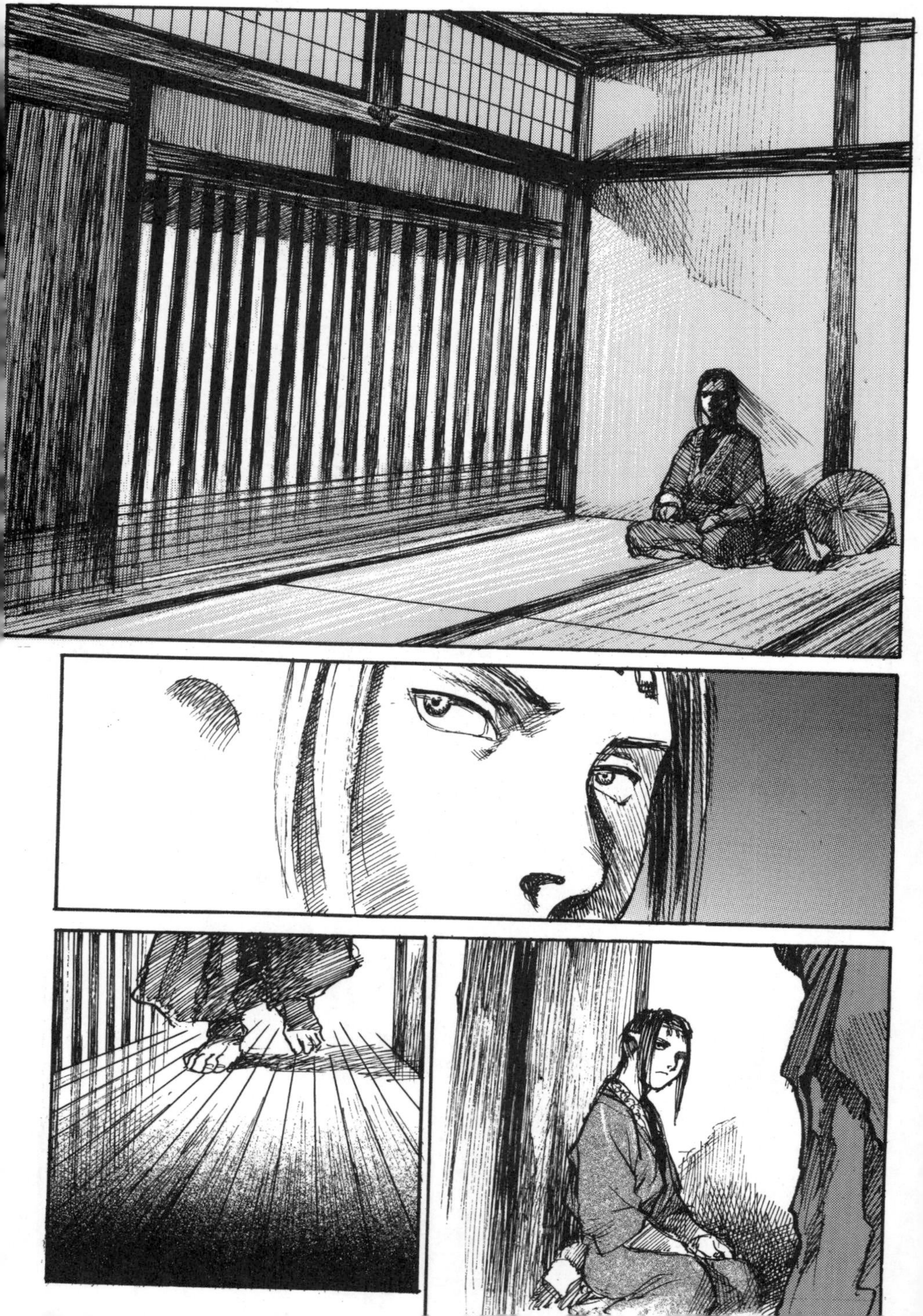

I'M SORRY ABOUT PUTTING YOU IN THIS SMALL OUTER ROOM.

BUT AS YOU'VE SEEN FOR YOUR-SELF... ≷Sighh≷

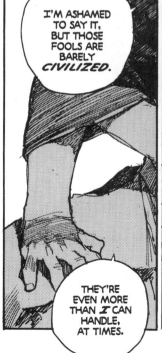

I'M ASHAMED TO SAY IT, BUT THOSE FOOLS ARE BARELY *CIVILIZED*.

THEY'RE EVEN MORE THAN *I* CAN HANDLE, AT TIMES.

AN IMPORTANT *GUEST*... A REMOTE, COUNTRY *DŌJŌ*...

THERE WILL BE AN ENORMOUS TEMPTATION FOR THEM TO EAVESDROP.

BUT AT LEAST IF WE USE A CORNER ROOM WITH THE DOORS ALL OPEN...

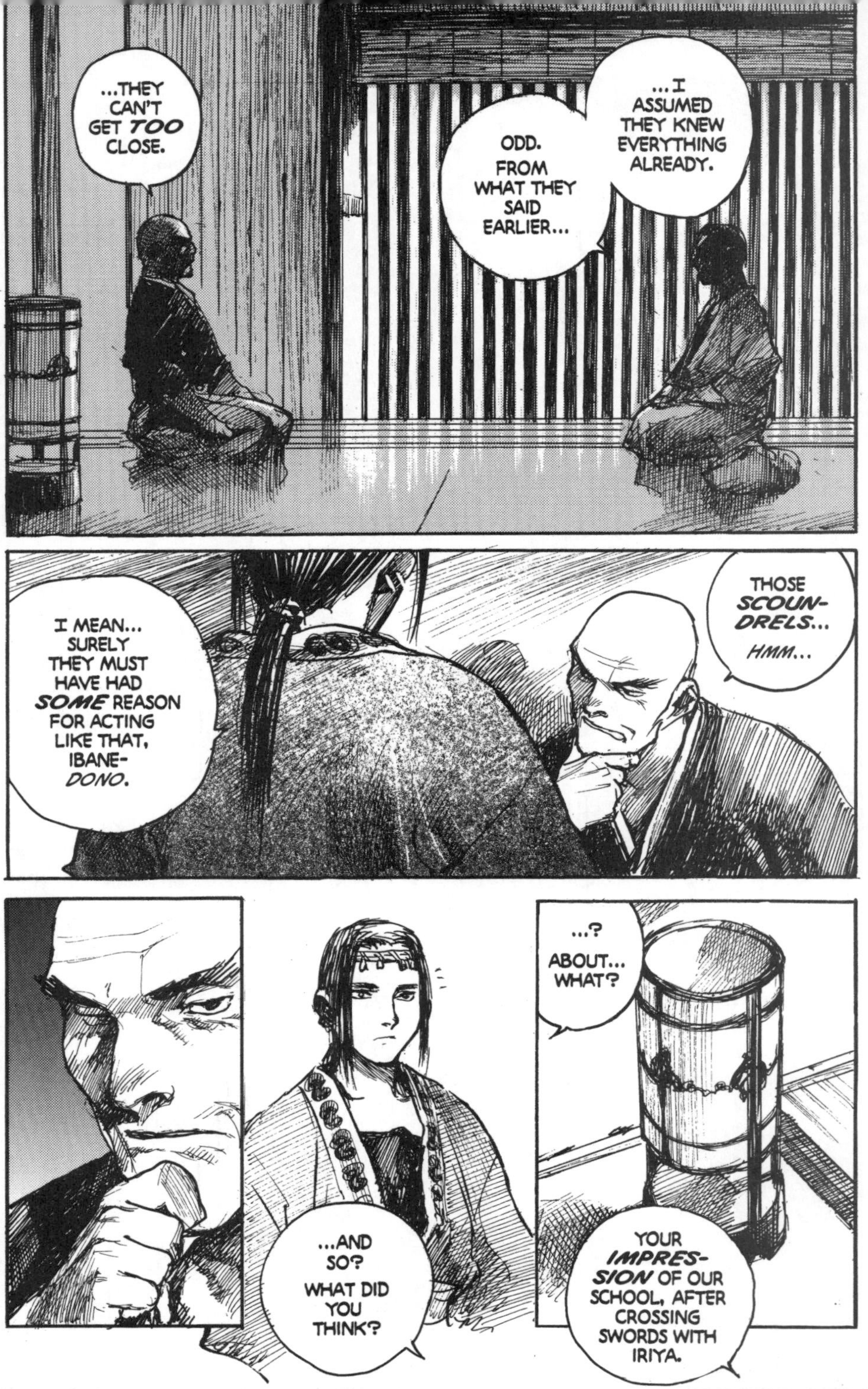
...THEY CAN'T GET *TOO* CLOSE.
ODD. FROM WHAT THEY SAID EARLIER...
...I ASSUMED THEY KNEW EVERYTHING ALREADY.
I MEAN... SURELY THEY MUST HAVE HAD *SOME* REASON FOR ACTING LIKE THAT, IBANE-*DONO*.
THOSE *SCOUNDRELS*... *HMM*...
...AND SO? WHAT DID YOU THINK?
...? ABOUT... WHAT?
YOUR *IMPRESSION* OF OUR SCHOOL, AFTER CROSSING SWORDS WITH IRIYA.

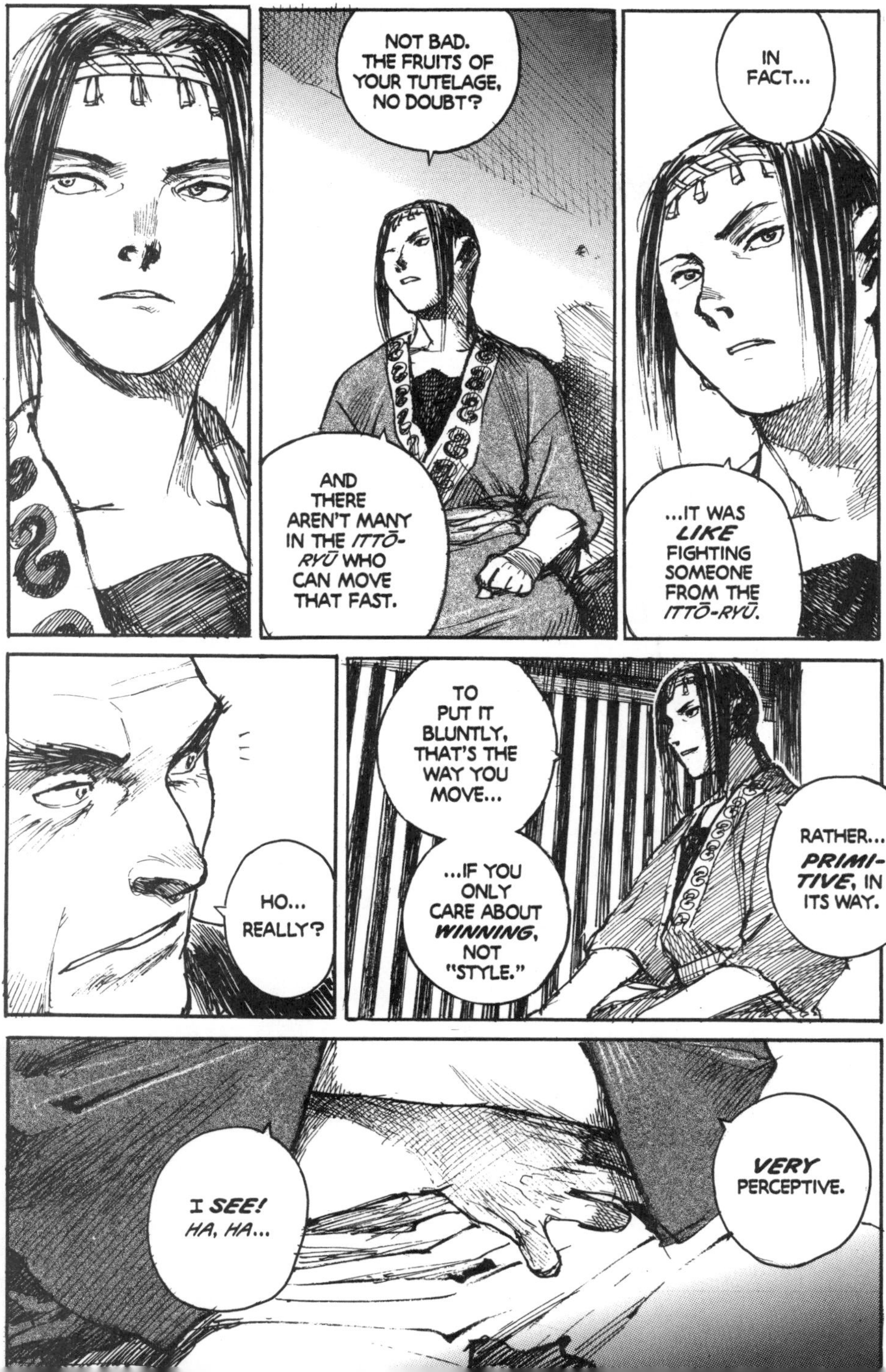
NOT BAD. THE FRUITS OF YOUR TUTELAGE, NO DOUBT?
AND THERE AREN'T MANY IN THE *ITTŌ-RYŪ* WHO CAN MOVE THAT FAST.
IN FACT...
...IT WAS *LIKE* FIGHTING SOMEONE FROM THE *ITTŌ-RYŪ*.
HO... REALLY?
TO PUT IT BLUNTLY, THAT'S THE WAY YOU MOVE...
...IF YOU ONLY CARE ABOUT *WINNING*, NOT "STYLE."
RATHER... *PRIMI-TIVE*, IN ITS WAY.
I *SEE!* HA, HA...
VERY PERCEPTIVE.

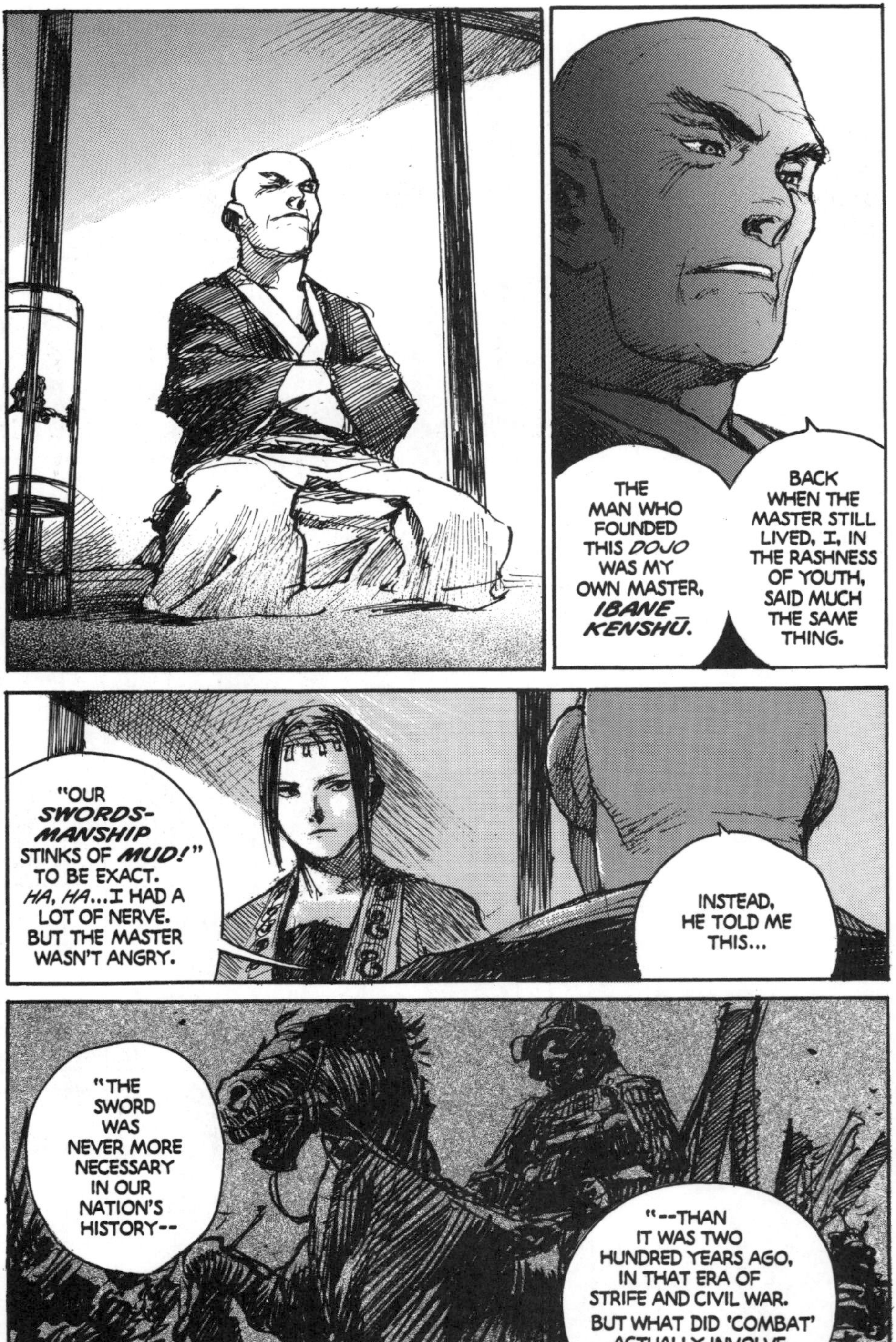
THE MAN WHO FOUNDED THIS DOJO WAS MY OWN MASTER, IBANE KENSHŪ.
BACK WHEN THE MASTER STILL LIVED, I, IN THE RASHNESS OF YOUTH, SAID MUCH THE SAME THING.
"OUR SWORDSMANSHIP STINKS OF MUD!" TO BE EXACT. HA, HA... I HAD A LOT OF NERVE. BUT THE MASTER WASN'T ANGRY.
INSTEAD, HE TOLD ME THIS...
"THE SWORD WAS NEVER MORE NECESSARY IN OUR NATION'S HISTORY--
"--THAN IT WAS TWO HUNDRED YEARS AGO, IN THAT ERA OF STRIFE AND CIVIL WAR. BUT WHAT DID 'COMBAT' ACTUALLY INVOLVE IN THOSE FAR-OFF DAYS?

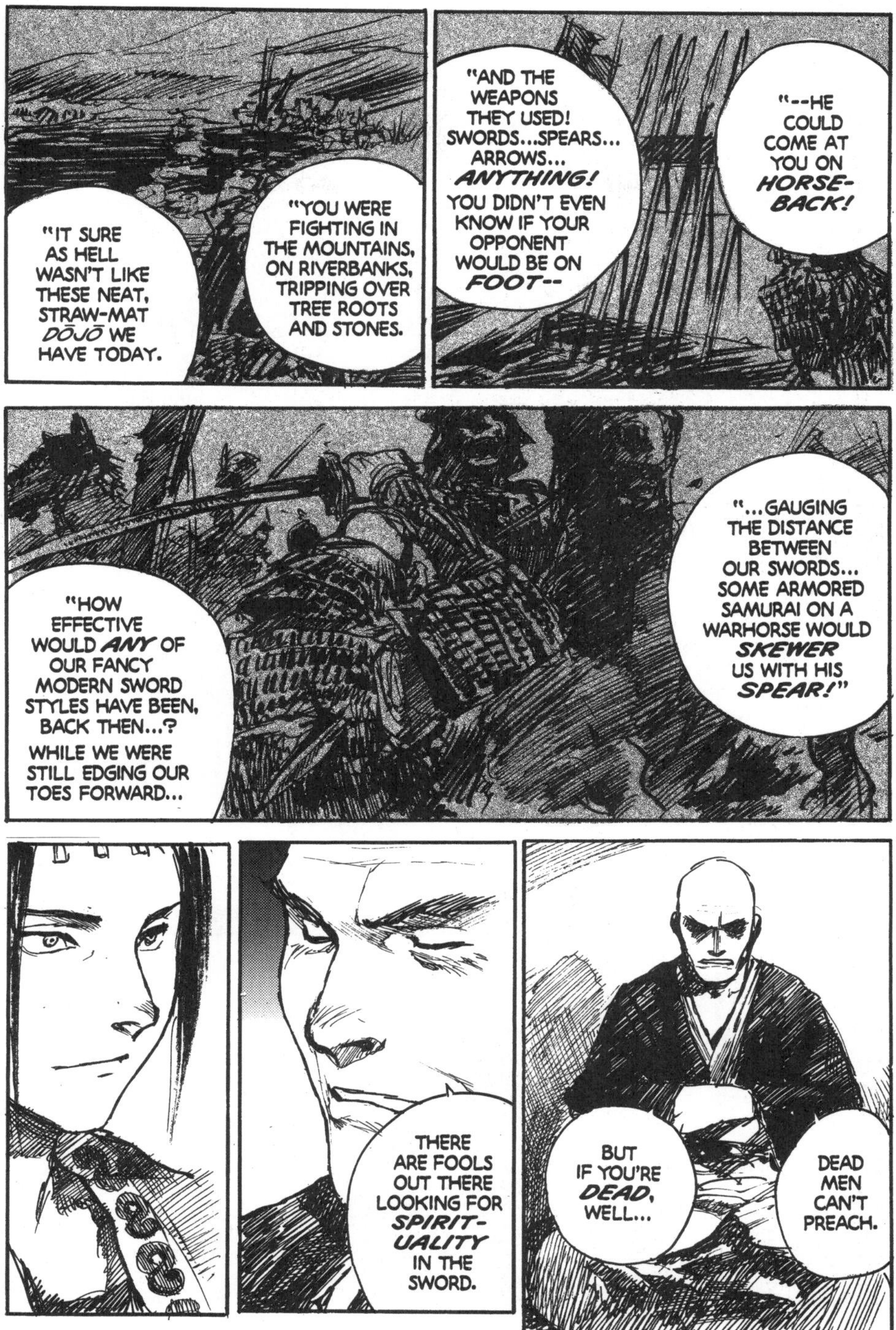
"IT SURE AS HELL WASN'T LIKE THESE NEAT, STRAW-MAT DŌJŌ WE HAVE TODAY.
"YOU WERE FIGHTING IN THE MOUNTAINS, ON RIVERBANKS, TRIPPING OVER TREE ROOTS AND STONES.
"AND THE WEAPONS THEY USED! SWORDS...SPEARS... ARROWS... ANYTHING! YOU DIDN'T EVEN KNOW IF YOUR OPPONENT WOULD BE ON FOOT--
"--HE COULD COME AT YOU ON HORSE-BACK!
"HOW EFFECTIVE WOULD ANY OF OUR FANCY MODERN SWORD STYLES HAVE BEEN, BACK THEN...? WHILE WE WERE STILL EDGING OUR TOES FORWARD...
"...GAUGING THE DISTANCE BETWEEN OUR SWORDS... SOME ARMORED SAMURAI ON A WARHORSE WOULD SKEWER US WITH HIS SPEAR!"
THERE ARE FOOLS OUT THERE LOOKING FOR SPIRIT-UALITY IN THE SWORD.
BUT IF YOU'RE DEAD, WELL...
DEAD MEN CAN'T PREACH.

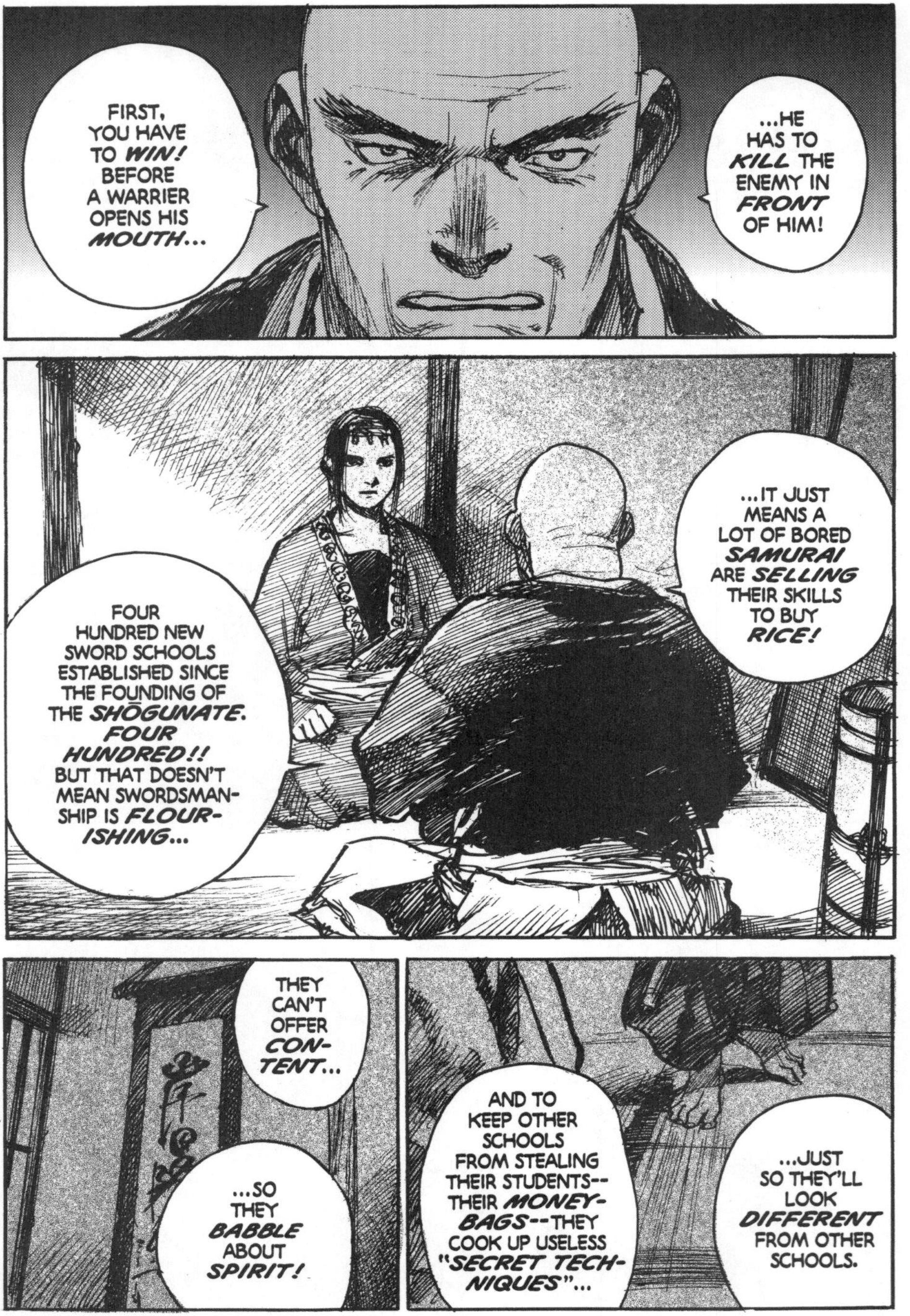
FIRST, YOU HAVE TO WIN! BEFORE A WARRIER OPENS HIS MOUTH...
...HE HAS TO KILL THE ENEMY IN FRONT OF HIM!
FOUR HUNDRED NEW SWORD SCHOOLS ESTABLISHED SINCE THE FOUNDING OF THE SHŌGUNATE. FOUR HUNDRED!! BUT THAT DOESN'T MEAN SWORDSMAN-SHIP IS FLOUR-ISHING...
...IT JUST MEANS A LOT OF BORED SAMURAI ARE SELLING THEIR SKILLS TO BUY RICE!
THEY CAN'T OFFER CON-TENT...
...SO THEY BABBLE ABOUT SPIRIT!
AND TO KEEP OTHER SCHOOLS FROM STEALING THEIR STUDENTS--THEIR MONEY-BAGS--THEY COOK UP USELESS "SECRET TECH-NIQUES"...
...JUST SO THEY'LL LOOK DIFFERENT FROM OTHER SCHOOLS.

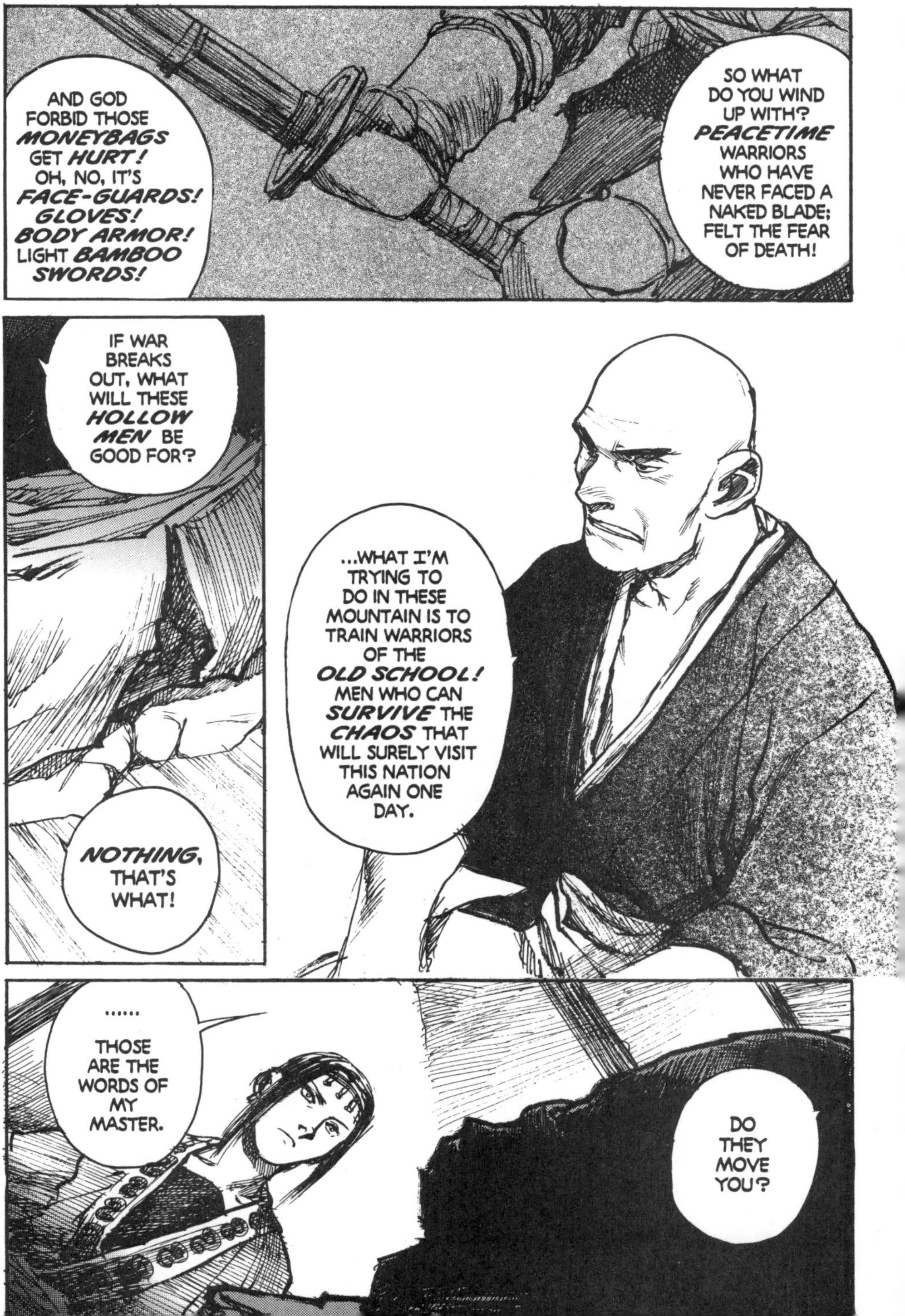
AND GOD FORBID THOSE MONEYBAGS GET HURT! OH, NO, IT'S FACE-GUARDS! GLOVES! BODY ARMOR! LIGHT BAMBOO SWORDS!
SO WHAT DO YOU WIND UP WITH? PEACETIME WARRIORS WHO HAVE NEVER FACED A NAKED BLADE; FELT THE FEAR OF DEATH!
IF WAR BREAKS OUT, WHAT WILL THESE HOLLOW MEN BE GOOD FOR?
NOTHING, THAT'S WHAT!
...WHAT I'M TRYING TO DO IN THESE MOUNTAIN IS TO TRAIN WARRIORS OF THE OLD SCHOOL! MEN WHO CAN SURVIVE THE CHAOS THAT WILL SURELY VISIT THIS NATION AGAIN ONE DAY.
......
THOSE ARE THE WORDS OF MY MASTER.
DO THEY MOVE YOU?

THEY STRIKE ME TO THE DEPTHS OF MY *SOUL!*

I WISH I HAD MET HIM BEFORE HE DIED.

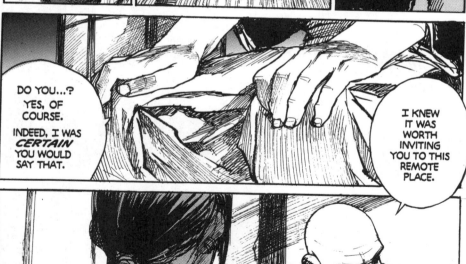

DO YOU...? YES, OF COURSE.

INDEED, I WAS *CERTAIN* YOU WOULD SAY THAT.

I KNEW IT WAS WORTH INVITING YOU TO THIS REMOTE PLACE.

AND *YET*, IBANE-DONO...

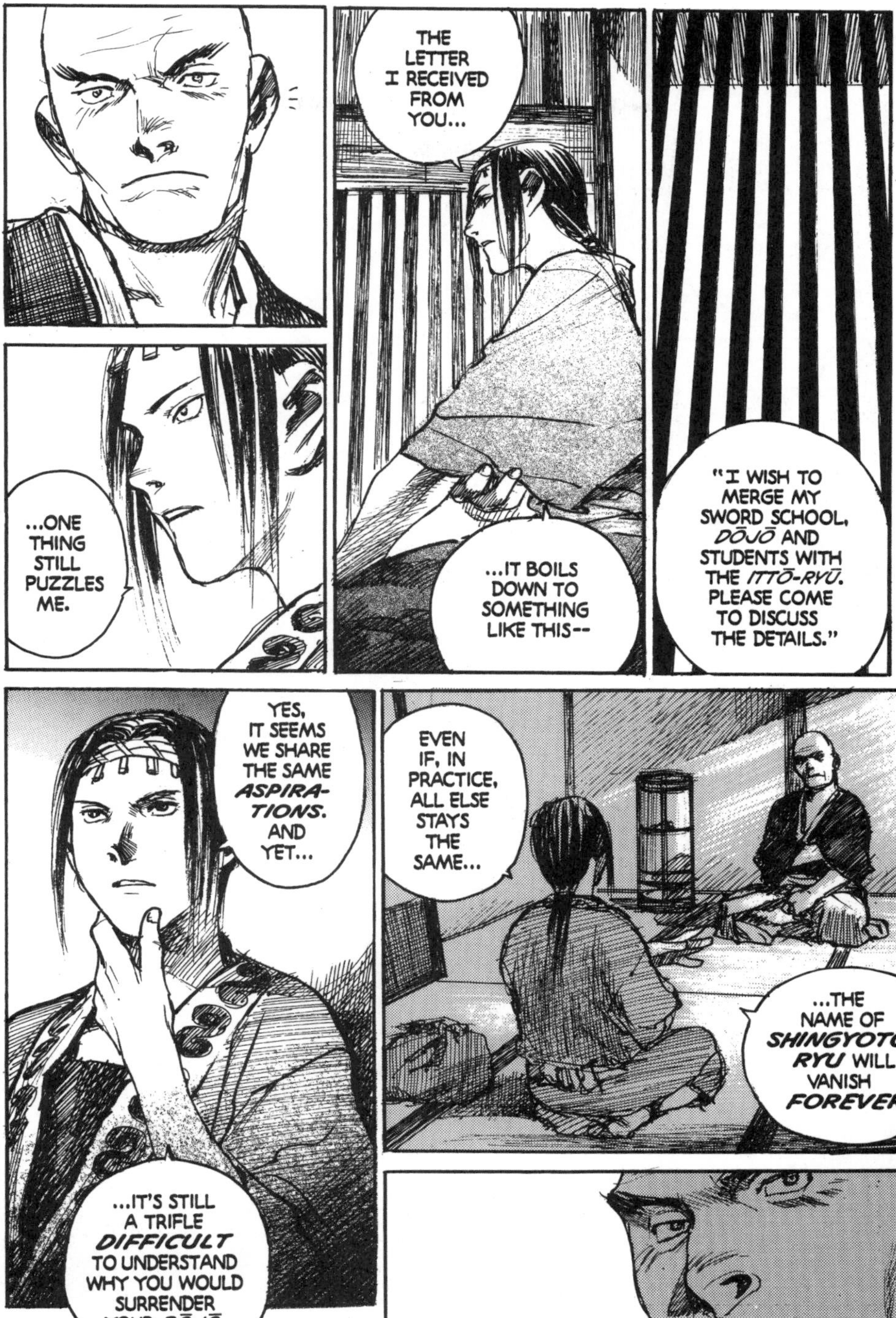
...ONE THING STILL PUZZLES ME.
THE LETTER I RECEIVED FROM YOU...
...IT BOILS DOWN TO SOMETHING LIKE THIS--
"I WISH TO MERGE MY SWORD SCHOOL, *DŌJŌ* AND STUDENTS WITH THE *ITTŌ-RYŪ*. PLEASE COME TO DISCUSS THE DETAILS."
YES, IT SEEMS WE SHARE THE SAME *ASPIRATIONS*. AND YET...
...IT'S STILL A TRIFLE *DIFFICULT* TO UNDERSTAND WHY YOU WOULD SURRENDER YOUR *DŌJŌ*.
EVEN IF, IN PRACTICE, ALL ELSE STAYS THE SAME...
...THE NAME OF *SHINGYOTO-RYU* WILL VANISH *FOREVER*.

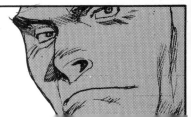

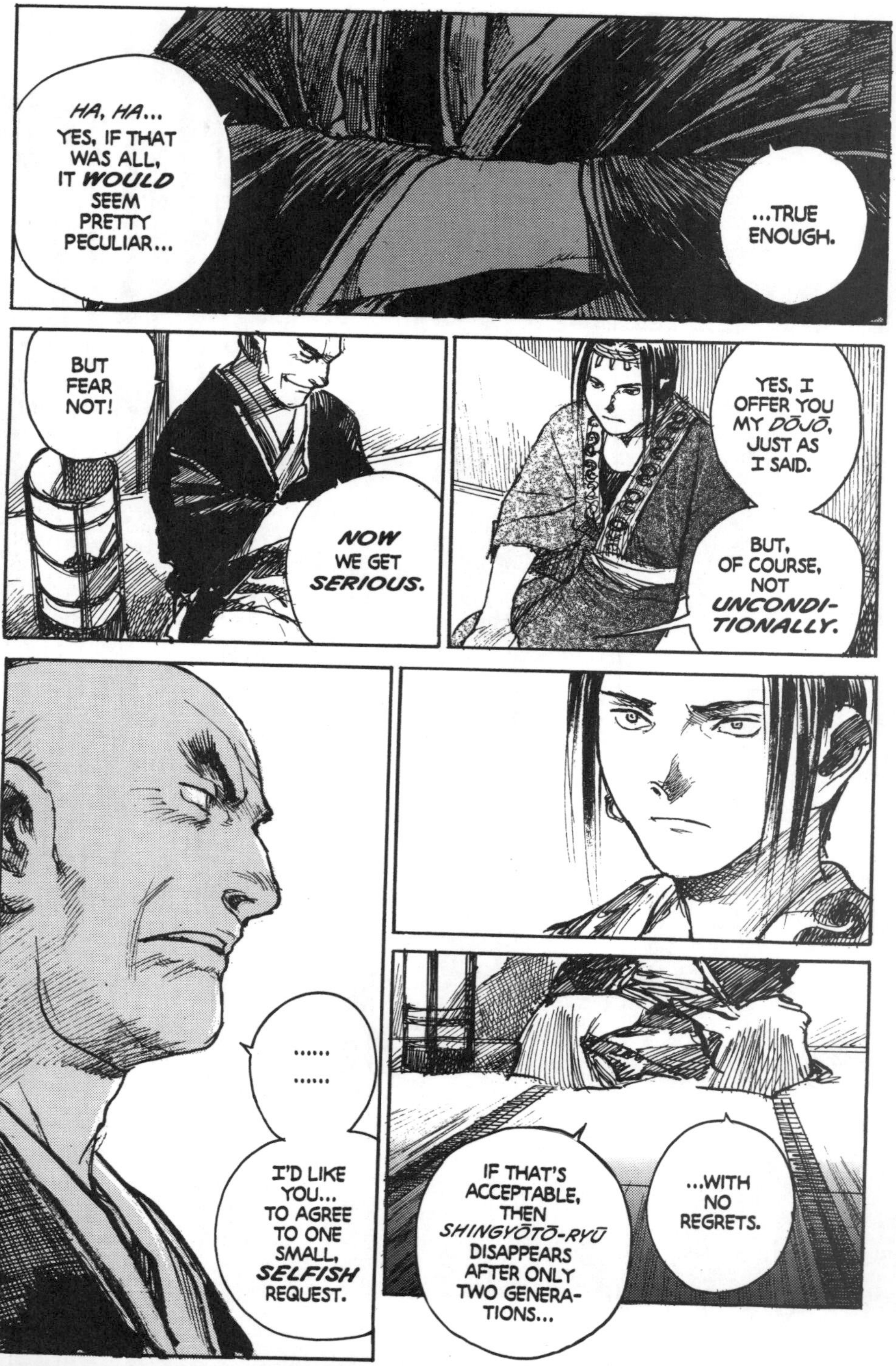
HA, HA... YES, IF THAT WAS ALL, IT WOULD SEEM PRETTY PECULIAR...
...TRUE ENOUGH.
BUT FEAR NOT!
NOW WE GET SERIOUS.
YES, I OFFER YOU MY DŌJŌ, JUST AS I SAID.
BUT, OF COURSE, NOT UNCONDITIONALLY.
......
......
I'D LIKE YOU... TO AGREE TO ONE SMALL, SELFISH REQUEST.
IF THAT'S ACCEPTABLE, THEN SHINGYŌTŌ-RYŪ DISAPPEARS AFTER ONLY TWO GENERATIONS...
...WITH NO REGRETS.

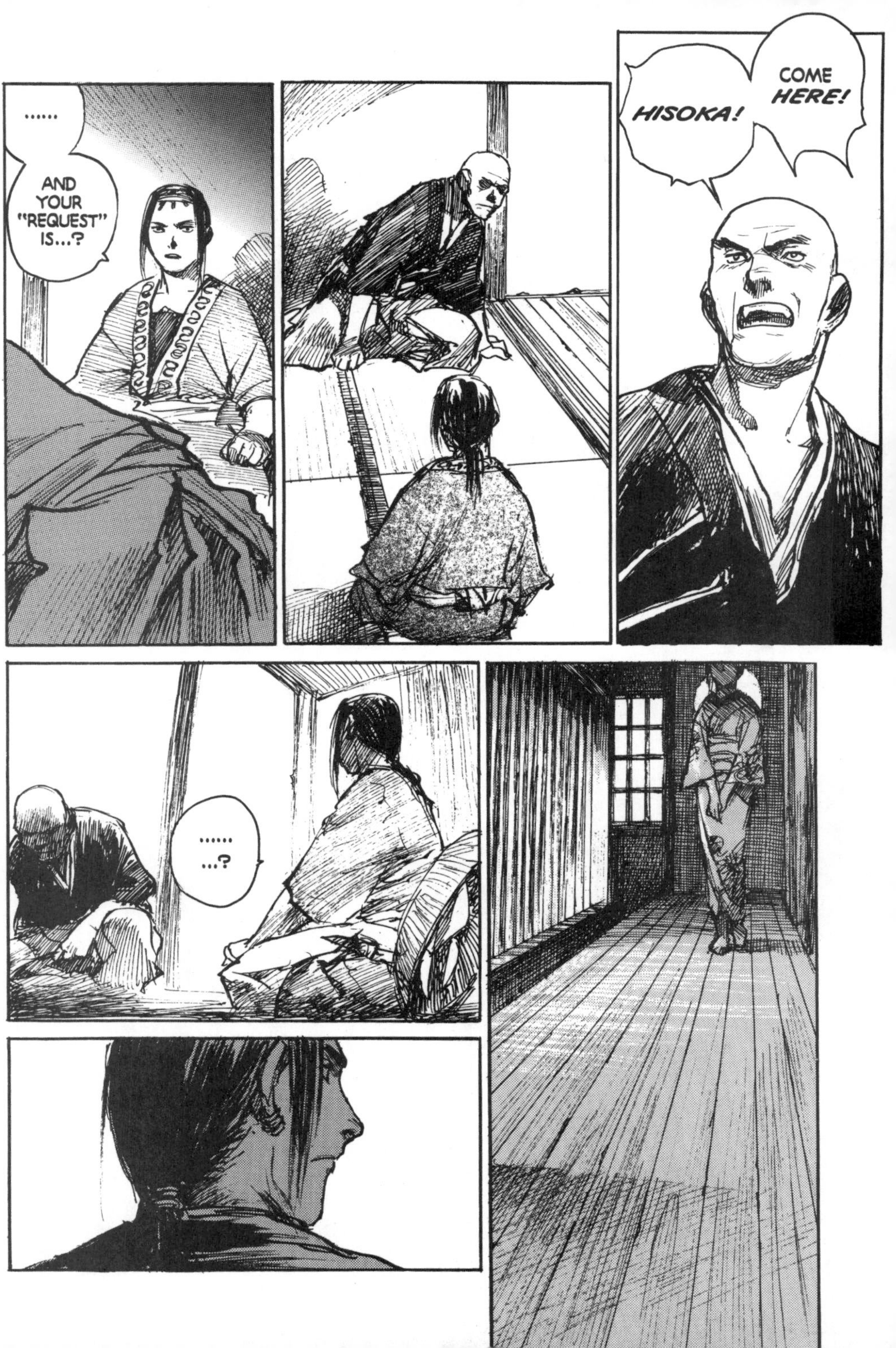
......
AND YOUR "REQUEST" IS...?
HISOKA!
COME HERE!
......
...?

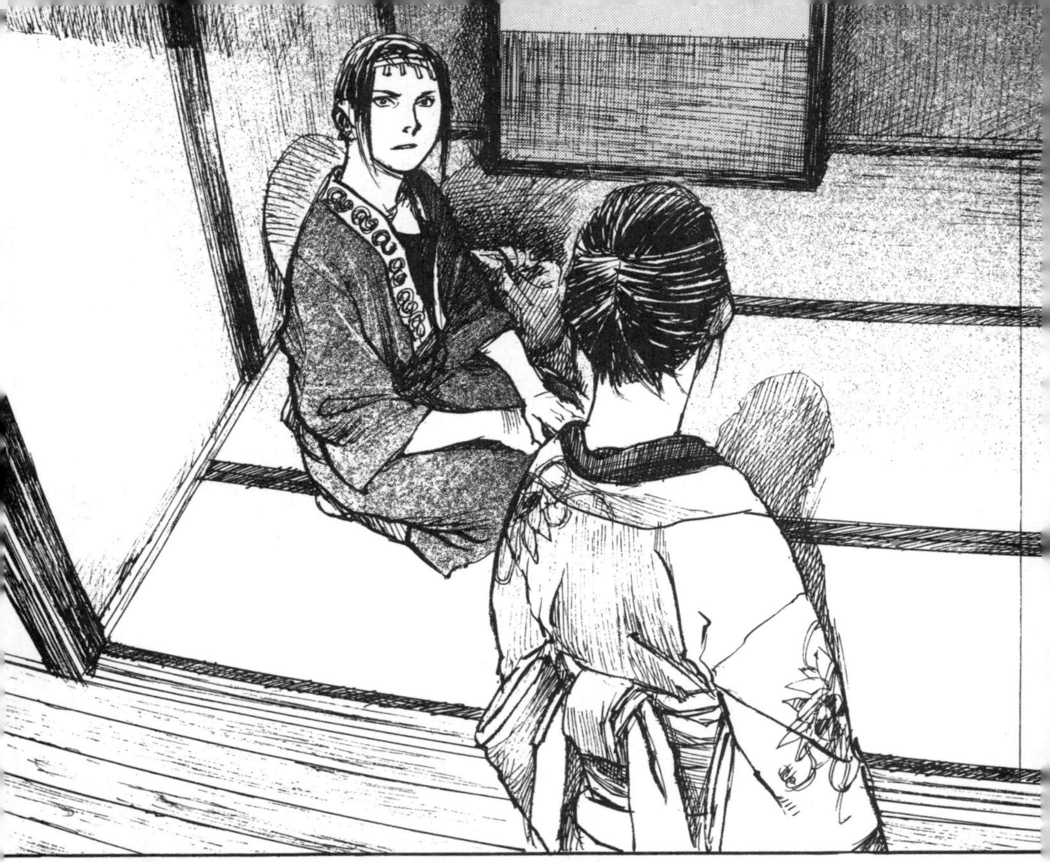
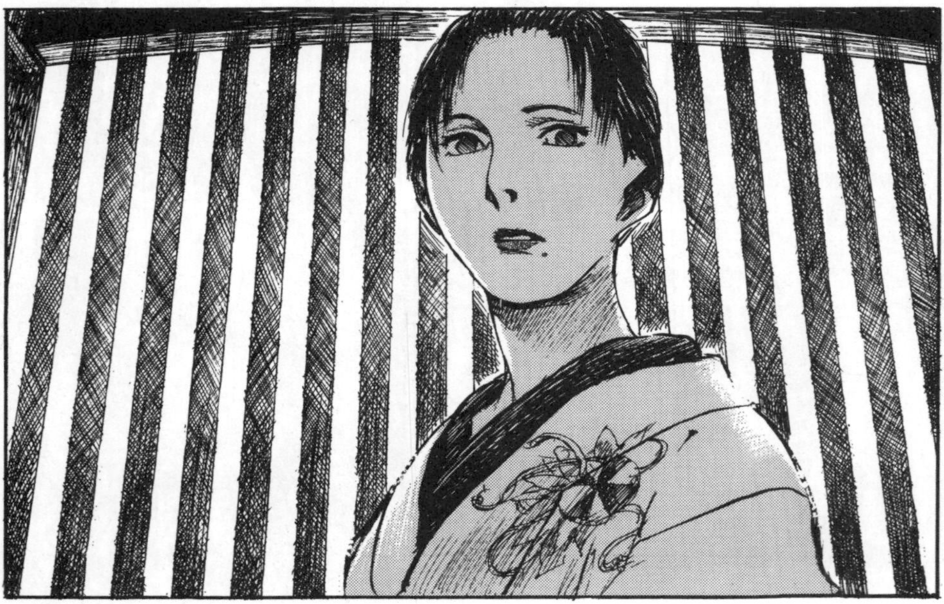

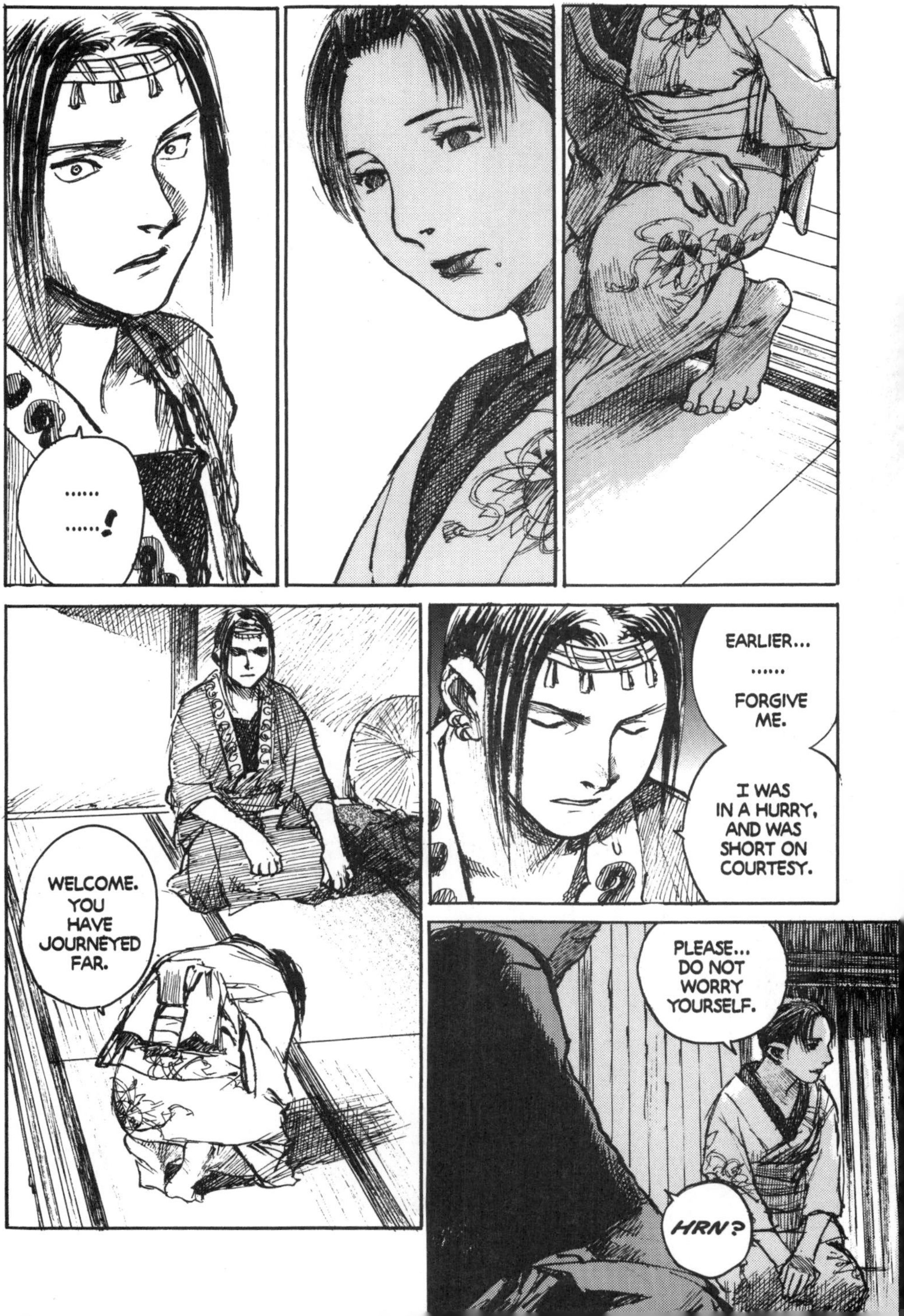
......
......!
WELCOME. YOU HAVE JOURNEYED FAR.
EARLIER... ...... FORGIVE ME.
I WAS IN A HURRY, AND WAS SHORT ON COURTESY.
PLEASE... DO NOT WORRY YOURSELF.
HRN?

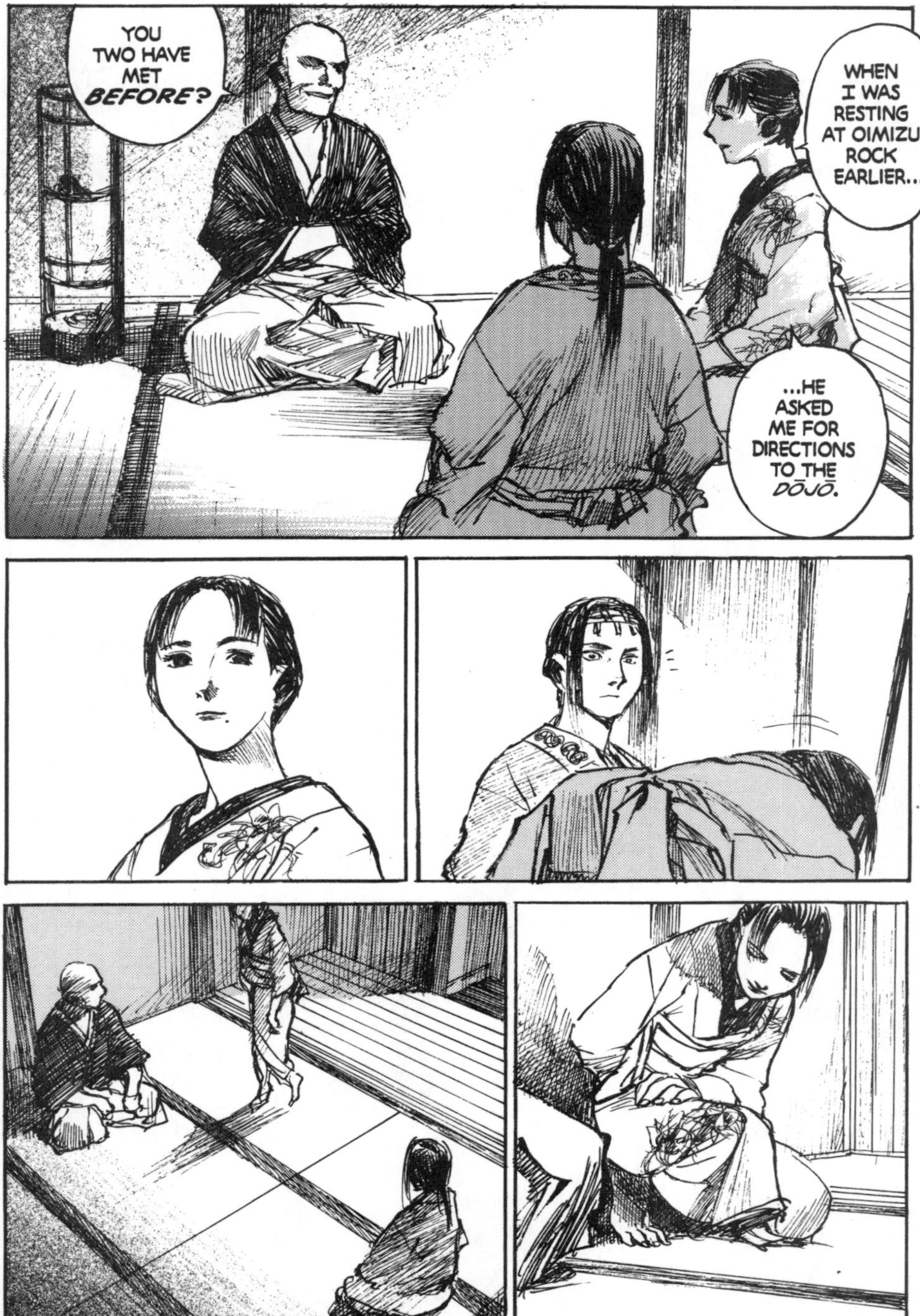
YOU TWO HAVE MET *BEFORE?*
WHEN I WAS RESTING AT OIMIZU ROCK EARLIER...
...HE ASKED ME FOR DIRECTIONS TO THE *DŌJŌ*.

HRMM... WELL, IF YOU'VE MET HER ALREADY, THAT HELPS.

THIS IS *HISOKA*-- MY ONLY DAUGHTER.

I HAD WONDERED ABOUT THAT.

I SAW NO OTHER RESIDENCES NEARBY.

AND SO...? ABOUT YOUR DAUGHTER?

WELL... *HMM*... HOW BEST TO PUT THIS, ANOTSU-*DONO*...?

WOULD IT BE TOO MUCH TO ASK FOR YOU TO TAKE HER WITH YOU?

?

I MEAN, WHEN YOU RETURN TO *EDO* AFTER YOUR STAY HERE.

NO, WAIT... THAT'S *TOO* VAGUE.

DAMN, I'M *LOUSY* AT THIS. LOOK--I'LL JUST *SAY* IT--

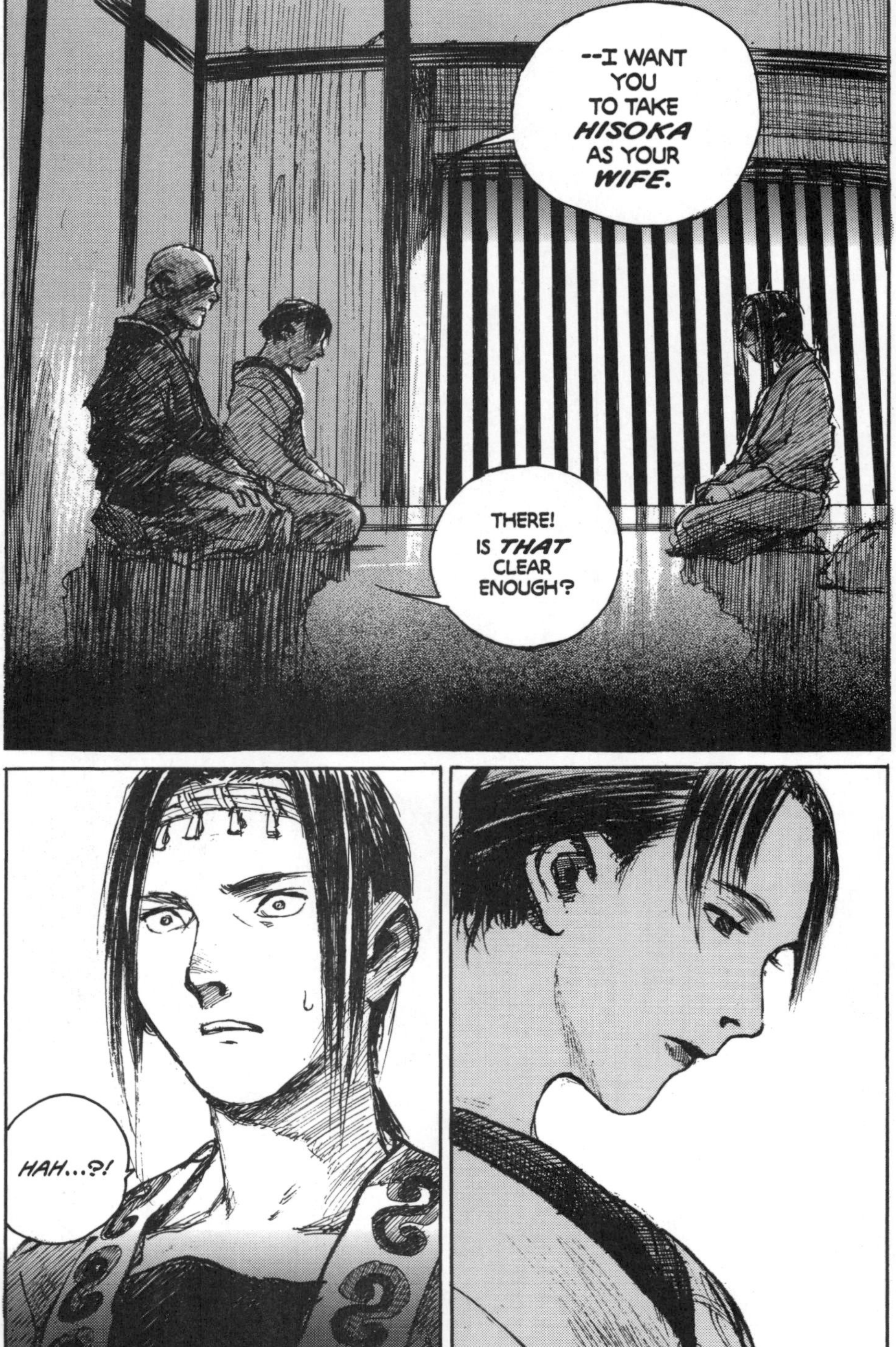

--I WANT YOU TO TAKE *HISOKA* AS YOUR *WIFE*.
THERE! IS *THAT* CLEAR ENOUGH?
HAH...?!

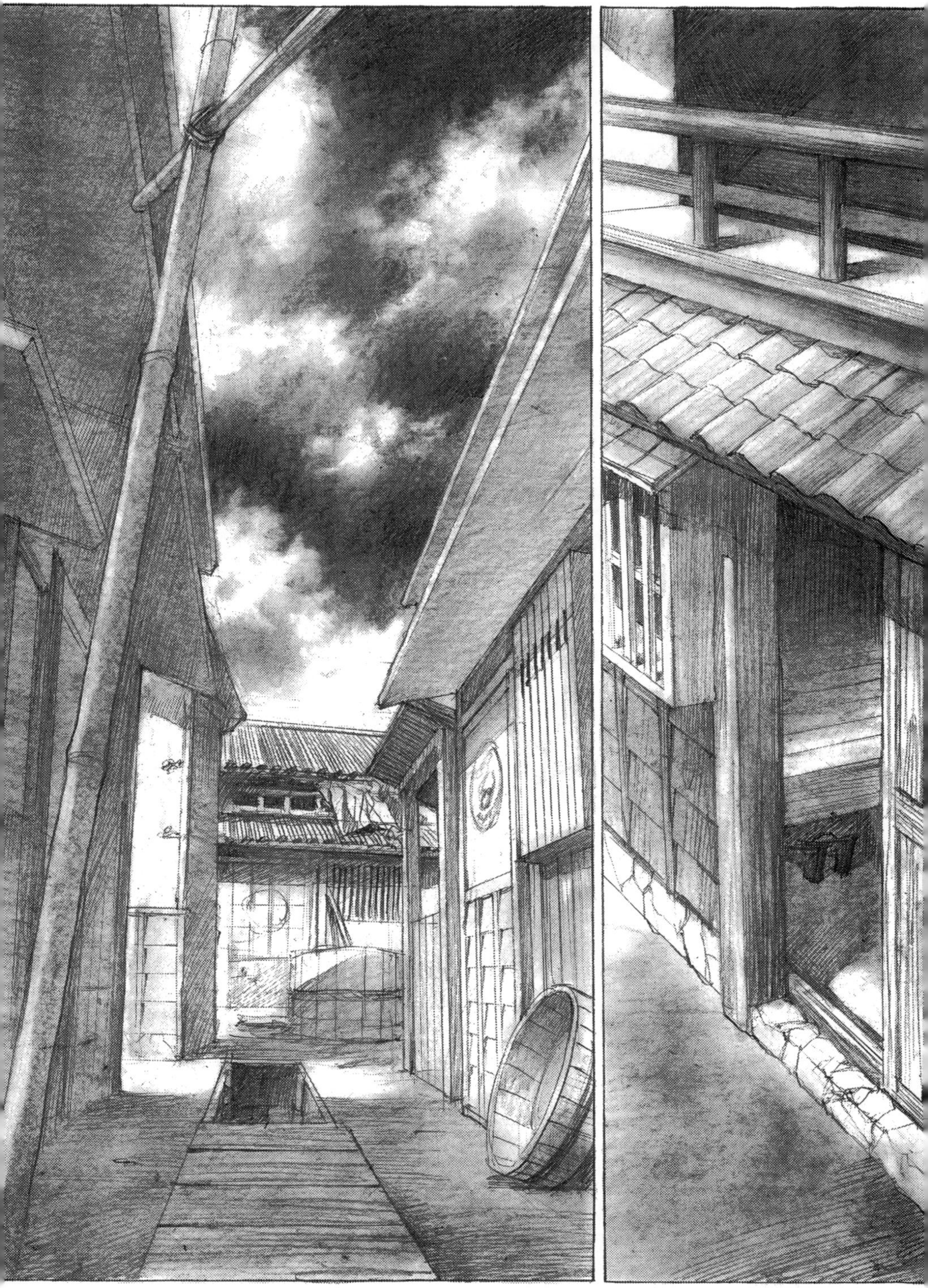

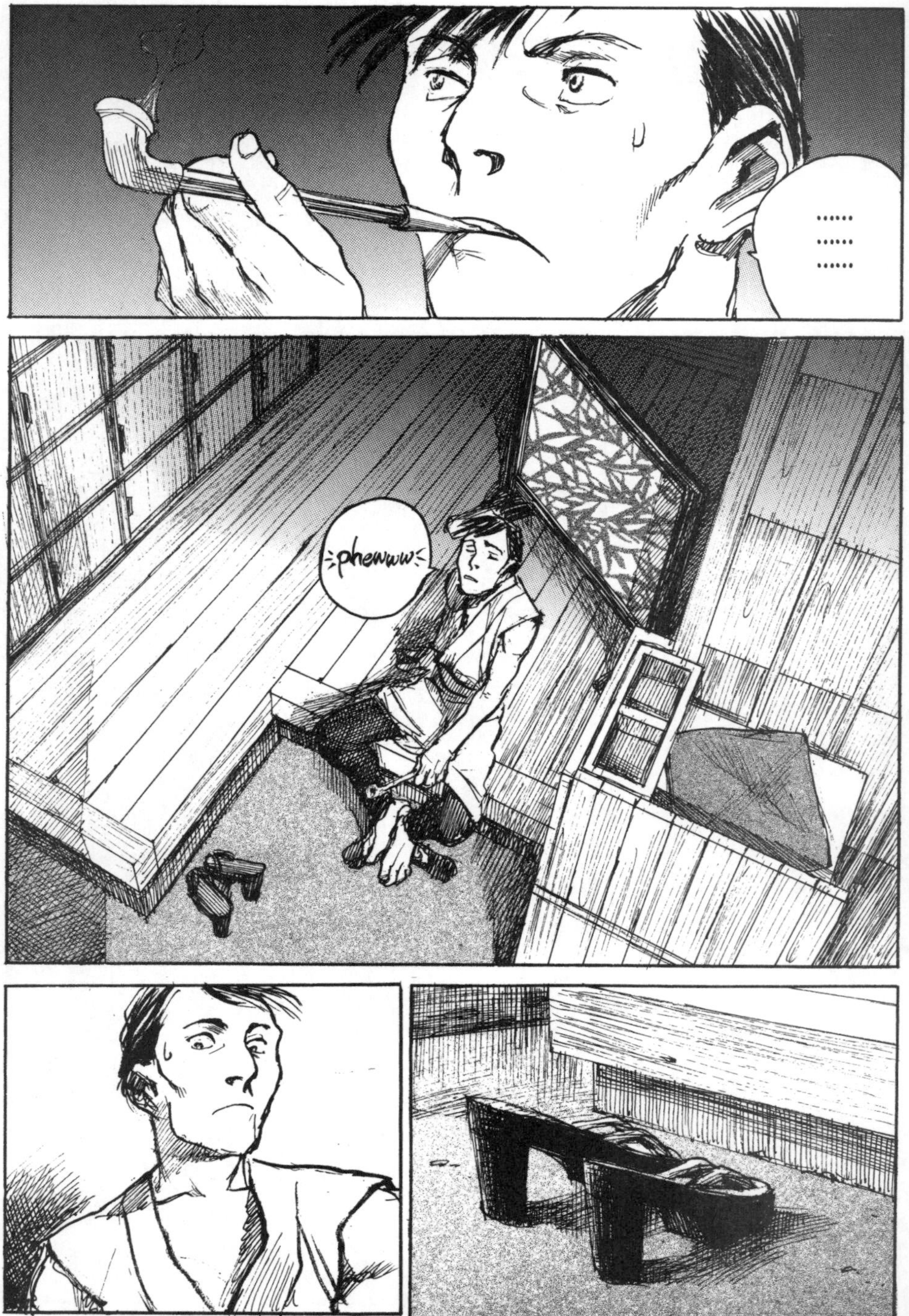
......
......
......
phewww

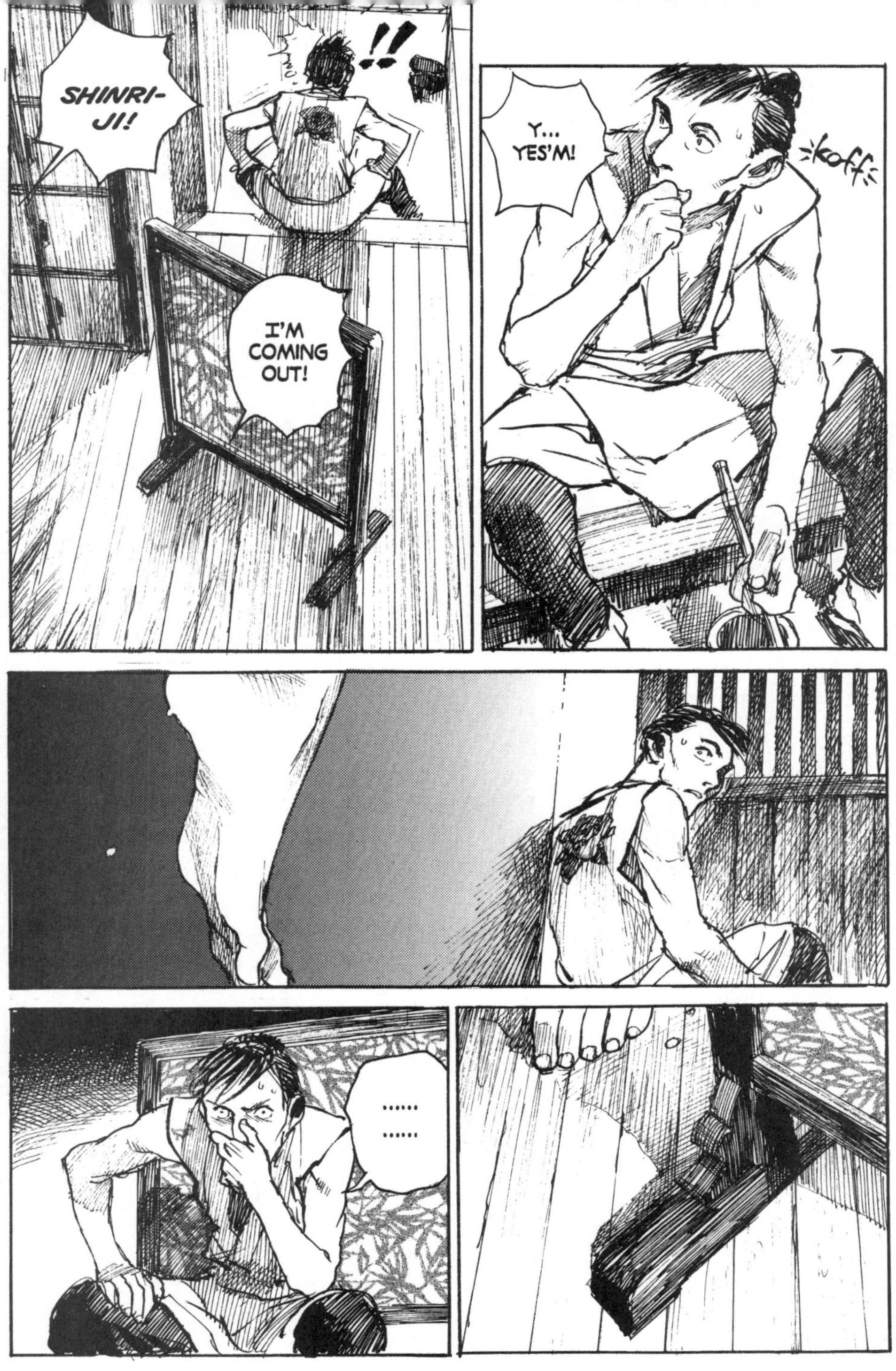
SHINRI-JI!
!!
I'M COMING OUT!
Y... YES'M!
koff
......
......

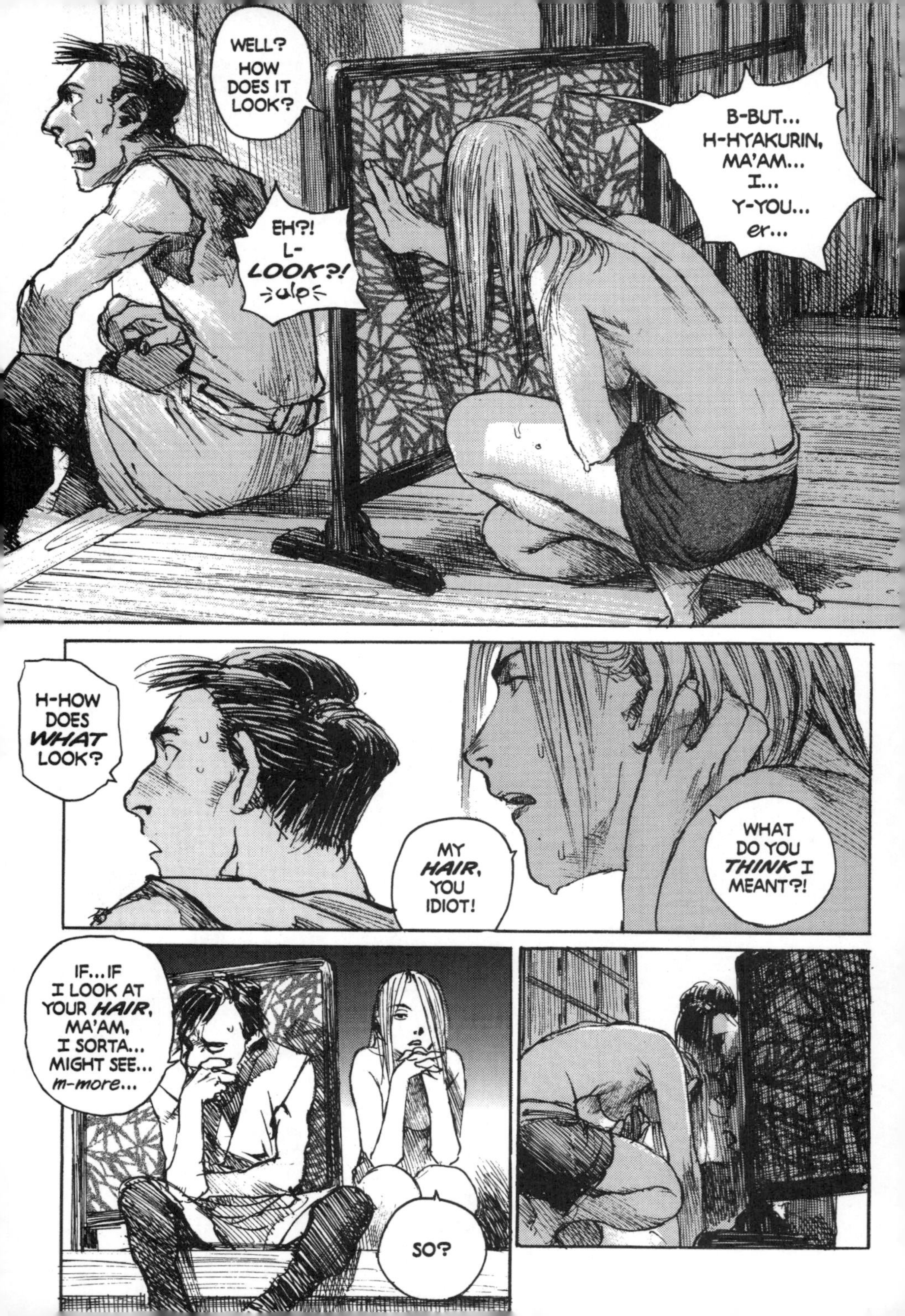
WELL? HOW DOES IT LOOK?
EH?! L- LOOK?! ulp
B-BUT... H-HYAKURIN, MA'AM... I... Y-YOU... er...
H-HOW DOES WHAT LOOK?
MY HAIR, YOU IDIOT!
WHAT DO YOU THINK I MEANT?!
IF...IF I LOOK AT YOUR HAIR, MA'AM, I SORTA... MIGHT SEE... m-more...
SO?

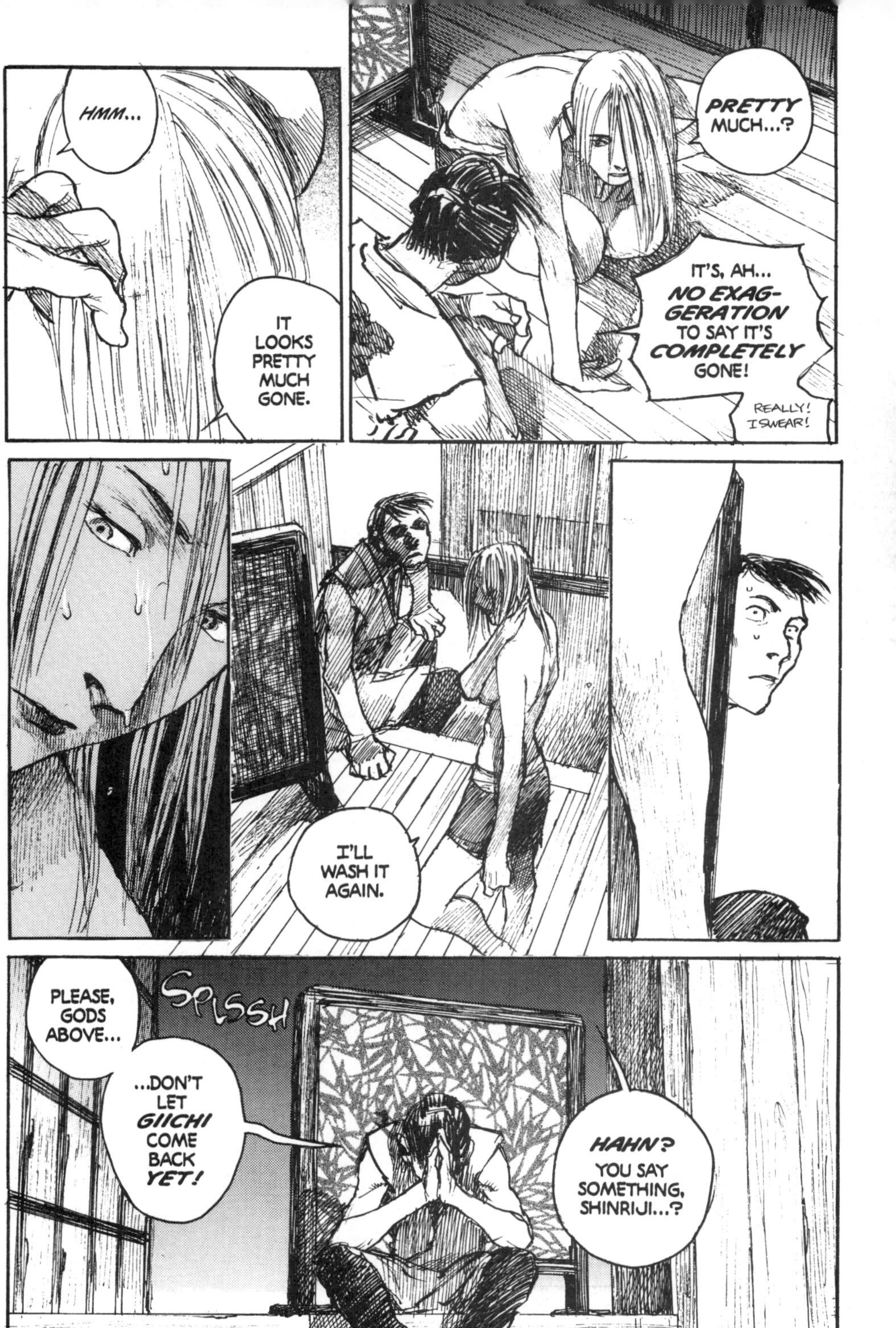
HMM...
IT LOOKS PRETTY MUCH GONE.
PRETTY MUCH...?
IT'S, AH... NO EXAGGERATION TO SAY IT'S COMPLETELY GONE!
REALLY! I SWEAR!
I'LL WASH IT AGAIN.
PLEASE, GODS ABOVE...
SPLSSH
...DON'T LET GIICHI COME BACK YET!
HAHN? YOU SAY SOMETHING, SHINRIJI...?

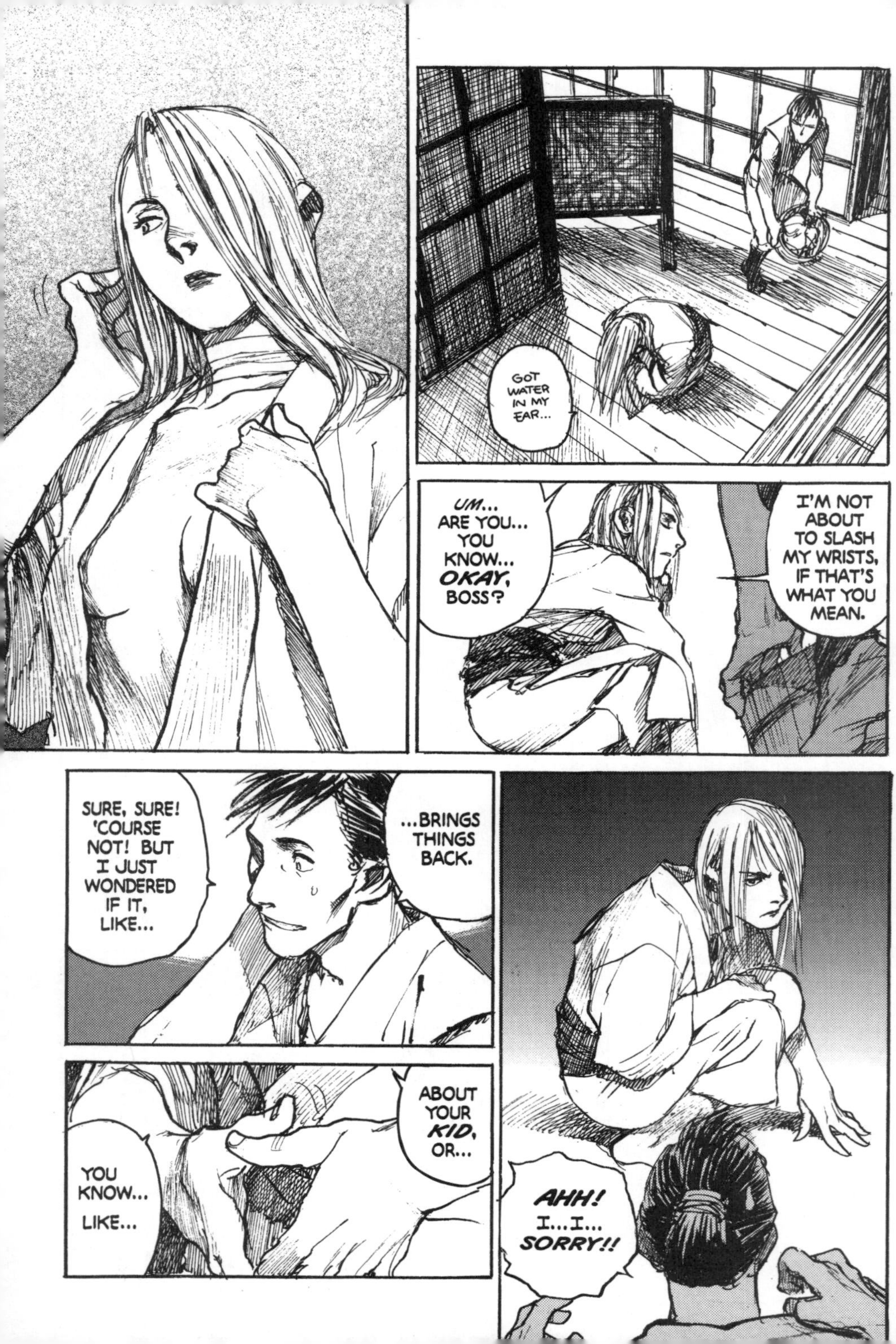
GOT WATER IN MY EAR...
UM... ARE YOU... YOU KNOW... OKAY, BOSS?
I'M NOT ABOUT TO SLASH MY WRISTS, IF THAT'S WHAT YOU MEAN.
SURE, SURE! 'COURSE NOT! BUT I JUST WONDERED IF IT, LIKE...
...BRINGS THINGS BACK.
ABOUT YOUR KID, OR...
YOU KNOW... LIKE...
AHH! I...I... SORRY!!

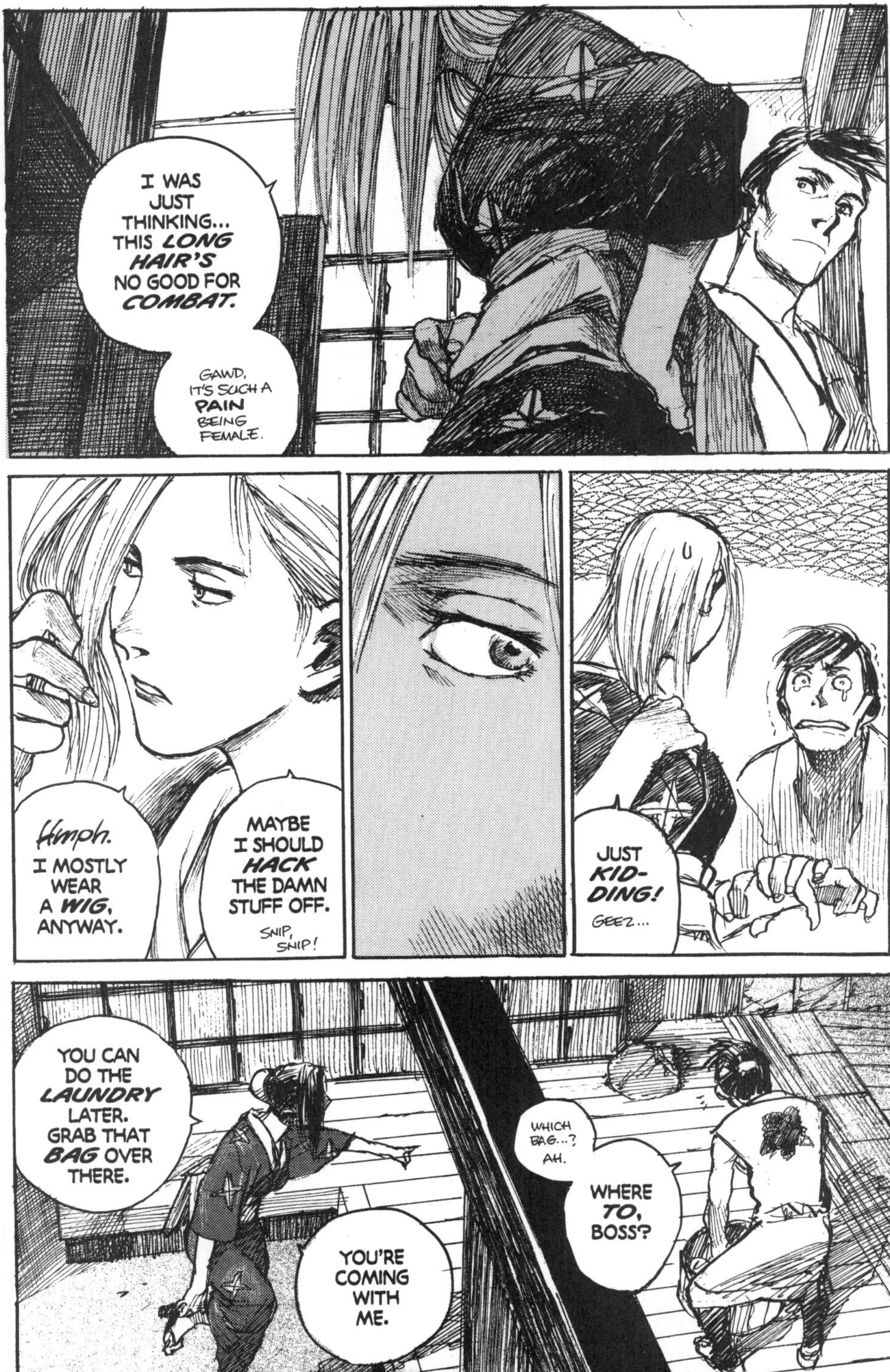
I WAS JUST THINKING... THIS LONG HAIR'S NO GOOD FOR COMBAT.
GAWD, IT'S SUCH A PAIN BEING FEMALE.
Hmph. I MOSTLY WEAR A WIG, ANYWAY.
MAYBE I SHOULD HACK THE DAMN STUFF OFF.
SNIP, SNIP!
JUST KID-DING!
GEEZ...
YOU CAN DO THE LAUNDRY LATER. GRAB THAT BAG OVER THERE.
WHICH BAG...? AH.
WHERE TO, BOSS?
YOU'RE COMING WITH ME.

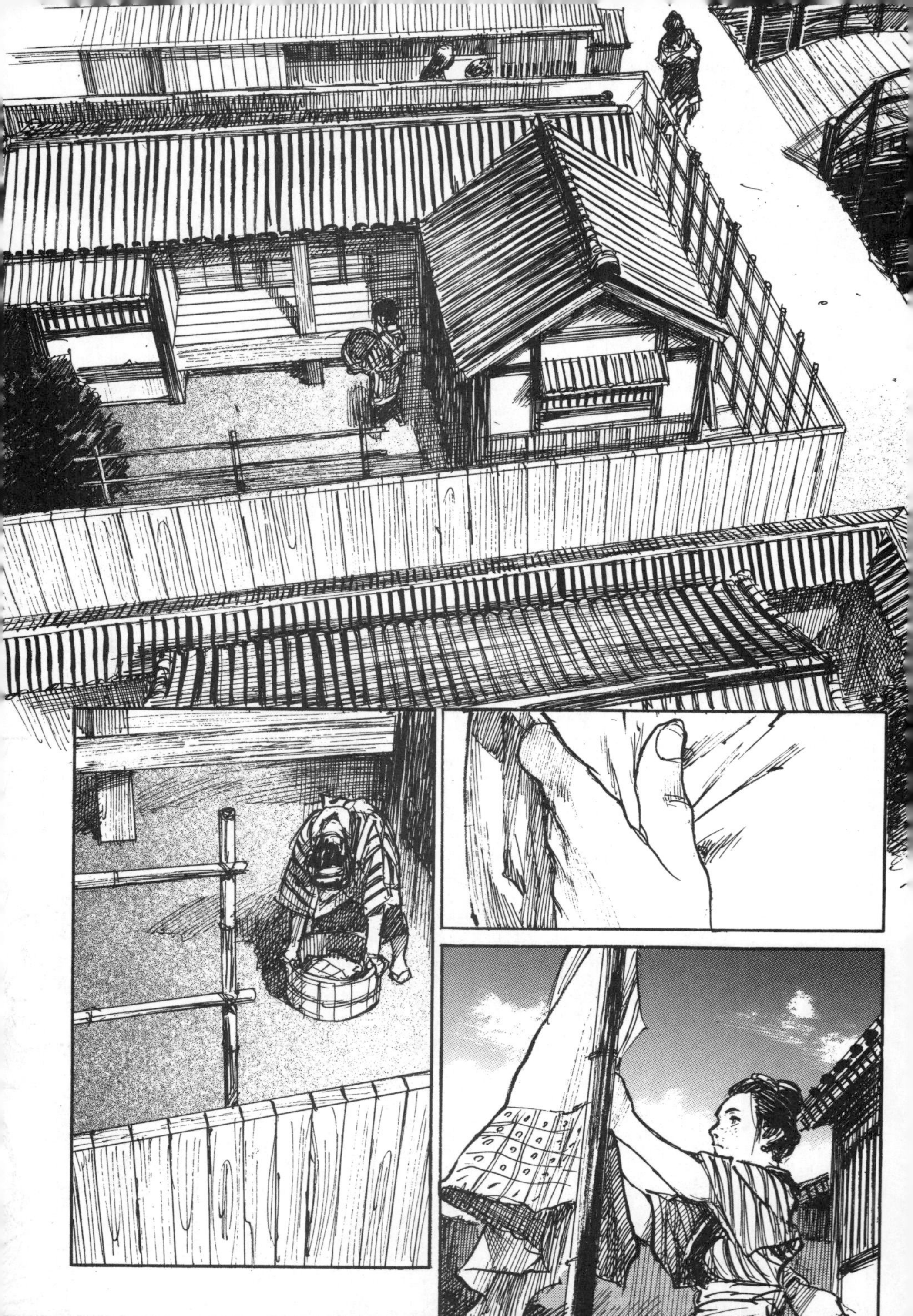

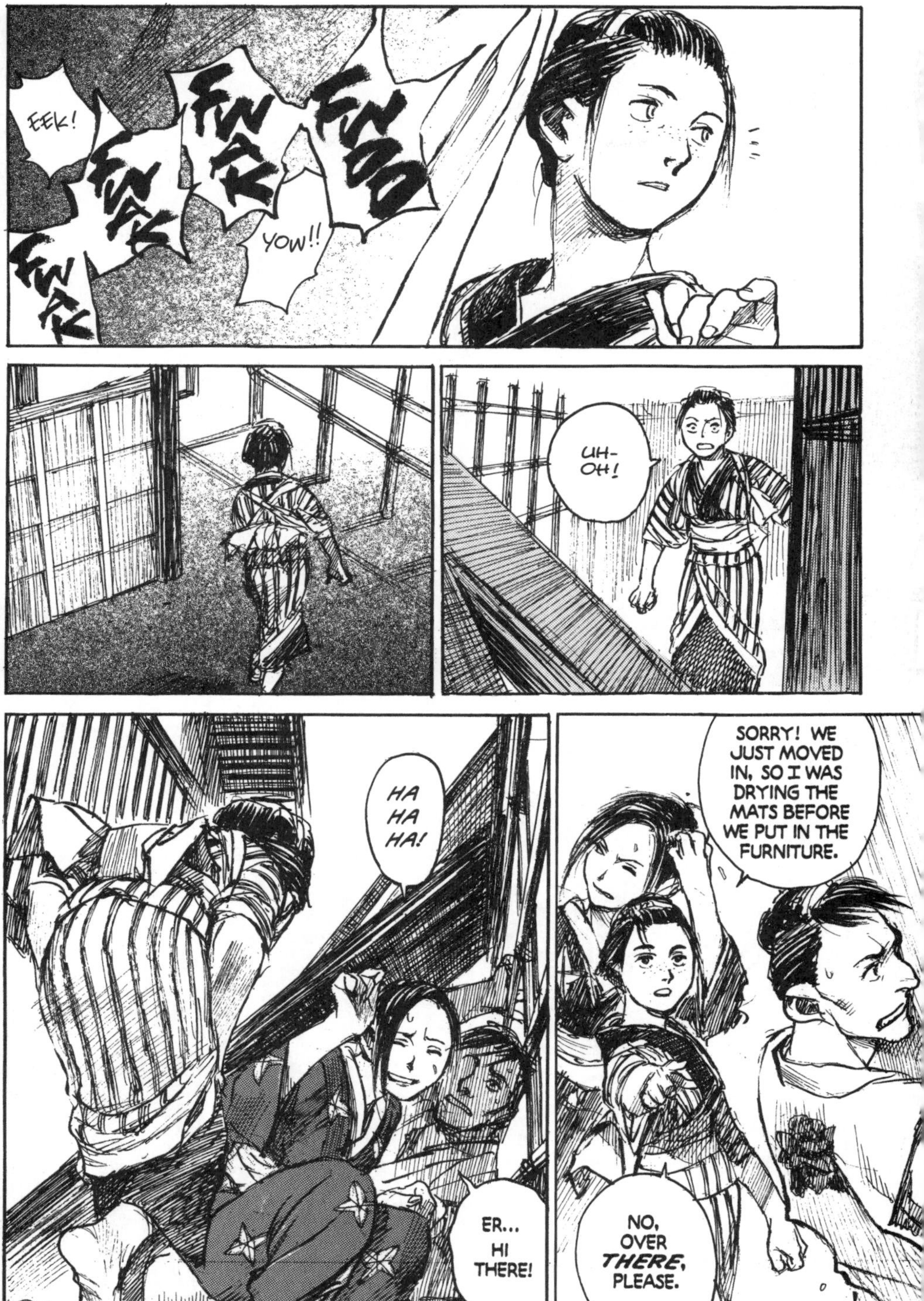
EEK!
FWAK
FWAK
FWAK
FWOOO
YOW!!
UH-OH!
HA HA HA!
ER... HI THERE!
SORRY! WE JUST MOVED IN, SO I WAS DRYING THE MATS BEFORE WE PUT IN THE FURNITURE.
NO, OVER *THERE*, PLEASE.

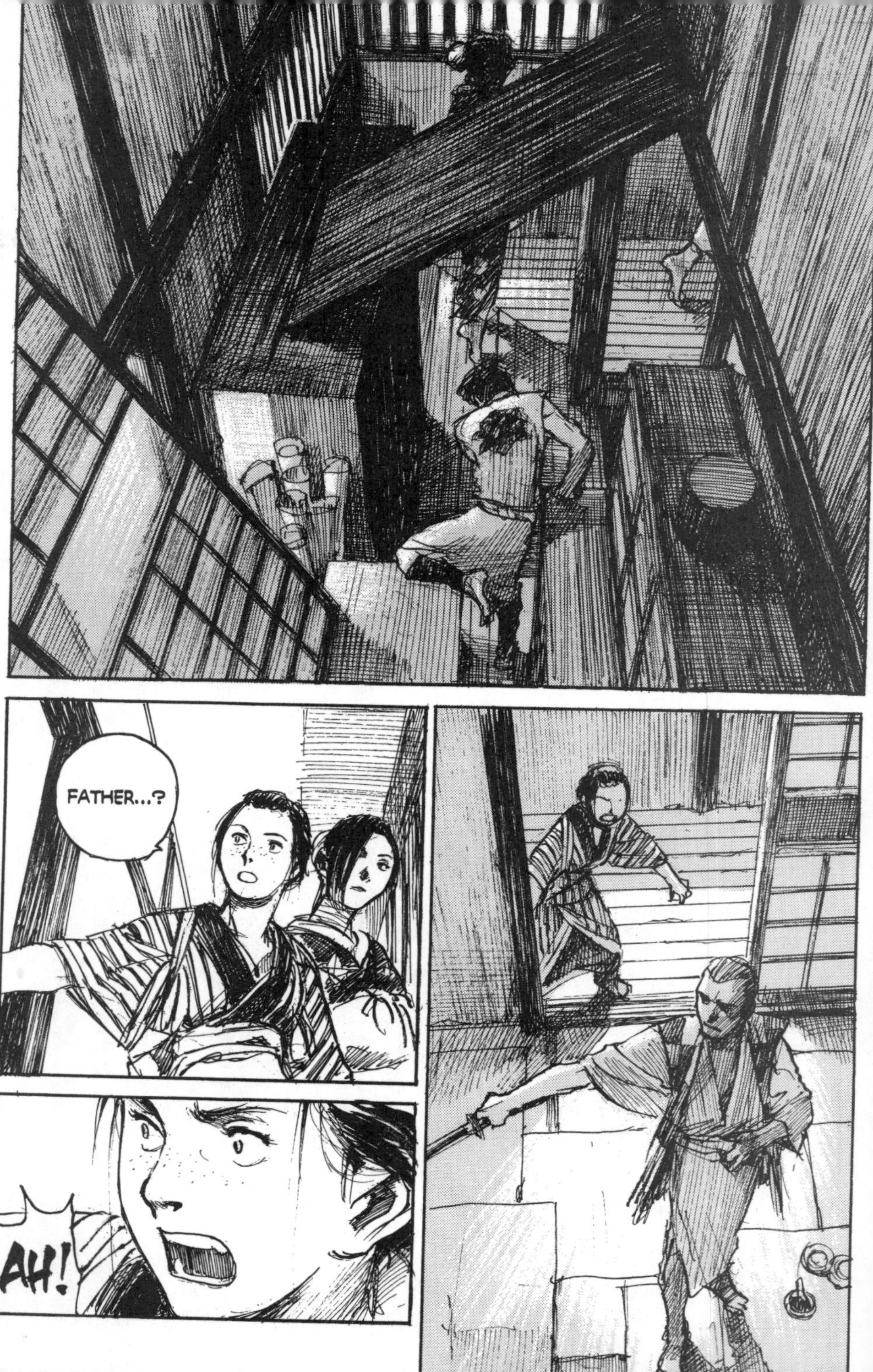
FATHER...?
AH!

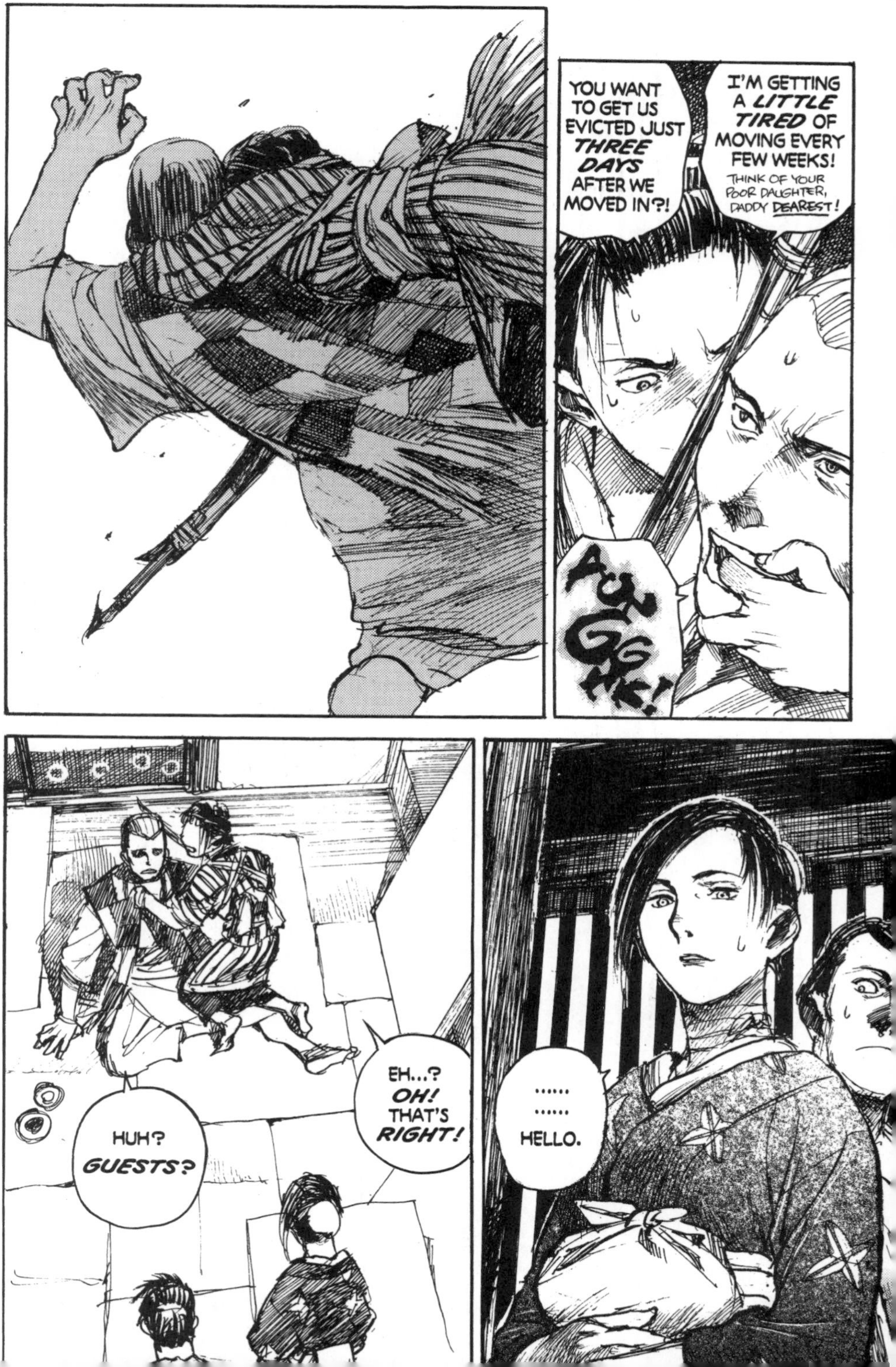
YOU WANT TO GET US EVICTED JUST THREE DAYS AFTER WE MOVED IN?!
I'M GETTING A LITTLE TIRED OF MOVING EVERY FEW WEEKS! THINK OF YOUR POOR DAUGHTER, DADDY DEAREST!
AUGGHK!
HUH? GUESTS?
EH...? OH! THAT'S RIGHT!
.... HELLO.

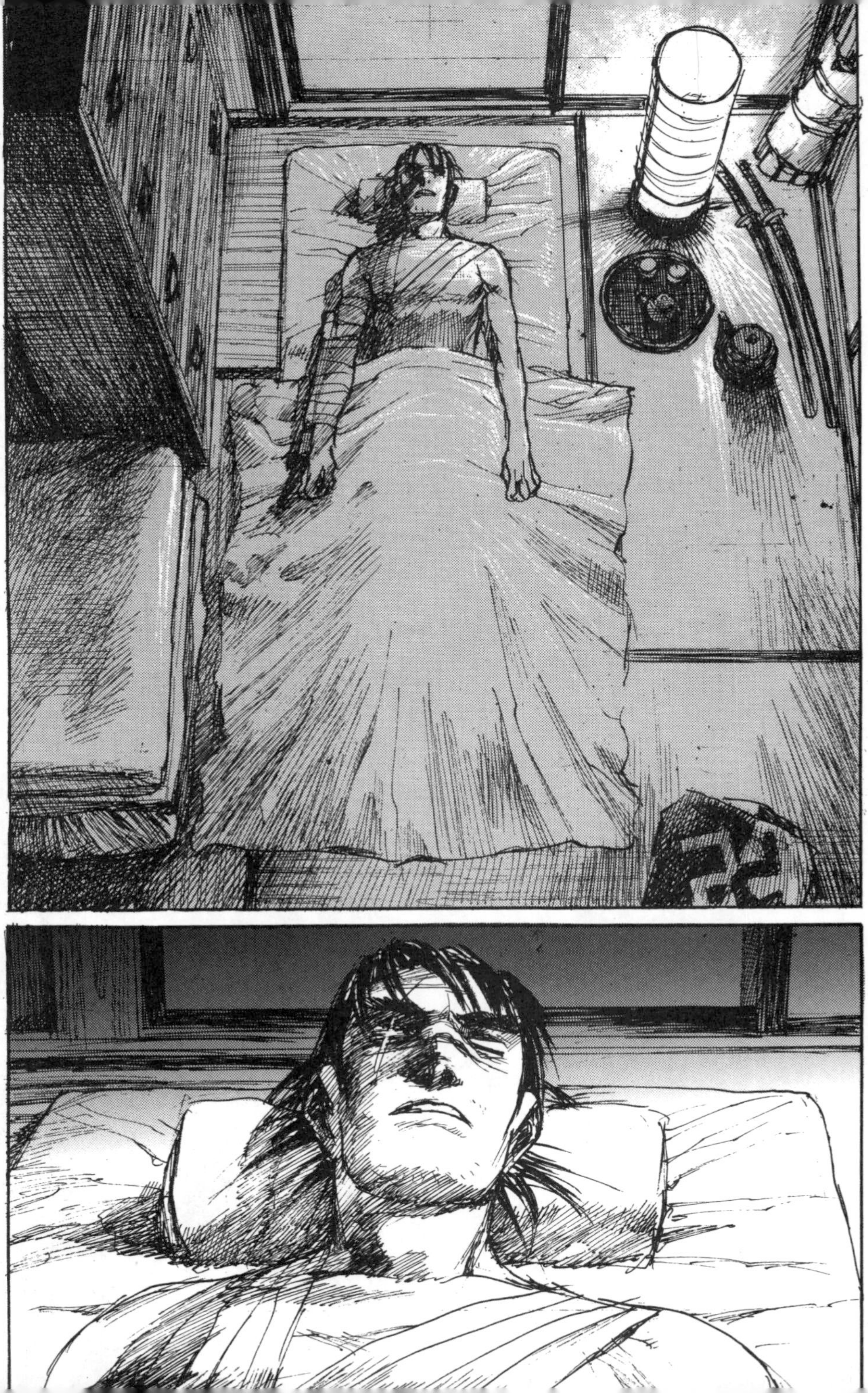

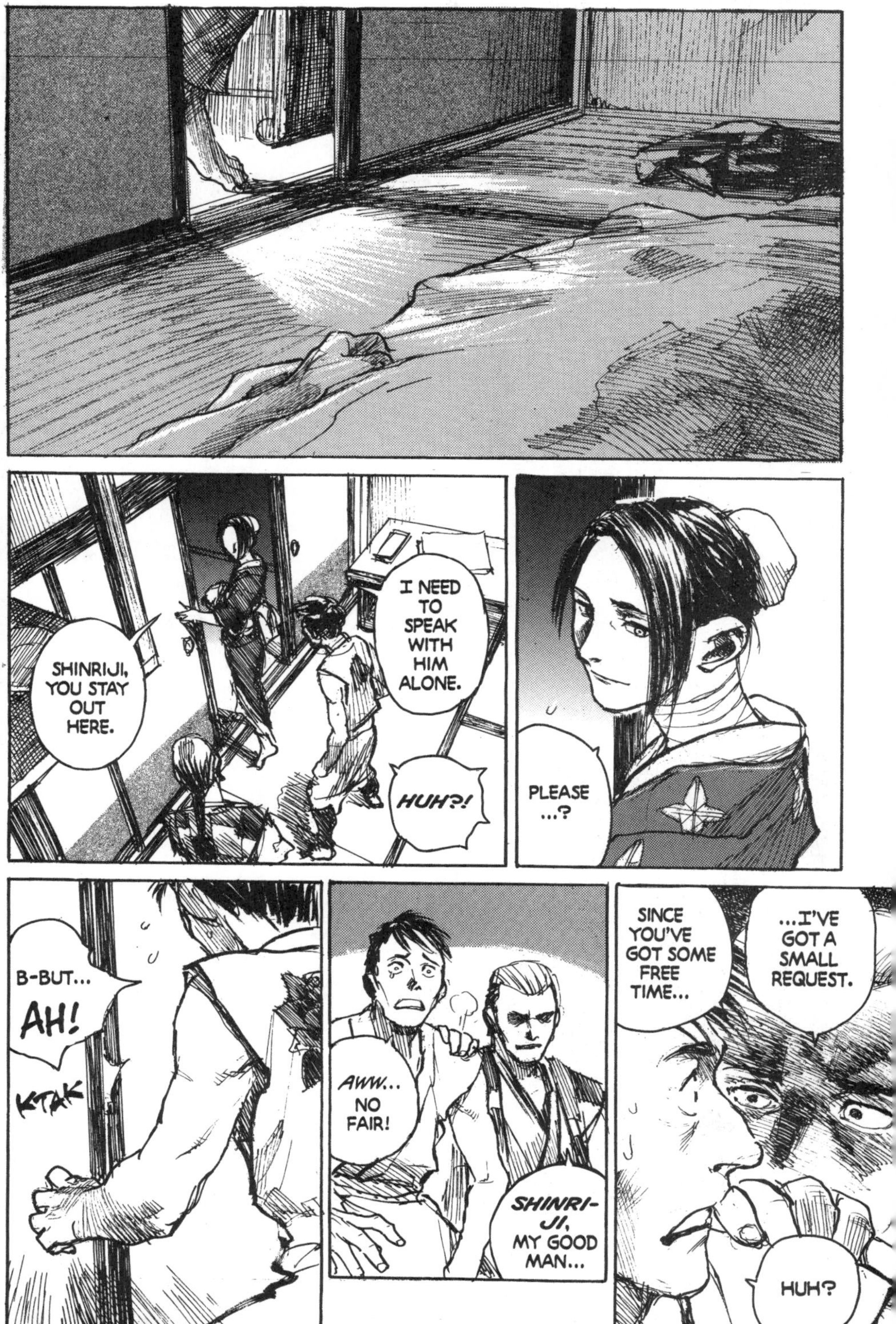
I NEED TO SPEAK WITH HIM ALONE.
SHINRIJI, YOU STAY OUT HERE.
HUH?!
PLEASE ...?
B-BUT...
AH!
KTAK
AWW... NO FAIR!
SHINRI-JI, MY GOOD MAN...
SINCE YOU'VE GOT SOME FREE TIME...
...I'VE GOT A SMALL REQUEST.
HUH?

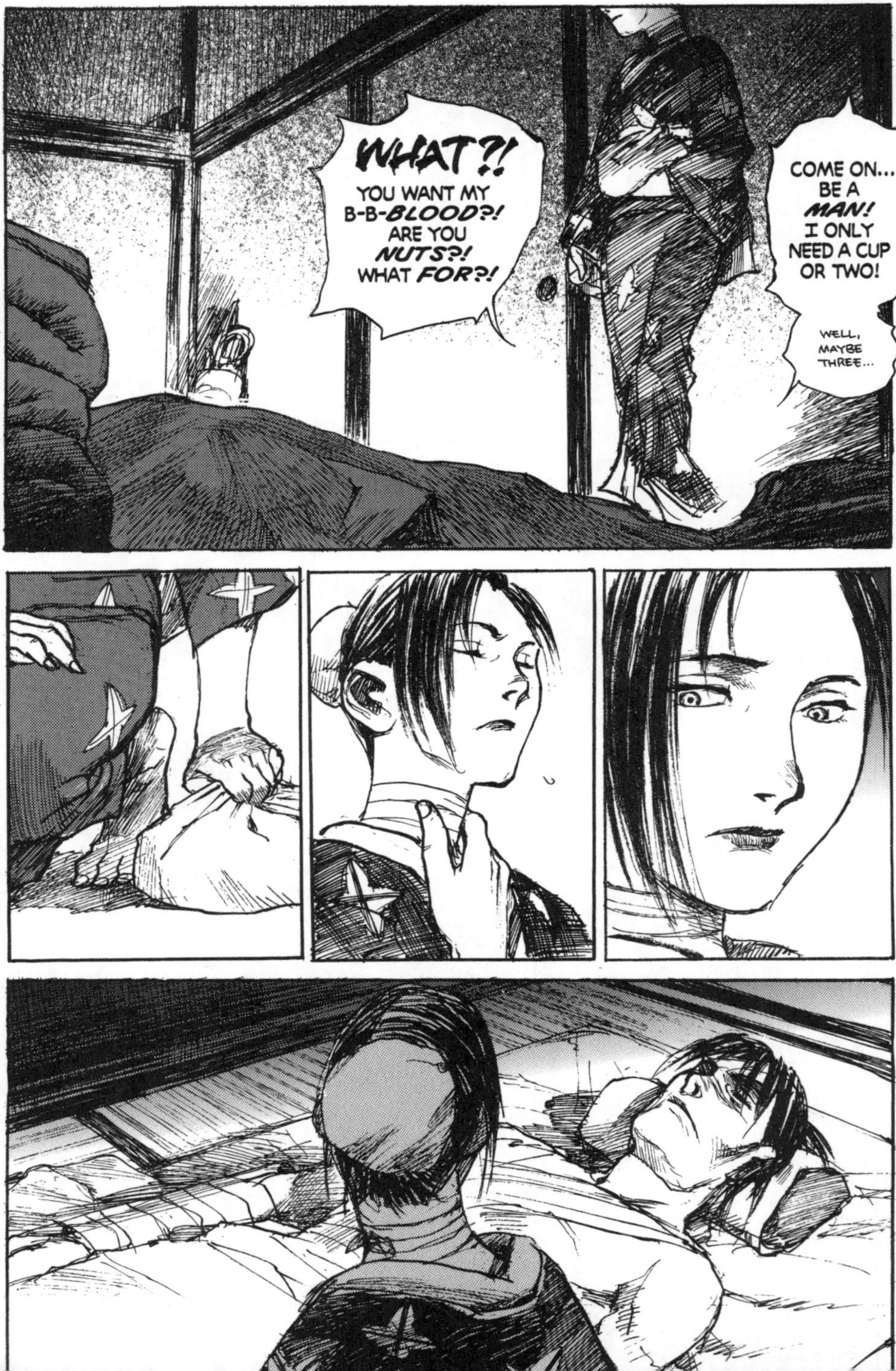
WHAT?! YOU WANT MY B-B-BLOOD?! ARE YOU NUTS?! WHAT FOR?!
COME ON... BE A MAN! I ONLY NEED A CUP OR TWO!
WELL, MAYBE THREE...

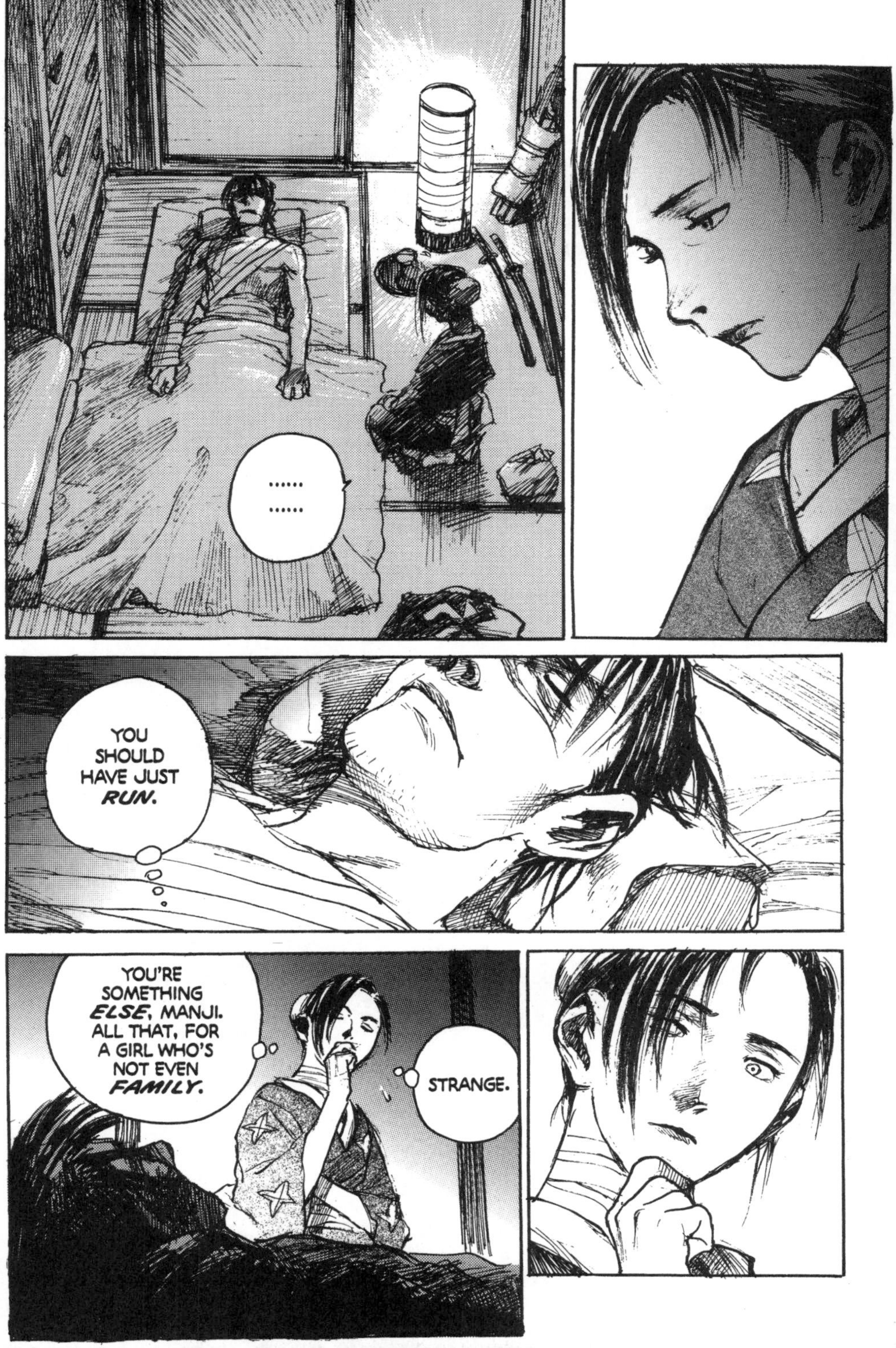
......
......
YOU SHOULD HAVE JUST RUN.
YOU'RE SOMETHING ELSE, MANJI. ALL THAT, FOR A GIRL WHO'S NOT EVEN FAMILY.
STRANGE.

HEY.

YAIEEK!

HYAKU-RIN...?

HA HA HA! SHEESH!

YOU WERE *AWAKE* ALL ALONG?

......

......

WHAT...

...WHAT *TIME* IS IT?

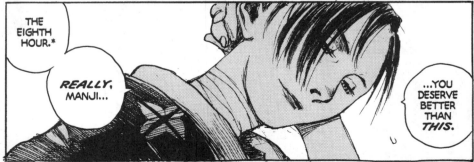

THE EIGHTH HOUR.*

REALLY, MANJI...

...YOU DESERVE BETTER THAN *THIS.*

*: APPROXIMATELY TWO IN THE AFTERNOON.

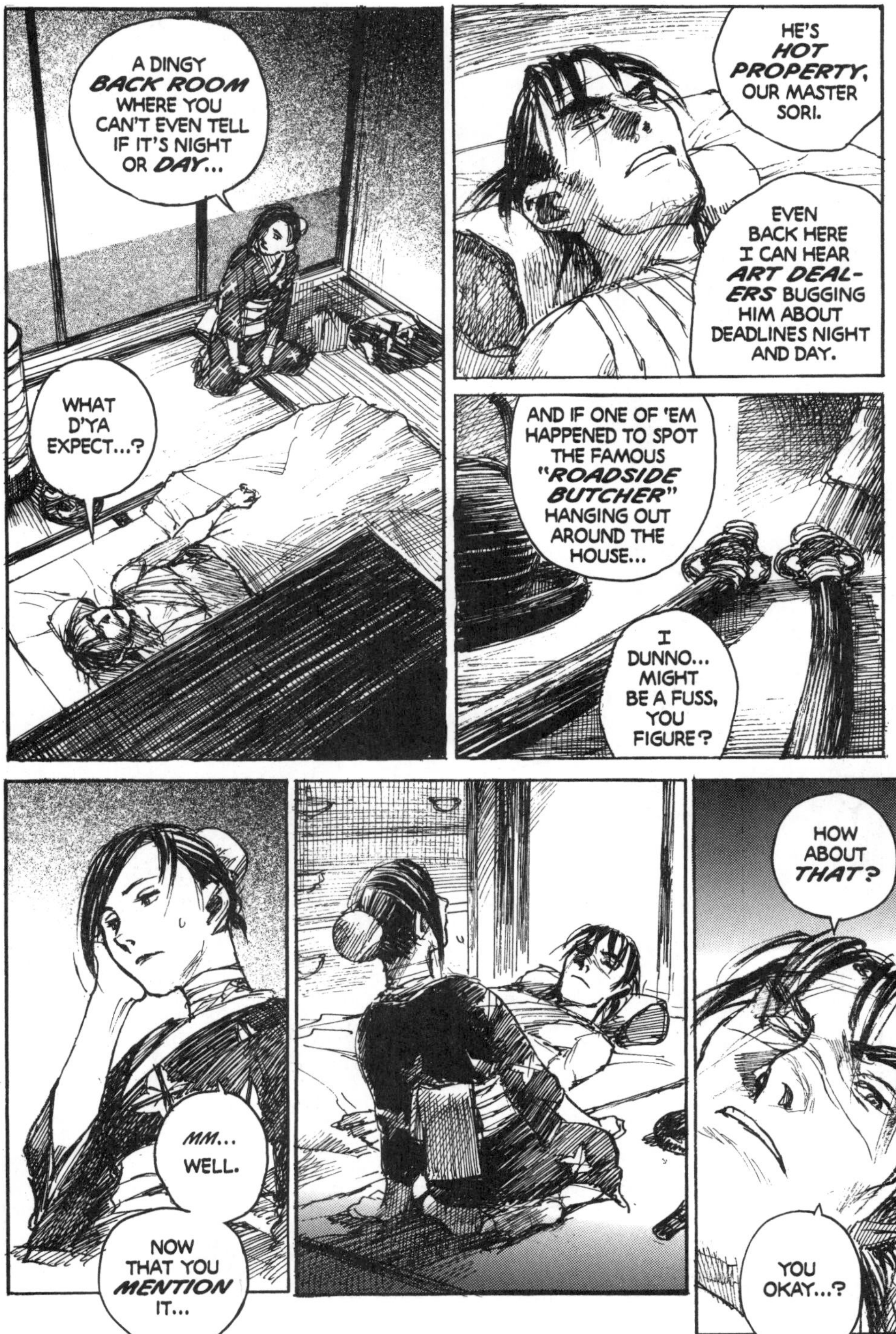
A DINGY BACK ROOM WHERE YOU CAN'T EVEN TELL IF IT'S NIGHT OR DAY...
WHAT D'YA EXPECT...?
HE'S HOT PROPERTY, OUR MASTER SORI.
EVEN BACK HERE I CAN HEAR ART DEALERS BUGGING HIM ABOUT DEADLINES NIGHT AND DAY.
AND IF ONE OF 'EM HAPPENED TO SPOT THE FAMOUS "ROADSIDE BUTCHER" HANGING OUT AROUND THE HOUSE...
I DUNNO... MIGHT BE A FUSS, YOU FIGURE?
MM... WELL.
NOW THAT YOU MENTION IT...
HOW ABOUT THAT?
YOU OKAY...?

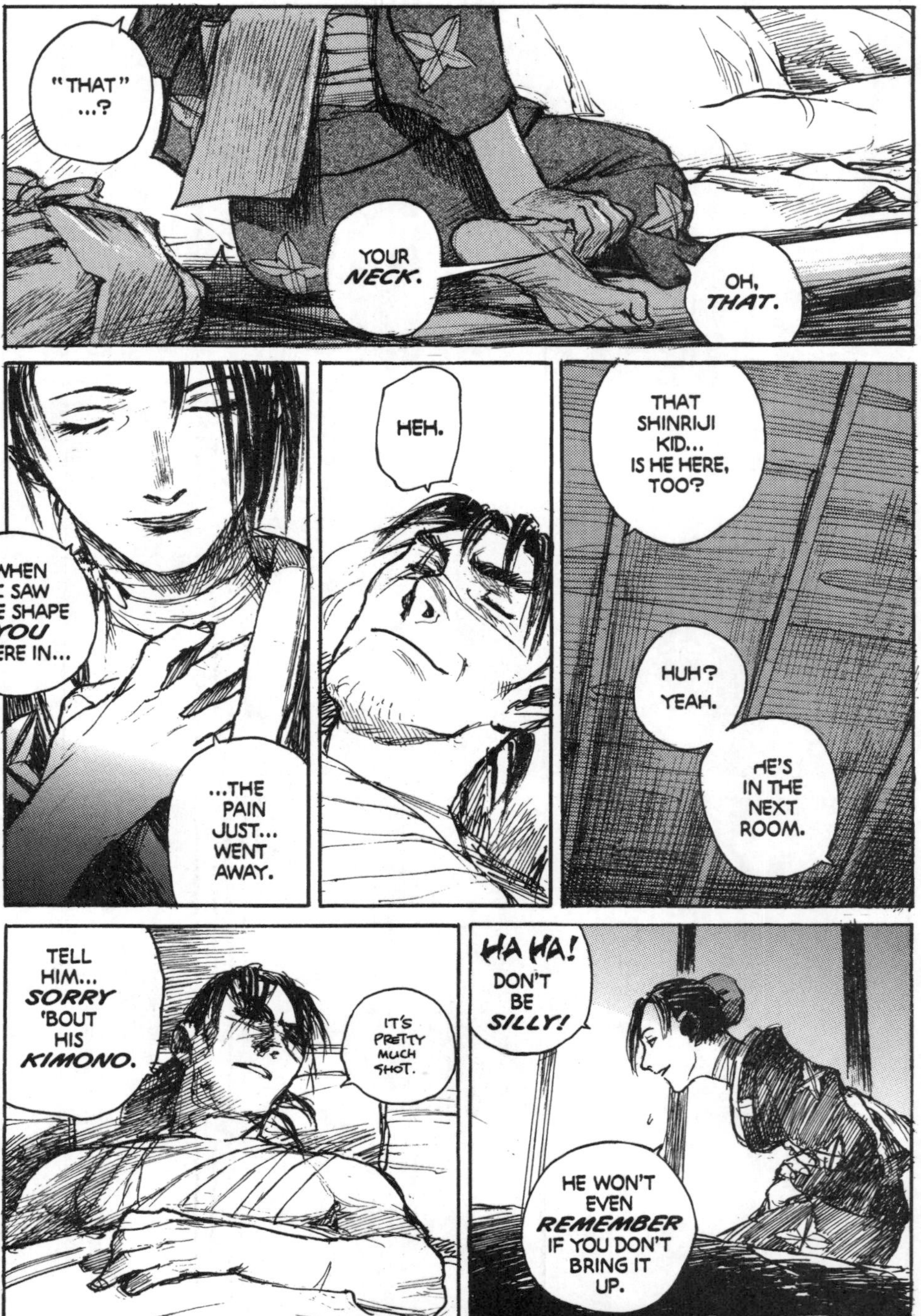
"THAT" ...?
YOUR NECK.
OH, THAT.
WHEN I SAW THE SHAPE YOU WERE IN...
...THE PAIN JUST... WENT AWAY.
HEH.
THAT SHINRIJI KID... IS HE HERE, TOO?
HUH? YEAH.
HE'S IN THE NEXT ROOM.
TELL HIM... SORRY 'BOUT HIS KIMONO.
IT'S PRETTY MUCH SHOT.
HA HA! DON'T BE SILLY!
HE WON'T EVEN REMEMBER IF YOU DON'T BRING IT UP.

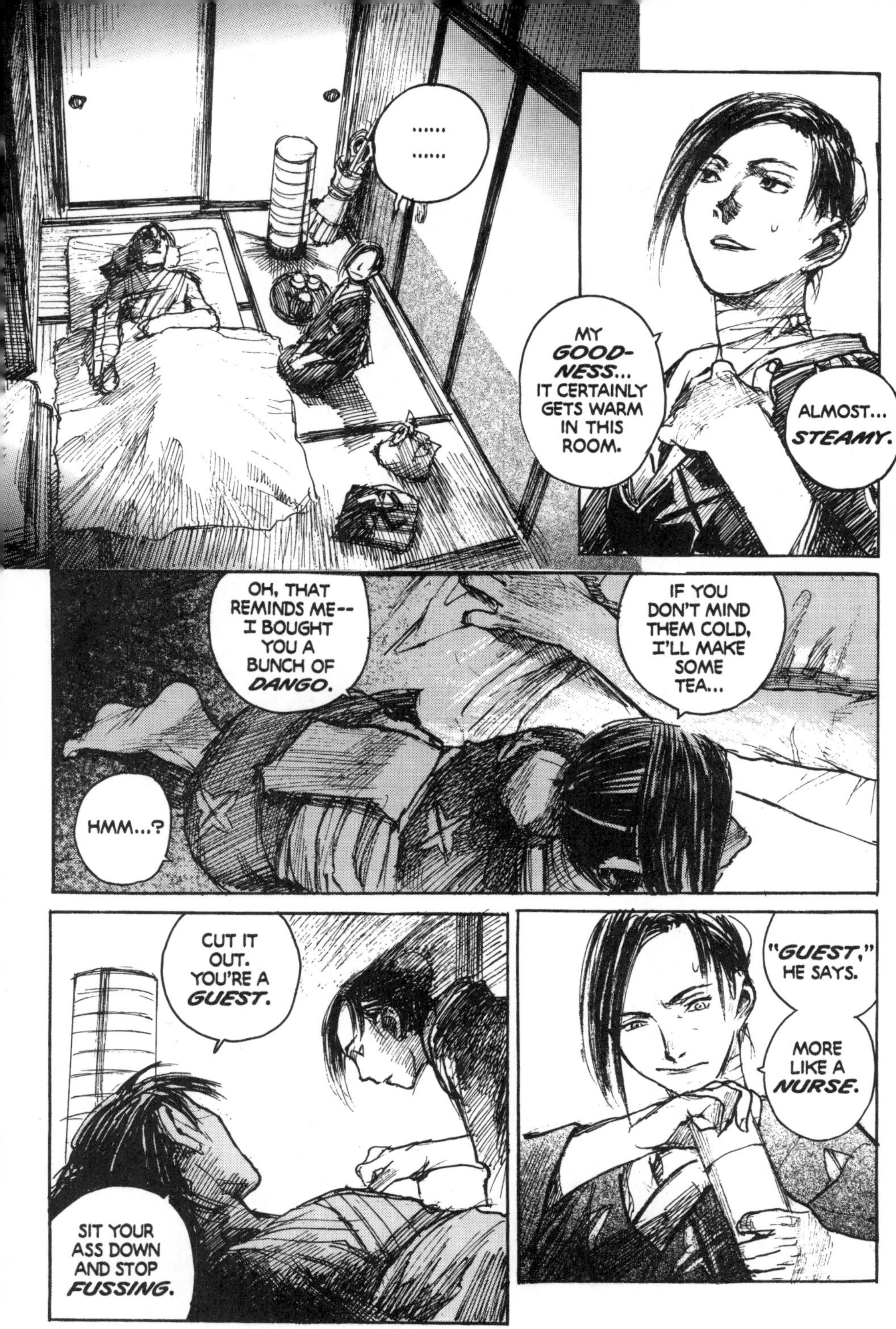
......
......
MY GOODNESS... IT CERTAINLY GETS WARM IN THIS ROOM.
ALMOST... STEAMY.
OH, THAT REMINDS ME-- I BOUGHT YOU A BUNCH OF DANGO.
IF YOU DON'T MIND THEM COLD, I'LL MAKE SOME TEA...
HMM...?
CUT IT OUT. YOU'RE A GUEST.
SIT YOUR ASS DOWN AND STOP FUSSING.
"GUEST," HE SAYS.
MORE LIKE A NURSE.

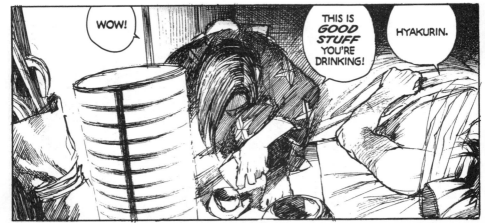

WOW! THIS IS **GOOD STUFF** YOU'RE DRINKING! HYAKURIN.

THE *TEGATA*.

WHERE IS IT?

COME ON.

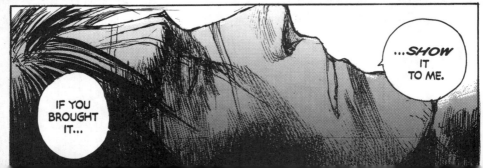

IF YOU BROUGHT IT...

...**SHOW** IT TO ME.

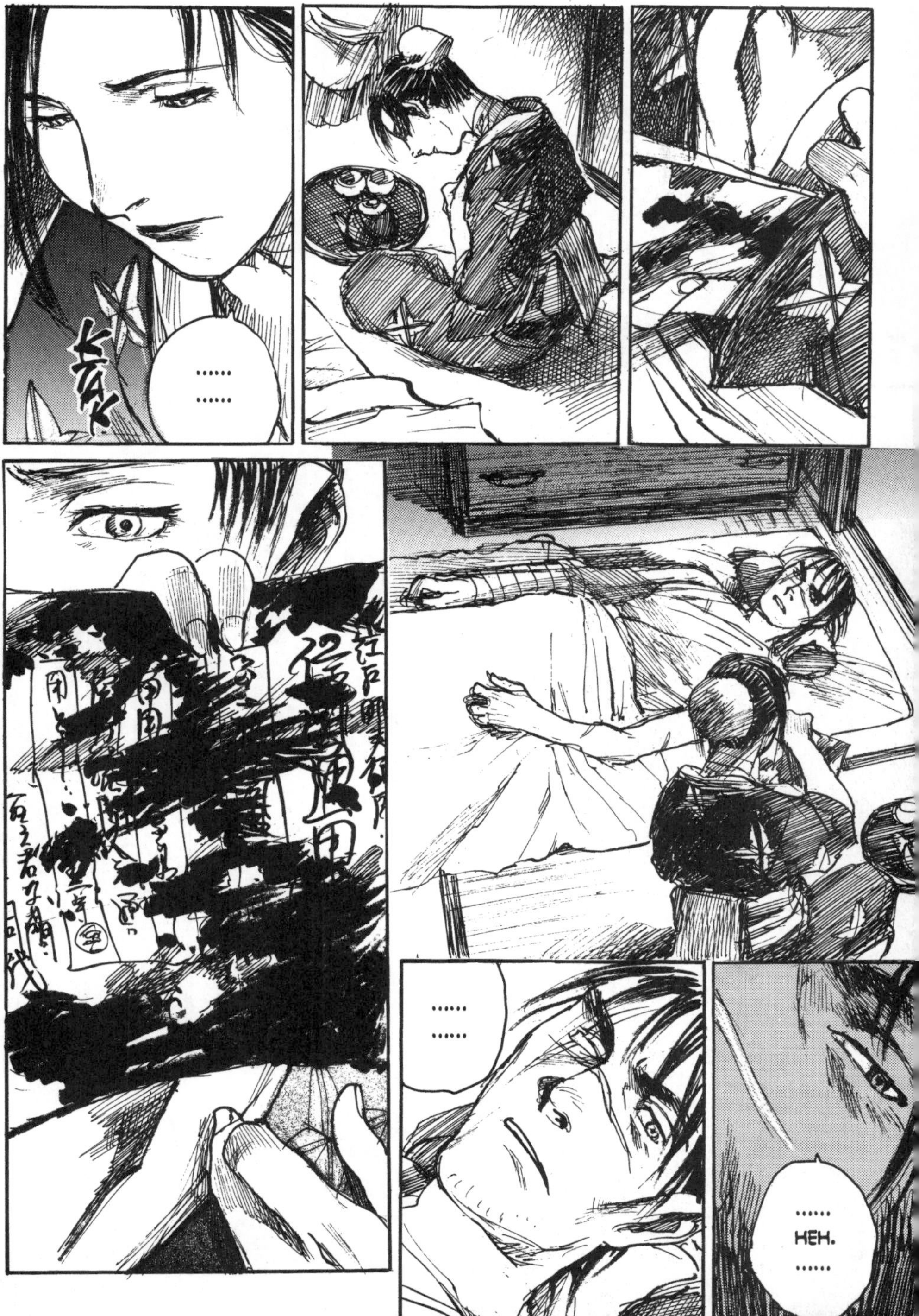
KLAK
......
......
......
......
......
HEH.
......

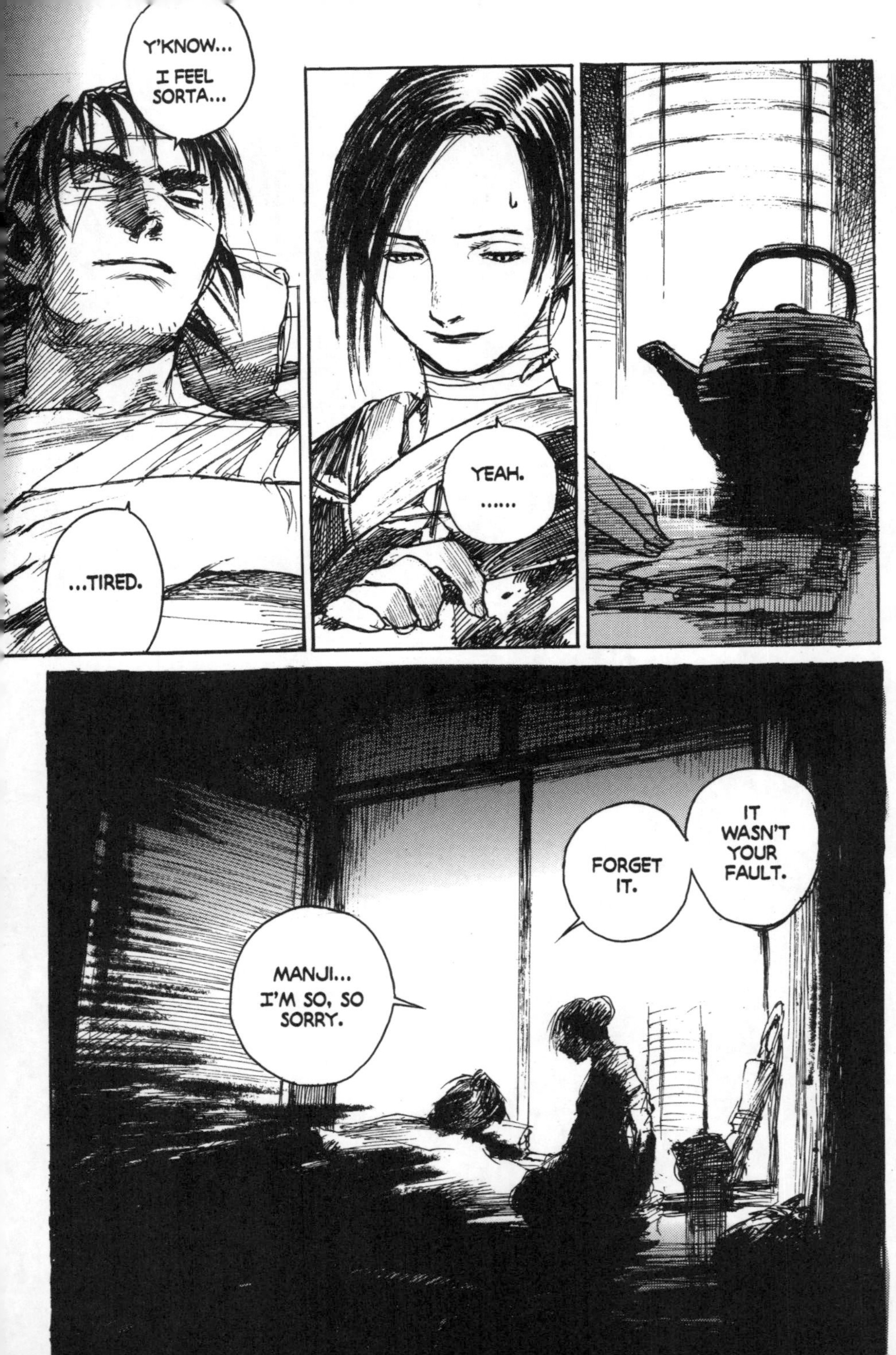
Y'KNOW... I FEEL SORTA...
...TIRED.
YEAH. ......
MANJI... I'M SO, SO SORRY.
FORGET IT.
IT WASN'T YOUR FAULT.

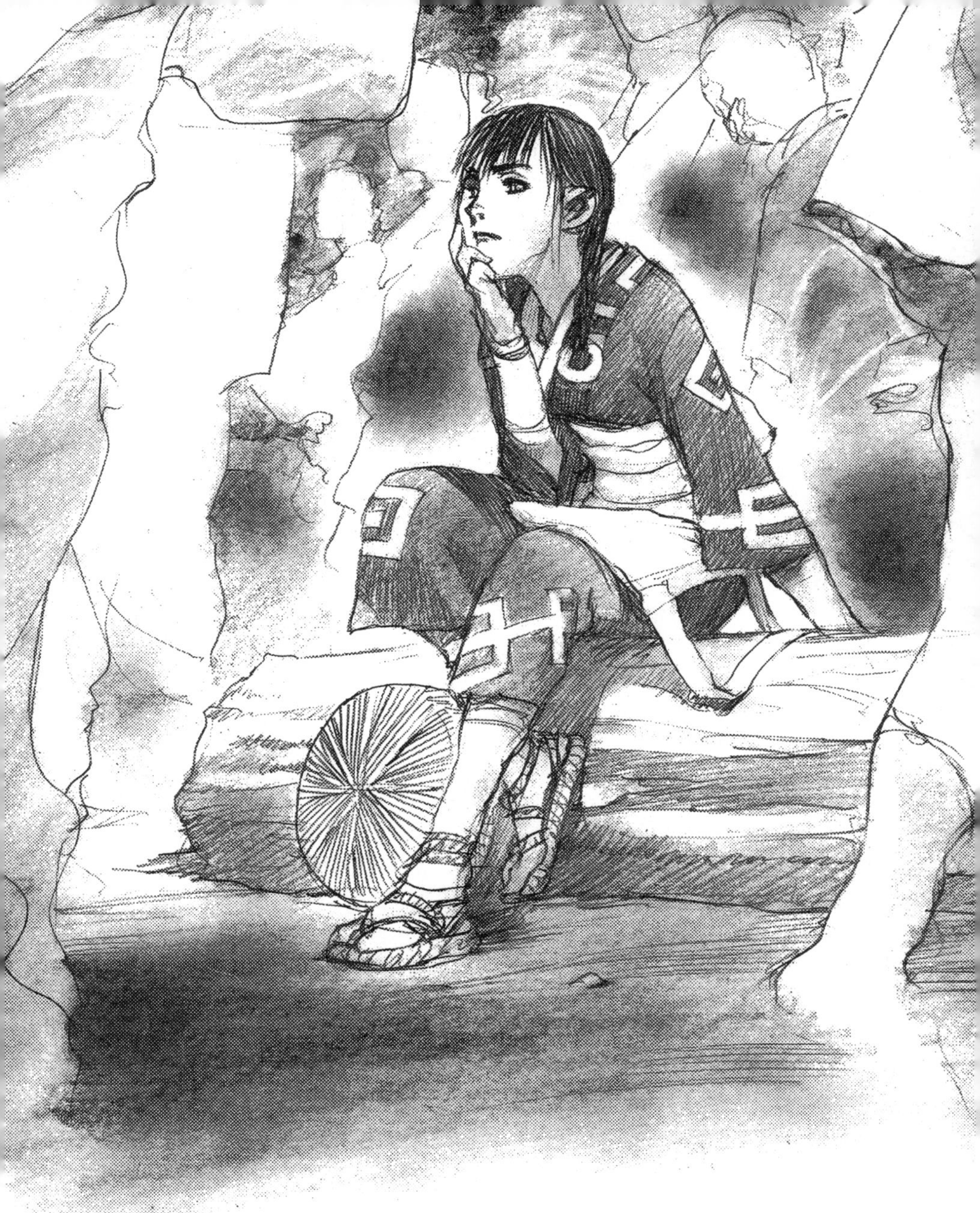

STIGMATA

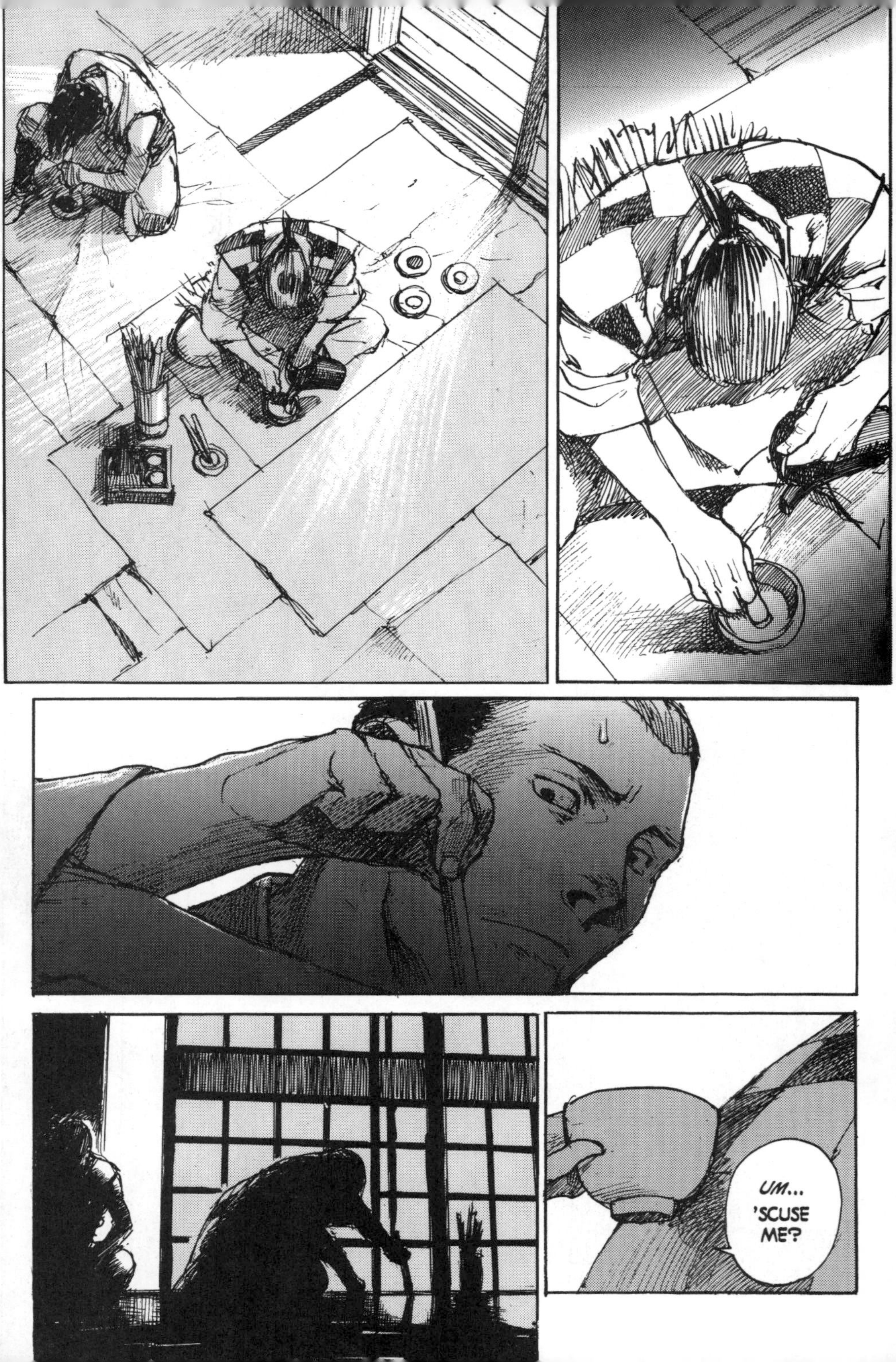
UM... 'SCUSE ME?

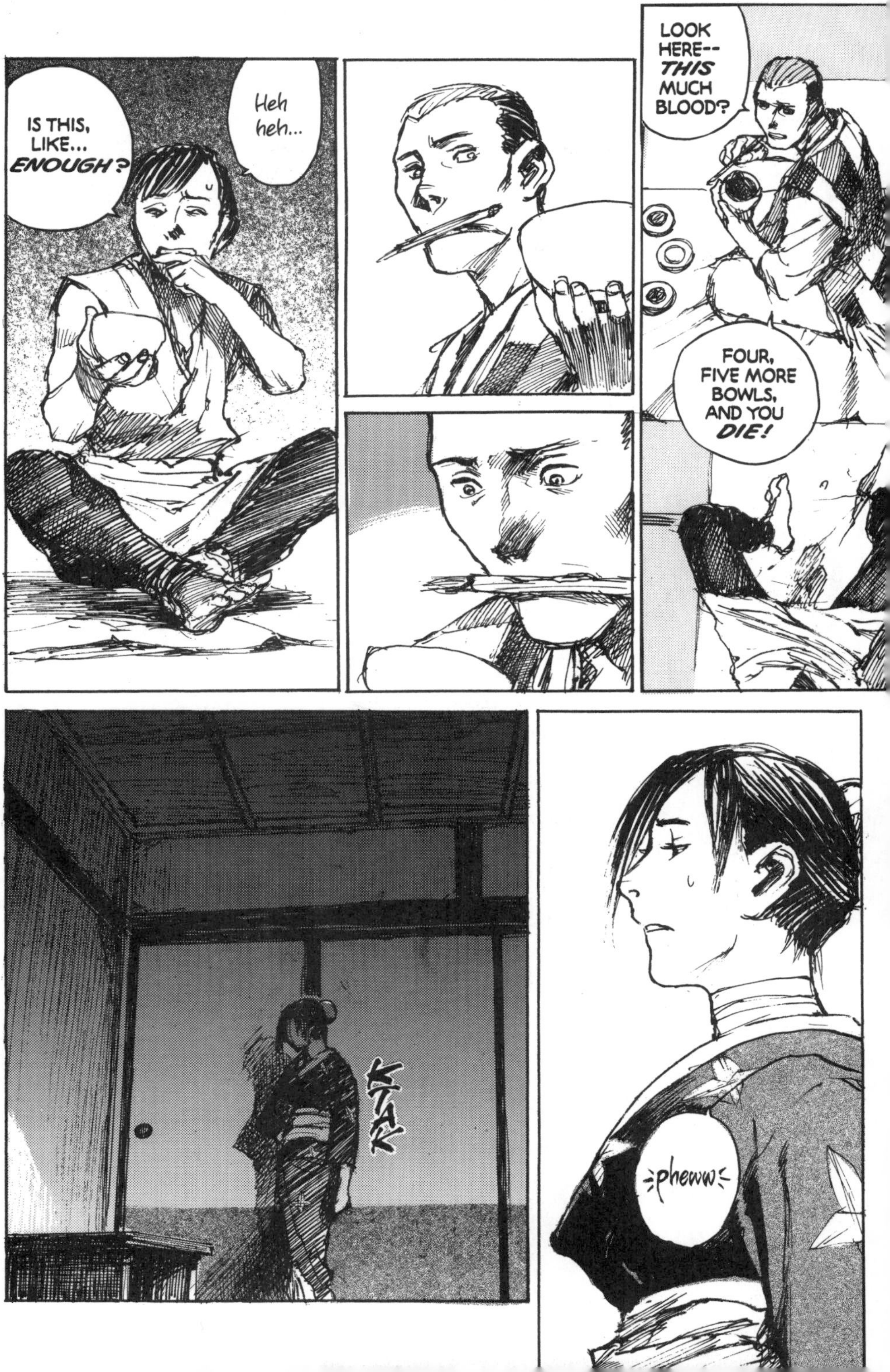
IS THIS, LIKE... ENOUGH?
Heh heh...
LOOK HERE-- THIS MUCH BLOOD?
FOUR, FIVE MORE BOWLS, AND YOU DIE!
KTAK
phewww

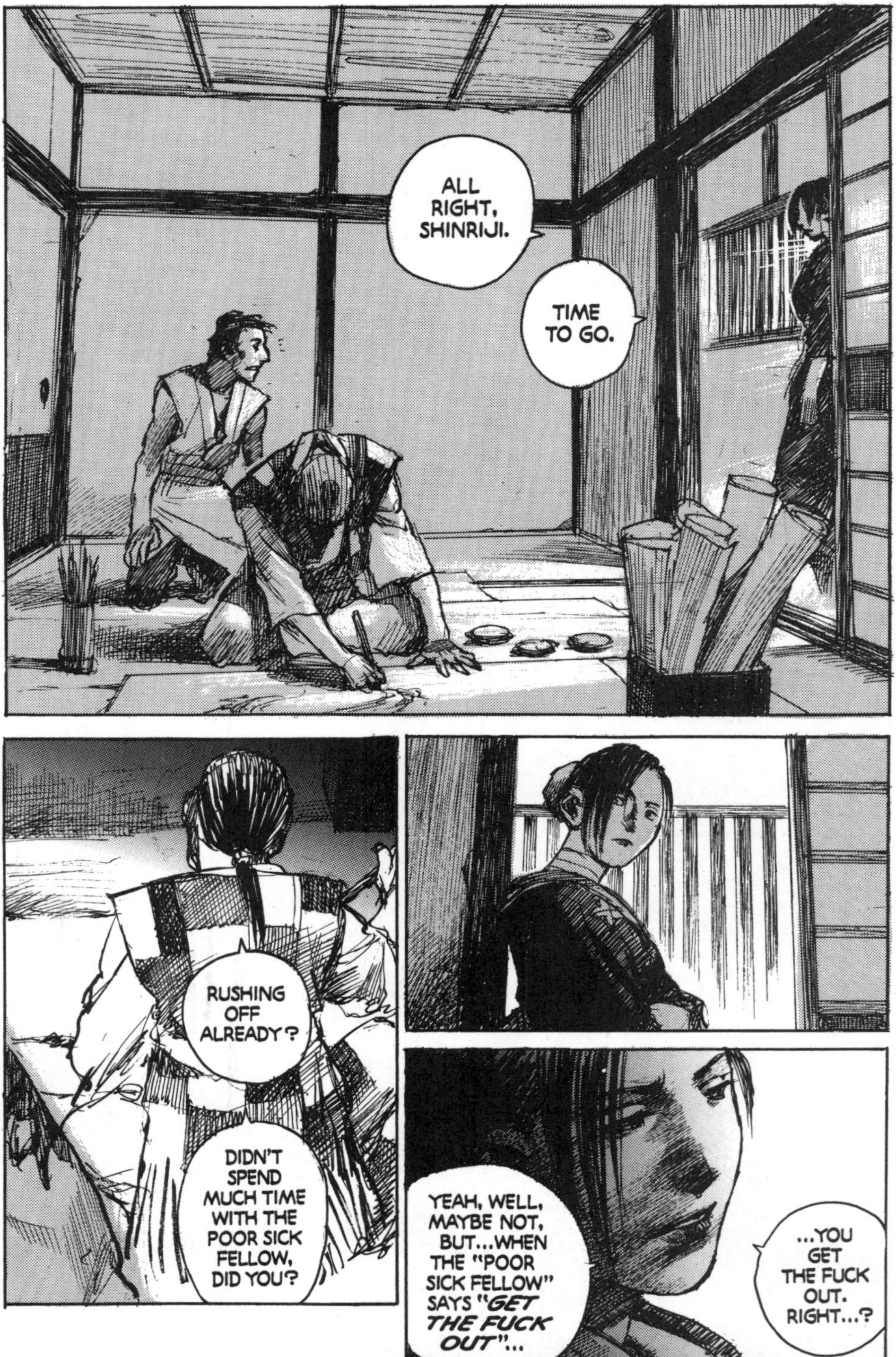
ALL RIGHT, SHINRIJI.
TIME TO GO.
RUSHING OFF ALREADY?
DIDN'T SPEND MUCH TIME WITH THE POOR SICK FELLOW, DID YOU?
YEAH, WELL, MAYBE NOT, BUT...WHEN THE "POOR SICK FELLOW" SAYS "GET THE FUCK OUT"...
...YOU GET THE FUCK OUT. RIGHT...?

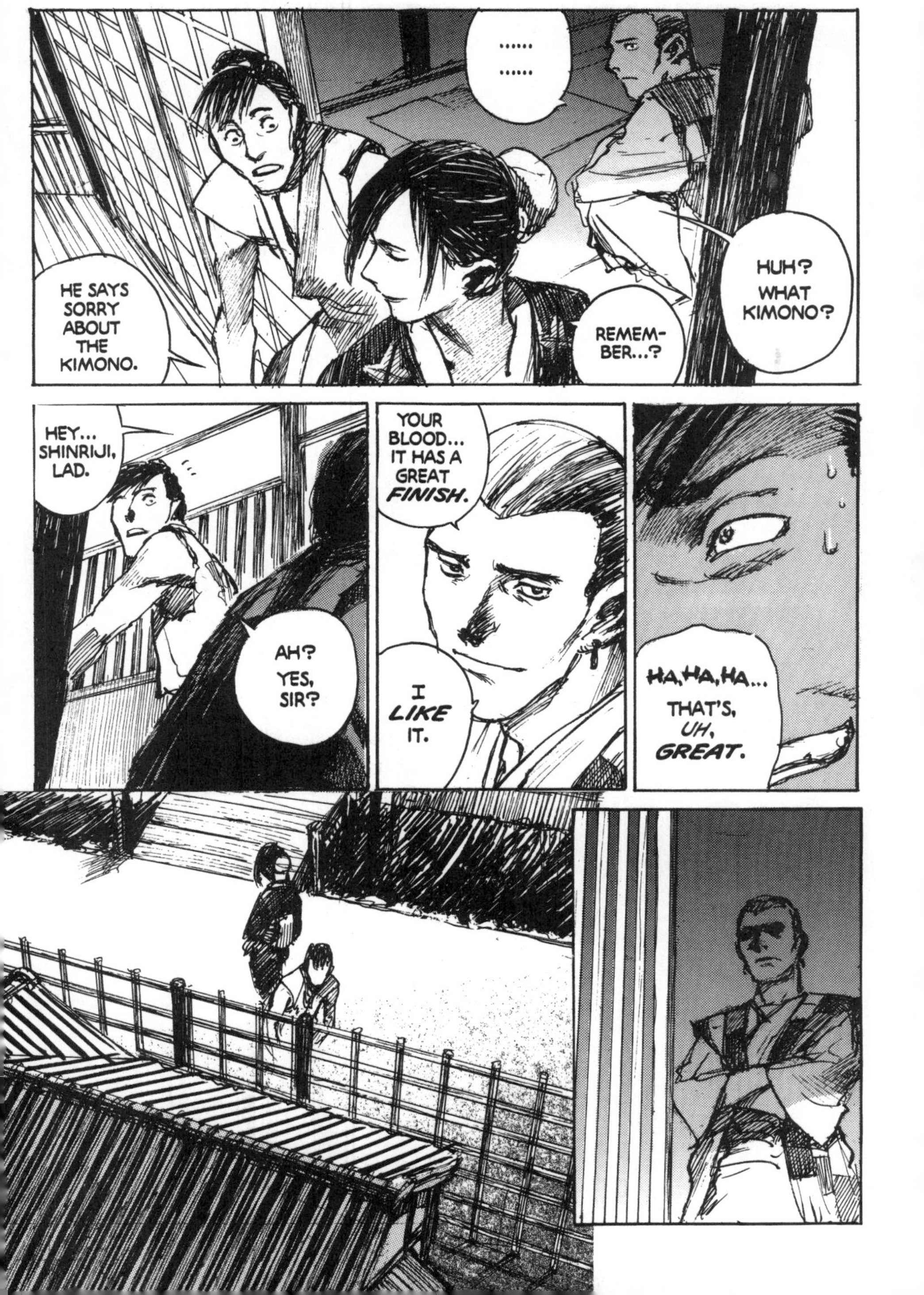
......
......
HE SAYS SORRY ABOUT THE KIMONO.
REMEMBER...?
HUH? WHAT KIMONO?
HEY... SHINRIJI, LAD.
AH? YES, SIR?
YOUR BLOOD... IT HAS A GREAT *FINISH*.
I *LIKE* IT.
HA,HA,HA... THAT'S, *UH*, *GREAT*.

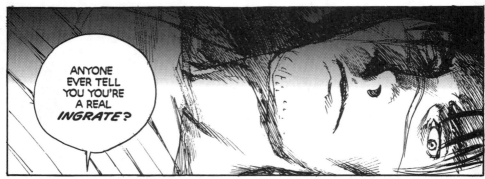

ANYONE EVER TELL YOU YOU'RE A REAL *INGRATE?*

SOME-ONE WORRIES ABOUT YOU...

...AND YOU TREAT THEM LIKE *DIRT.*

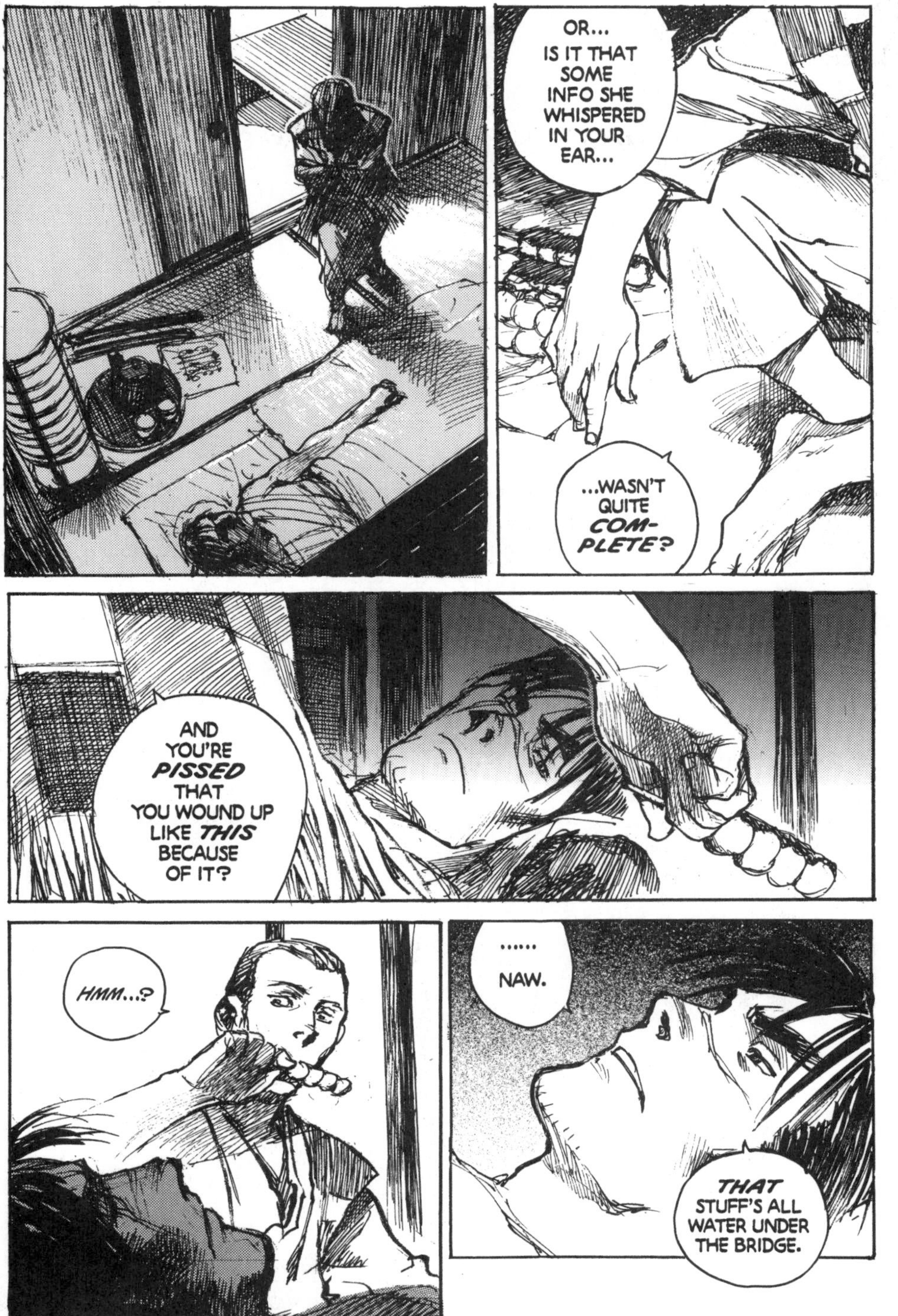
OR... IS IT THAT SOME INFO SHE WHISPERED IN YOUR EAR...
...WASN'T QUITE COM-PLETE?
AND YOU'RE PISSED THAT YOU WOUND UP LIKE THIS BECAUSE OF IT?
HMM...?
......
NAW.
THAT STUFF'S ALL WATER UNDER THE BRIDGE.

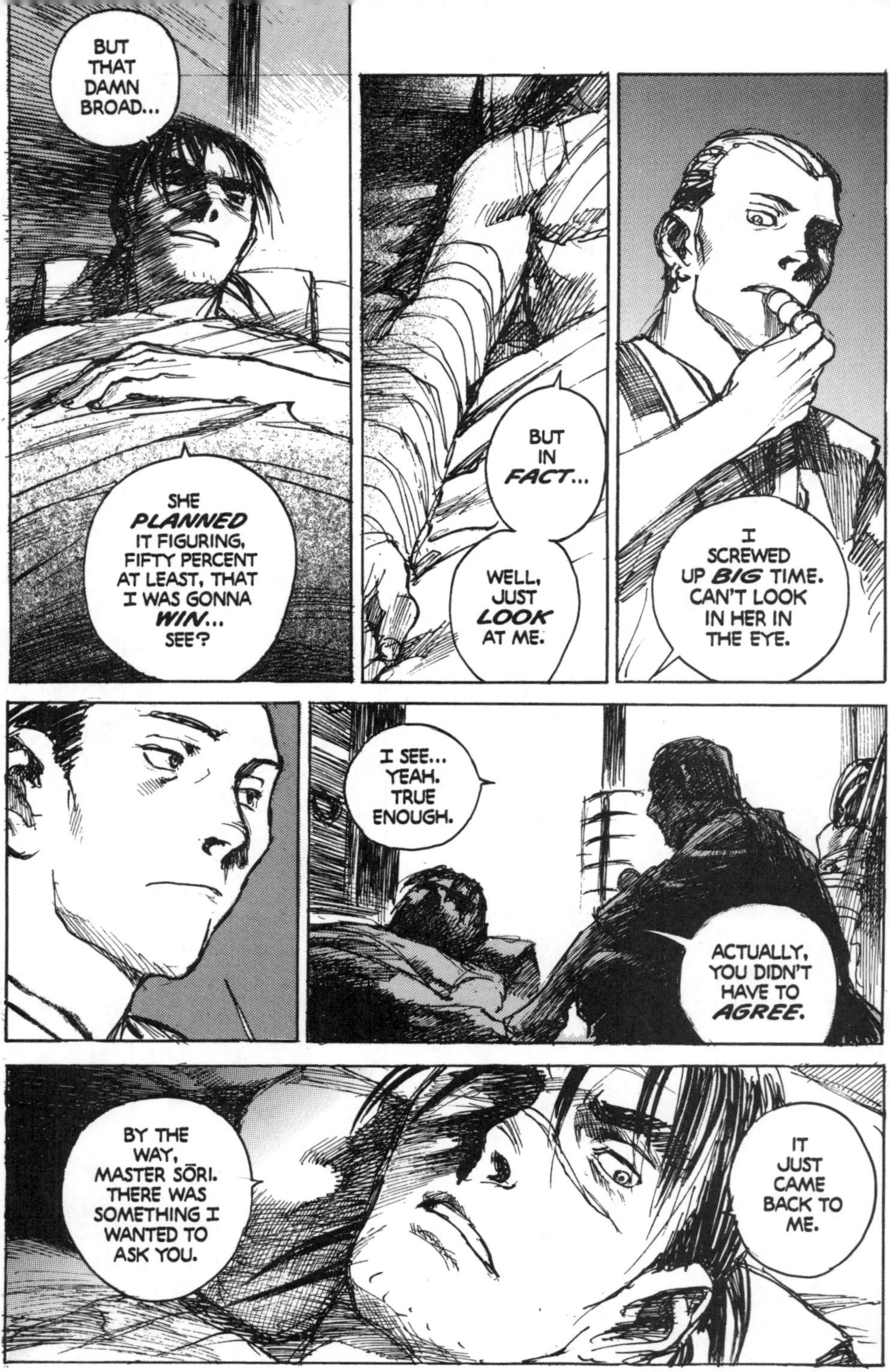
BUT THAT DAMN BROAD...
SHE PLANNED IT FIGURING, FIFTY PERCENT AT LEAST, THAT I WAS GONNA WIN... SEE?
BUT IN FACT...
WELL, JUST LOOK AT ME.
I SCREWED UP BIG TIME. CAN'T LOOK IN HER IN THE EYE.
I SEE... YEAH. TRUE ENOUGH.
ACTUALLY, YOU DIDN'T HAVE TO AGREE.
BY THE WAY, MASTER SŌRI. THERE WAS SOMETHING I WANTED TO ASK YOU.
IT JUST CAME BACK TO ME.

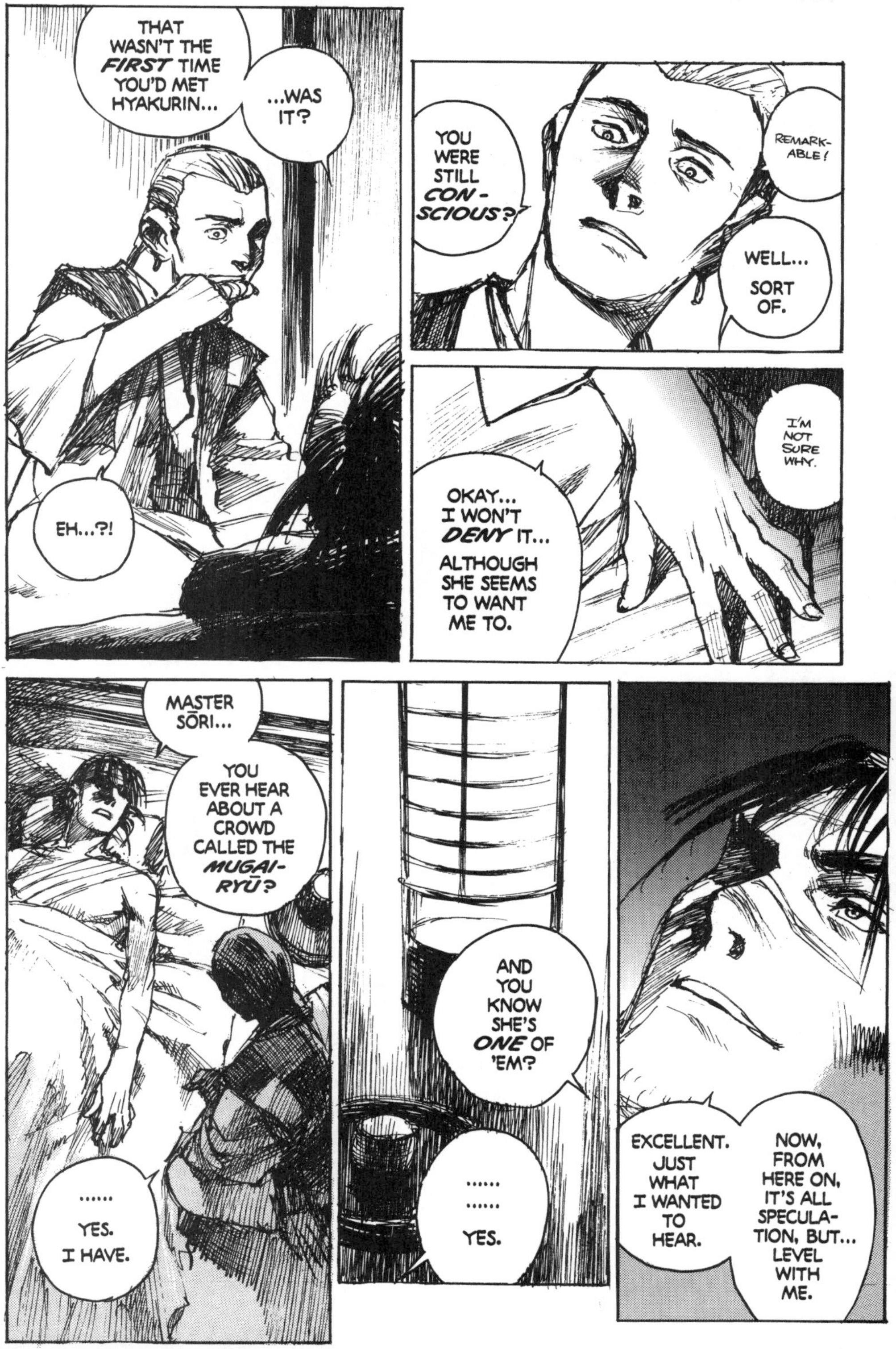
THAT WASN'T THE FIRST TIME YOU'D MET HYAKURIN...
...WAS IT?
EH...?!
YOU WERE STILL CON-SCIOUS?
REMARK-ABLE!
WELL... SORT OF.
OKAY... I WON'T DENY IT... ALTHOUGH SHE SEEMS TO WANT ME TO.
I'M NOT SURE WHY.
MASTER SŌRI...
YOU EVER HEAR ABOUT A CROWD CALLED THE MUGAI-RYŪ?
...... YES. I HAVE.
AND YOU KNOW SHE'S ONE OF 'EM?
.... YES.
EXCELLENT. JUST WHAT I WANTED TO HEAR.
NOW, FROM HERE ON, IT'S ALL SPECULA-TION, BUT... LEVEL WITH ME.

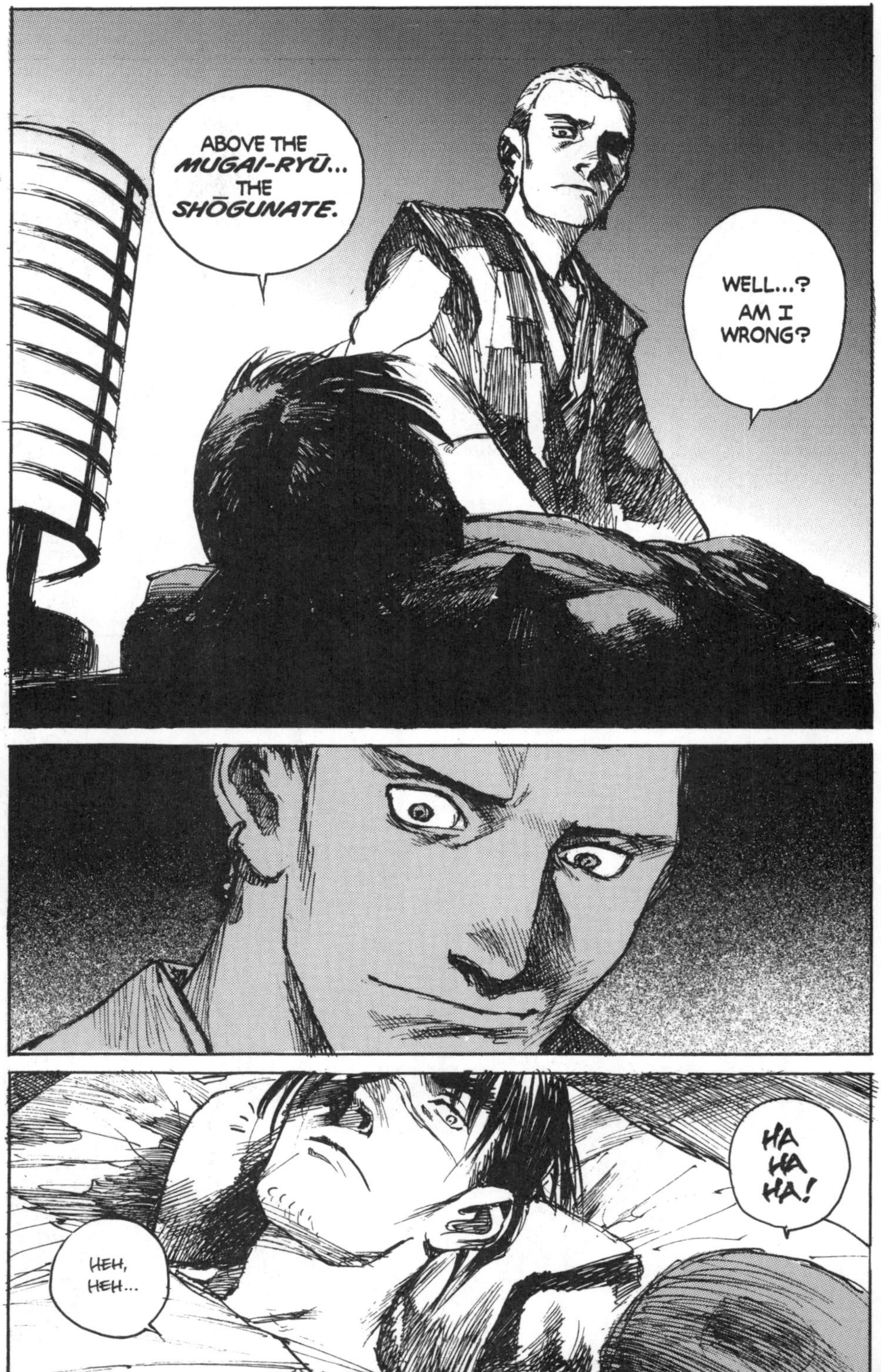
ABOVE THE *MUGAI-RYŪ*... THE *SHŌGUNATE*.
WELL...? AM I WRONG?
HEH, HEH...
HA HA HA!

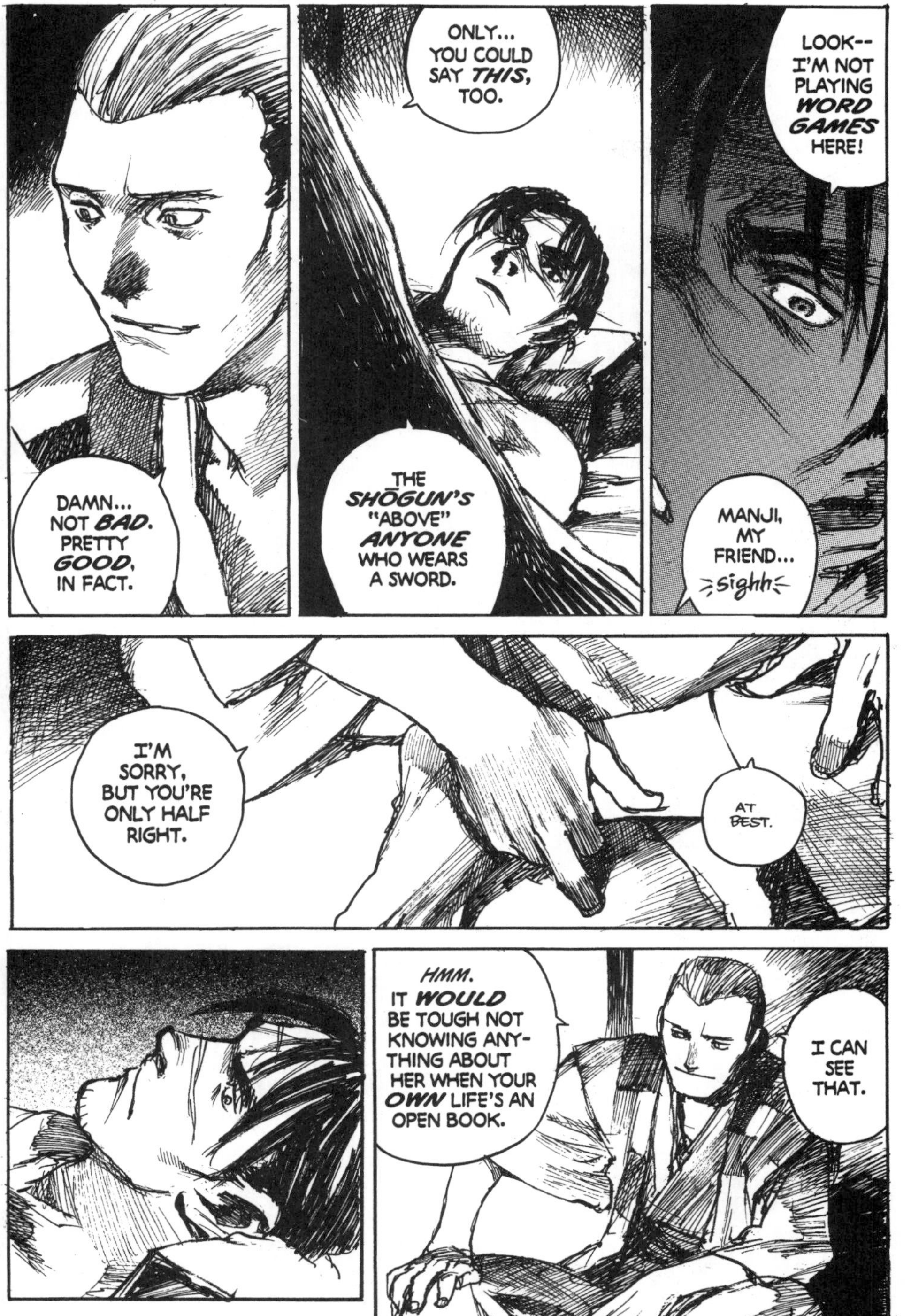
DAMN... NOT BAD. PRETTY GOOD, IN FACT.
ONLY... YOU COULD SAY THIS, TOO.
THE SHŌGUN'S "ABOVE" ANYONE WHO WEARS A SWORD.
LOOK-- I'M NOT PLAYING WORD GAMES HERE!
MANJI, MY FRIEND... sighh
I'M SORRY, BUT YOU'RE ONLY HALF RIGHT.
AT BEST.
HMM. IT WOULD BE TOUGH NOT KNOWING ANY-THING ABOUT HER WHEN YOUR OWN LIFE'S AN OPEN BOOK.
I CAN SEE THAT.

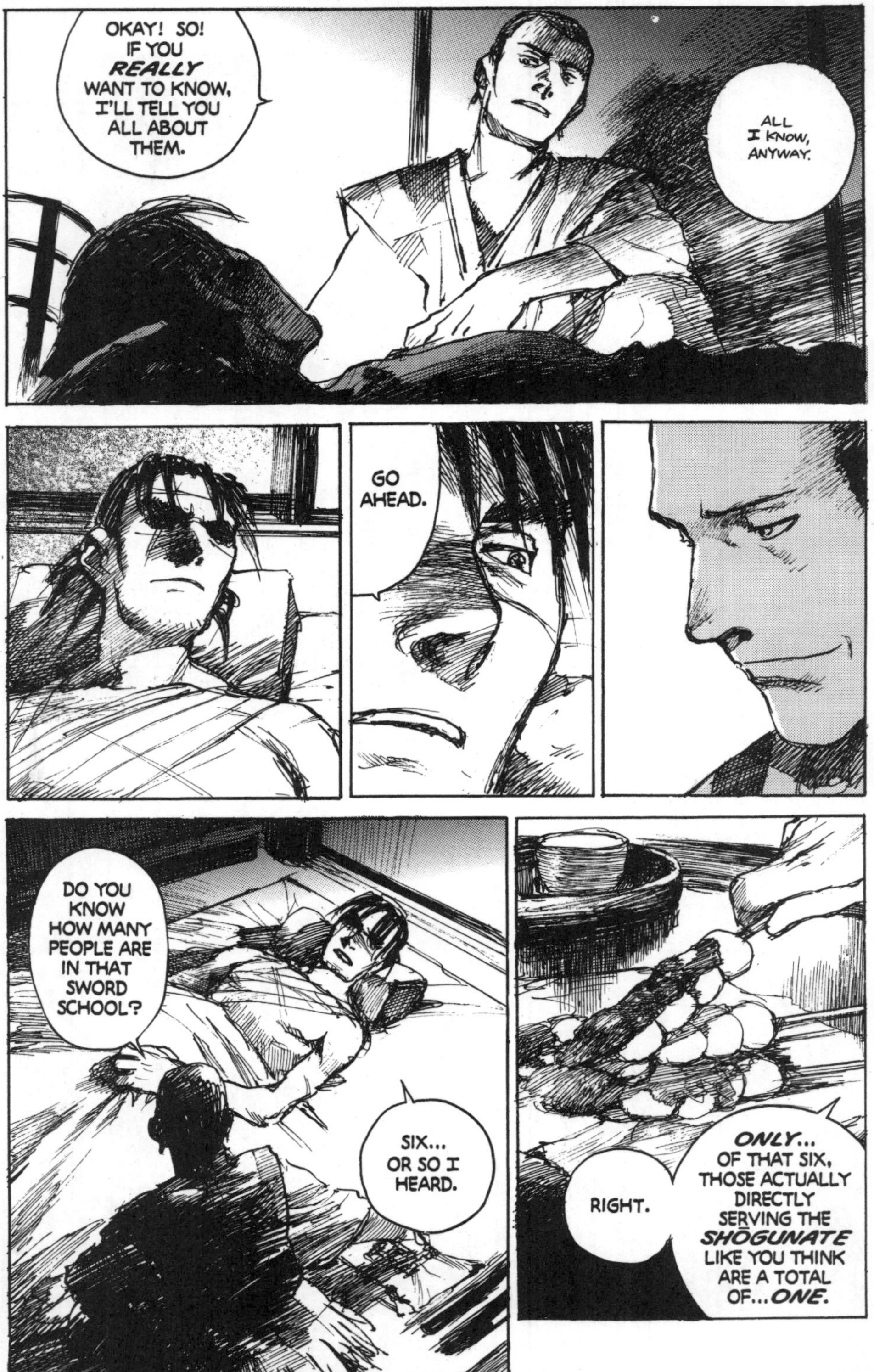
OKAY! SO! IF YOU *REALLY* WANT TO KNOW, I'LL TELL YOU ALL ABOUT THEM.
ALL I KNOW, ANYWAY.
GO AHEAD.
DO YOU KNOW HOW MANY PEOPLE ARE IN THAT SWORD SCHOOL?
SIX... OR SO I HEARD.
RIGHT.
ONLY... OF THAT SIX, THOSE ACTUALLY DIRECTLY SERVING THE *SHŌGUNATE* LIKE YOU THINK ARE A TOTAL OF... *ONE*.

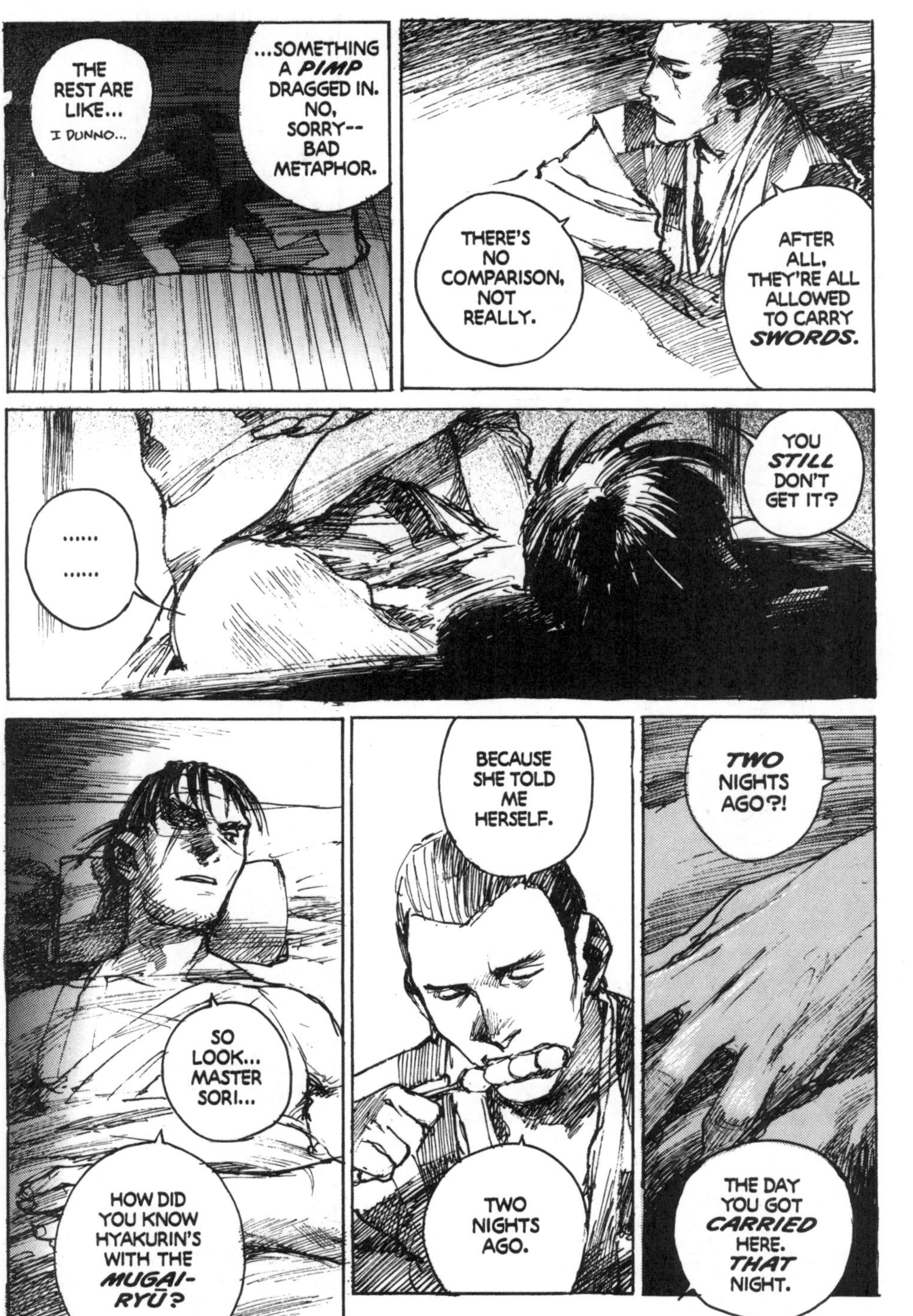
THE REST ARE LIKE... I DUNNO...
...SOMETHING A PIMP DRAGGED IN. NO, SORRY-- BAD METAPHOR.
THERE'S NO COMPARISON, NOT REALLY.
AFTER ALL, THEY'RE ALL ALLOWED TO CARRY SWORDS.
......
......
YOU STILL DON'T GET IT?
SO LOOK... MASTER SORI...
HOW DID YOU KNOW HYAKURIN'S WITH THE MUGAI-RYŪ?
BECAUSE SHE TOLD ME HERSELF.
TWO NIGHTS AGO.
TWO NIGHTS AGO?!
THE DAY YOU GOT CARRIED HERE. THAT NIGHT.

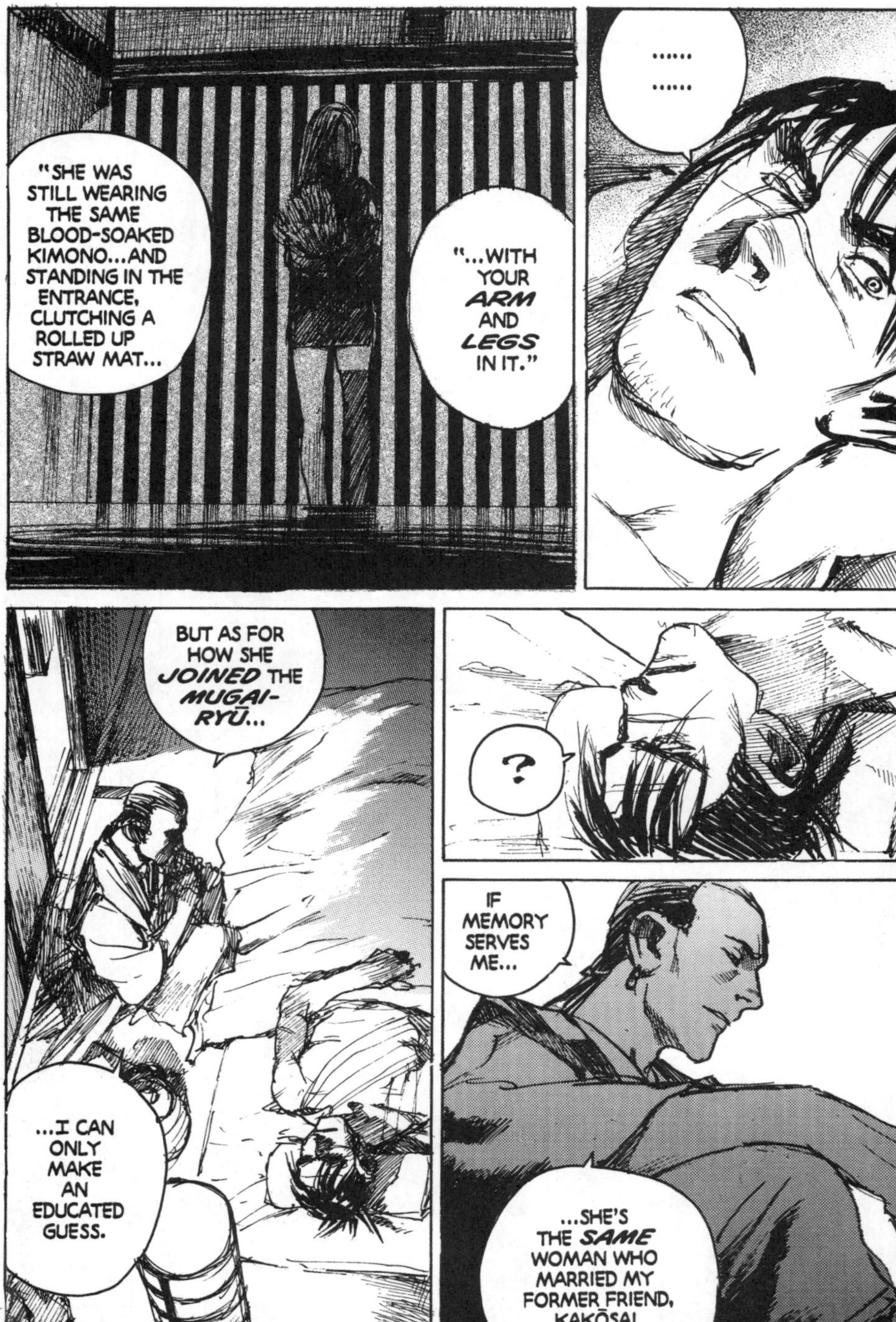
"SHE WAS STILL WEARING THE SAME BLOOD-SOAKED KIMONO...AND STANDING IN THE ENTRANCE, CLUTCHING A ROLLED UP STRAW MAT...
"...WITH YOUR *ARM* AND *LEGS* IN IT."
......
......
BUT AS FOR HOW SHE *JOINED* THE *MUGAI-RYŪ*...
...I CAN ONLY MAKE AN EDUCATED GUESS.
?
IF MEMORY SERVES ME...
...SHE'S THE *SAME* WOMAN WHO MARRIED MY FORMER FRIEND, KAKŌSAI GENKEI.

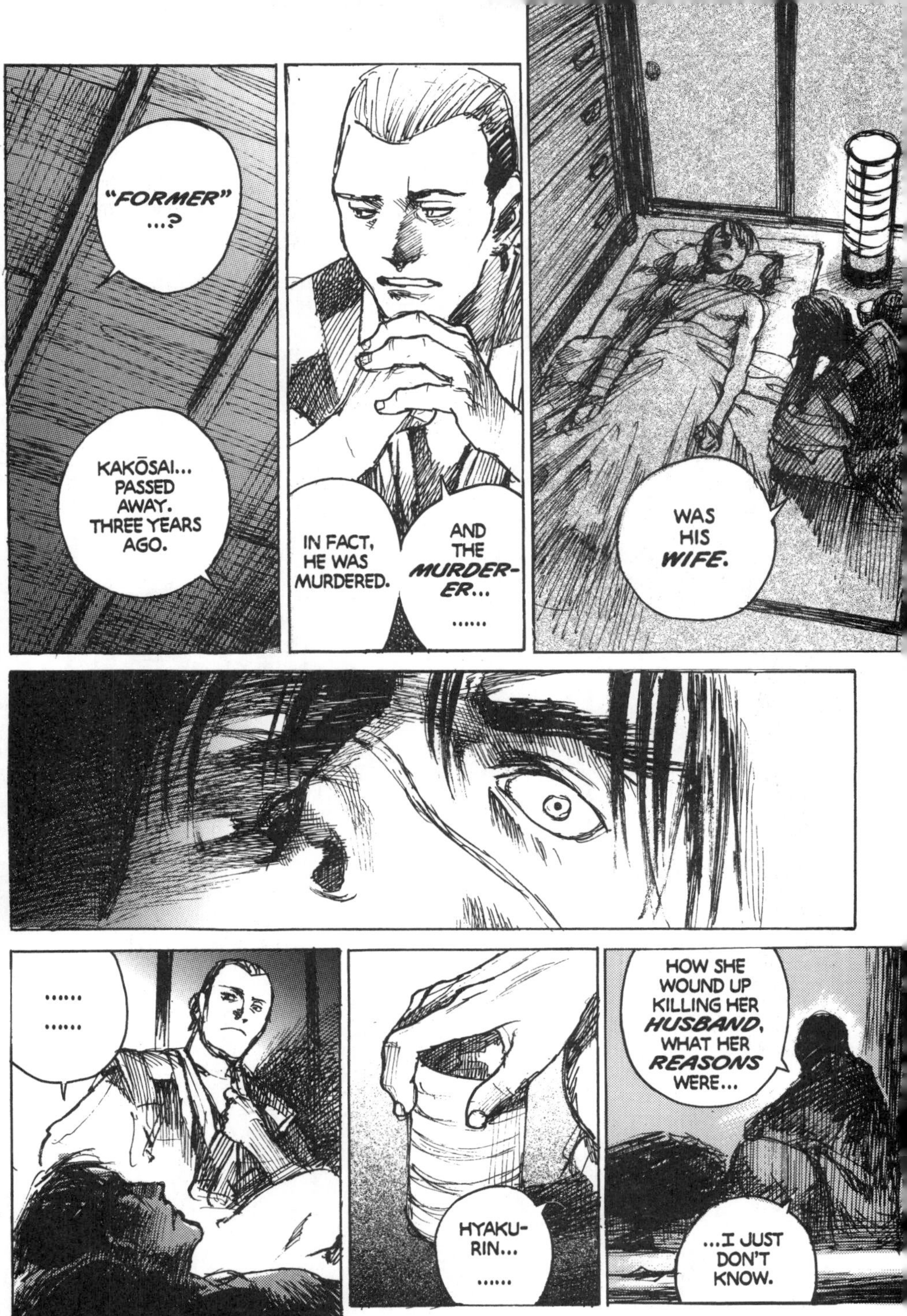
"FORMER" ...?
KAKŌSAI... PASSED AWAY. THREE YEARS AGO.
IN FACT, HE WAS MURDERED.
AND THE MURDERER...
......
WAS HIS WIFE.
......
......
HYAKURIN...
......
HOW SHE WOUND UP KILLING HER HUSBAND, WHAT HER REASONS WERE...
...I JUST DON'T KNOW.

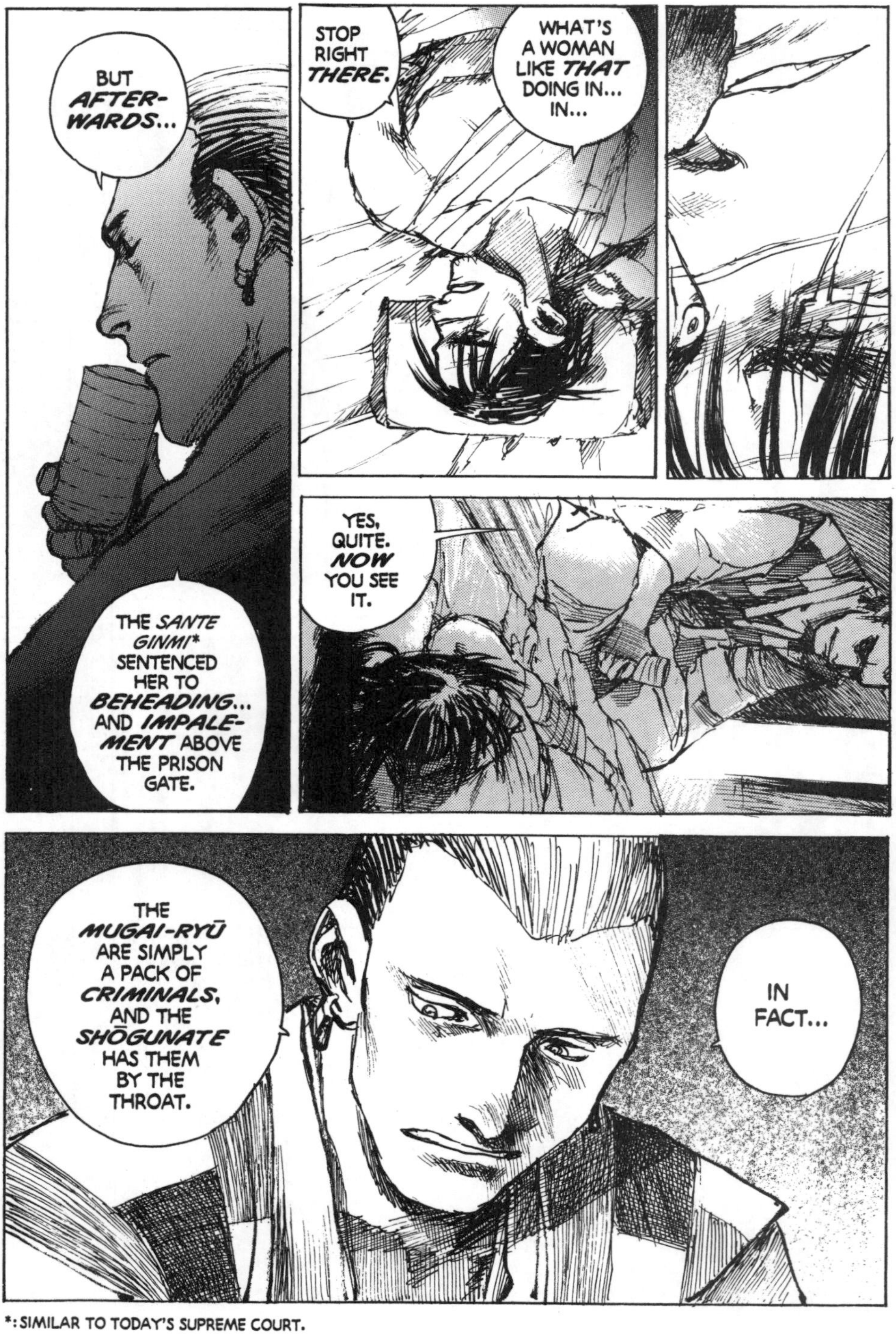
BUT AFTER-WARDS...
THE SANTE GINMI* SENTENCED HER TO BEHEADING... AND IMPALE-MENT ABOVE THE PRISON GATE.
STOP RIGHT THERE.
WHAT'S A WOMAN LIKE THAT DOING IN... IN...
YES, QUITE. NOW YOU SEE IT.
THE MUGAI-RYŪ ARE SIMPLY A PACK OF CRIMINALS, AND THE SHŌGUNATE HAS THEM BY THE THROAT.
IN FACT...

*: SIMILAR TO TODAY'S SUPREME COURT.

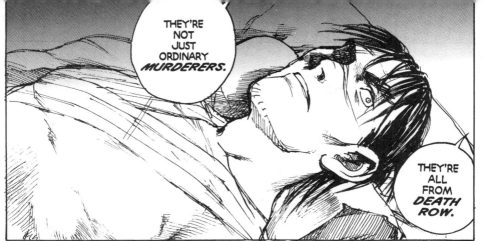

THEY'RE NOT JUST ORDINARY *MURDERERS.*

THEY'RE ALL FROM *DEATH ROW.*

WE *MUGAI-RYŪ* FOLK... CAN'T EVER TRAVEL TO ANOTHER *HAN.*

EVEN IF WE SECRETLY APPLIED FOR A *TEGATA...*

...WE'D BE CAUGHT AND STOPPED FROM ON HIGH.

OR IN THE WORST CASE... WE'D GET "DISAP-PEARED."

DOES THAT RING A BELL...?

....

ANYWAY, BECAUSE THEY *ARE...* THAT MAKES THEM EVEN *MORE* SECRETIVE AND SPECIALIZED THAN ORDINARY SPIES...

...LIKE *ME.*

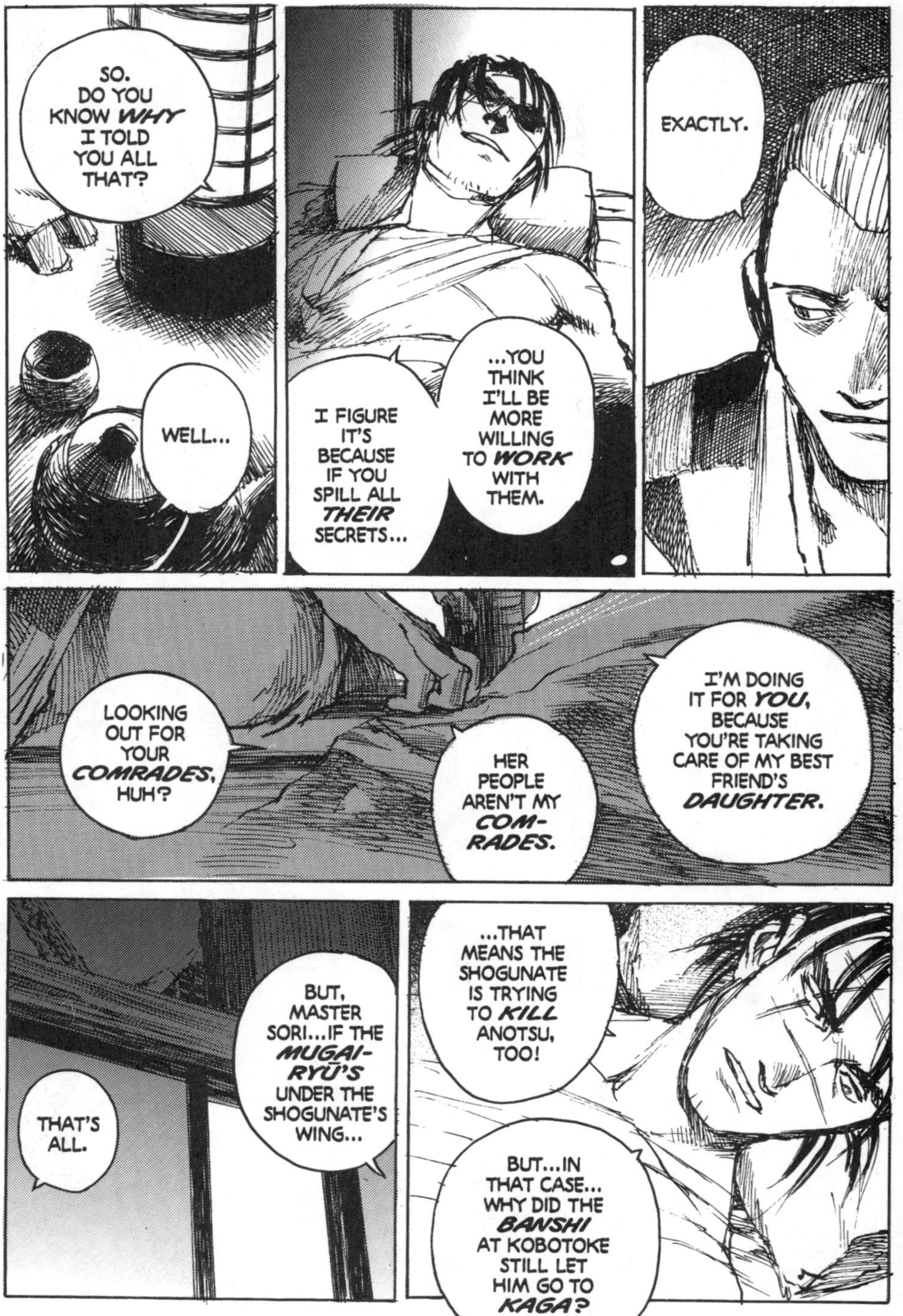
SO. DO YOU KNOW WHY I TOLD YOU ALL THAT?
WELL...
I FIGURE IT'S BECAUSE IF YOU SPILL ALL THEIR SECRETS...
...YOU THINK I'LL BE MORE WILLING TO WORK WITH THEM.
EXACTLY.
LOOKING OUT FOR YOUR COMRADES, HUH?
HER PEOPLE AREN'T MY COM-RADES.
I'M DOING IT FOR YOU, BECAUSE YOU'RE TAKING CARE OF MY BEST FRIEND'S DAUGHTER.
THAT'S ALL.
BUT, MASTER SORI...IF THE MUGAI-RYŪ'S UNDER THE SHOGUNATE'S WING...
...THAT MEANS THE SHOGUNATE IS TRYING TO KILL ANOTSU, TOO!
BUT...IN THAT CASE... WHY DID THE BANSHI AT KOBOTOKE STILL LET HIM GO TO KAGA?

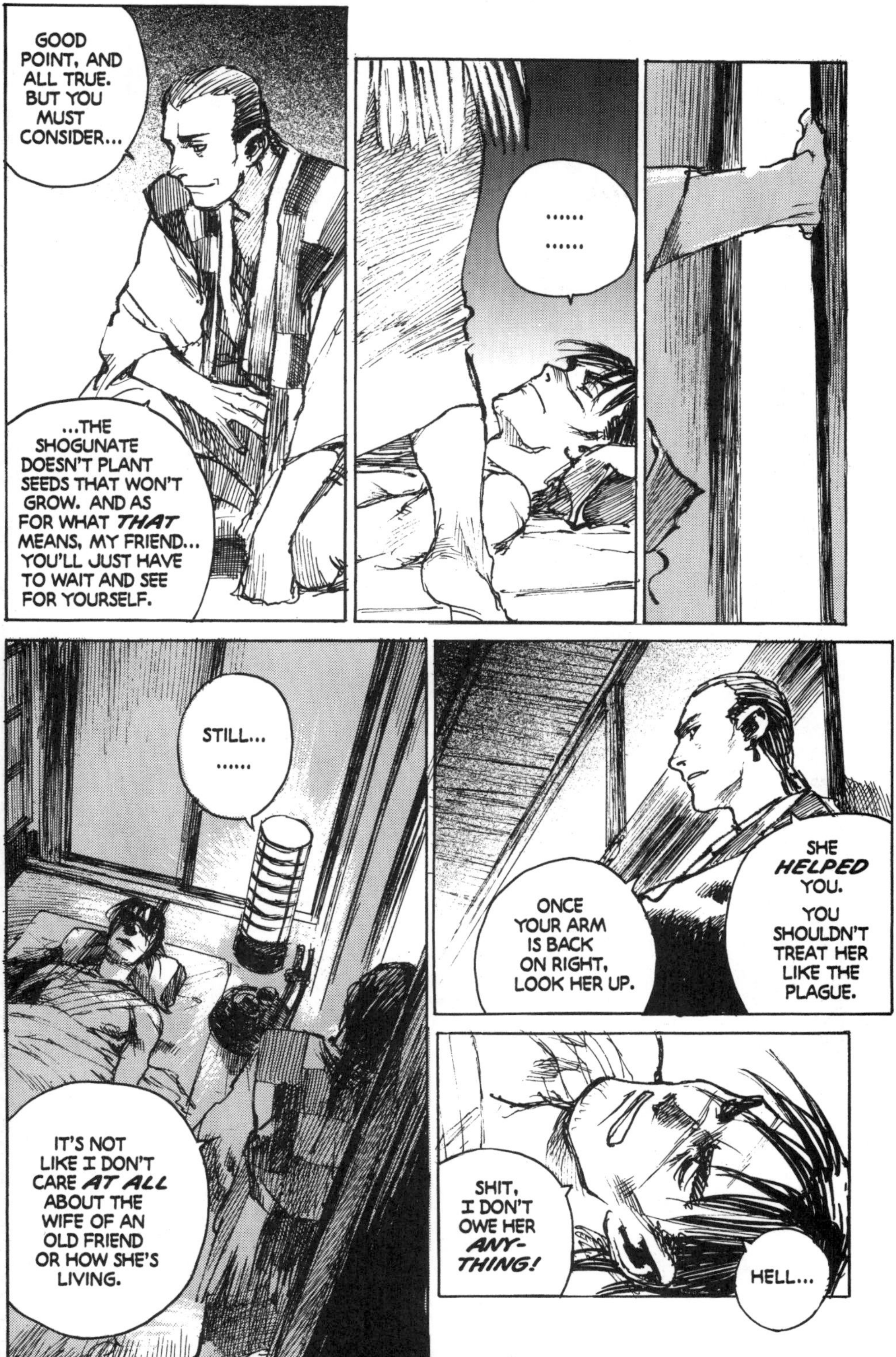
GOOD POINT, AND ALL TRUE. BUT YOU MUST CONSIDER...
...THE SHOGUNATE DOESN'T PLANT SEEDS THAT WON'T GROW. AND AS FOR WHAT *THAT* MEANS, MY FRIEND... YOU'LL JUST HAVE TO WAIT AND SEE FOR YOURSELF.
....
STILL... ......
IT'S NOT LIKE I DON'T CARE *AT ALL* ABOUT THE WIFE OF AN OLD FRIEND OR HOW SHE'S LIVING.
ONCE YOUR ARM IS BACK ON RIGHT, LOOK HER UP.
SHE *HELPED* YOU.
YOU SHOULDN'T TREAT HER LIKE THE PLAGUE.
SHIT, I DON'T OWE HER *ANY-THING!*
HELL...

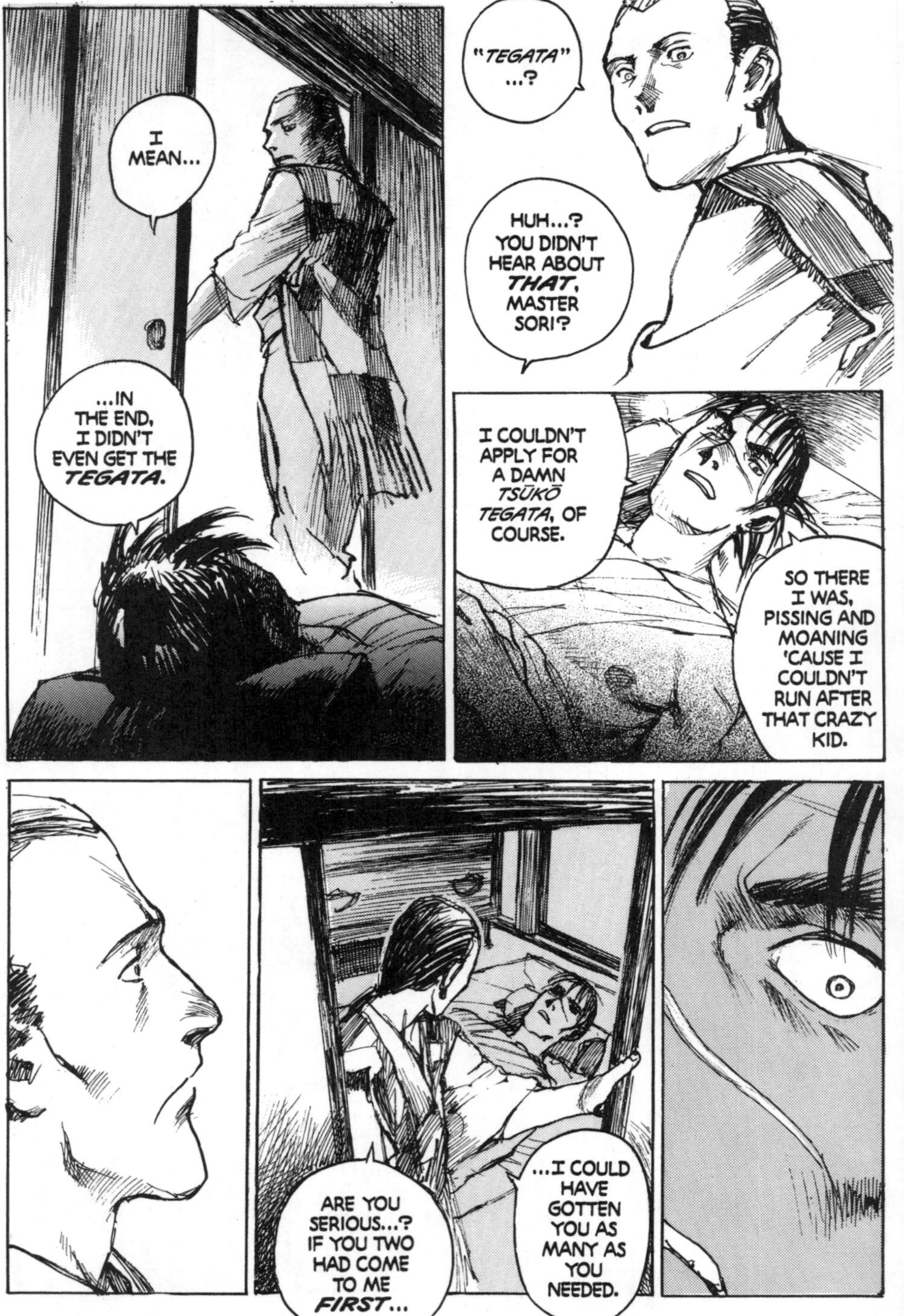
I MEAN...
...IN THE END, I DIDN'T EVEN GET THE *TEGATA*.
"*TEGATA*" ...?
HUH...? YOU DIDN'T HEAR ABOUT *THAT*, MASTER SORI?
I COULDN'T APPLY FOR A DAMN *TSŪKŌ TEGATA*, OF COURSE.
SO THERE I WAS, PISSING AND MOANING 'CAUSE I COULDN'T RUN AFTER THAT CRAZY KID.
ARE YOU SERIOUS...? IF YOU TWO HAD COME TO ME *FIRST*...
...I COULD HAVE GOTTEN YOU AS MANY AS YOU NEEDED.

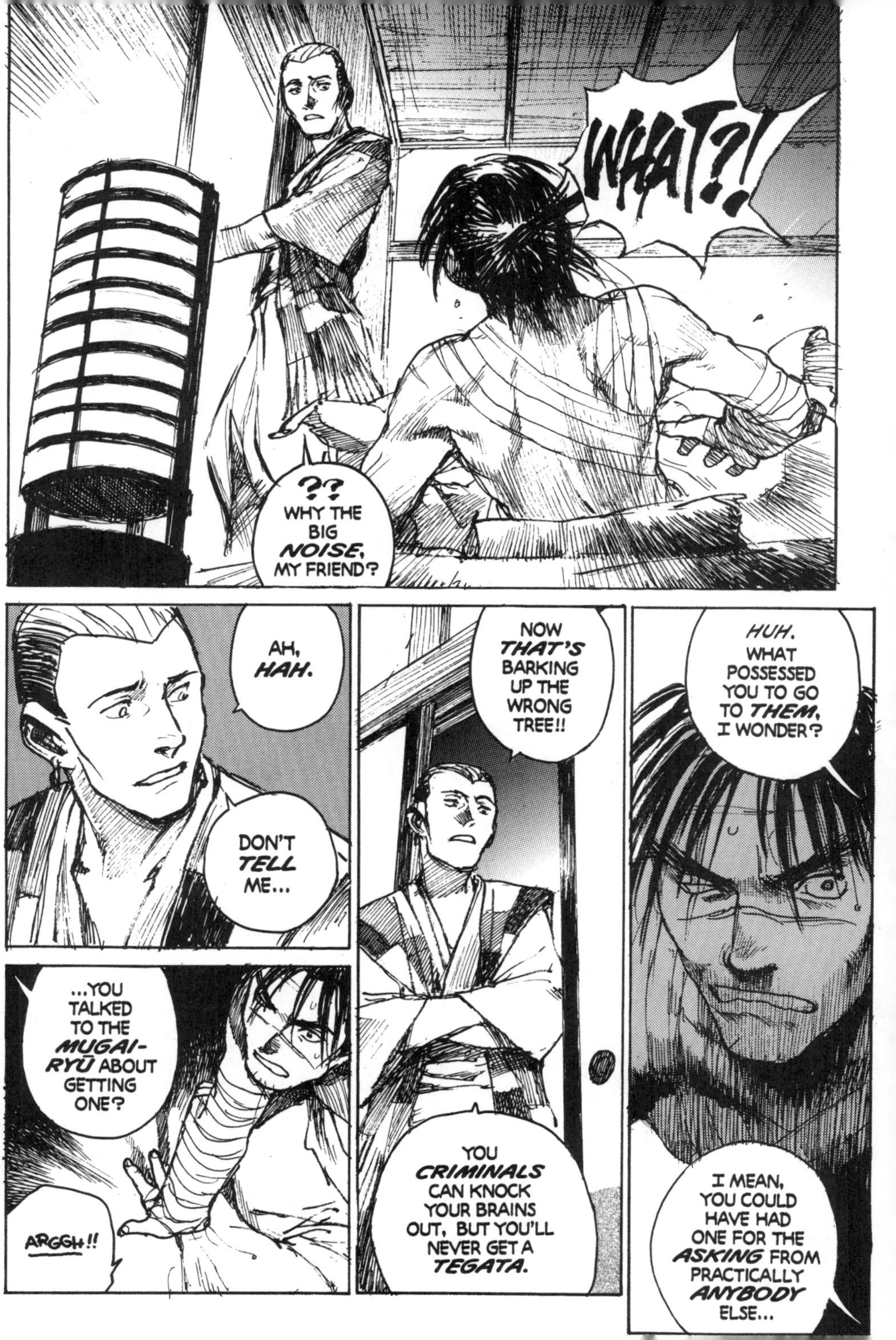
WHAT?!
?? WHY THE BIG NOISE, MY FRIEND?
AH, HAH.
DON'T TELL ME...
...YOU TALKED TO THE MUGAI-RYŪ ABOUT GETTING ONE?
ARGGH!!
NOW THAT'S BARKING UP THE WRONG TREE!!
YOU CRIMINALS CAN KNOCK YOUR BRAINS OUT, BUT YOU'LL NEVER GET A TEGATA.
HUH. WHAT POSSESSED YOU TO GO TO THEM, I WONDER?
I MEAN, YOU COULD HAVE HAD ONE FOR THE ASKING FROM PRACTICALLY ANYBODY ELSE...

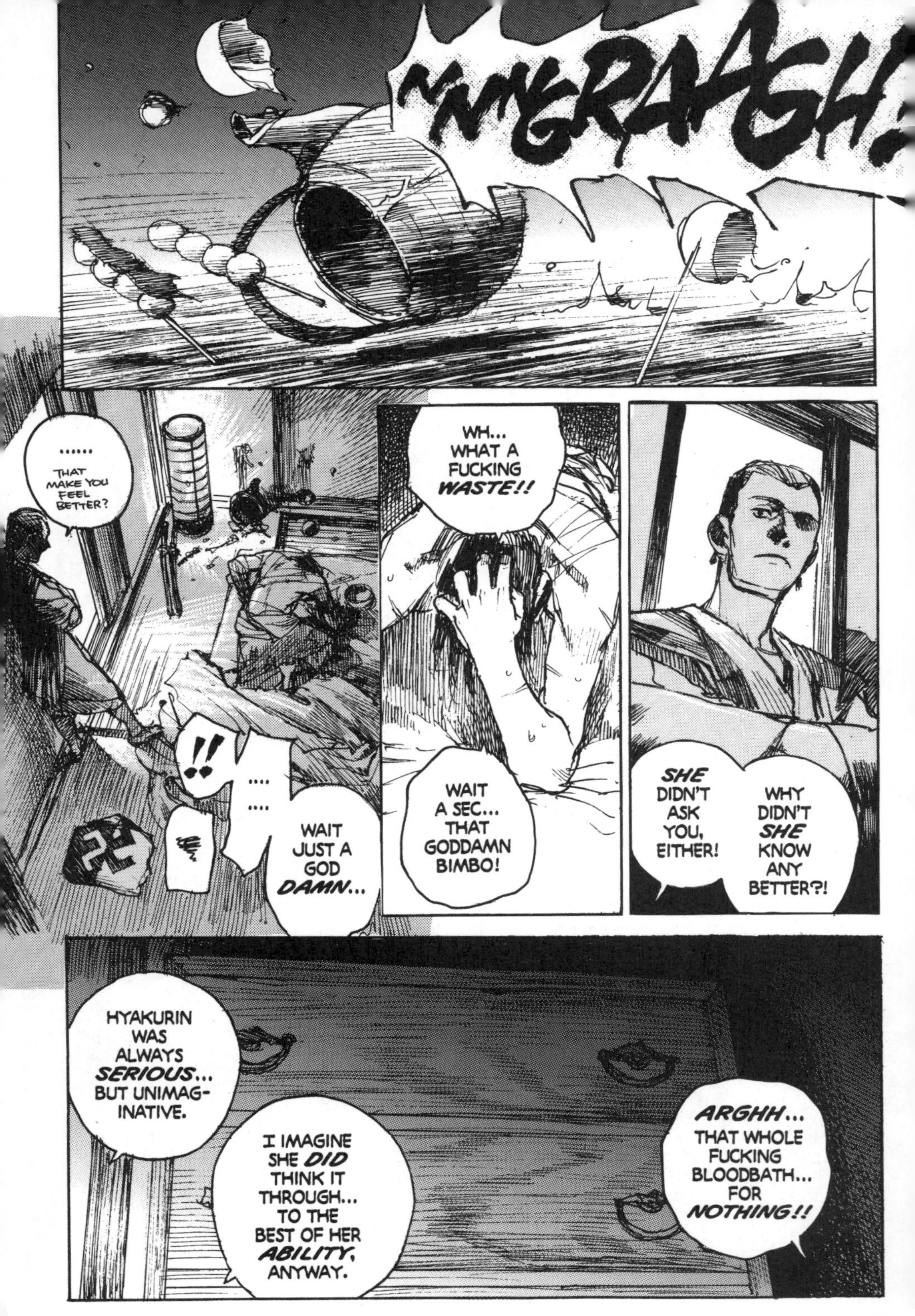

MMGRAAGH!
......
THAT MAKE YOU FEEL BETTER?
!!
....
....
WAIT JUST A GOD DAMN...
WH... WHAT A FUCKING WASTE!!
WAIT A SEC... THAT GODDAMN BIMBO!
SHE DIDN'T ASK YOU, EITHER!
WHY DIDN'T SHE KNOW ANY BETTER?!
HYAKURIN WAS ALWAYS SERIOUS... BUT UNIMAG-INATIVE.
I IMAGINE SHE DID THINK IT THROUGH... TO THE BEST OF HER ABILITY, ANYWAY.
ARGHH... THAT WHOLE FUCKING BLOODBATH... FOR NOTHING!!

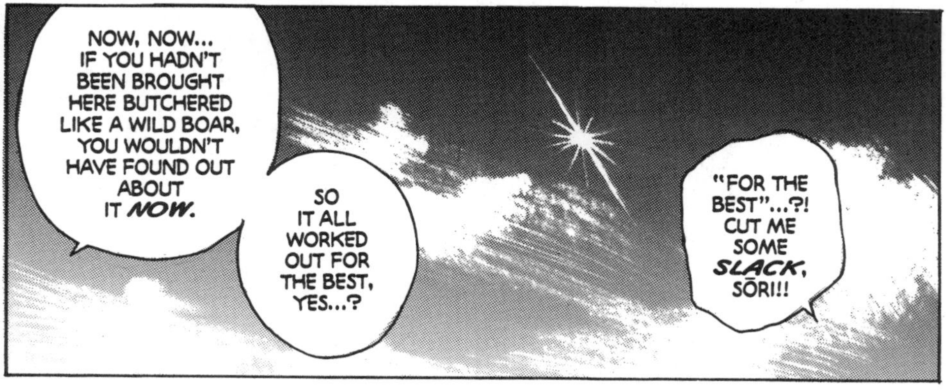
NOW, NOW... IF YOU HADN'T BEEN BROUGHT HERE BUTCHERED LIKE A WILD BOAR, YOU WOULDN'T HAVE FOUND OUT ABOUT IT *NOW*.
SO IT ALL WORKED OUT FOR THE BEST, YES...?
"FOR THE BEST"...?! CUT ME SOME *SLACK*, SŌRI!!

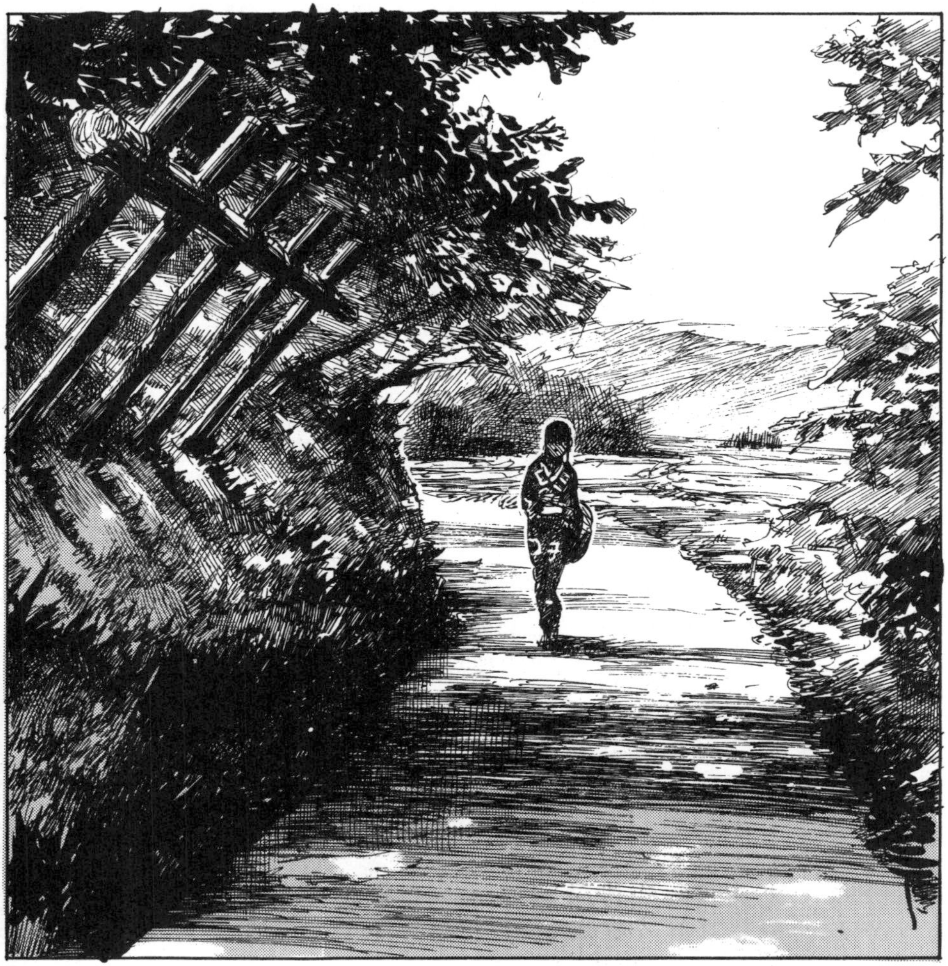

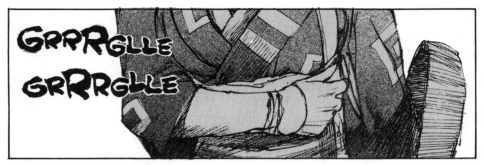

GRRRGLLE
GRRRGLLE

I'VE BEEN *WONDER-ING*... LATELY...

...WAS I *BORN* WITH A BIGGER STOMACH THAN OTHER GIRLS?

ANOTHER TEA SHOP. THAT MAKES THREE...

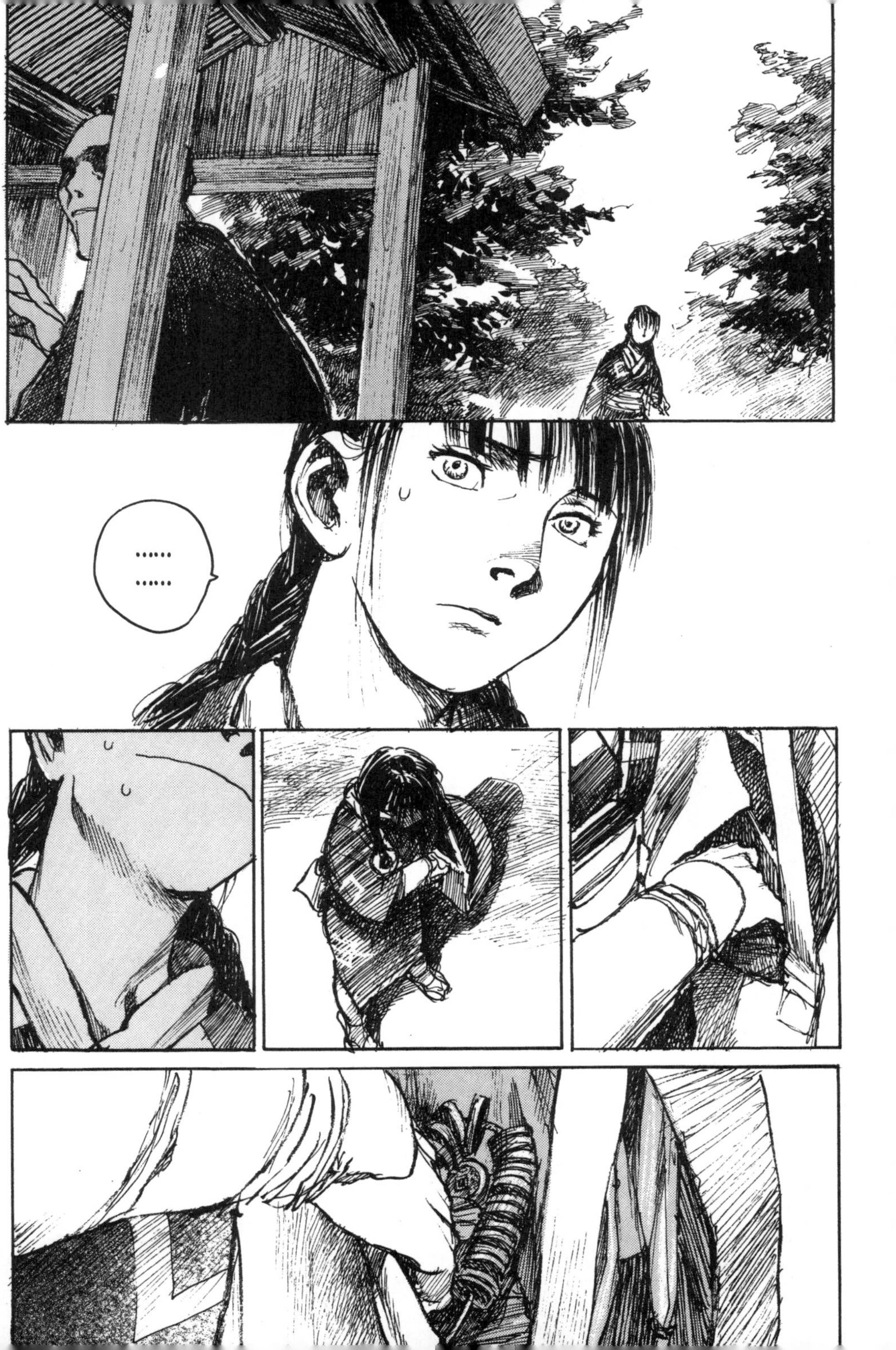
……
……

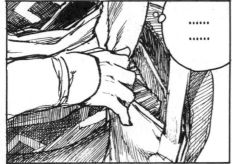

......
......

NO...
BETTER
GO
ANOTHER
THREE
RI.

ON
SECOND
THOUGHT,
MAKE THAT
TWO...

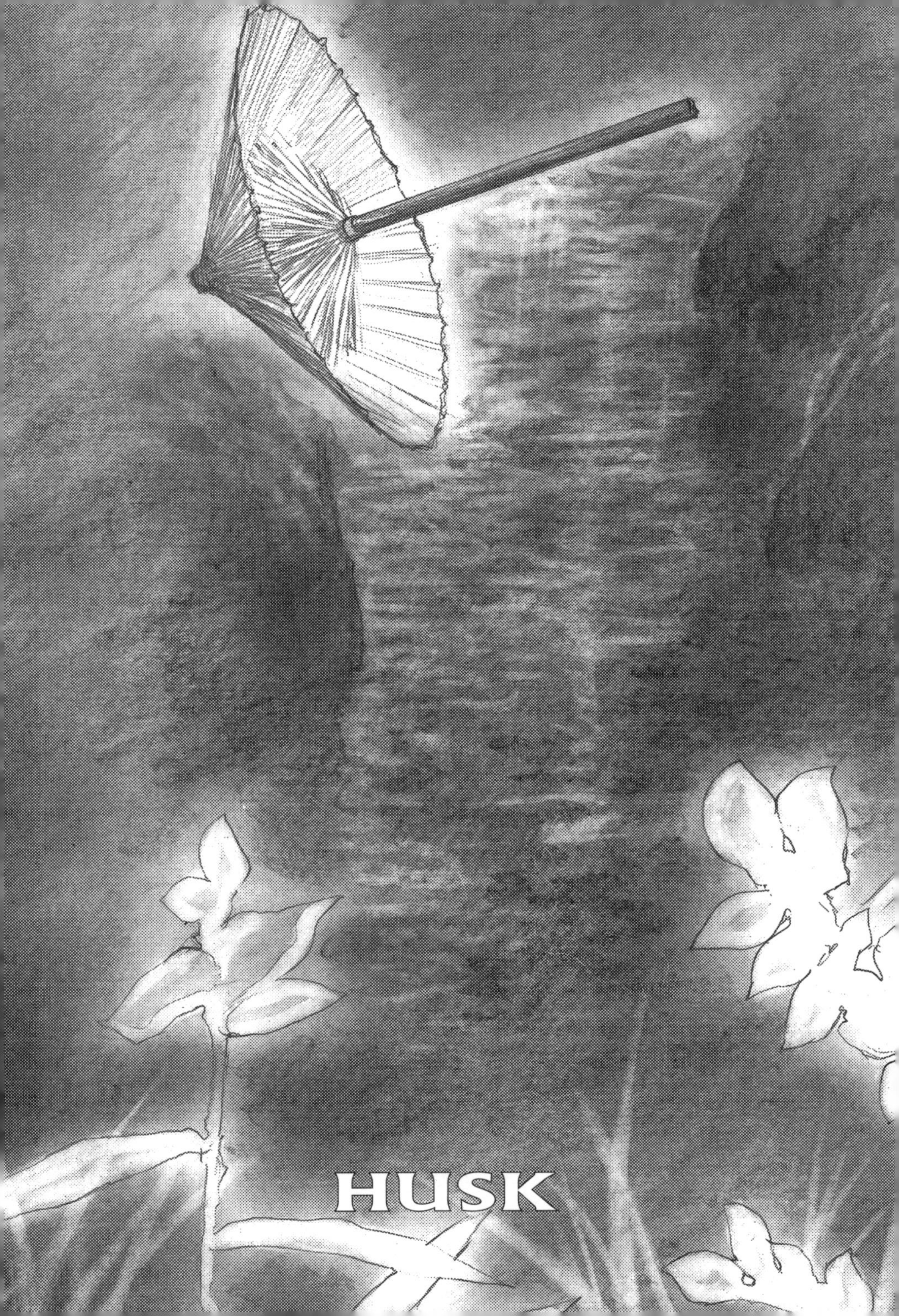
HUSK

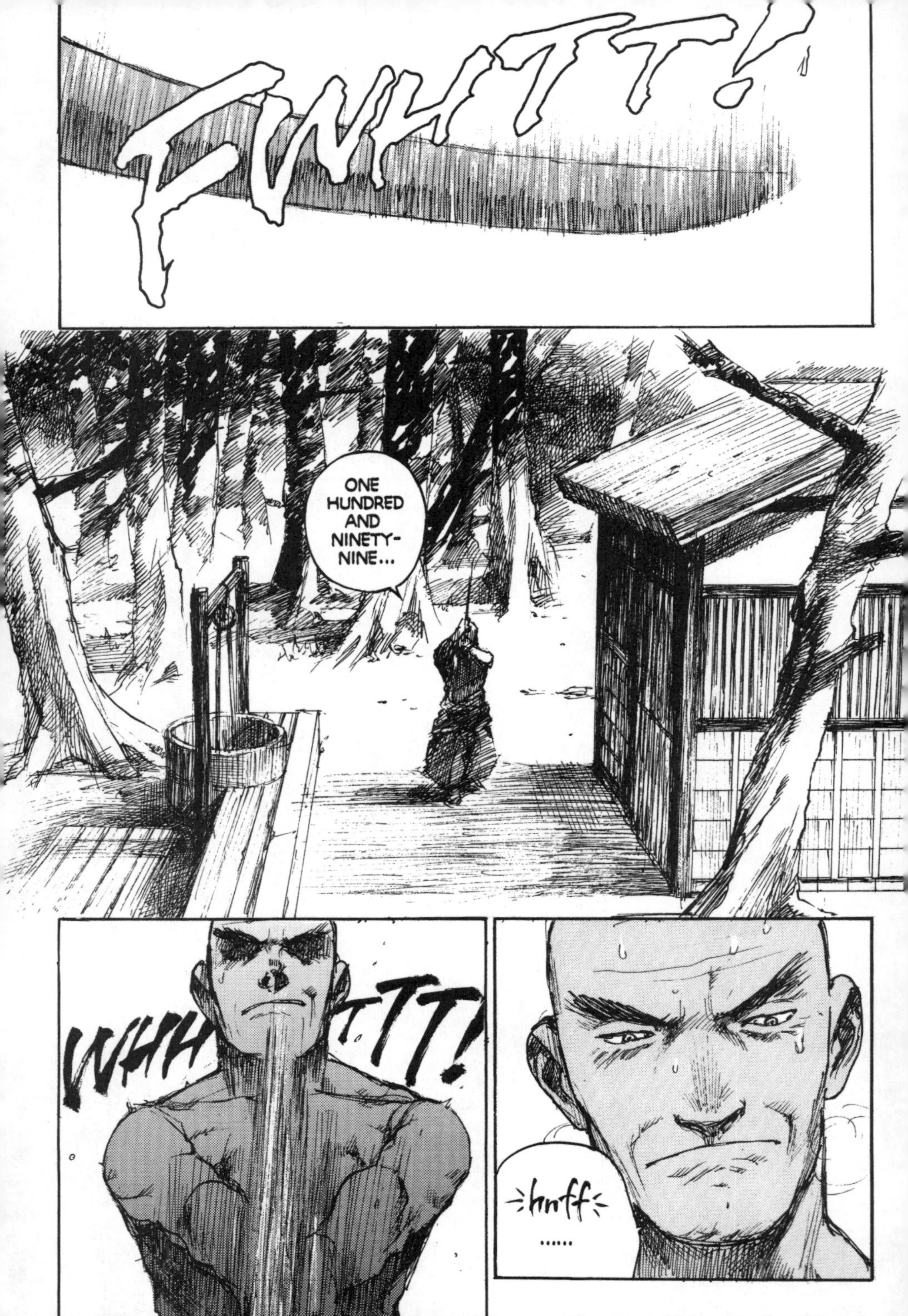
FWHTT!
ONE HUNDRED AND NINETY-NINE...
WHH TT!
hnff
......

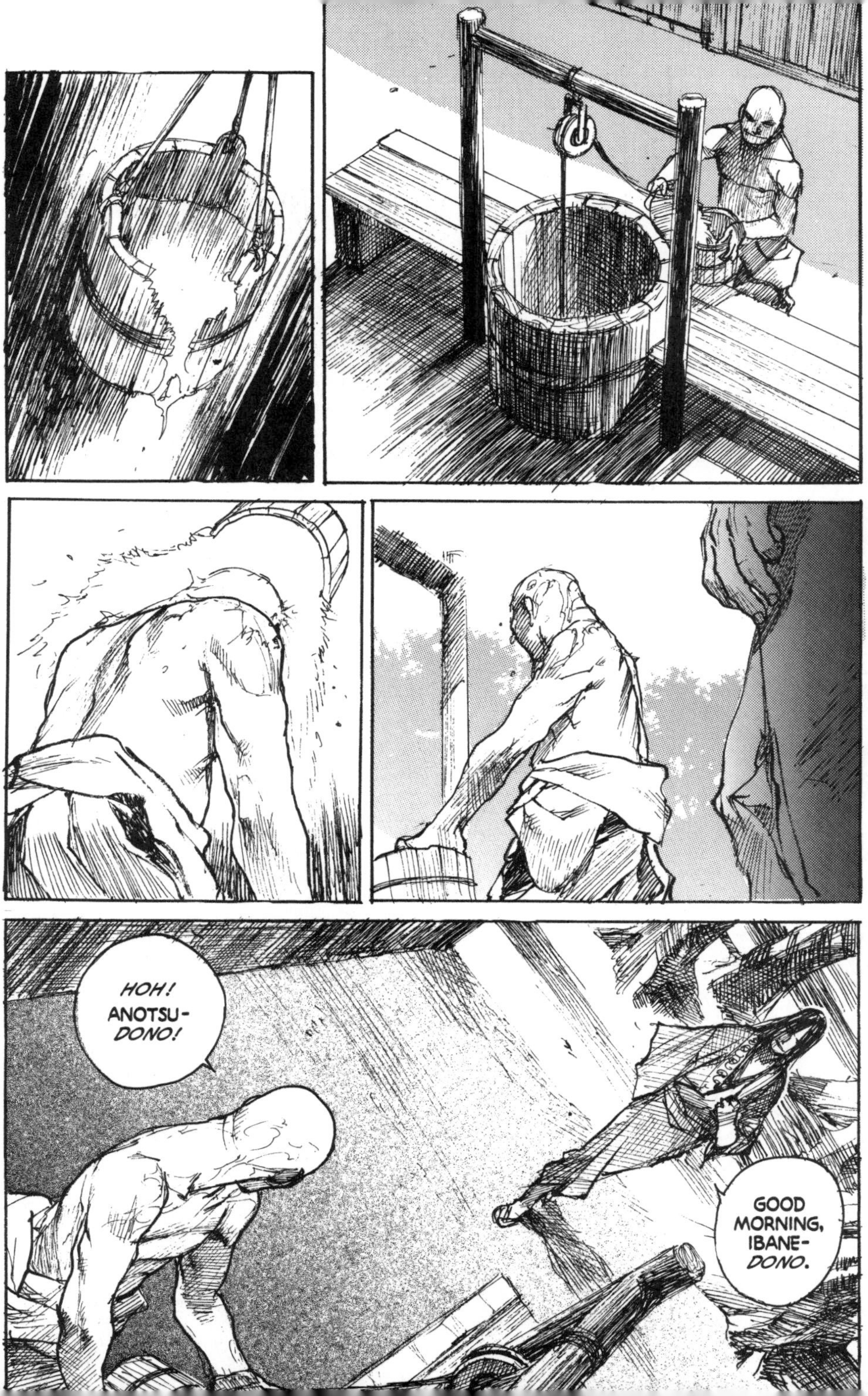
HOH! ANOTSU-DONO!
GOOD MORNING, IBANE-DONO.

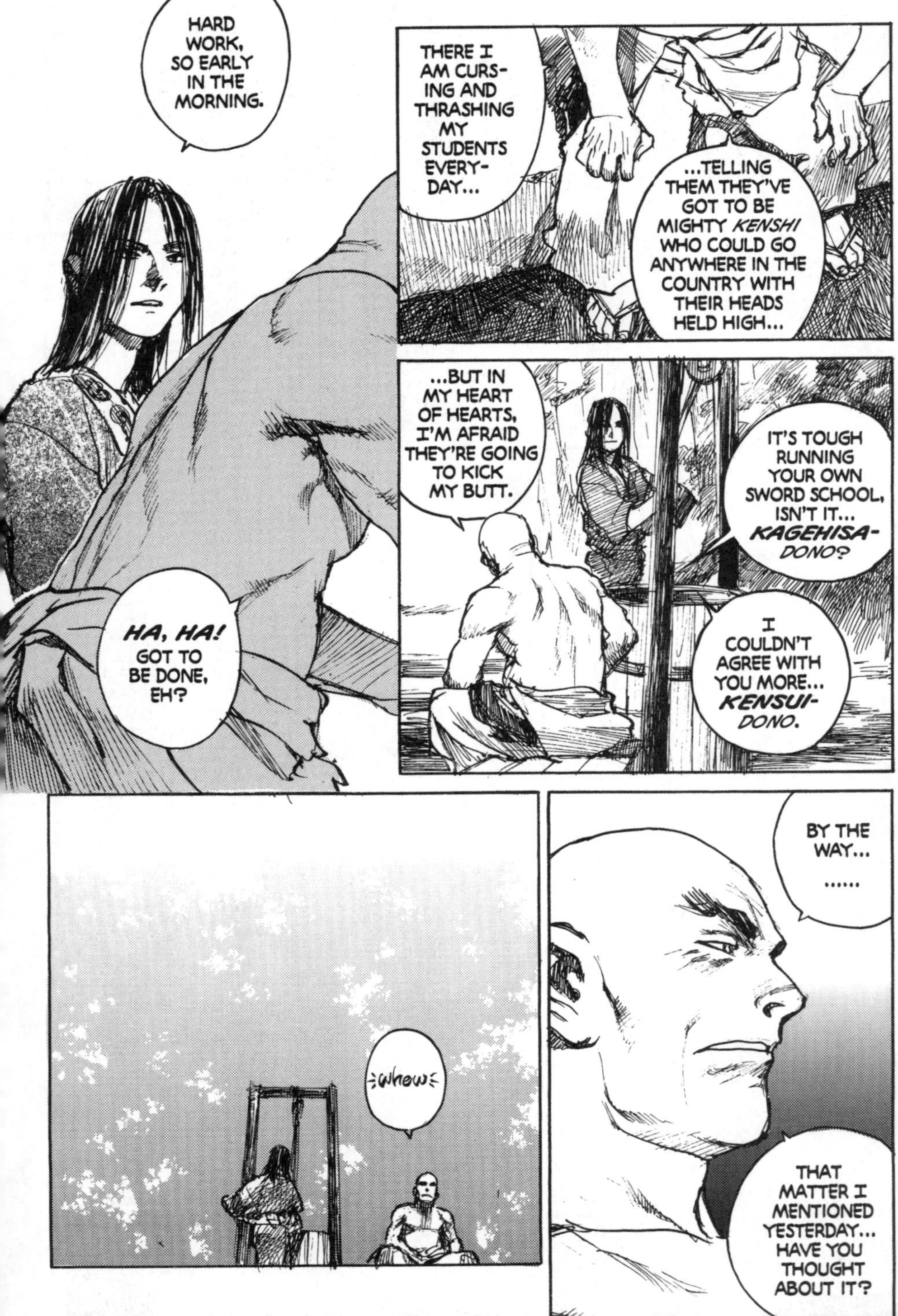
HARD WORK, SO EARLY IN THE MORNING.
HA, HA! GOT TO BE DONE, EH?
THERE I AM CURSING AND THRASHING MY STUDENTS EVERYDAY...
...TELLING THEM THEY'VE GOT TO BE MIGHTY *KENSHI* WHO COULD GO ANYWHERE IN THE COUNTRY WITH THEIR HEADS HELD HIGH...
...BUT IN MY HEART OF HEARTS, I'M AFRAID THEY'RE GOING TO KICK MY BUTT.
IT'S TOUGH RUNNING YOUR OWN SWORD SCHOOL, ISN'T IT... *KAGEHISA-DONO?*
I COULDN'T AGREE WITH YOU MORE... *KENSUI-DONO.*
whew
BY THE WAY... ......
THAT MATTER I MENTIONED YESTERDAY... HAVE YOU THOUGHT ABOUT IT?

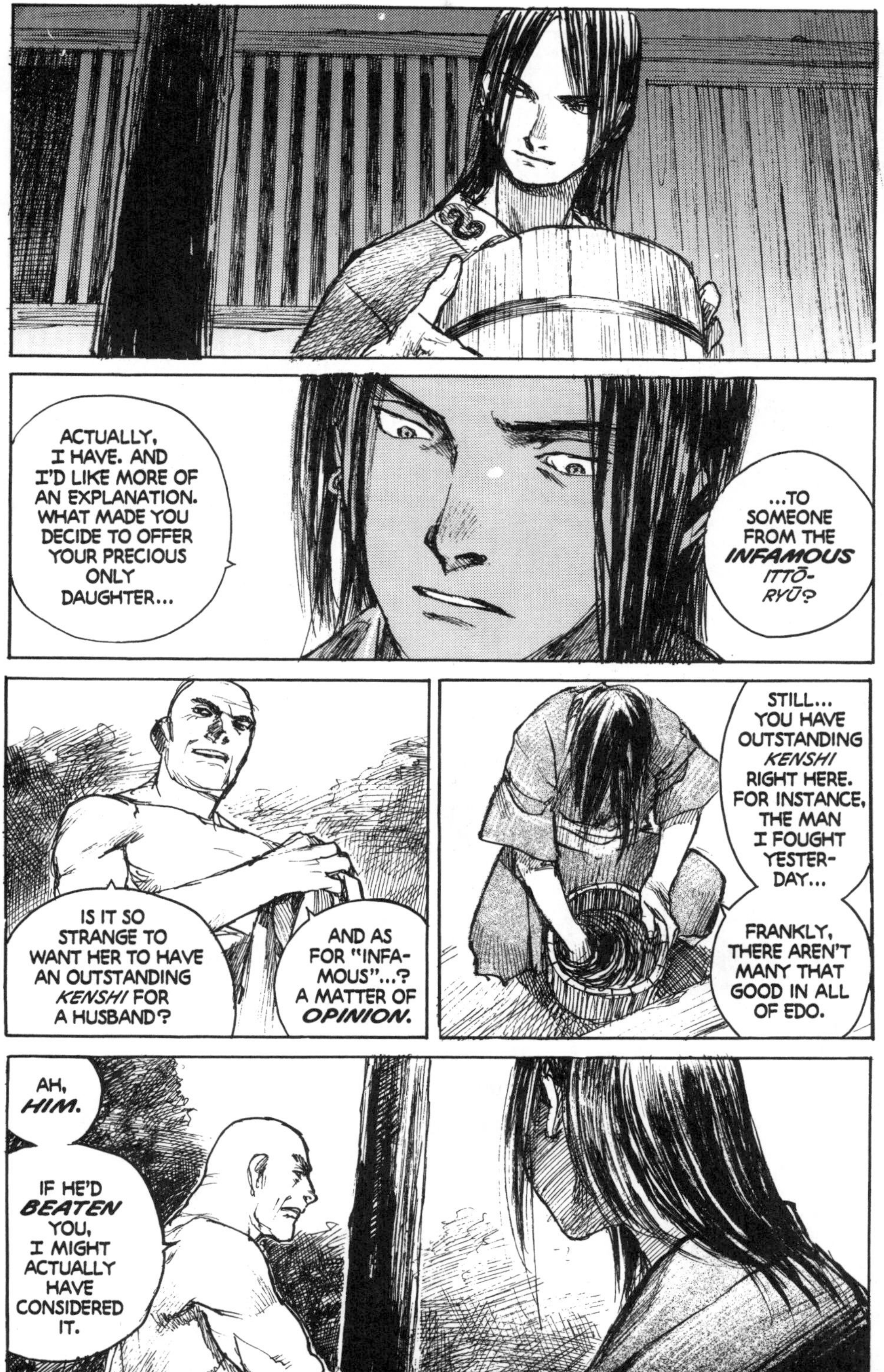

ACTUALLY, I HAVE. AND I'D LIKE MORE OF AN EXPLANATION. WHAT MADE YOU DECIDE TO OFFER YOUR PRECIOUS ONLY DAUGHTER...
...TO SOMEONE FROM THE INFAMOUS ITTŌ-RYŪ?
IS IT SO STRANGE TO WANT HER TO HAVE AN OUTSTANDING KENSHI FOR A HUSBAND?
AND AS FOR "INFA-MOUS"...? A MATTER OF OPINION.
STILL... YOU HAVE OUTSTANDING KENSHI RIGHT HERE. FOR INSTANCE, THE MAN I FOUGHT YESTER-DAY...
FRANKLY, THERE AREN'T MANY THAT GOOD IN ALL OF EDO.
AH, HIM.
IF HE'D BEATEN YOU, I MIGHT ACTUALLY HAVE CONSIDERED IT.

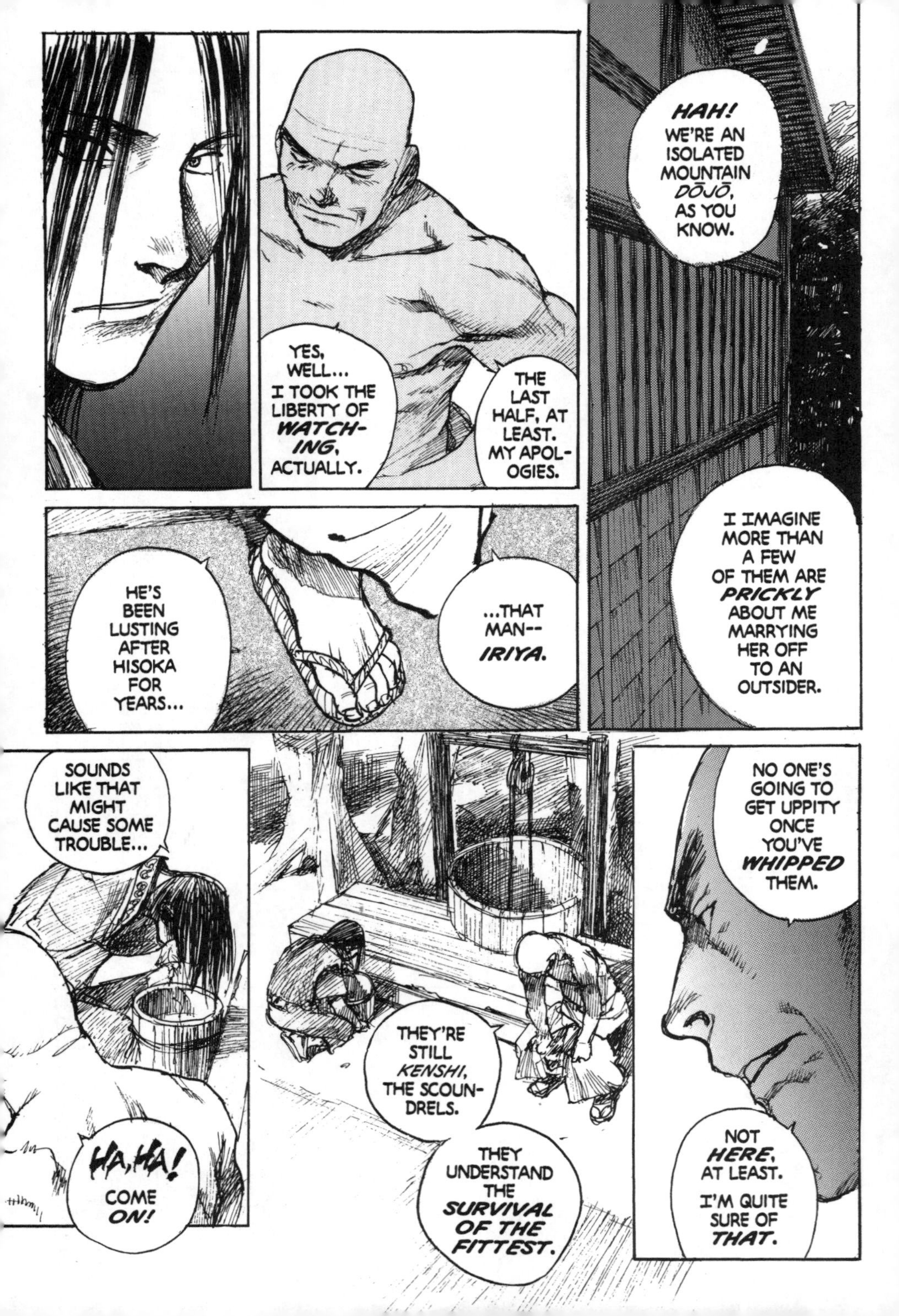
YES, WELL... I TOOK THE LIBERTY OF *WATCHING*, ACTUALLY.
THE LAST HALF, AT LEAST. MY APOLOGIES.
HE'S BEEN LUSTING AFTER HISOKA FOR YEARS...
...THAT MAN-- *IRIYA*.
HAH! WE'RE AN ISOLATED MOUNTAIN *DŌJŌ*, AS YOU KNOW.
I IMAGINE MORE THAN A FEW OF THEM ARE *PRICKLY* ABOUT ME MARRYING HER OFF TO AN OUTSIDER.
SOUNDS LIKE THAT MIGHT CAUSE SOME TROUBLE...
HA, HA! COME *ON!*
THEY'RE STILL *KENSHI*, THE SCOUNDRELS.
THEY UNDERSTAND THE *SURVIVAL OF THE FITTEST*.
NO ONE'S GOING TO GET UPPITY ONCE YOU'VE *WHIPPED* THEM.
NOT *HERE*, AT LEAST.
I'M QUITE SURE OF *THAT*.

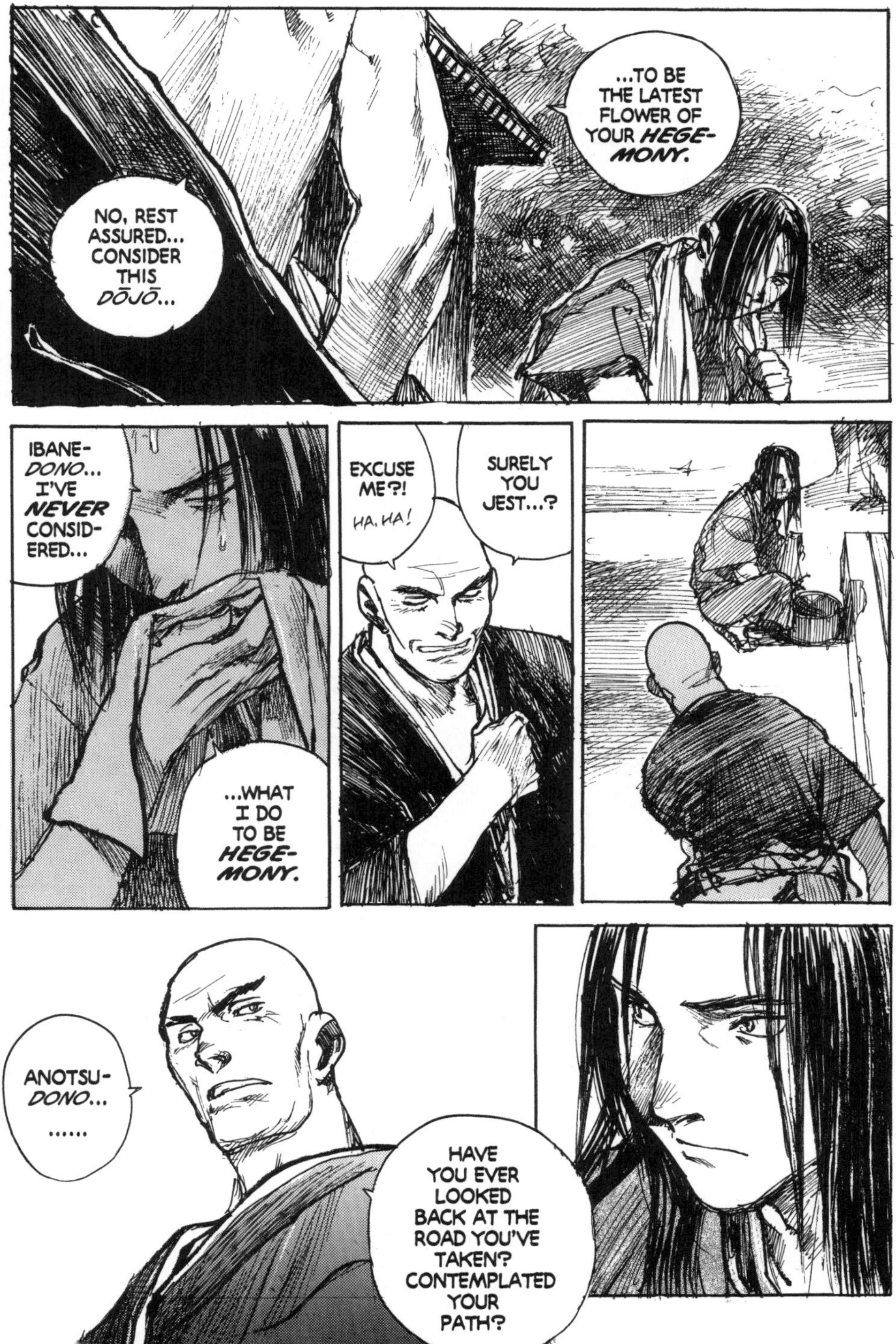
NO, REST ASSURED... CONSIDER THIS *DŌJŌ*...
...TO BE THE LATEST FLOWER OF YOUR ***HEGEMONY***.
IBANE-*DONO*... I'VE ***NEVER*** CONSIDERED...
...WHAT I DO TO BE ***HEGEMONY***.
EXCUSE ME?!
HA, HA!
SURELY YOU JEST...?
ANOTSU-*DONO*... ......
HAVE YOU EVER LOOKED BACK AT THE ROAD YOU'VE TAKEN? CONTEMPLATED YOUR PATH?

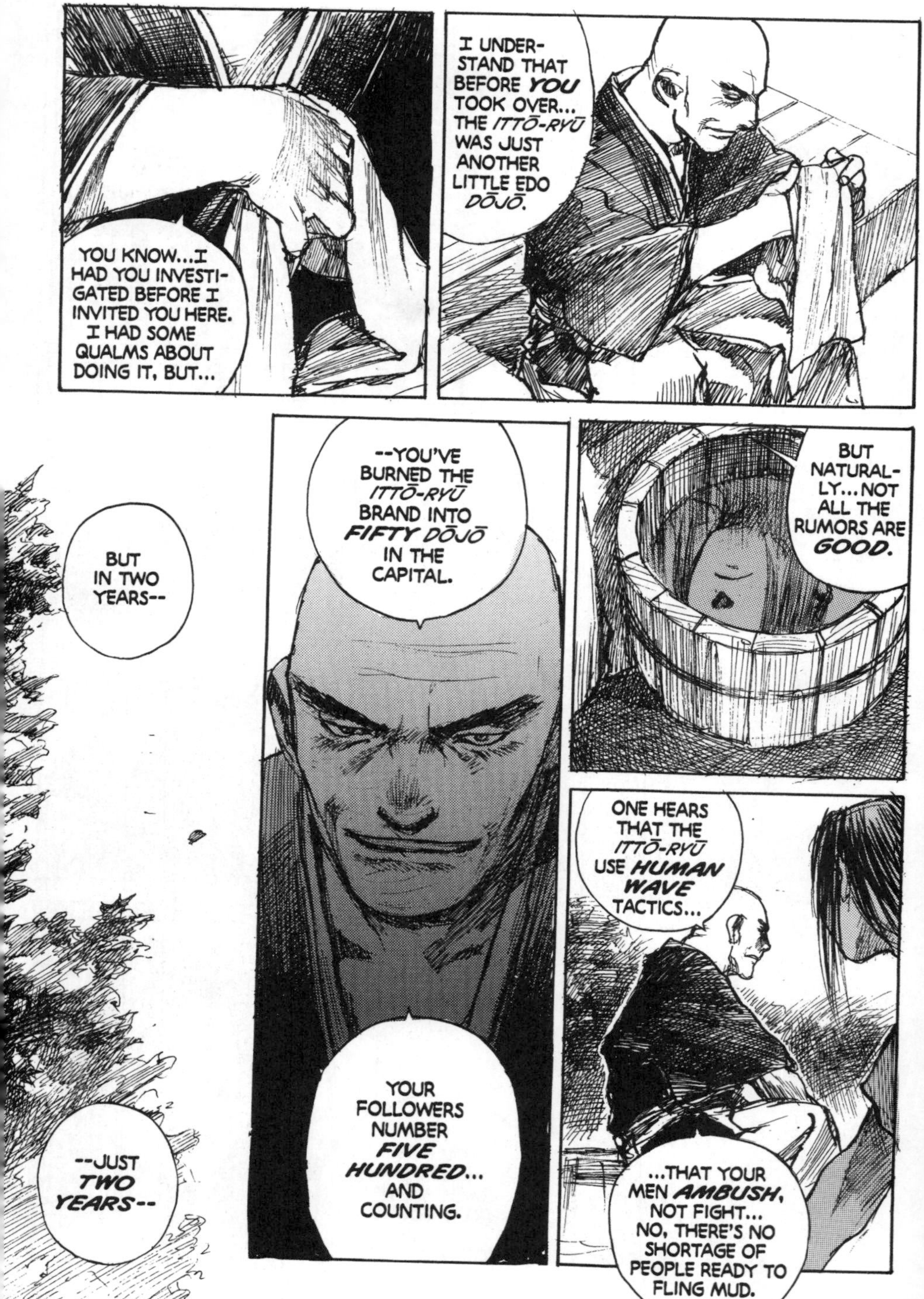
YOU KNOW...I HAD YOU INVESTIGATED BEFORE I INVITED YOU HERE. I HAD SOME QUALMS ABOUT DOING IT, BUT...
I UNDERSTAND THAT BEFORE YOU TOOK OVER... THE ITTŌ-RYŪ WAS JUST ANOTHER LITTLE EDO DŌJŌ.
BUT IN TWO YEARS--
--YOU'VE BURNED THE ITTŌ-RYŪ BRAND INTO FIFTY DŌJŌ IN THE CAPITAL.
YOUR FOLLOWERS NUMBER FIVE HUNDRED... AND COUNTING.
--JUST TWO YEARS--
BUT NATURALLY...NOT ALL THE RUMORS ARE GOOD.
ONE HEARS THAT THE ITTŌ-RYŪ USE HUMAN WAVE TACTICS...
...THAT YOUR MEN AMBUSH, NOT FIGHT... NO, THERE'S NO SHORTAGE OF PEOPLE READY TO FLING MUD.

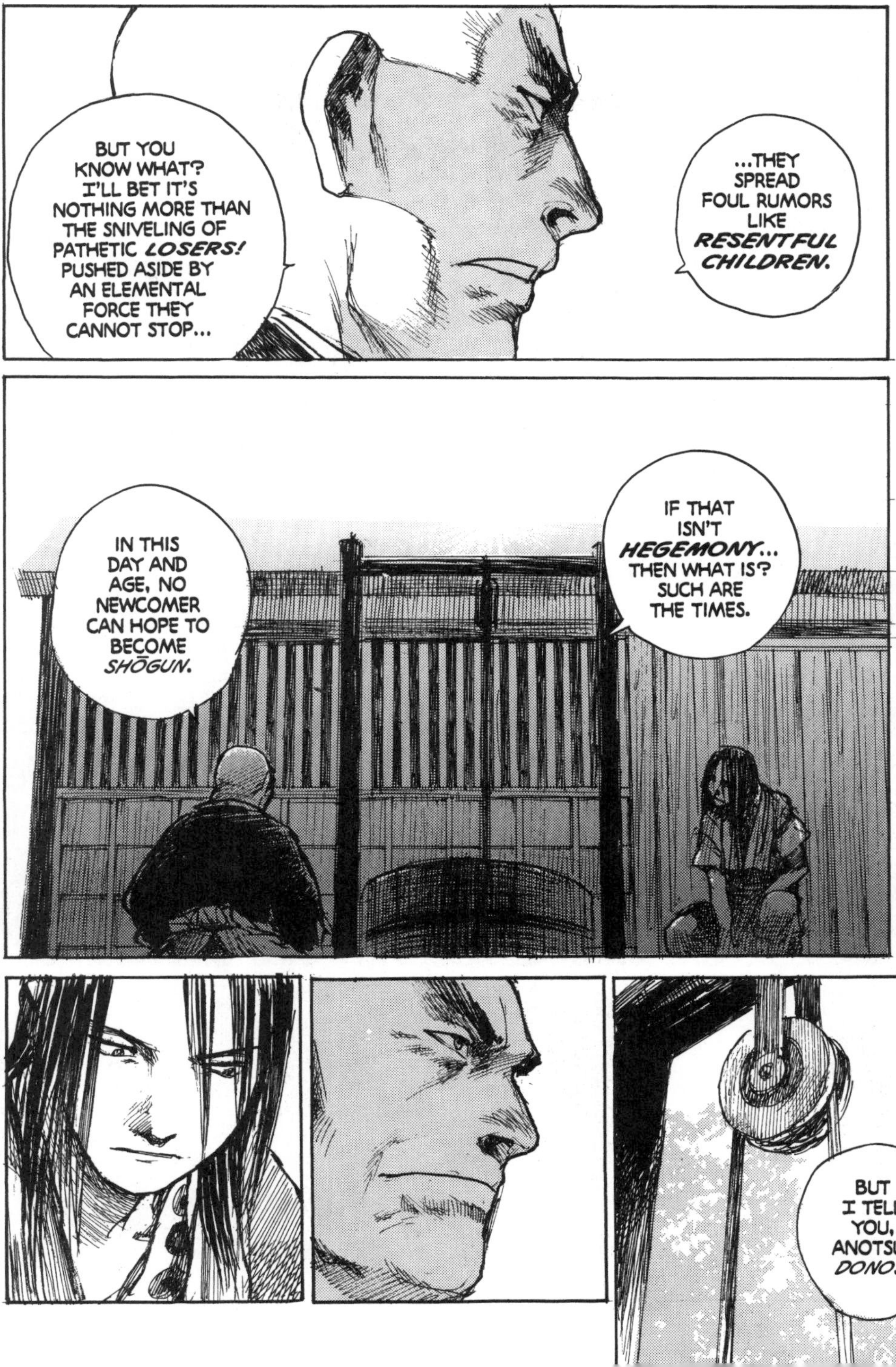
BUT YOU KNOW WHAT? I'LL BET IT'S NOTHING MORE THAN THE SNIVELING OF PATHETIC *LOSERS!* PUSHED ASIDE BY AN ELEMENTAL FORCE THEY CANNOT STOP...
...THEY SPREAD FOUL RUMORS LIKE *RESENTFUL CHILDREN.*
IN THIS DAY AND AGE, NO NEWCOMER CAN HOPE TO BECOME *SHŌGUN.*
IF THAT ISN'T *HEGEMONY*... THEN WHAT IS? SUCH ARE THE TIMES.
BUT I TELL YOU, ANOTSU-*DONO*...

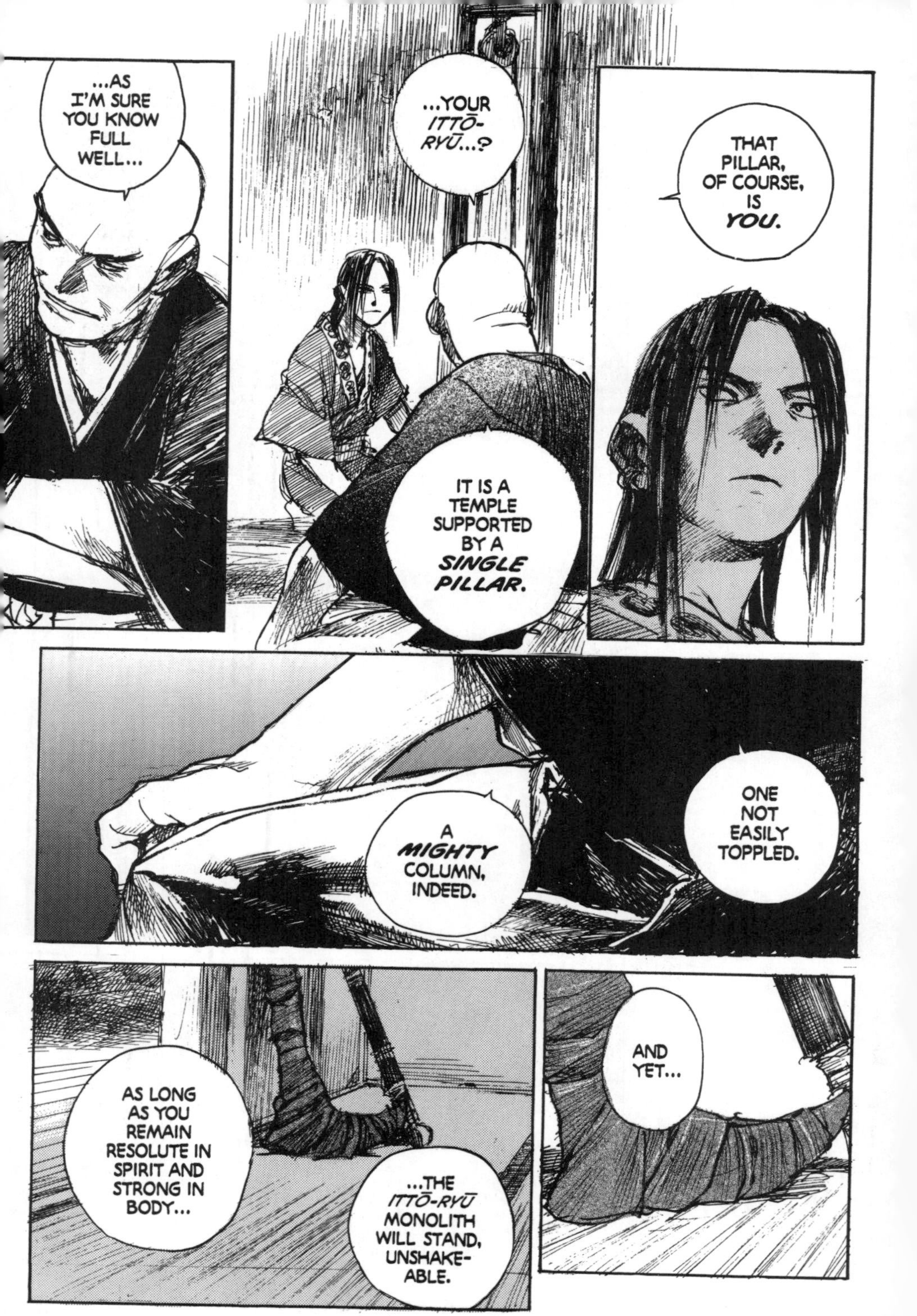
...AS I'M SURE YOU KNOW FULL WELL...
...YOUR *ITTŌ-RYŪ*...?
IT IS A TEMPLE SUPPORTED BY A *SINGLE PILLAR*.
THAT PILLAR, OF COURSE, IS *YOU*.
A *MIGHTY* COLUMN, INDEED.
ONE NOT EASILY TOPPLED.
AS LONG AS YOU REMAIN RESOLUTE IN SPIRIT AND STRONG IN BODY...
...THE *ITTŌ-RYŪ* MONOLITH WILL STAND, UNSHAKE-ABLE.
AND YET...

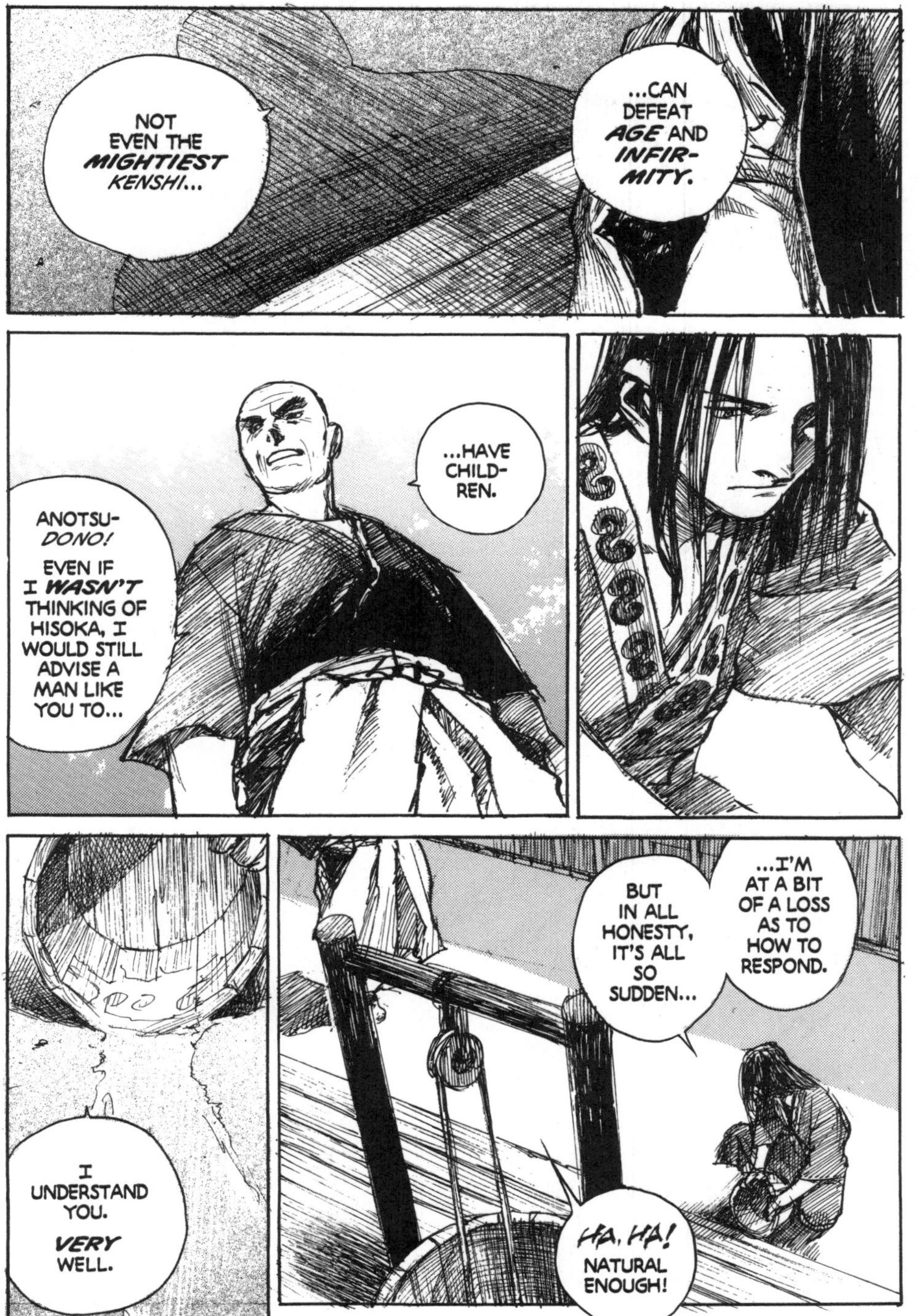
NOT EVEN THE MIGHTIEST KENSHI...
...CAN DEFEAT AGE AND INFIRMITY.
ANOTSU-DONO! EVEN IF I WASN'T THINKING OF HISOKA, I WOULD STILL ADVISE A MAN LIKE YOU TO...
...HAVE CHILDREN.
I UNDERSTAND YOU. VERY WELL.
BUT IN ALL HONESTY, IT'S ALL SO SUDDEN...
...I'M AT A BIT OF A LOSS AS TO HOW TO RESPOND.
HA, HA! NATURAL ENOUGH!

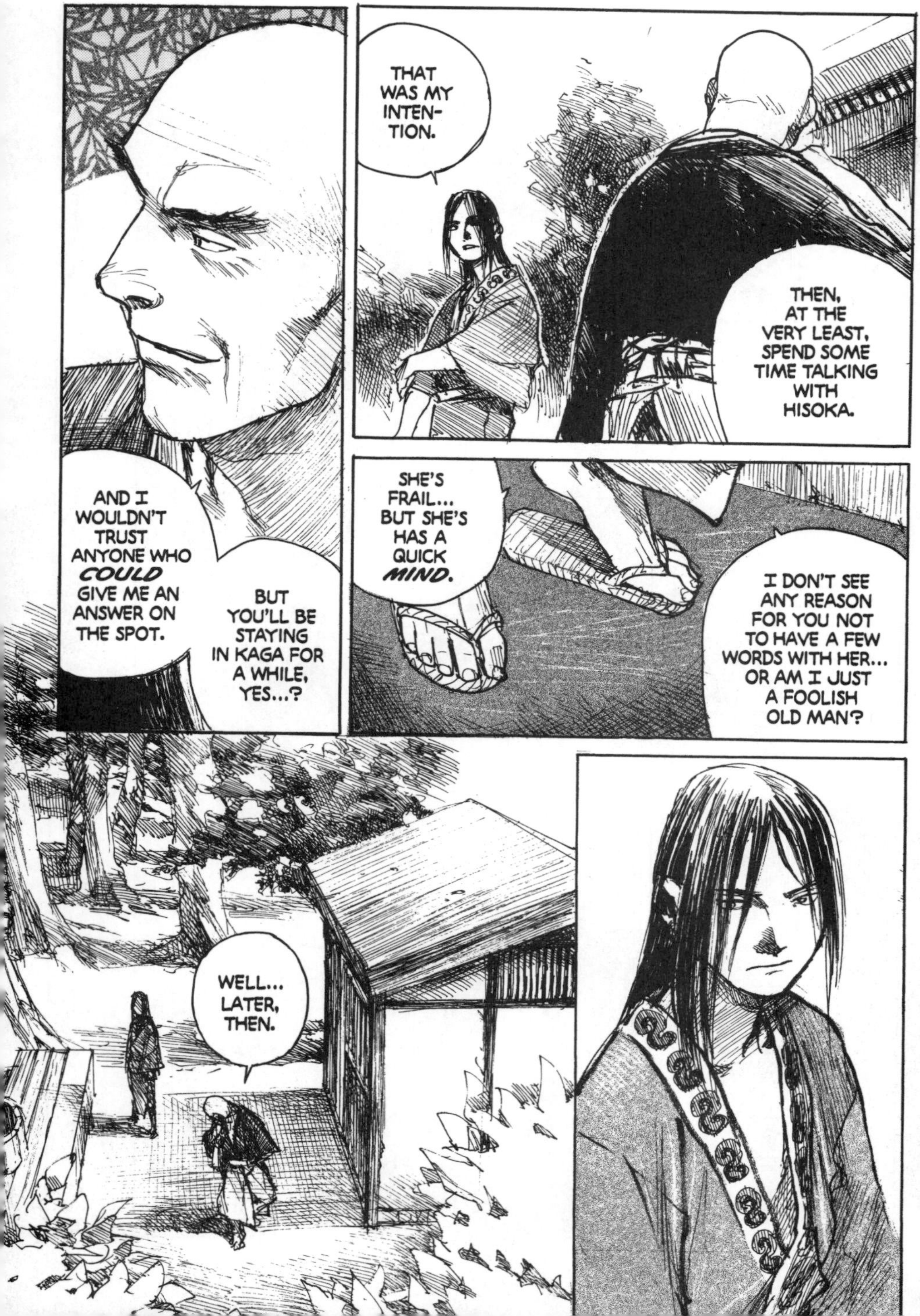
AND I WOULDN'T TRUST ANYONE WHO COULD GIVE ME AN ANSWER ON THE SPOT.
BUT YOU'LL BE STAYING IN KAGA FOR A WHILE, YES...?
THAT WAS MY INTEN-TION.
THEN, AT THE VERY LEAST, SPEND SOME TIME TALKING WITH HISOKA.
SHE'S FRAIL... BUT SHE'S HAS A QUICK MIND.
I DON'T SEE ANY REASON FOR YOU NOT TO HAVE A FEW WORDS WITH HER... OR AM I JUST A FOOLISH OLD MAN?
WELL... LATER, THEN.

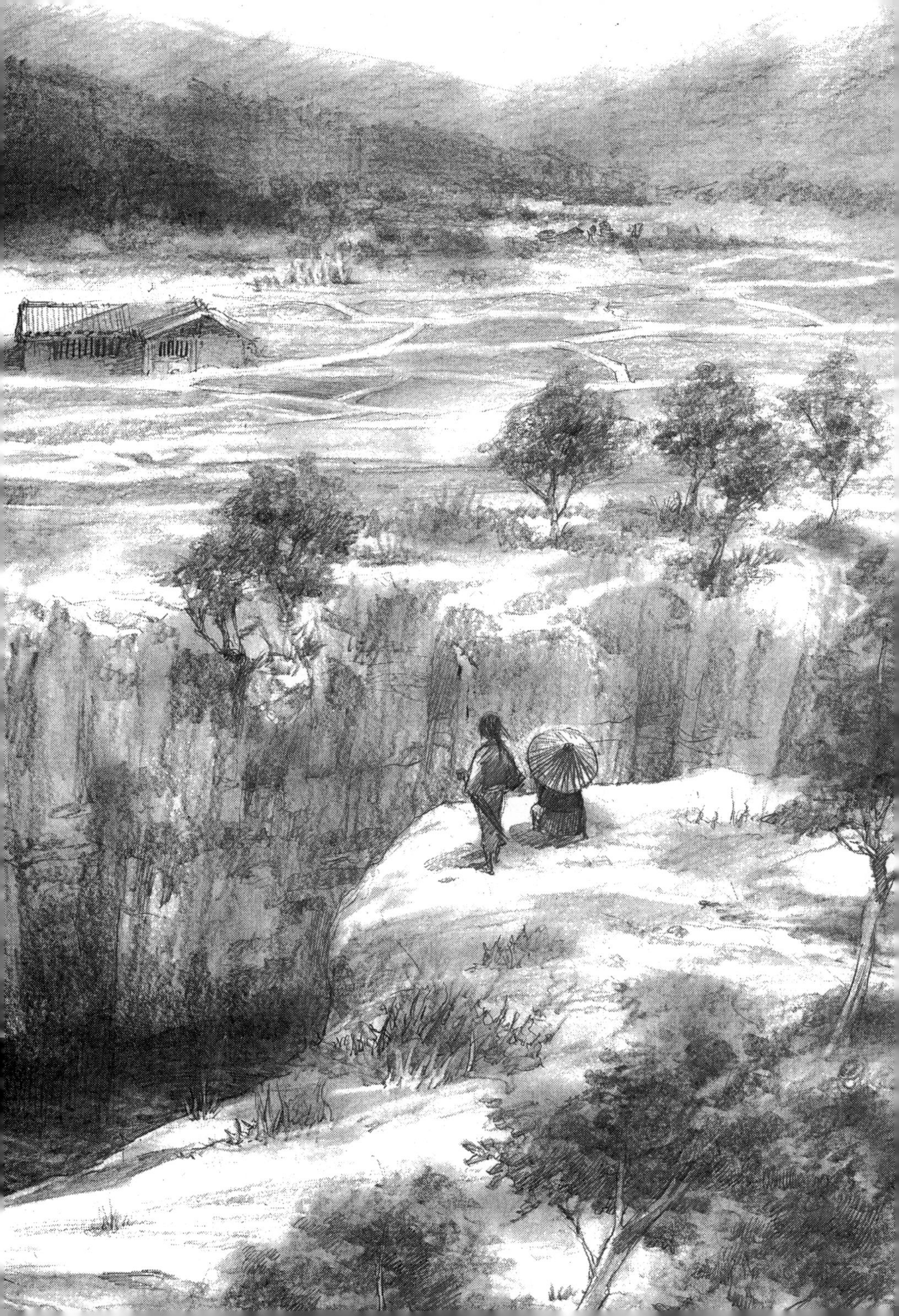

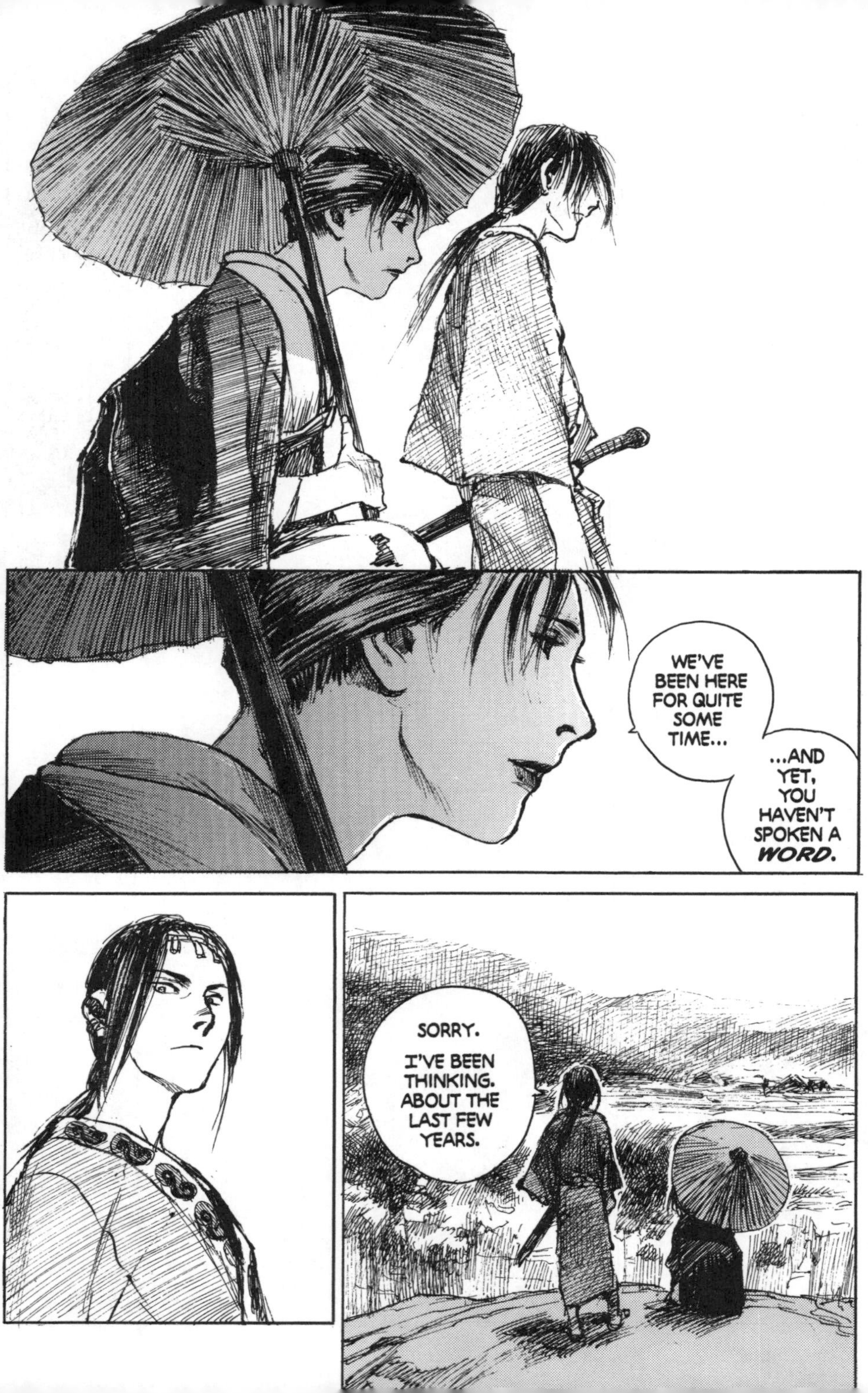
WE'VE BEEN HERE FOR QUITE SOME TIME...
...AND YET, YOU HAVEN'T SPOKEN A WORD.
SORRY.
I'VE BEEN THINKING. ABOUT THE LAST FEW YEARS.

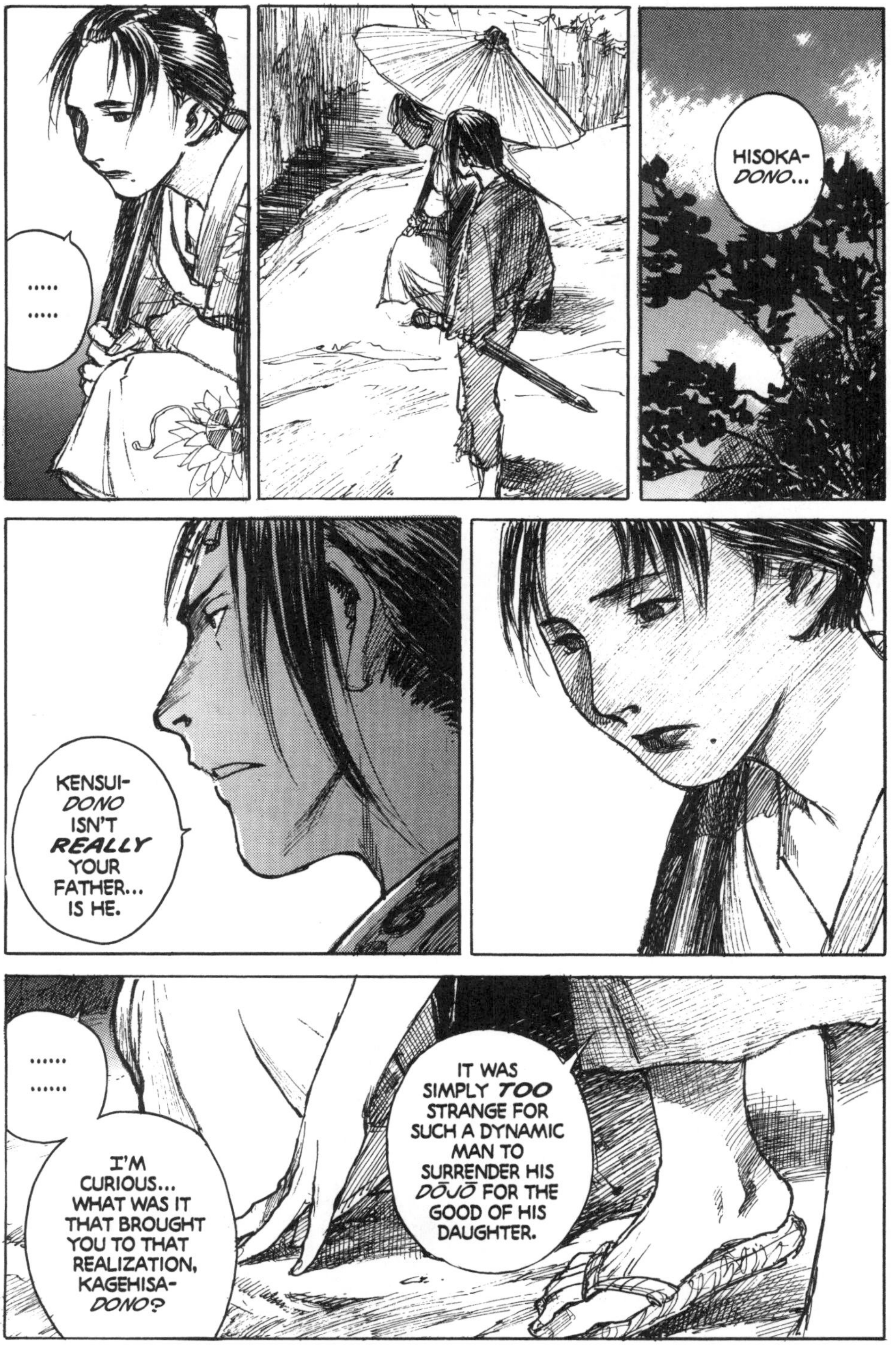
......
......
HISOKA-DONO...
KENSUI-DONO ISN'T REALLY YOUR FATHER... IS HE.
......
......
I'M CURIOUS... WHAT WAS IT THAT BROUGHT YOU TO THAT REALIZATION, KAGEHISA-DONO?
IT WAS SIMPLY TOO STRANGE FOR SUCH A DYNAMIC MAN TO SURRENDER HIS DŌJŌ FOR THE GOOD OF HIS DAUGHTER.

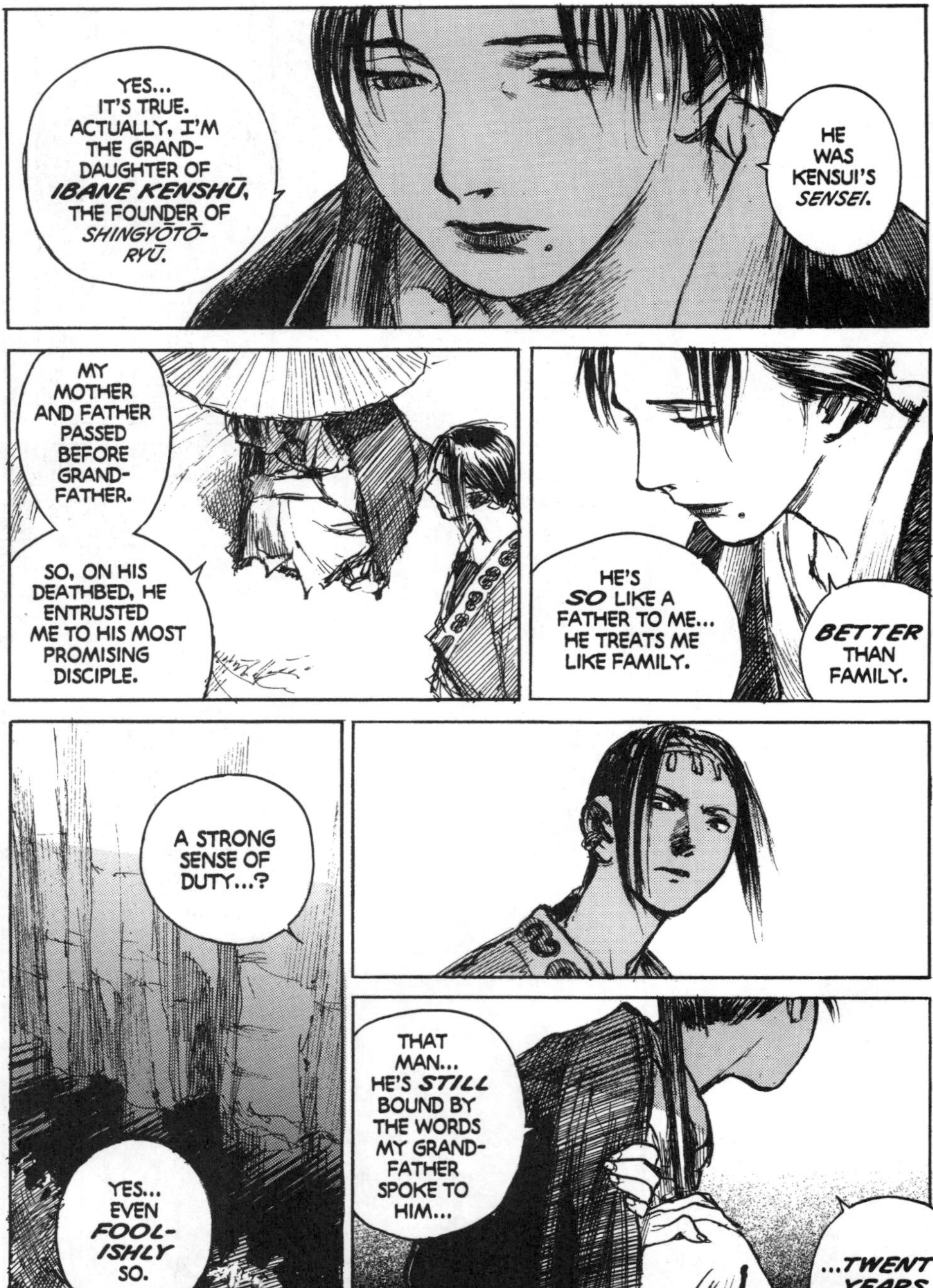
YES... IT'S TRUE. ACTUALLY, I'M THE GRAND-DAUGHTER OF IBANE KENSHŪ, THE FOUNDER OF SHINGYŌTŌ-RYŪ.
HE WAS KENSUI'S SENSEI.
MY MOTHER AND FATHER PASSED BEFORE GRAND-FATHER.
SO, ON HIS DEATHBED, HE ENTRUSTED ME TO HIS MOST PROMISING DISCIPLE.
HE'S SO LIKE A FATHER TO ME... HE TREATS ME LIKE FAMILY.
BETTER THAN FAMILY.
A STRONG SENSE OF DUTY...?
YES... EVEN FOOL-ISHLY SO.
THAT MAN... HE'S STILL BOUND BY THE WORDS MY GRAND-FATHER SPOKE TO HIM...
...TWENTY YEARS AGO.

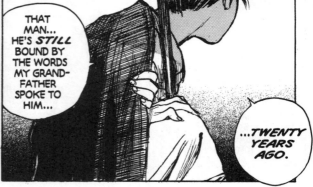

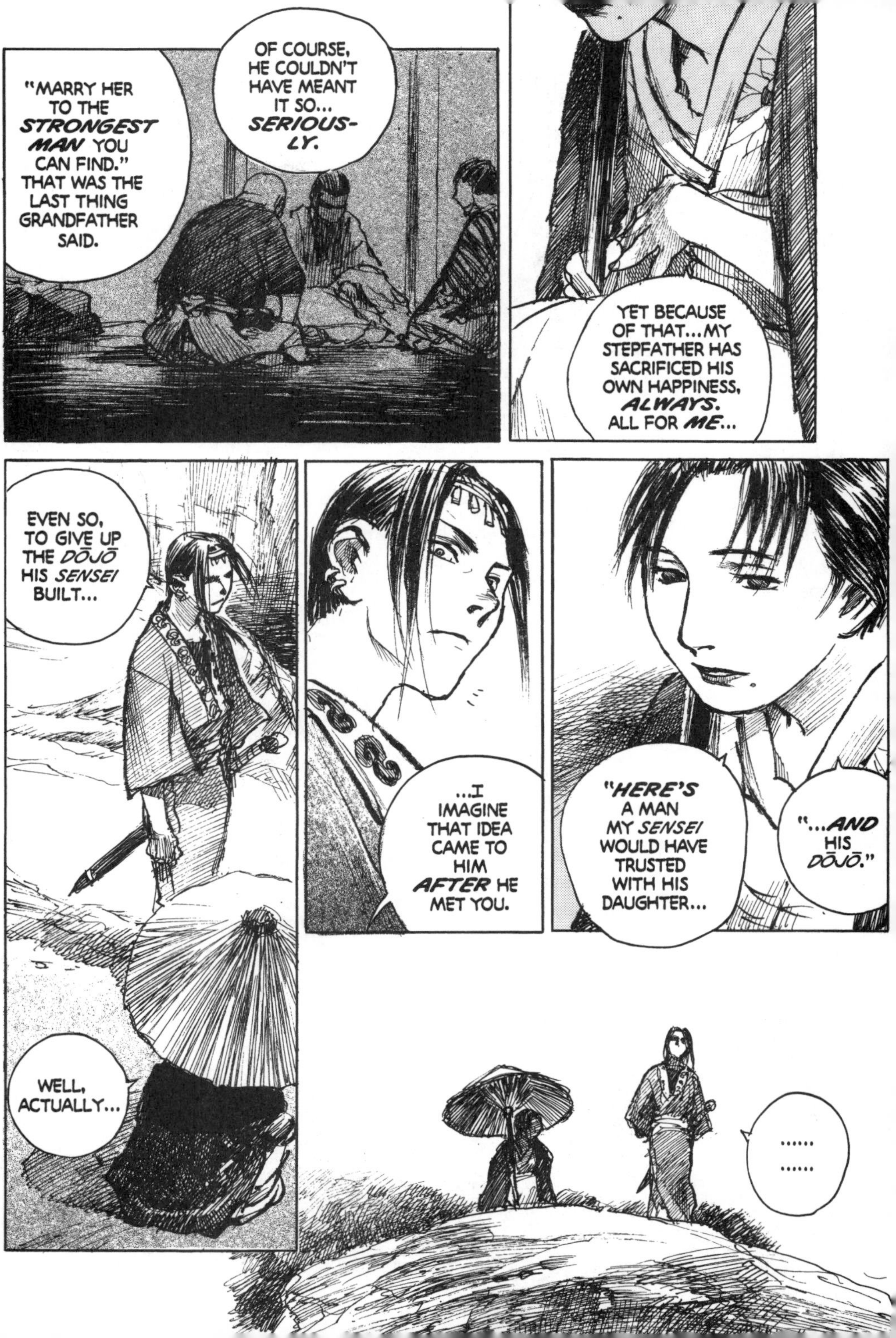
"MARRY HER TO THE STRONGEST MAN YOU CAN FIND." THAT WAS THE LAST THING GRANDFATHER SAID.
OF COURSE, HE COULDN'T HAVE MEANT IT SO... SERIOUS-LY.
YET BECAUSE OF THAT...MY STEPFATHER HAS SACRIFICED HIS OWN HAPPINESS, ALWAYS. ALL FOR ME...
EVEN SO, TO GIVE UP THE DŌJŌ HIS SENSEI BUILT...
...I IMAGINE THAT IDEA CAME TO HIM AFTER HE MET YOU.
"HERE'S A MAN MY SENSEI WOULD HAVE TRUSTED WITH HIS DAUGHTER...
"...AND HIS DŌJŌ."
WELL, ACTUALLY...
......
......

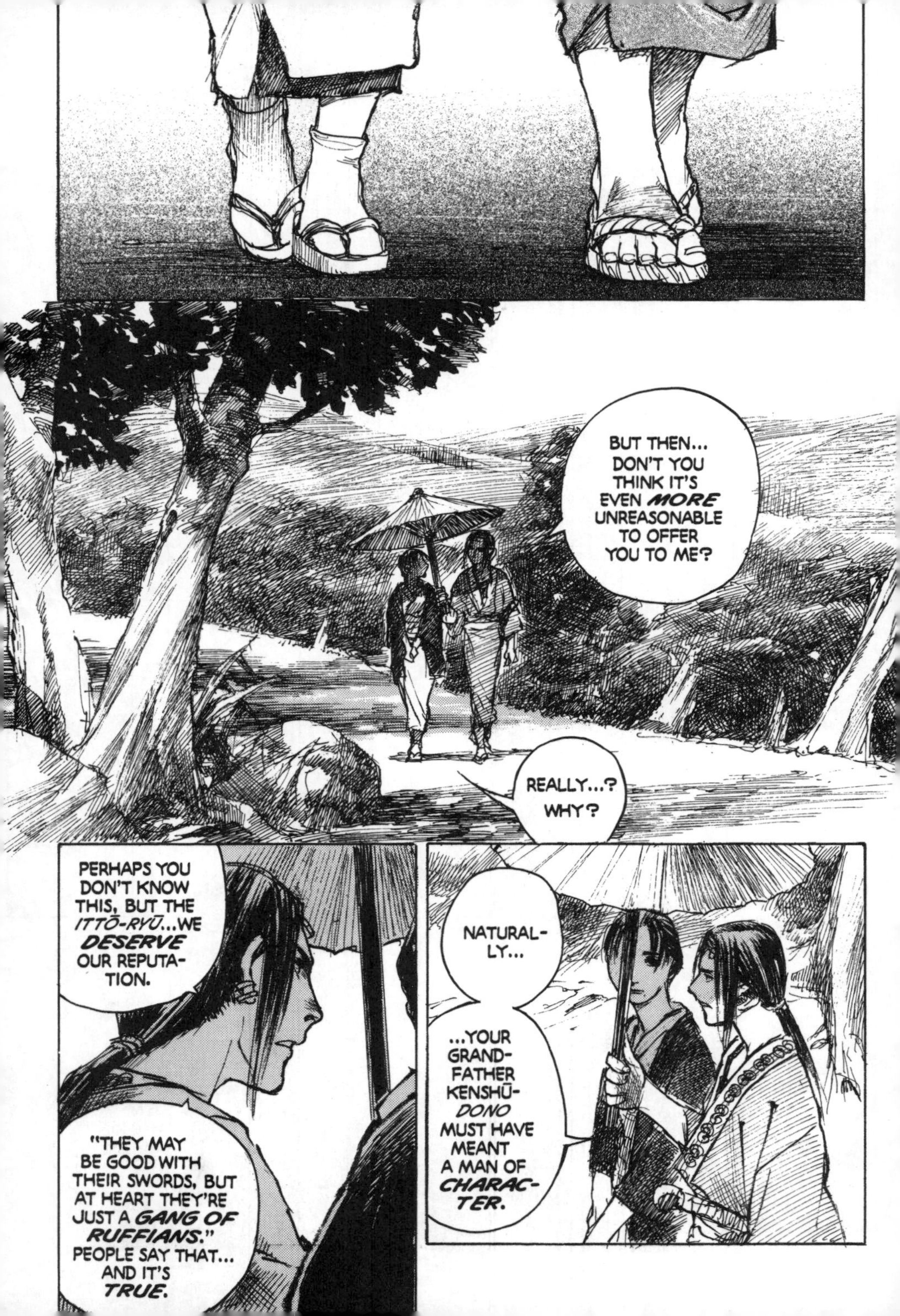
BUT THEN... DON'T YOU THINK IT'S EVEN *MORE* UNREASONABLE TO OFFER YOU TO ME?
REALLY...? WHY?
PERHAPS YOU DON'T KNOW THIS, BUT THE *ITTŌ-RYŪ*...WE ***DESERVE*** OUR REPUTATION.
"THEY MAY BE GOOD WITH THEIR SWORDS, BUT AT HEART THEY'RE JUST A ***GANG OF RUFFIANS.***" PEOPLE SAY THAT... AND IT'S ***TRUE.***
NATURALLY...
...YOUR GRANDFATHER KENSHŪ-*DONO* MUST HAVE MEANT A MAN OF ***CHARACTER.***

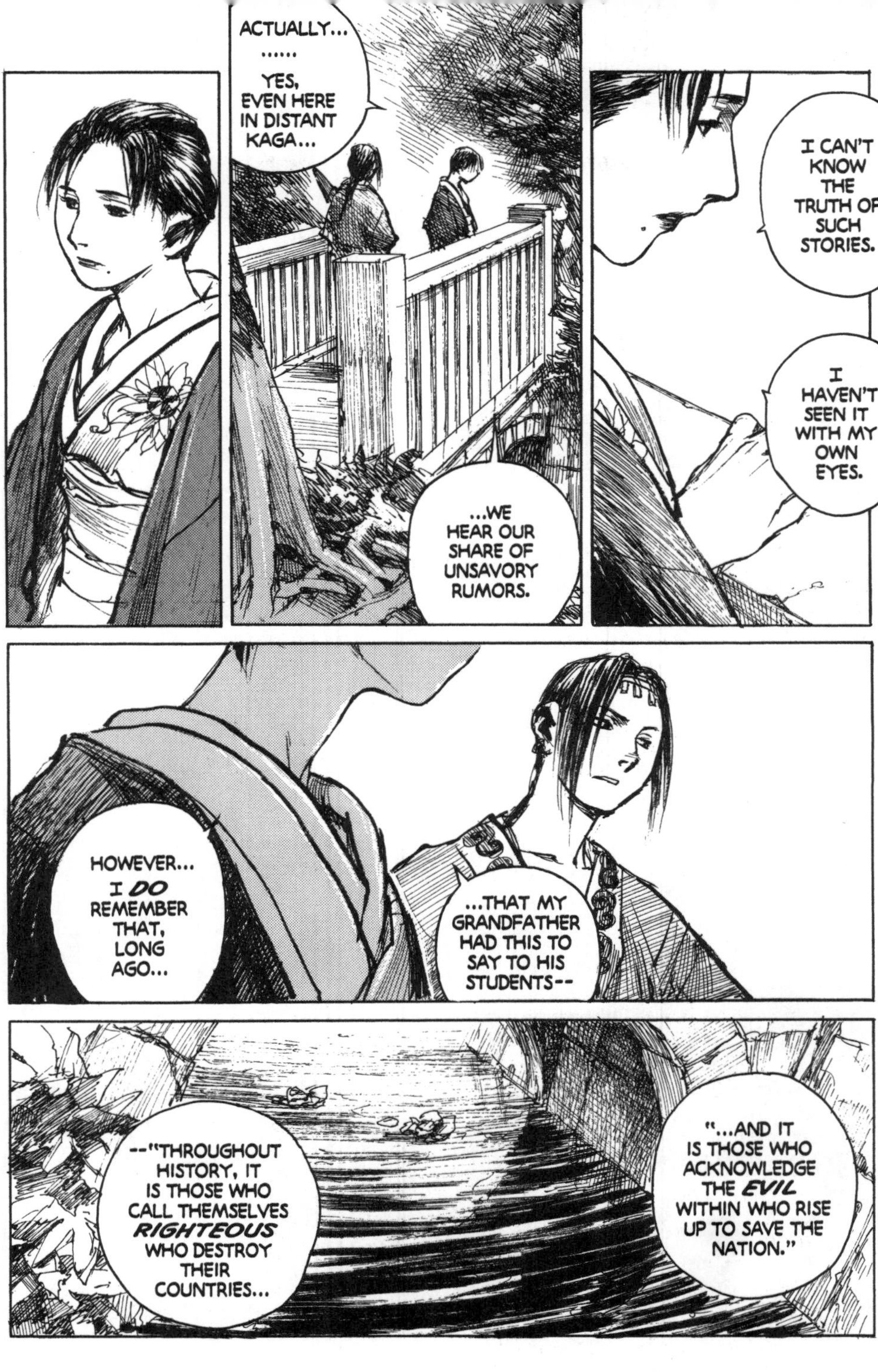
ACTUALLY... ...... YES, EVEN HERE IN DISTANT KAGA...
...WE HEAR OUR SHARE OF UNSAVORY RUMORS.
I CAN'T KNOW THE TRUTH OF SUCH STORIES.
I HAVEN'T SEEN IT WITH MY OWN EYES.
HOWEVER... I *DO* REMEMBER THAT, LONG AGO...
...THAT MY GRANDFATHER HAD THIS TO SAY TO HIS STUDENTS--
--"THROUGHOUT HISTORY, IT IS THOSE WHO CALL THEMSELVES *RIGHTEOUS* WHO DESTROY THEIR COUNTRIES...
"...AND IT IS THOSE WHO ACKNOWLEDGE THE *EVIL* WITHIN WHO RISE UP TO SAVE THE NATION."

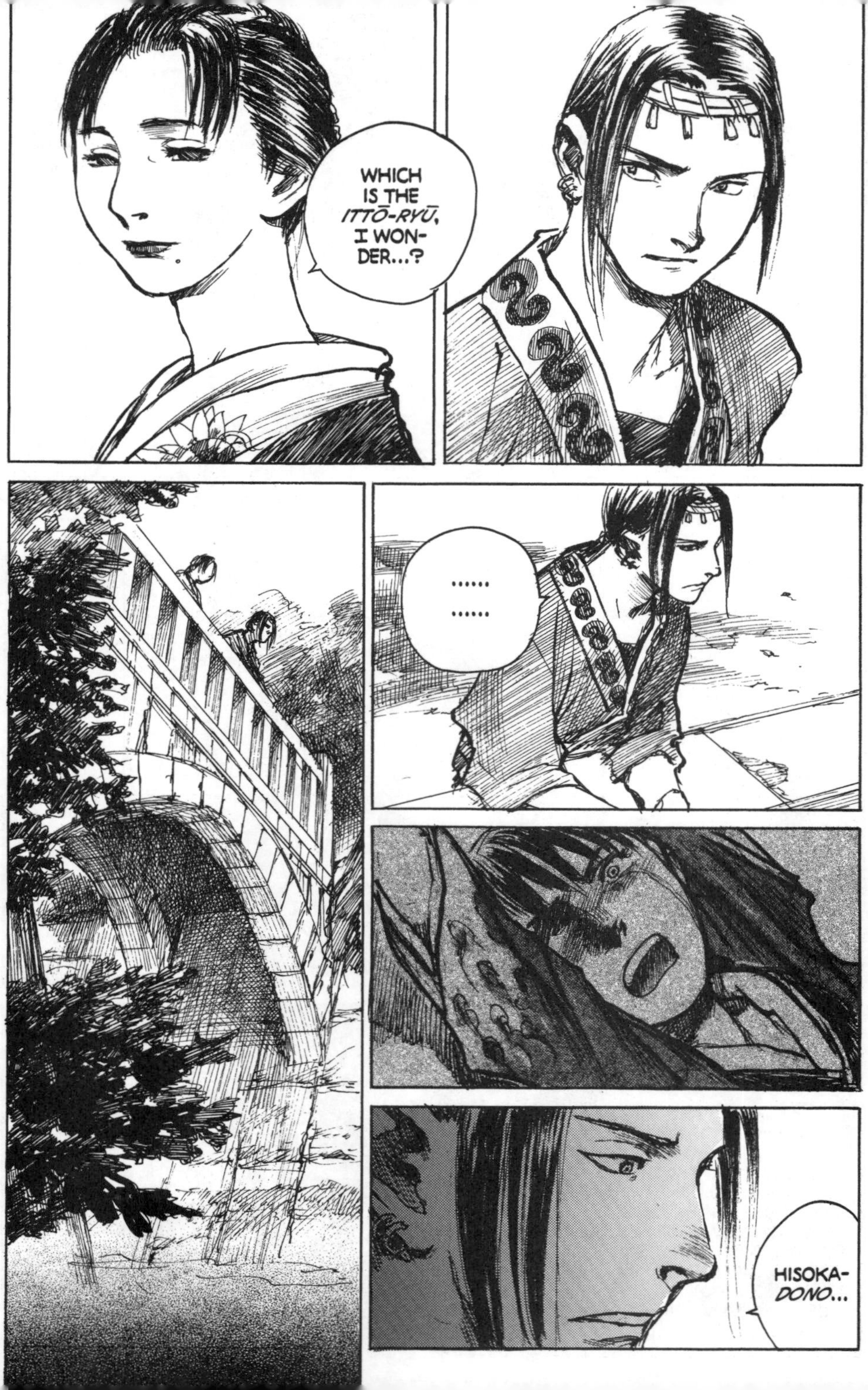
WHICH IS THE *ITTŌ-RYŪ*, I WONDER...?
......
......
HISOKA-*DONO*...

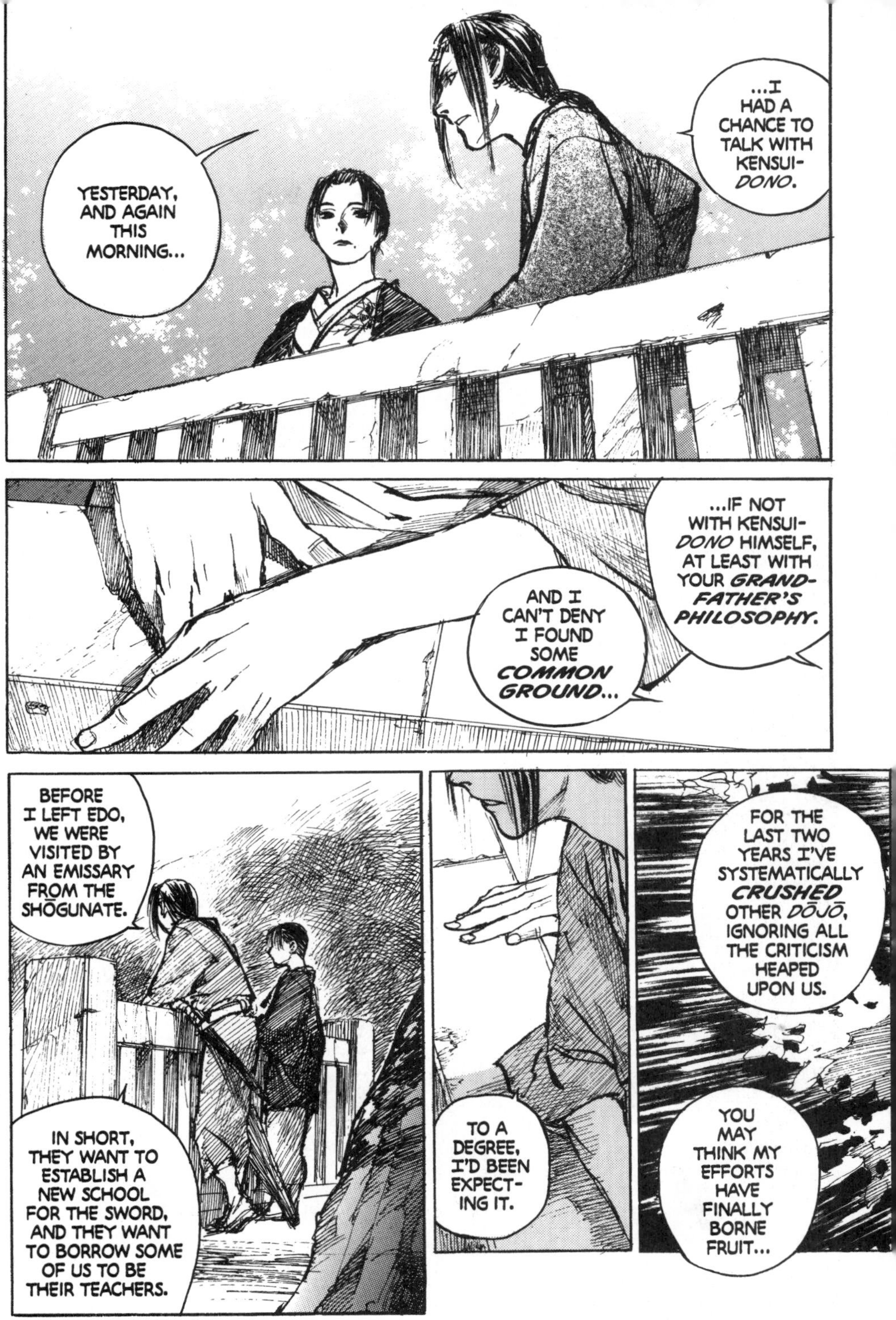
YESTERDAY, AND AGAIN THIS MORNING...
...I HAD A CHANCE TO TALK WITH KENSUI-*DONO*.
AND I CAN'T DENY I FOUND SOME ***COMMON GROUND***...
...IF NOT WITH KENSUI-*DONO* HIMSELF, AT LEAST WITH YOUR ***GRANDFATHER'S PHILOSOPHY***.
BEFORE I LEFT EDO, WE WERE VISITED BY AN EMISSARY FROM THE SHŌGUNATE.
IN SHORT, THEY WANT TO ESTABLISH A NEW SCHOOL FOR THE SWORD, AND THEY WANT TO BORROW SOME OF US TO BE THEIR TEACHERS.
TO A DEGREE, I'D BEEN EXPECTING IT.
FOR THE LAST TWO YEARS I'VE SYSTEMATICALLY ***CRUSHED*** OTHER *DŌJŌ*, IGNORING ALL THE CRITICISM HEAPED UPON US.
YOU MAY THINK MY EFFORTS HAVE FINALLY BORNE FRUIT...

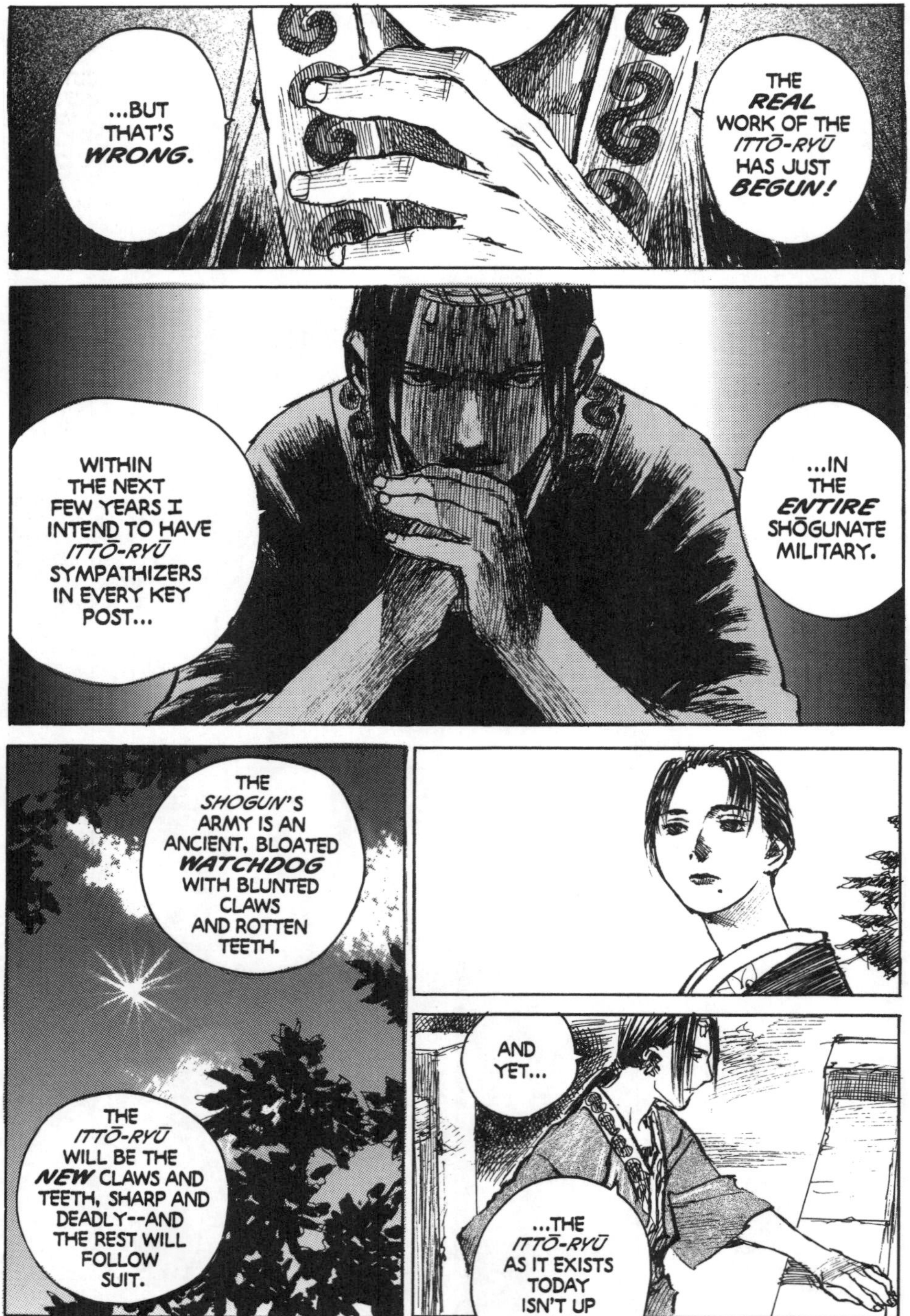
...BUT THAT'S WRONG.
THE REAL WORK OF THE ITTŌ-RYŪ HAS JUST BEGUN!
WITHIN THE NEXT FEW YEARS I INTEND TO HAVE ITTŌ-RYŪ SYMPATHIZERS IN EVERY KEY POST...
...IN THE ENTIRE SHŌGUNATE MILITARY.
THE SHOGUN'S ARMY IS AN ANCIENT, BLOATED WATCHDOG WITH BLUNTED CLAWS AND ROTTEN TEETH.
THE ITTŌ-RYŪ WILL BE THE NEW CLAWS AND TEETH, SHARP AND DEADLY--AND THE REST WILL FOLLOW SUIT.
AND YET...
...THE ITTŌ-RYŪ AS IT EXISTS TODAY ISN'T UP TO IT.

WE'RE NOT A TRUE SCHOOL. WE'RE NOT EVEN A PROPER *ORGANI-ZATION.*

WE'RE A *GANG. RABBLE!*

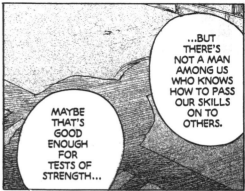

MAYBE THAT'S GOOD ENOUGH FOR TESTS OF STRENGTH...

...BUT THERE'S NOT A MAN AMONG US WHO KNOWS HOW TO PASS OUR SKILLS ON TO OTHERS.

HISOKA...
......

I BELIEVE MY *TRUE* WORK AS THE LEADER OF THE *ITTŌ-RYŪ*...

...HAS JUST *BEGUN!*

SHOULD I START A FAMILY NOW...

...I'D BE ONE OF THOSE FATHERS WHO *NEVER* LOOKS BACK.

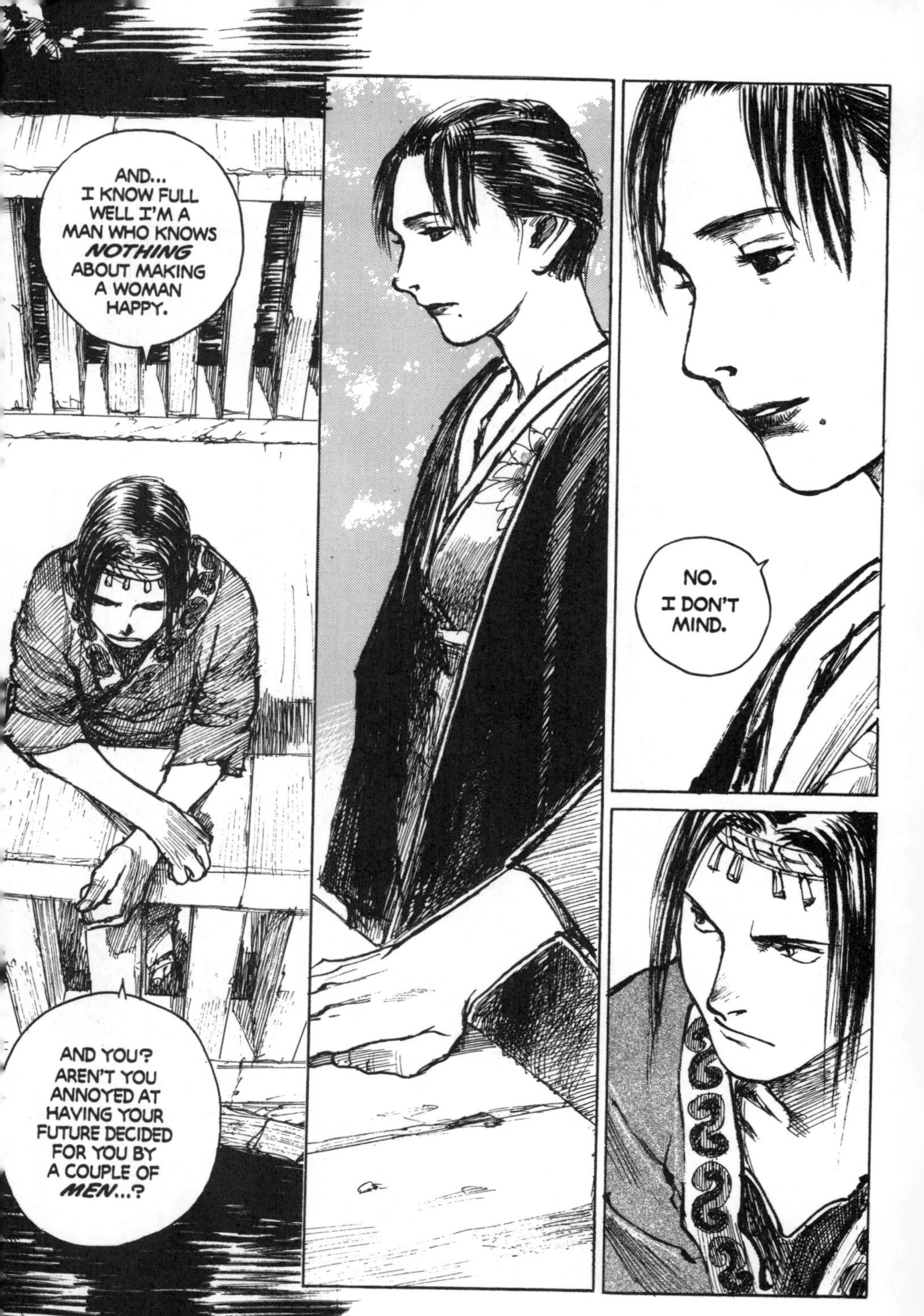
AND... I KNOW FULL WELL I'M A MAN WHO KNOWS *NOTHING* ABOUT MAKING A WOMAN HAPPY.
AND YOU? AREN'T YOU ANNOYED AT HAVING YOUR FUTURE DECIDED FOR YOU BY A COUPLE OF *MEN*...?
NO. I DON'T MIND.

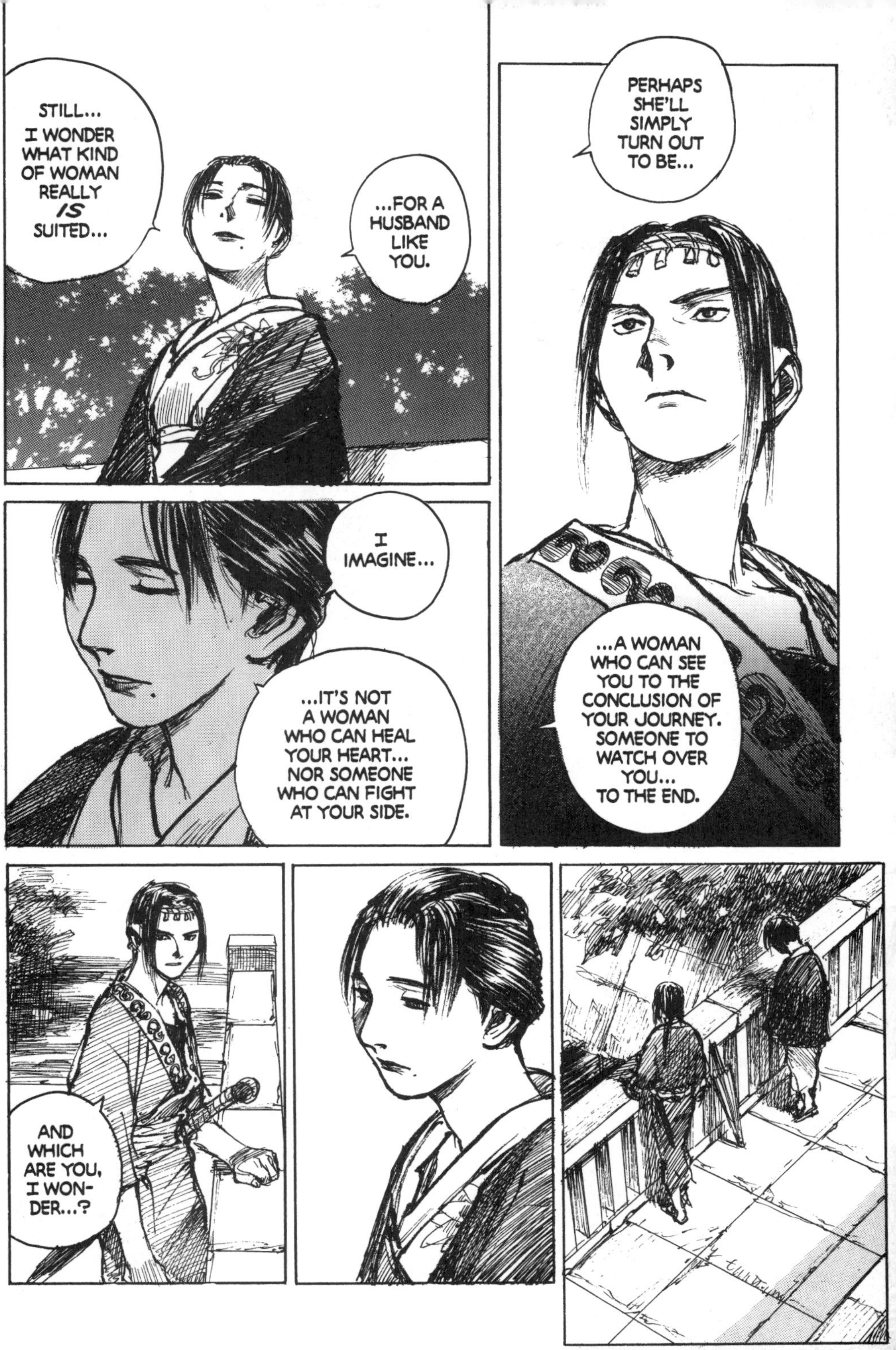
STILL... I WONDER WHAT KIND OF WOMAN REALLY *IS* SUITED...
...FOR A HUSBAND LIKE YOU.
I IMAGINE...
...IT'S NOT A WOMAN WHO CAN HEAL YOUR HEART... NOR SOMEONE WHO CAN FIGHT AT YOUR SIDE.
PERHAPS SHE'LL SIMPLY TURN OUT TO BE...
...A WOMAN WHO CAN SEE YOU TO THE CONCLUSION OF YOUR JOURNEY. SOMEONE TO WATCH OVER YOU... TO THE END.
AND WHICH ARE YOU, I WONDER...?

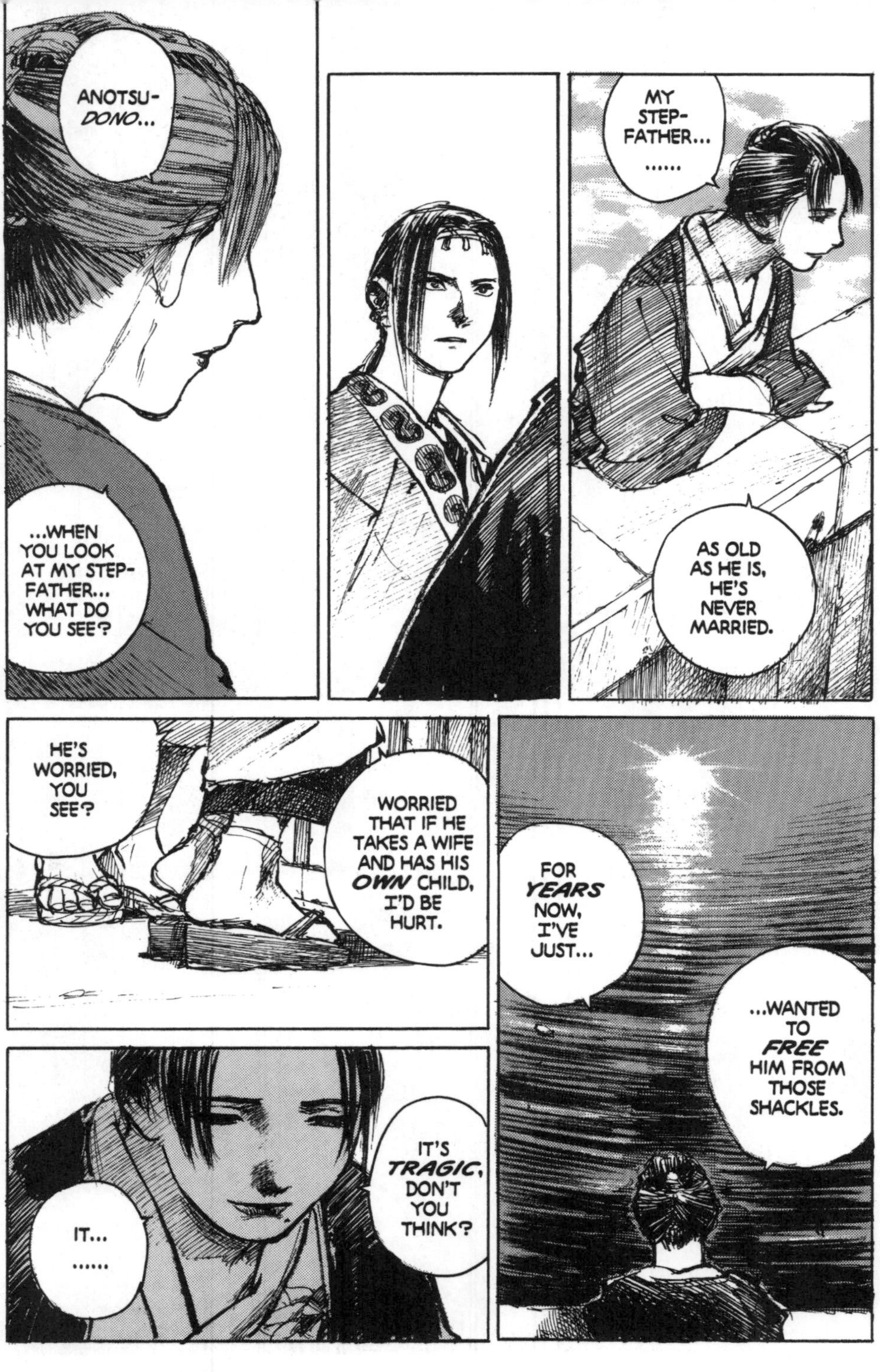
ANOTSU-DONO...
...WHEN YOU LOOK AT MY STEP-FATHER... WHAT DO YOU SEE?
MY STEP-FATHER... ......
AS OLD AS HE IS, HE'S NEVER MARRIED.
HE'S WORRIED, YOU SEE?
WORRIED THAT IF HE TAKES A WIFE AND HAS HIS OWN CHILD, I'D BE HURT.
FOR YEARS NOW, I'VE JUST...
...WANTED TO FREE HIM FROM THOSE SHACKLES.
IT'S TRAGIC, DON'T YOU THINK?
IT... ......

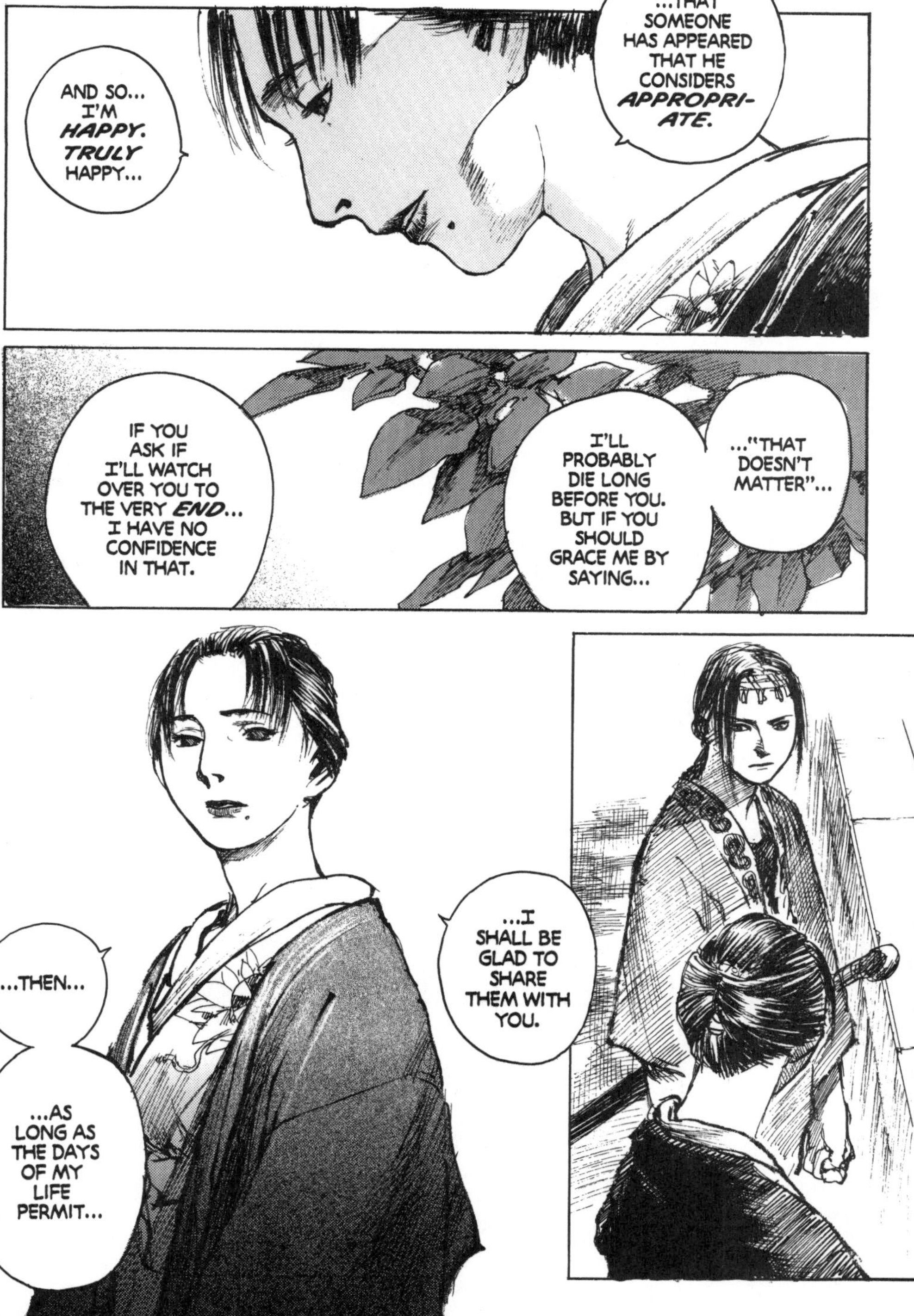
...THAT SOMEONE HAS APPEARED THAT HE CONSIDERS *APPROPRI-ATE.*
AND SO... I'M *HAPPY. TRULY* HAPPY...
IF YOU ASK IF I'LL WATCH OVER YOU TO THE VERY *END*... I HAVE NO CONFIDENCE IN THAT.
I'LL PROBABLY DIE LONG BEFORE YOU. BUT IF YOU SHOULD GRACE ME BY SAYING...
..."THAT DOESN'T MATTER"...
...THEN...
...AS LONG AS THE DAYS OF MY LIFE PERMIT...
...I SHALL BE GLAD TO SHARE THEM WITH YOU.

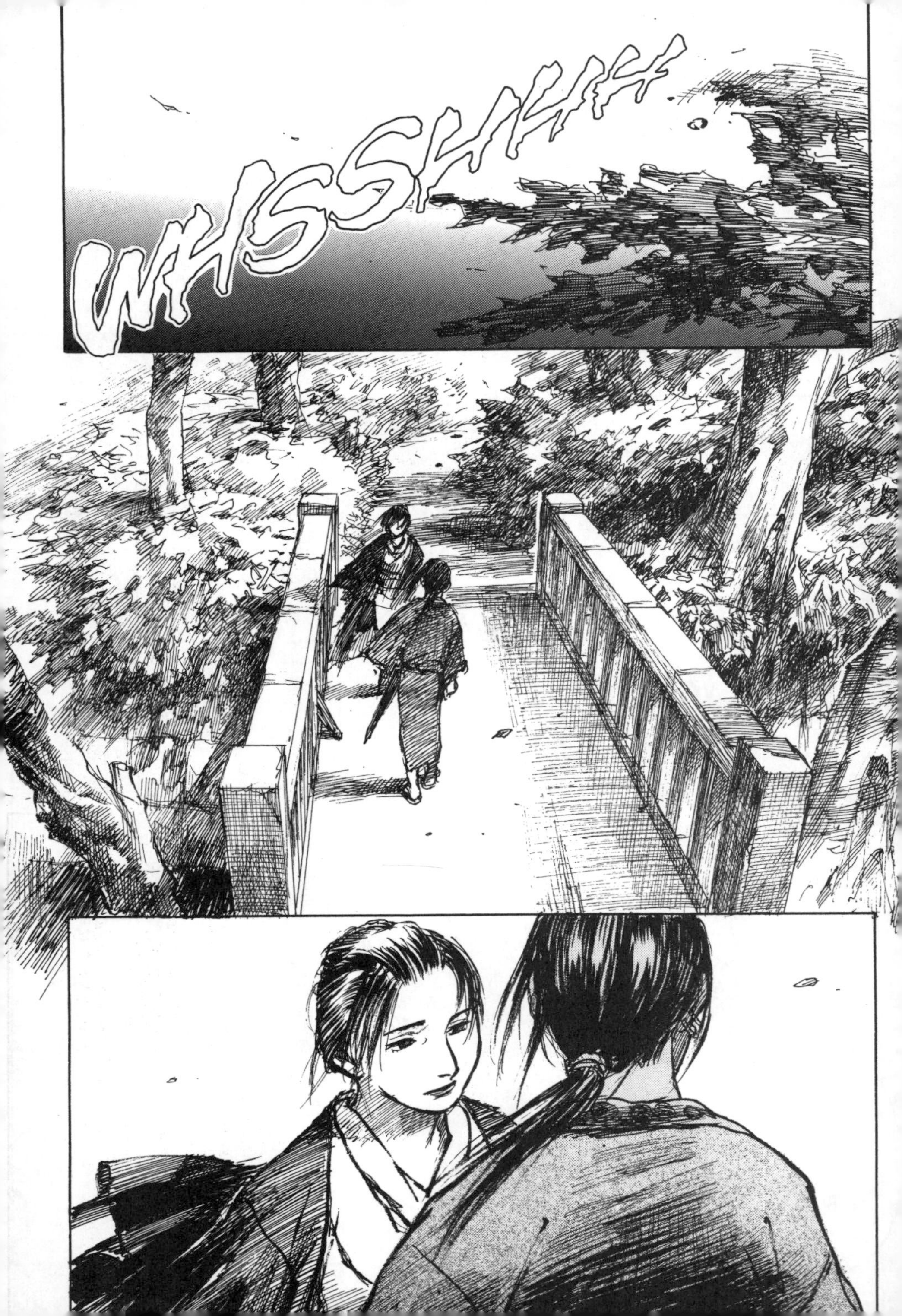
WHSSHHH

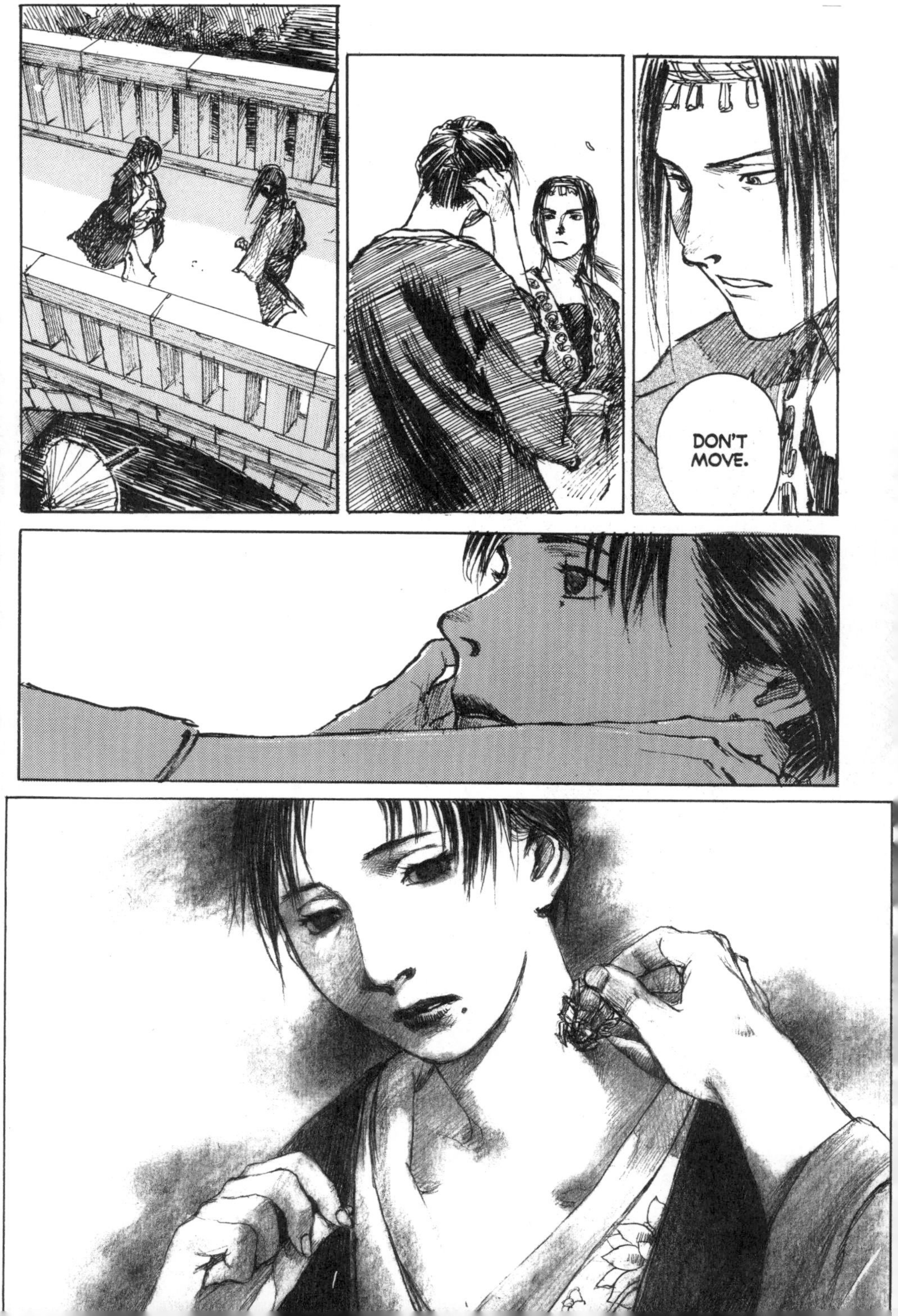
DON'T
MOVE.

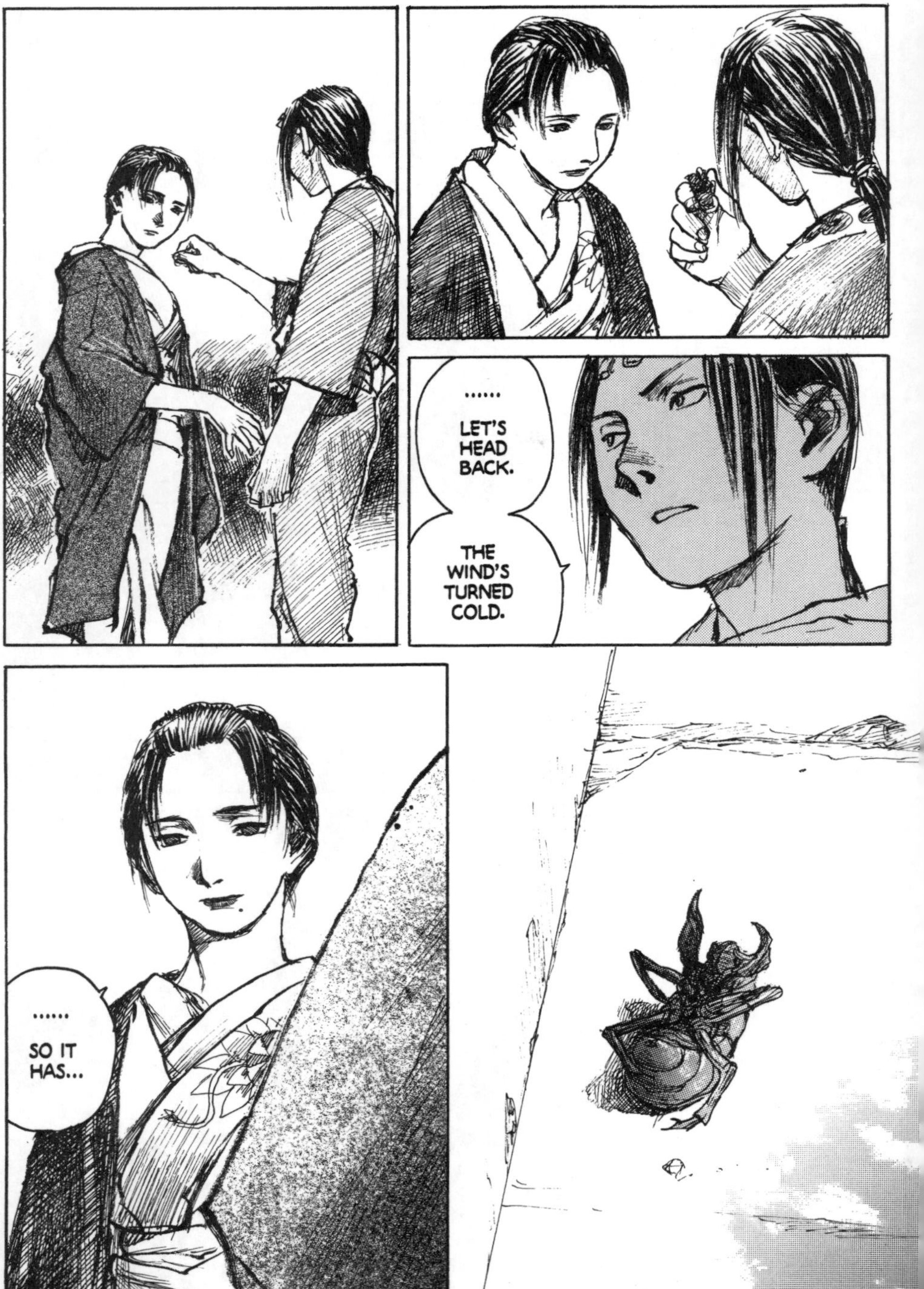
......
LET'S HEAD BACK.
THE WIND'S TURNED COLD.
......
SO IT HAS...

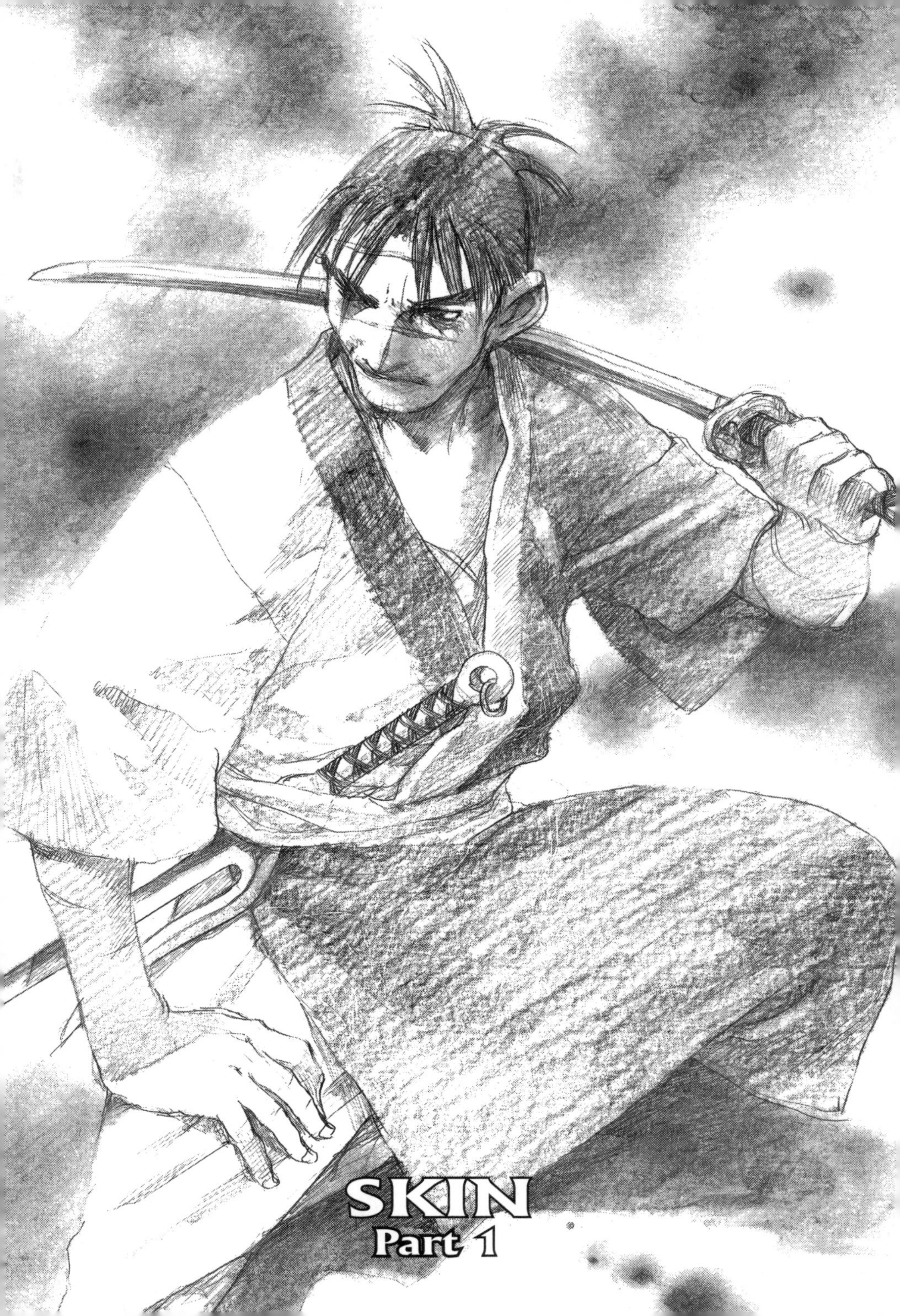

SKIN
Part 1

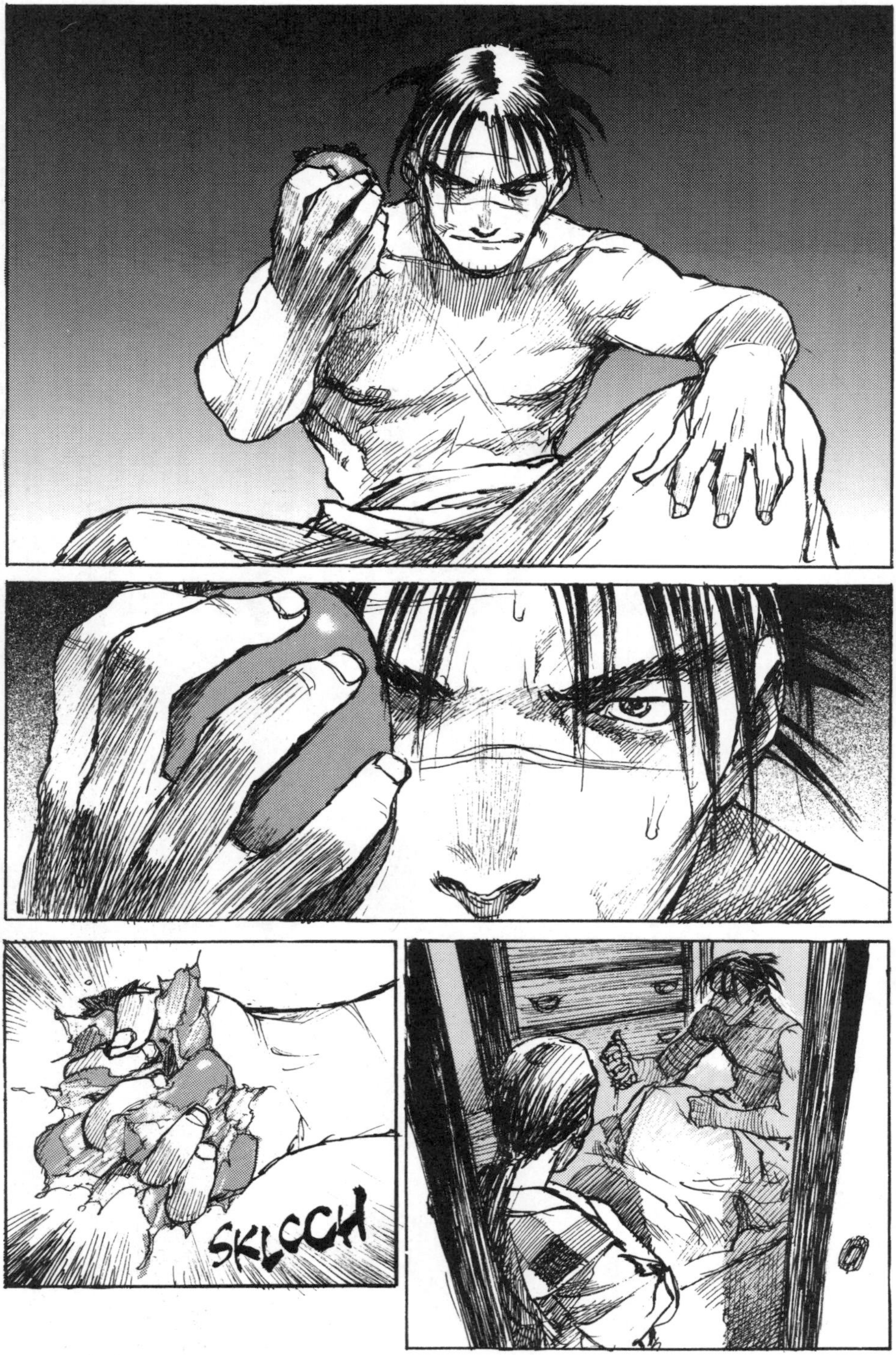
SKLCCH

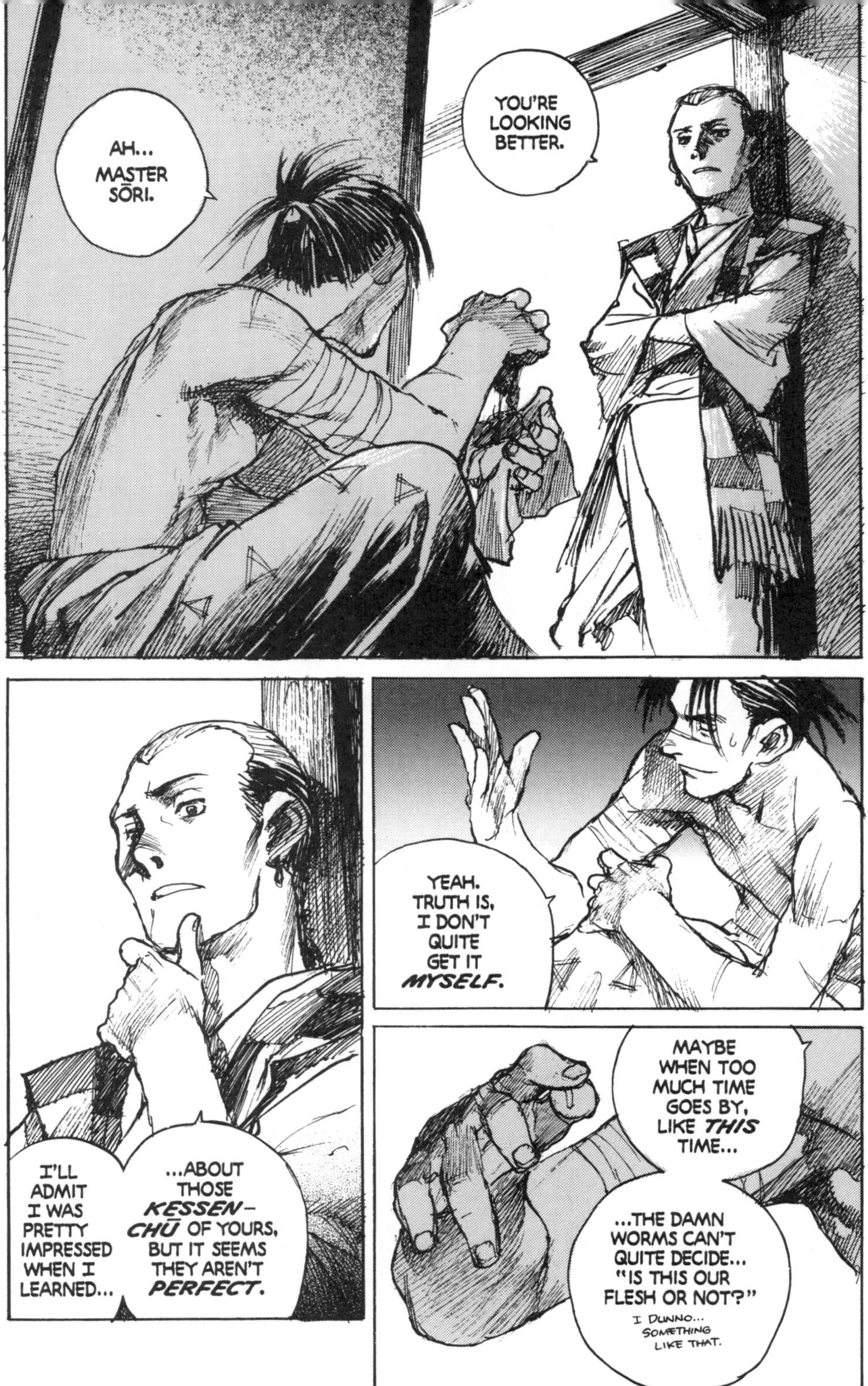
AH... MASTER SŌRI.
YOU'RE LOOKING BETTER.
I'LL ADMIT I WAS PRETTY IMPRESSED WHEN I LEARNED...
...ABOUT THOSE KESSEN-CHŪ OF YOURS, BUT IT SEEMS THEY AREN'T PERFECT.
YEAH. TRUTH IS, I DON'T QUITE GET IT MYSELF.
MAYBE WHEN TOO MUCH TIME GOES BY, LIKE THIS TIME...
...THE DAMN WORMS CAN'T QUITE DECIDE... "IS THIS OUR FLESH OR NOT?"
I DUNNO... SOMETHING LIKE THAT.

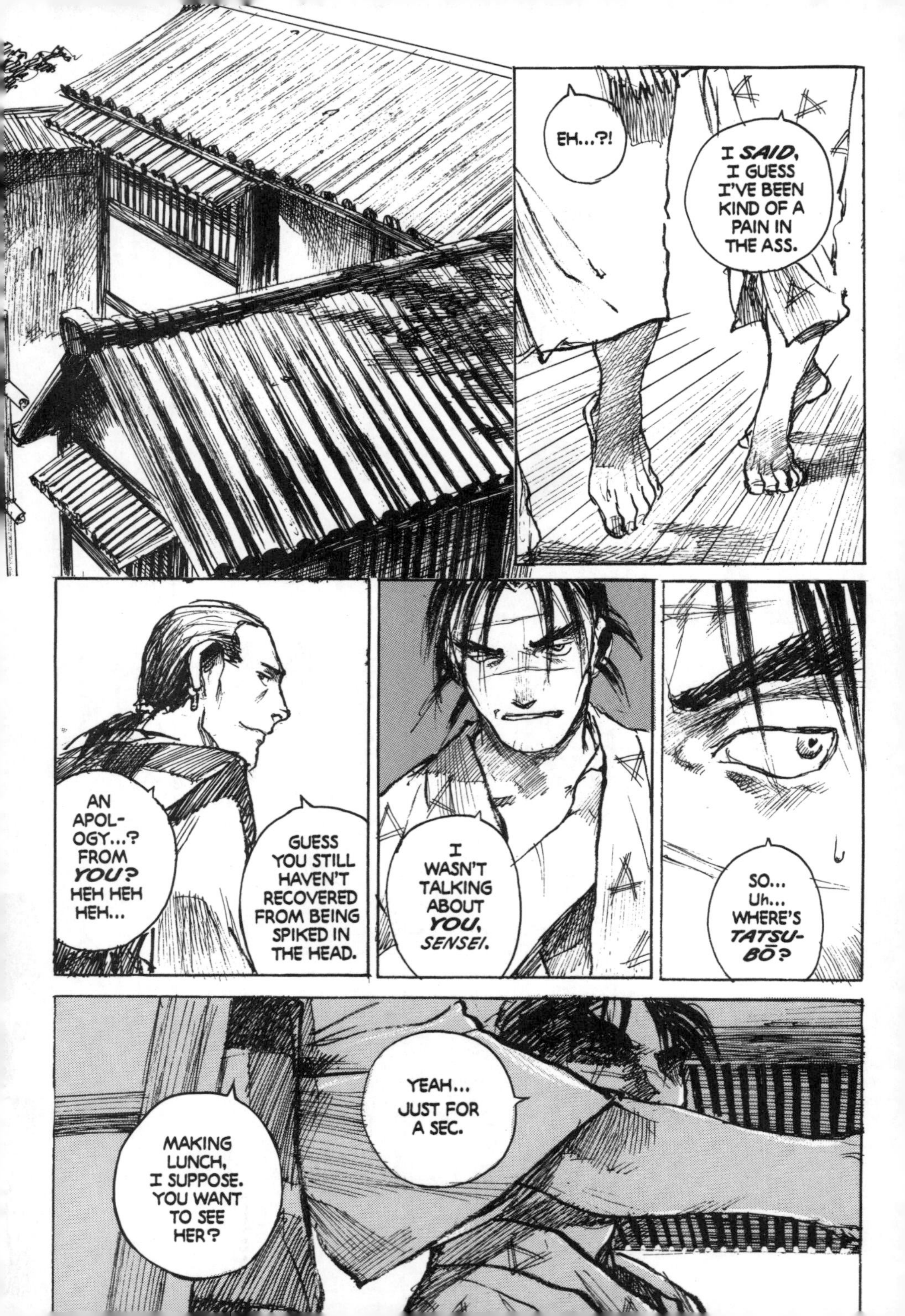
EH...?!
I SAID, I GUESS I'VE BEEN KIND OF A PAIN IN THE ASS.
AN APOLOGY...? FROM YOU? HEH HEH HEH...
GUESS YOU STILL HAVEN'T RECOVERED FROM BEING SPIKED IN THE HEAD.
I WASN'T TALKING ABOUT YOU, SENSEI.
SO... Uh... WHERE'S TATSUBŌ?
MAKING LUNCH, I SUPPOSE. YOU WANT TO SEE HER?
YEAH... JUST FOR A SEC.

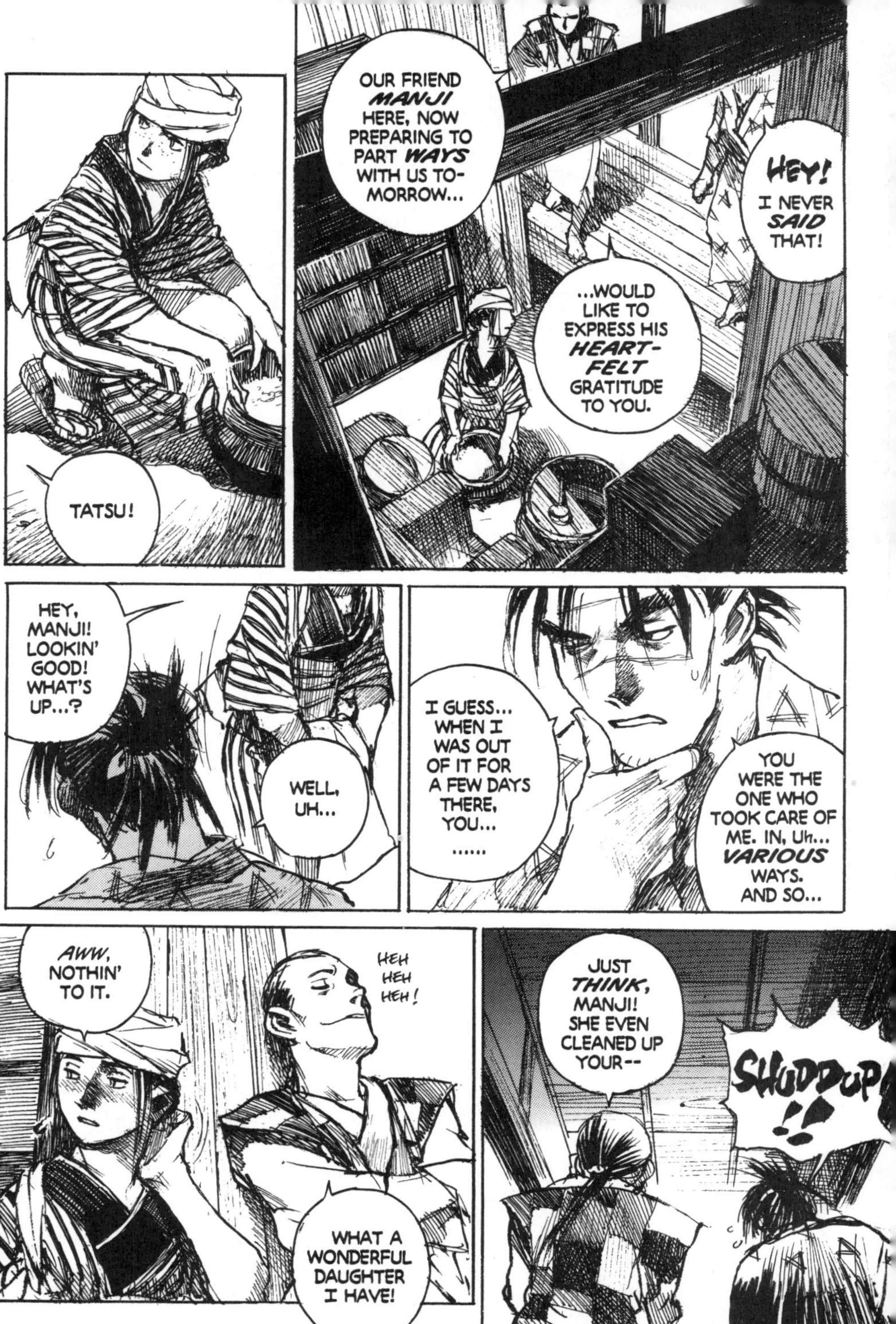
TATSU!
OUR FRIEND MANJI HERE, NOW PREPARING TO PART WAYS WITH US TO-MORROW...
...WOULD LIKE TO EXPRESS HIS HEART-FELT GRATITUDE TO YOU.
HEY! I NEVER SAID THAT!
HEY, MANJI! LOOKIN' GOOD! WHAT'S UP...?
WELL, UH...
I GUESS... WHEN I WAS OUT OF IT FOR A FEW DAYS THERE, YOU... ......
YOU WERE THE ONE WHO TOOK CARE OF ME. IN, UH... VARIOUS WAYS. AND SO...
AWW, NOTHIN' TO IT.
HEH HEH HEH!
WHAT A WONDERFUL DAUGHTER I HAVE!
JUST THINK, MANJI! SHE EVEN CLEANED UP YOUR--
SHUDDUP!!

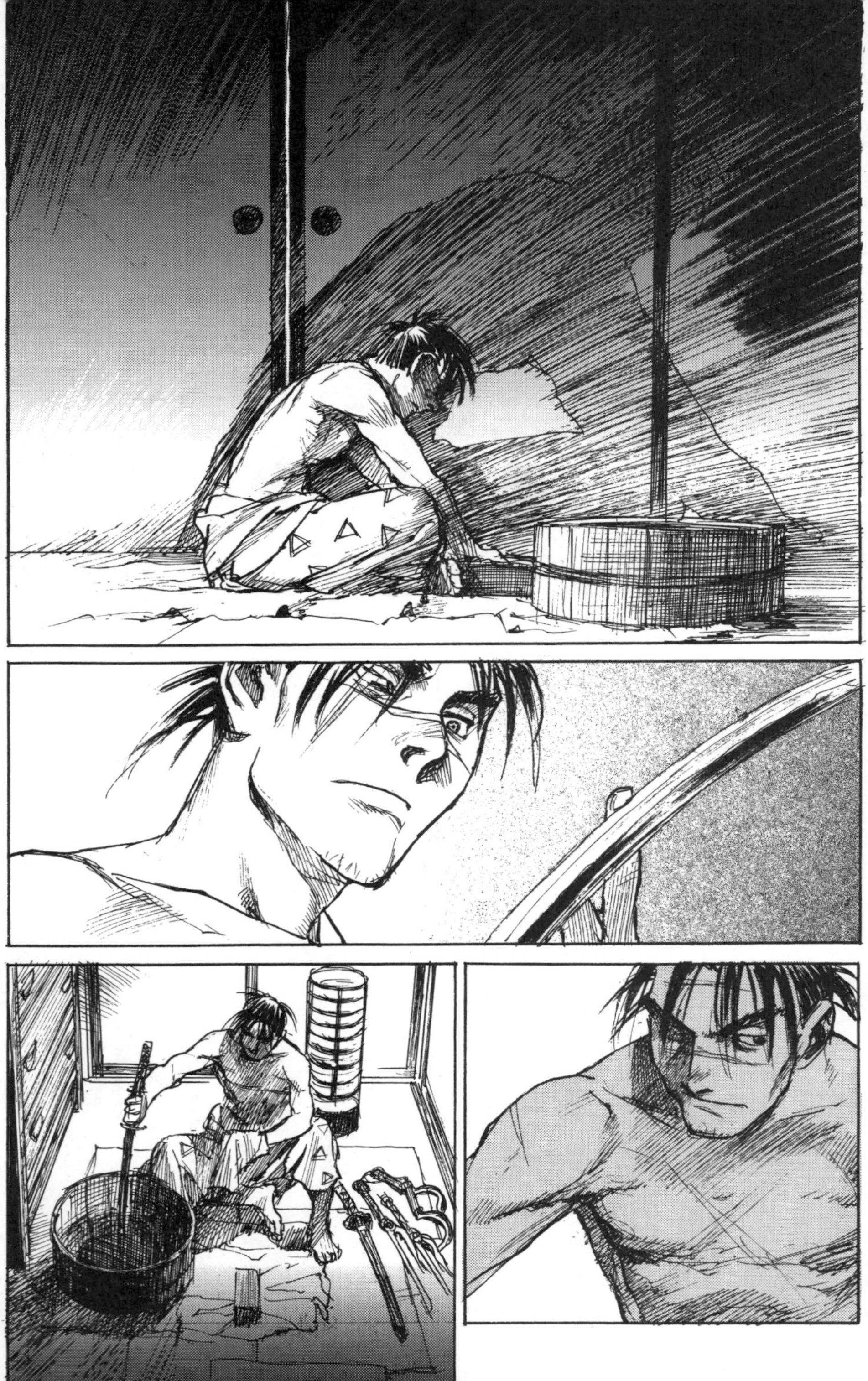

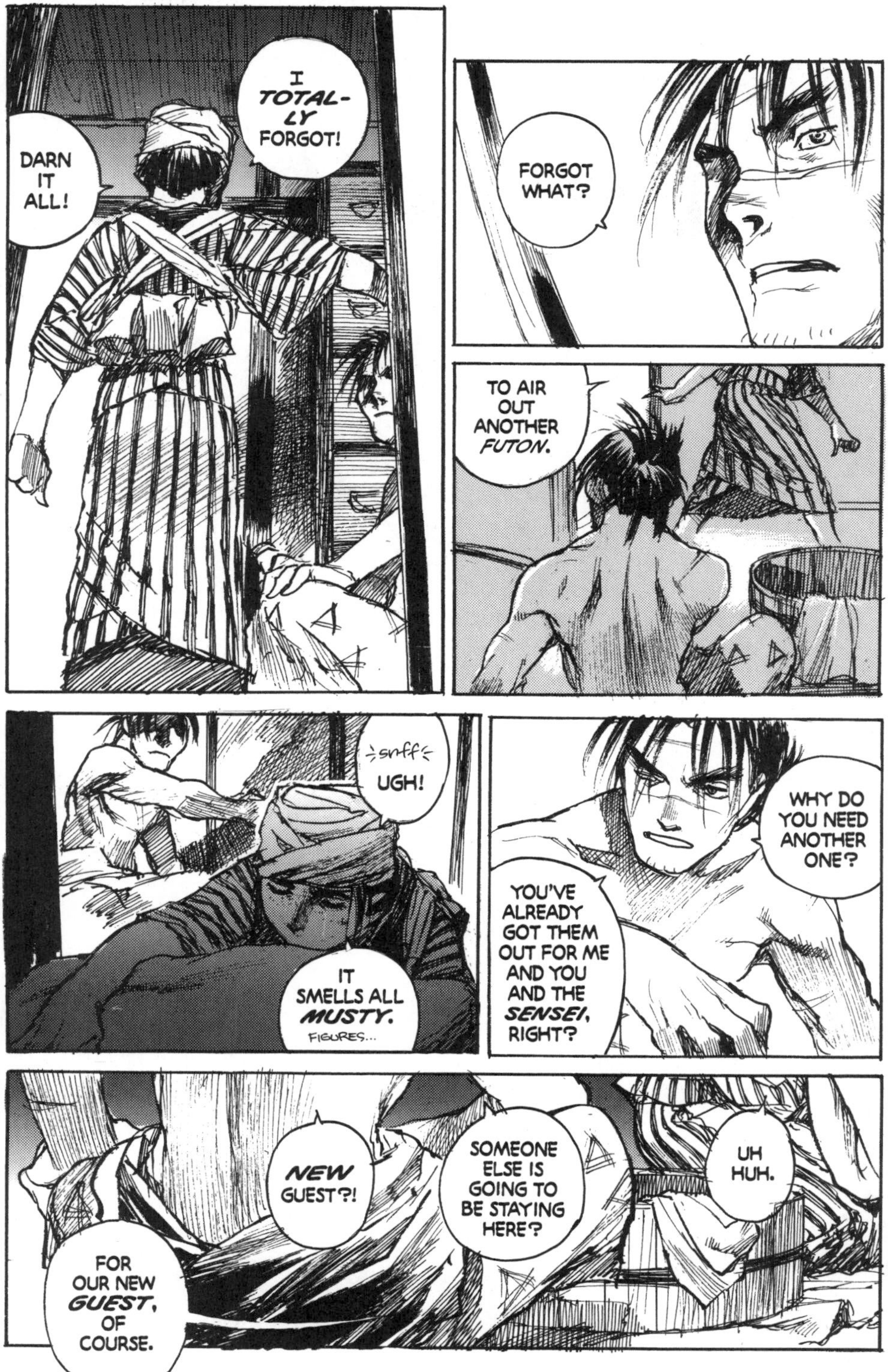
I *TOTAL-LY* FORGOT!
DARN IT ALL!
FORGOT WHAT?
TO AIR OUT ANOTHER *FUTON*.
snff
UGH!
IT SMELLS ALL ***MUSTY***.
FIGURES...
WHY DO YOU NEED ANOTHER ONE?
YOU'VE ALREADY GOT THEM OUT FOR ME AND YOU AND THE ***SENSEI***, RIGHT?
FOR OUR NEW ***GUEST***, OF COURSE.
NEW GUEST?!
SOMEONE ELSE IS GOING TO BE STAYING HERE?
UH HUH.

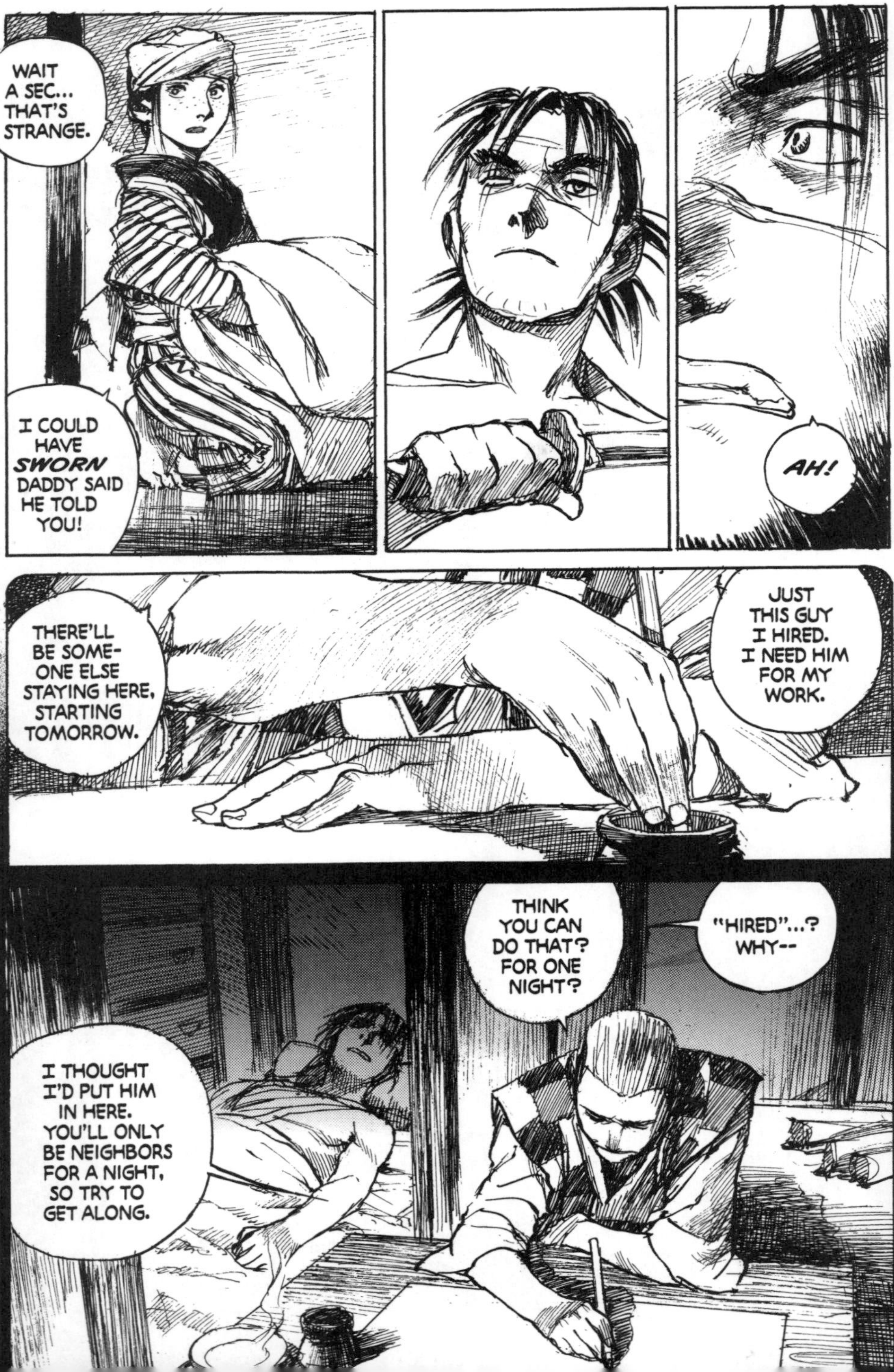
WAIT A SEC... THAT'S STRANGE.
I COULD HAVE *SWORN* DADDY SAID HE TOLD YOU!
AH!
THERE'LL BE SOME-ONE ELSE STAYING HERE, STARTING TOMORROW.
JUST THIS GUY I HIRED. I NEED HIM FOR MY WORK.
"HIRED"...? WHY--
I THOUGHT I'D PUT HIM IN HERE. YOU'LL ONLY BE NEIGHBORS FOR A NIGHT, SO TRY TO GET ALONG.
THINK YOU CAN DO THAT? FOR ONE NIGHT?

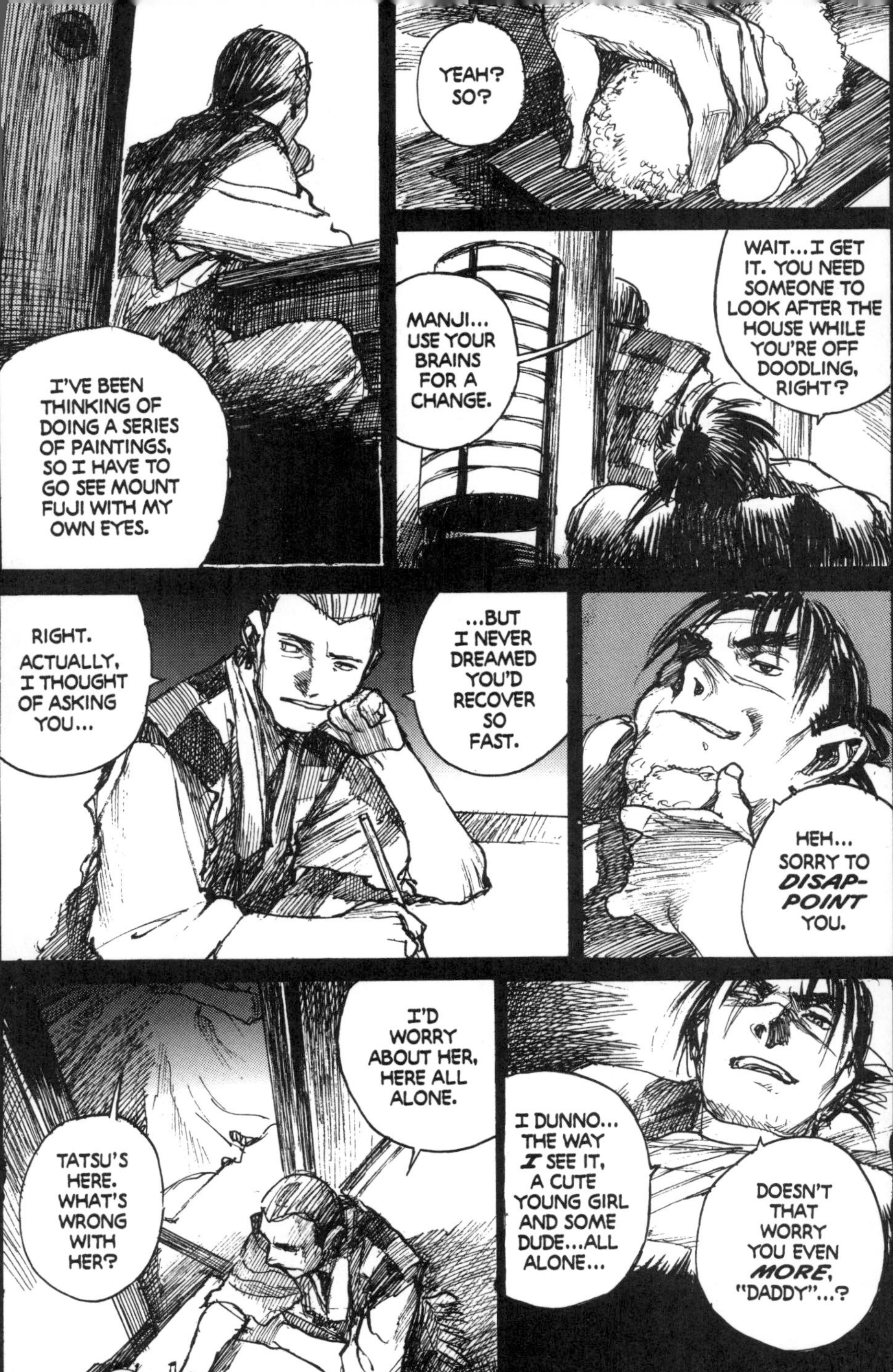

I'VE BEEN THINKING OF DOING A SERIES OF PAINTINGS, SO I HAVE TO GO SEE MOUNT FUJI WITH MY OWN EYES.
YEAH? SO?
MANJI... USE YOUR BRAINS FOR A CHANGE.
WAIT...I GET IT. YOU NEED SOMEONE TO LOOK AFTER THE HOUSE WHILE YOU'RE OFF DOODLING, RIGHT?
RIGHT. ACTUALLY, I THOUGHT OF ASKING YOU...
...BUT I NEVER DREAMED YOU'D RECOVER SO FAST.
HEH... SORRY TO *DISAPPOINT* YOU.
I'D WORRY ABOUT HER, HERE ALL ALONE.
TATSU'S HERE. WHAT'S WRONG WITH HER?
I DUNNO... THE WAY *I* SEE IT, A CUTE YOUNG GIRL AND SOME DUDE...ALL ALONE...
DOESN'T THAT WORRY YOU EVEN *MORE*, "DADDY"...?

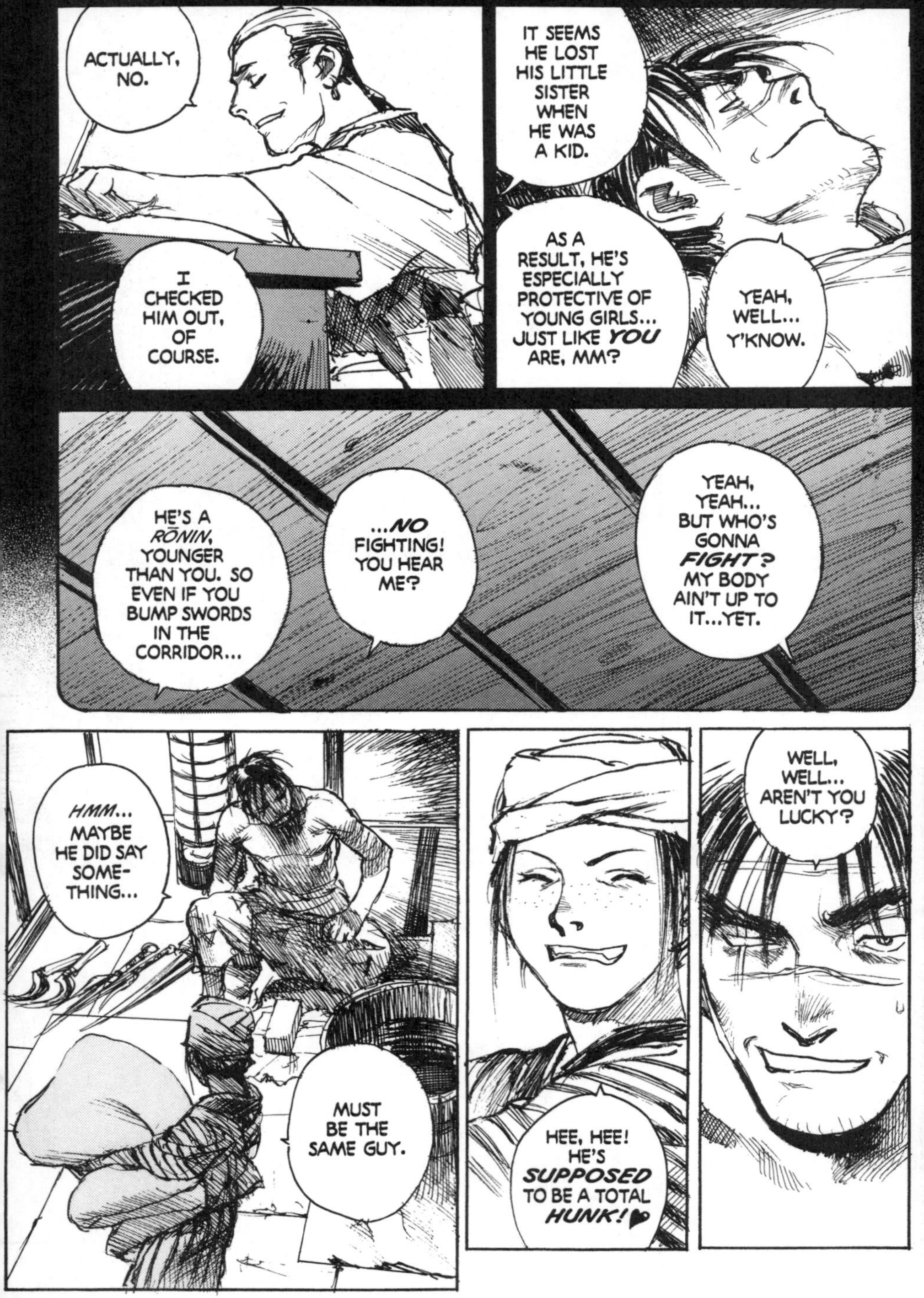
ACTUALLY, NO.
I CHECKED HIM OUT, OF COURSE.
IT SEEMS HE LOST HIS LITTLE SISTER WHEN HE WAS A KID.
AS A RESULT, HE'S ESPECIALLY PROTECTIVE OF YOUNG GIRLS... JUST LIKE *YOU* ARE, MM?
YEAH, WELL... Y'KNOW.
HE'S A *RŌNIN*, YOUNGER THAN YOU. SO EVEN IF YOU BUMP SWORDS IN THE CORRIDOR...
...*NO* FIGHTING! YOU HEAR ME?
YEAH, YEAH... BUT WHO'S GONNA *FIGHT*? MY BODY AIN'T UP TO IT...YET.
HMM... MAYBE HE DID SAY SOME-THING...
MUST BE THE SAME GUY.
HEE, HEE! HE'S *SUPPOSED* TO BE A TOTAL *HUNK!*♥
WELL, WELL... AREN'T YOU LUCKY?

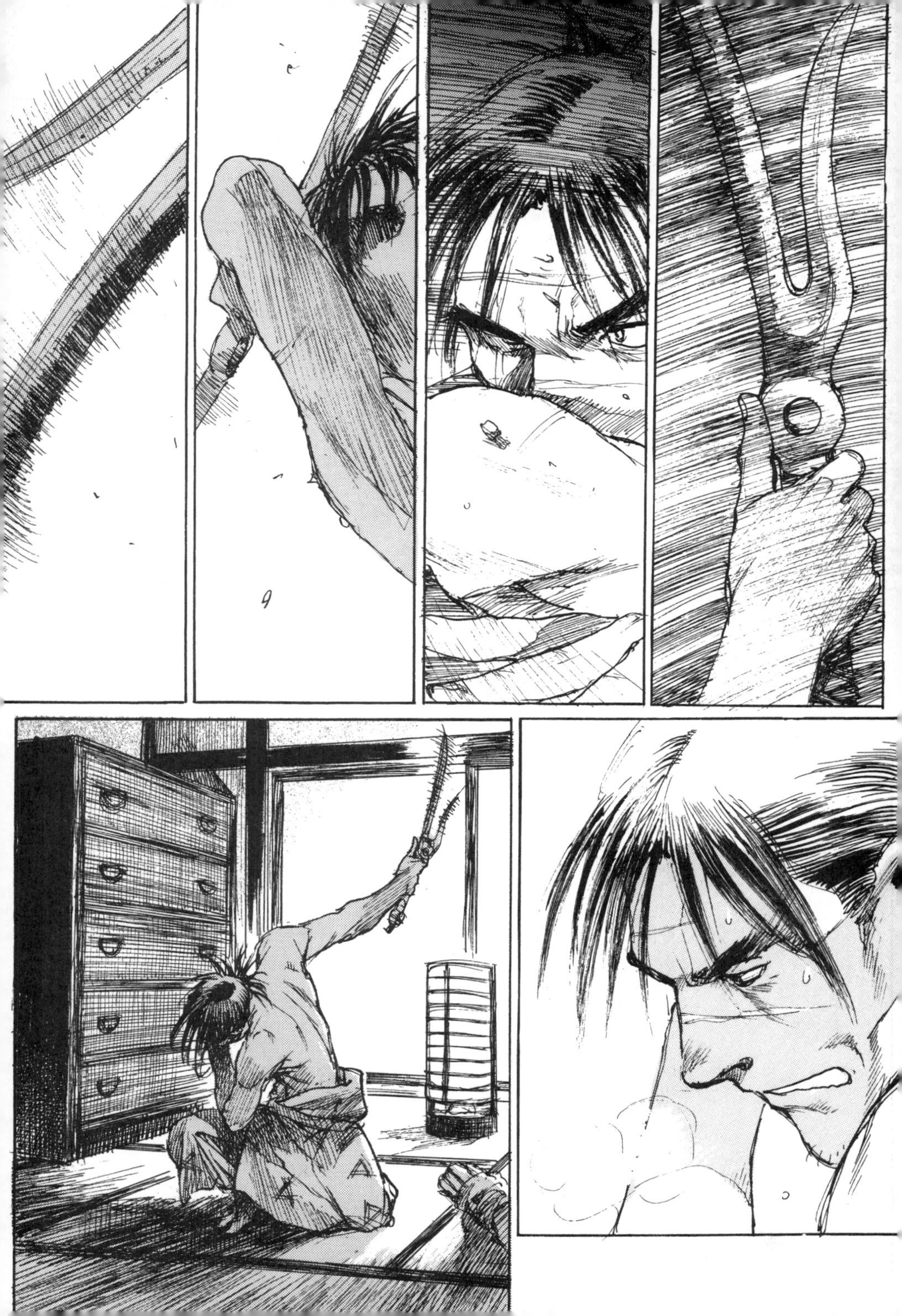

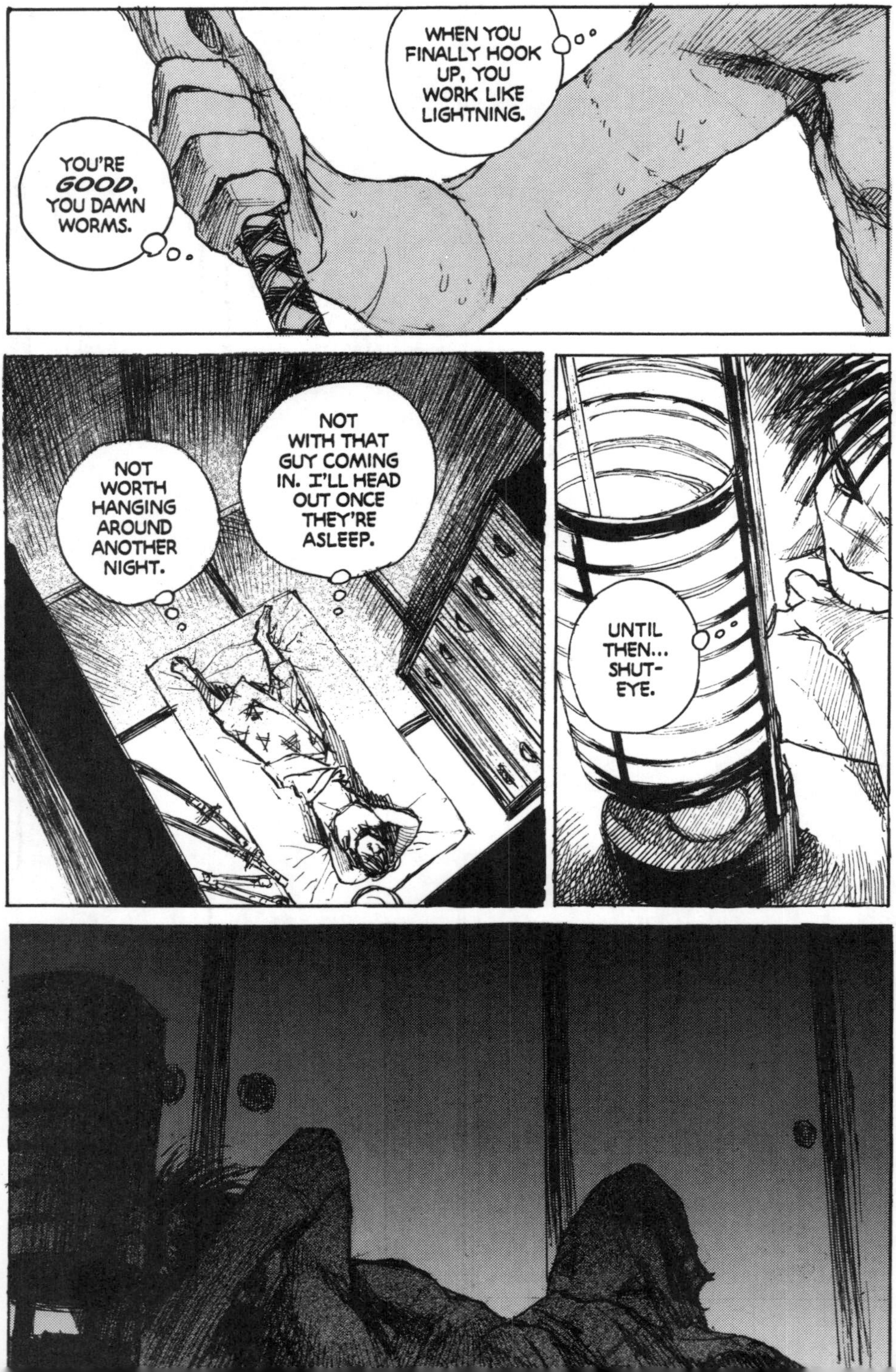
YOU'RE GOOD, YOU DAMN WORMS.
WHEN YOU FINALLY HOOK UP, YOU WORK LIKE LIGHTNING.
NOT WORTH HANGING AROUND ANOTHER NIGHT.
NOT WITH THAT GUY COMING IN. I'LL HEAD OUT ONCE THEY'RE ASLEEP.
UNTIL THEN... SHUT-EYE.

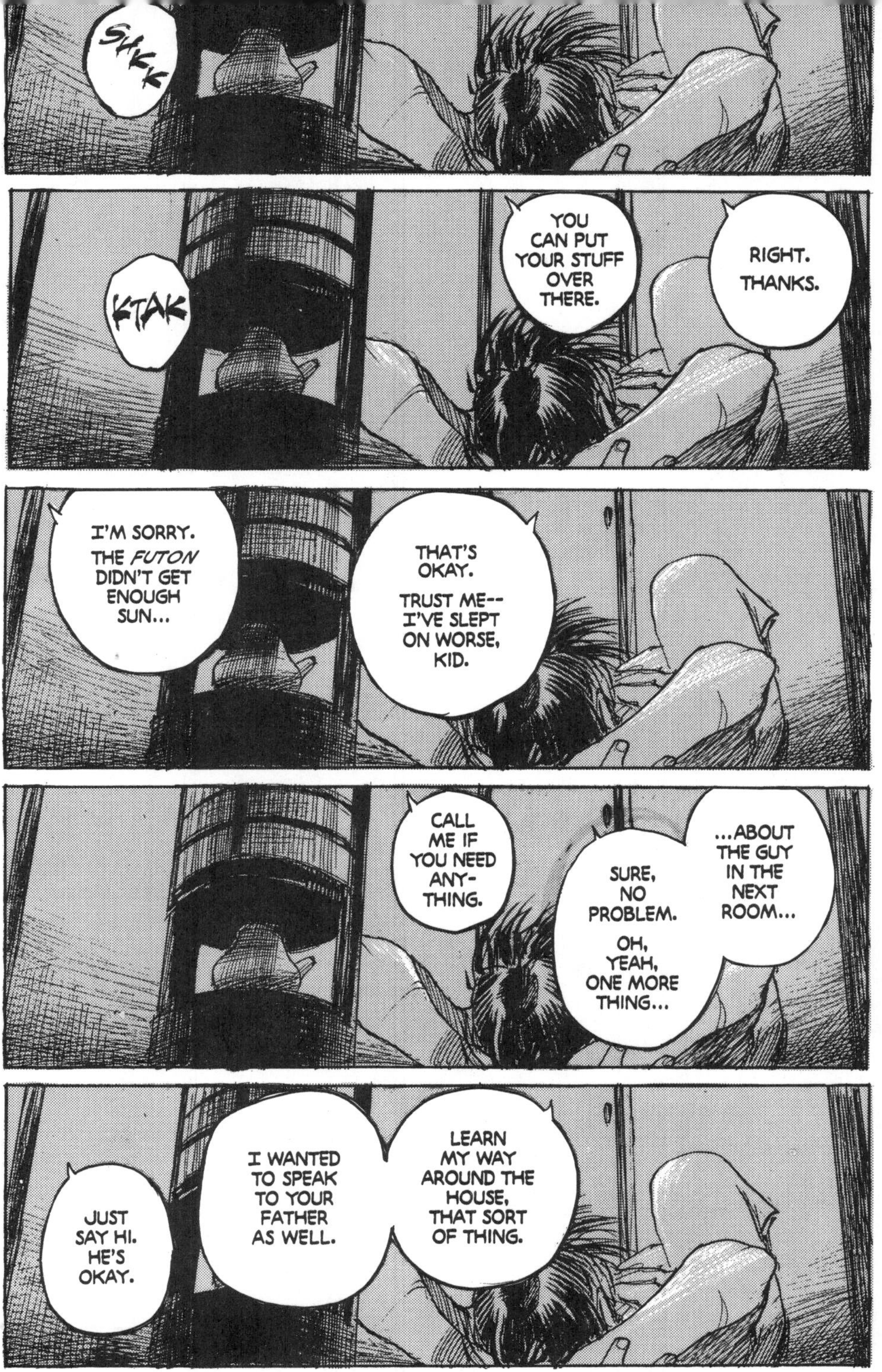
SHKK
KTAK
YOU CAN PUT YOUR STUFF OVER THERE.
RIGHT. THANKS.
I'M SORRY. THE *FUTON* DIDN'T GET ENOUGH SUN...
THAT'S OKAY. TRUST ME-- I'VE SLEPT ON WORSE, KID.
CALL ME IF YOU NEED ANY-THING.
SURE, NO PROBLEM. OH, YEAH, ONE MORE THING...
...ABOUT THE GUY IN THE NEXT ROOM...
JUST SAY HI. HE'S OKAY.
I WANTED TO SPEAK TO YOUR FATHER AS WELL.
LEARN MY WAY AROUND THE HOUSE, THAT SORT OF THING.

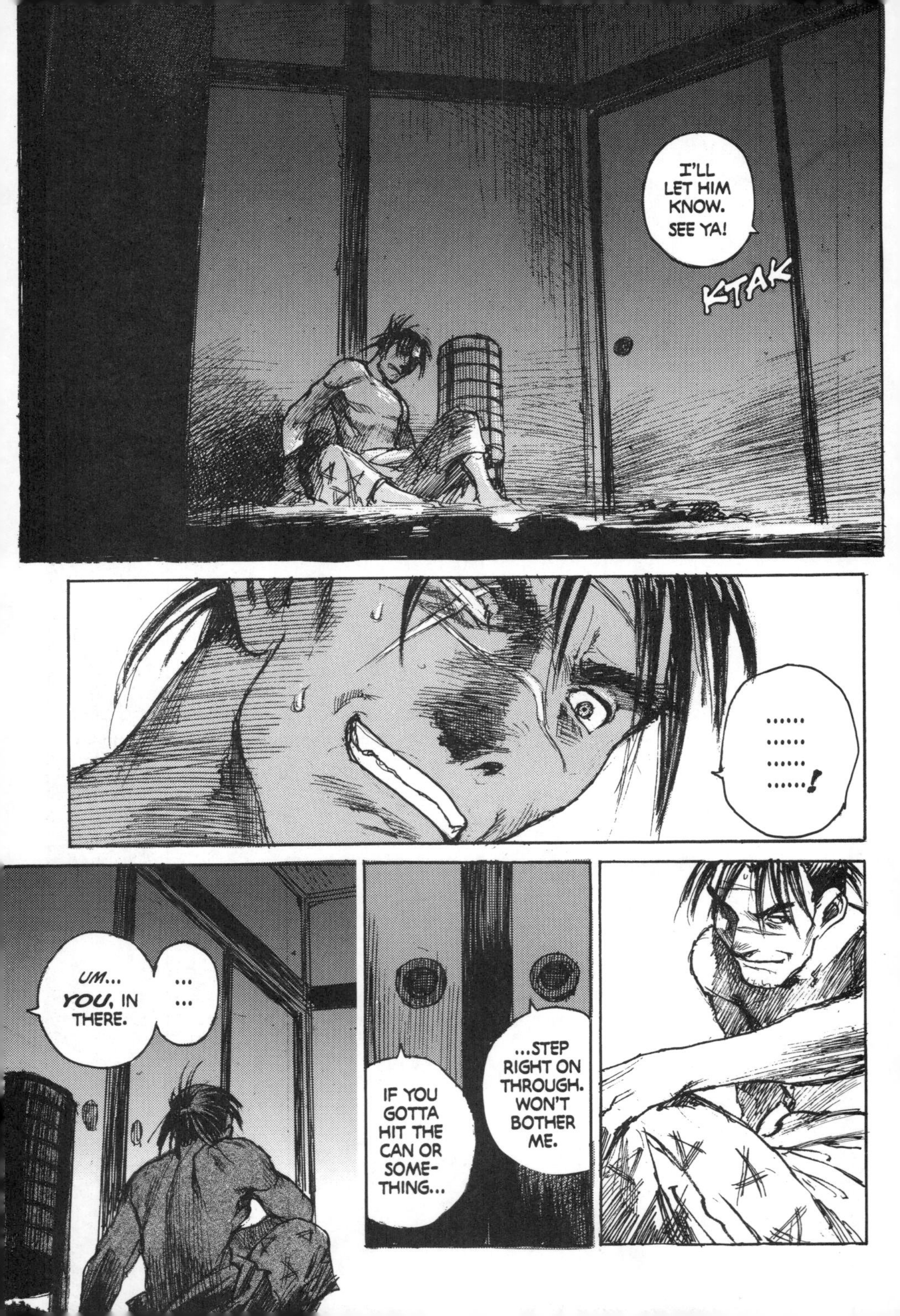
I'LL LET HIM KNOW. SEE YA!
KTAK
......
......
......
.......!
UM... YOU, IN THERE.
...
...
IF YOU GOTTA HIT THE CAN OR SOME-THING...
...STEP RIGHT ON THROUGH. WON'T BOTHER ME.

THANK YOU KINDLY.

I'LL TRY NOT TO...

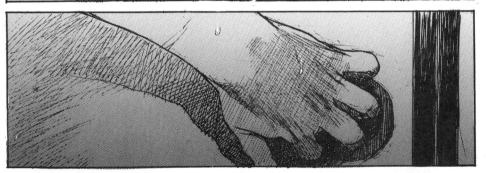

SLISSH

WHAM!

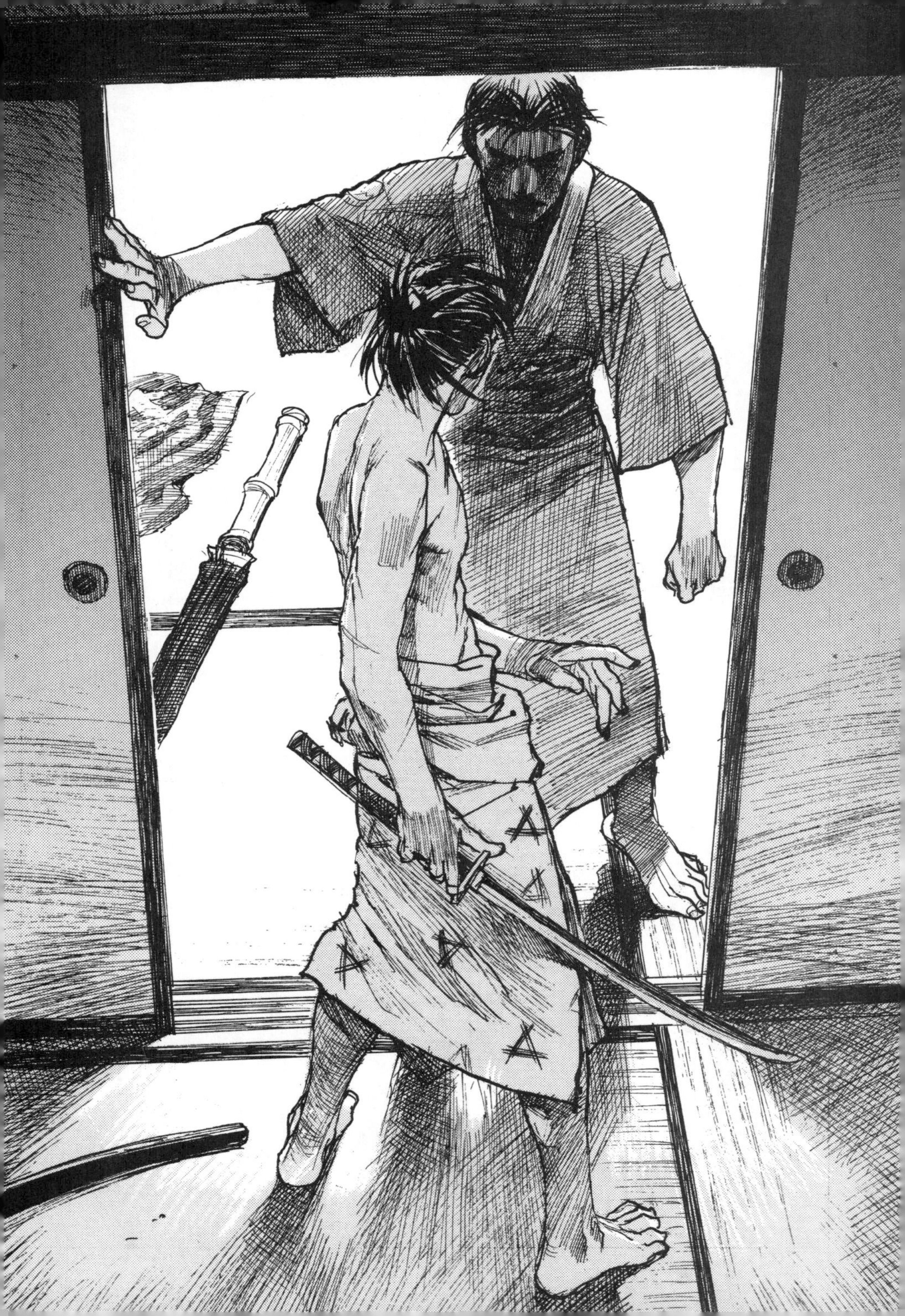

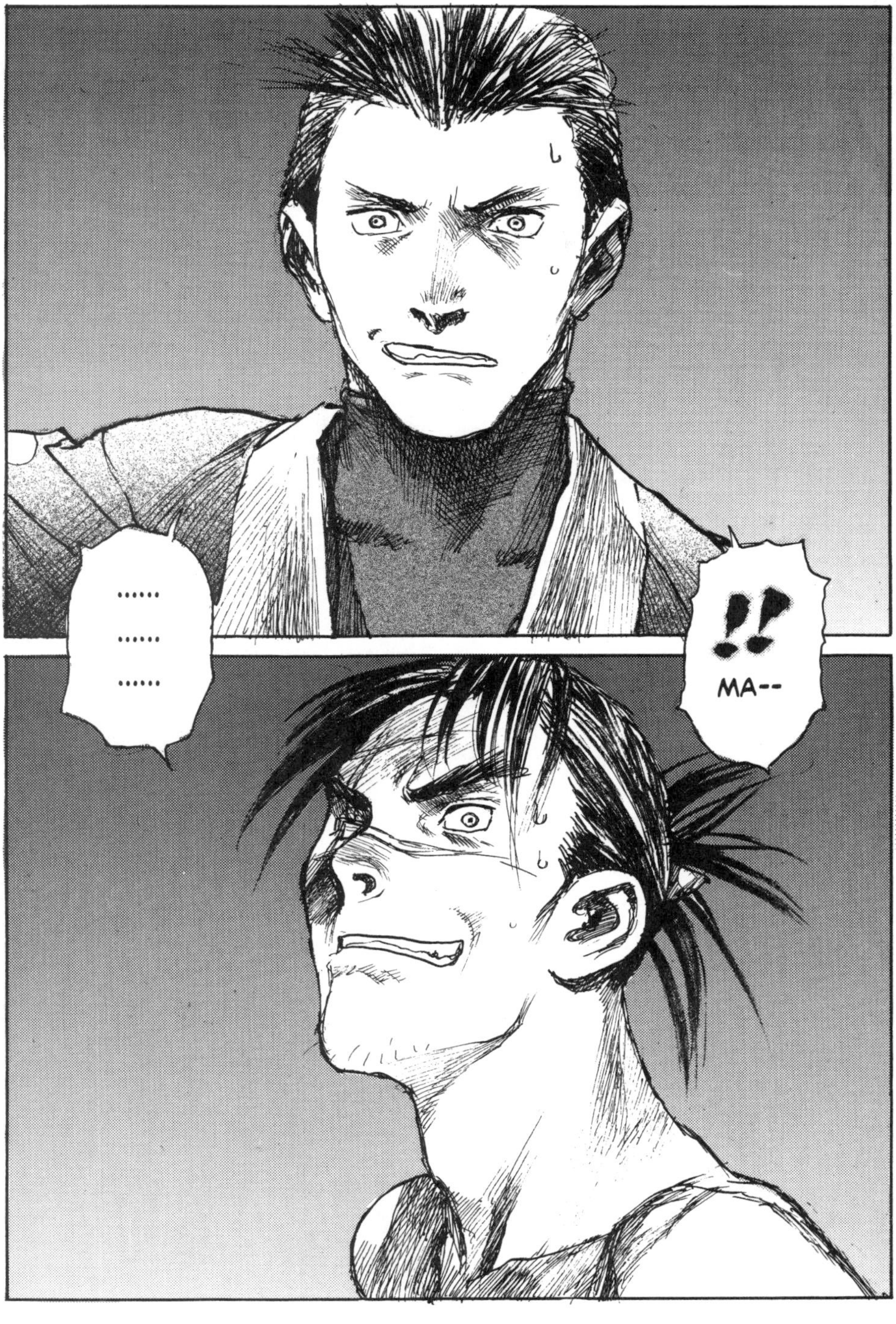
......
......
......
!!
MA--

OOPS!

I FORGOT TO TELL HIM...

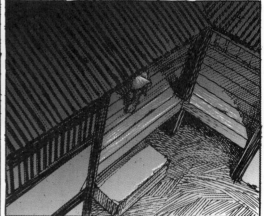

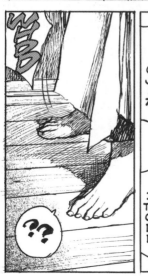

YOU'RE NOT GETTING OFF WITH JUST YOUR STOMACH *THIS* TIME, PAL!

HEY, I'M NOT THE *ONLY* ONE WHO DIDN'T DIE, DAMMIT!

ER...
WHAT
ARE YOU
DOING?

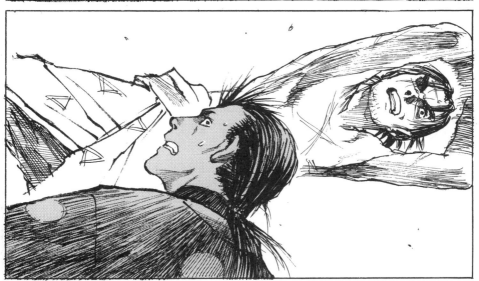

AH...
TATSUBŌ...

WE...
ER...
UM...

......
......
......

......
...?

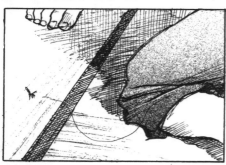

Uh...
YEAH!

KILLING
MOSQUI-
TOES!

YOU'VE
GOT
TO BE
KIDDING
ME!

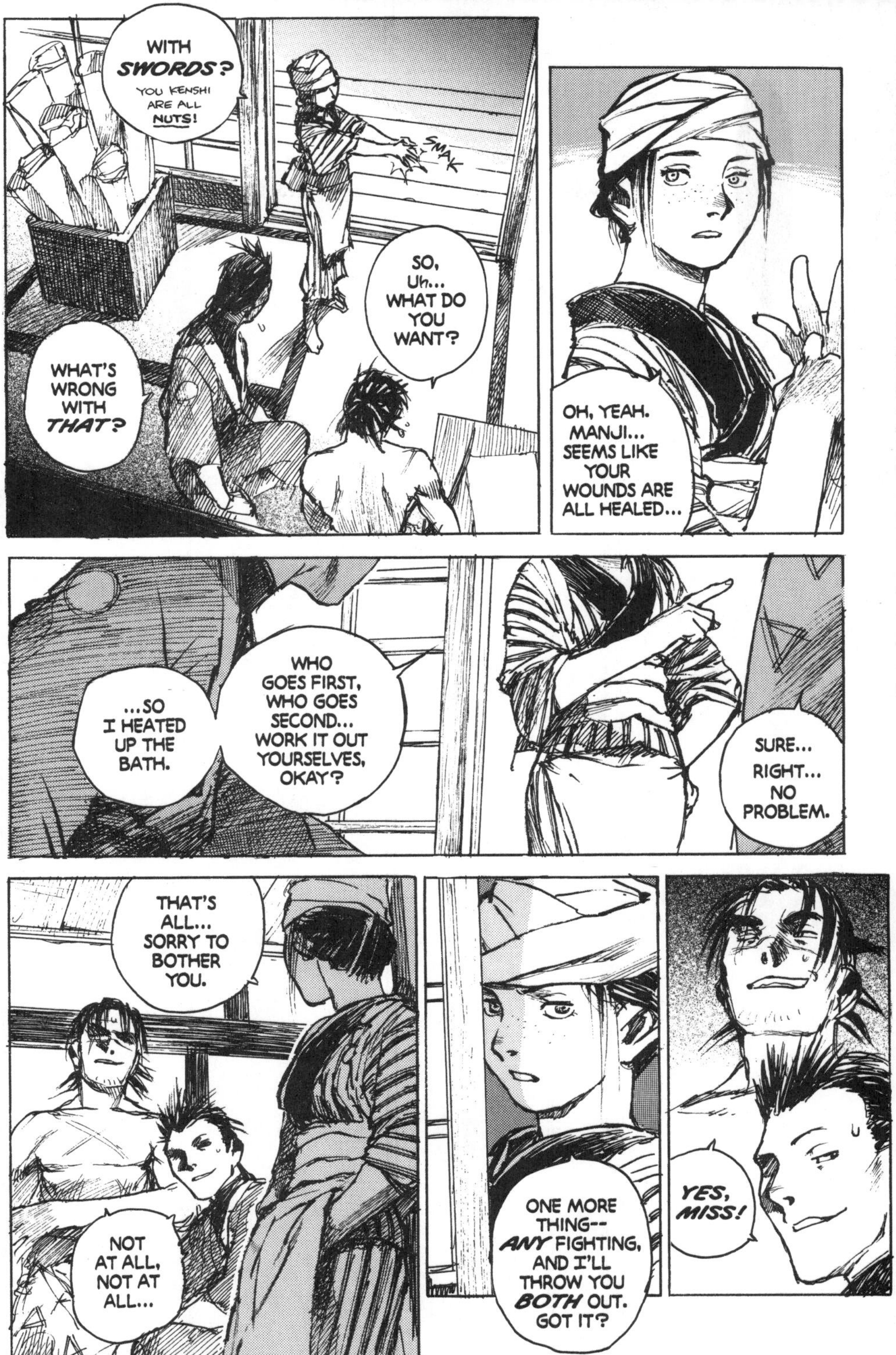
WITH SWORDS? YOU KENSHI ARE ALL NUTS!
SMAK
SO, Uh... WHAT DO YOU WANT?
WHAT'S WRONG WITH THAT?
OH, YEAH. MANJI... SEEMS LIKE YOUR WOUNDS ARE ALL HEALED...
...SO I HEATED UP THE BATH.
WHO GOES FIRST, WHO GOES SECOND... WORK IT OUT YOURSELVES, OKAY?
SURE... RIGHT... NO PROBLEM.
THAT'S ALL... SORRY TO BOTHER YOU.
NOT AT ALL, NOT AT ALL...
ONE MORE THING-- ANY FIGHTING, AND I'LL THROW YOU BOTH OUT. GOT IT?
YES, MISS!

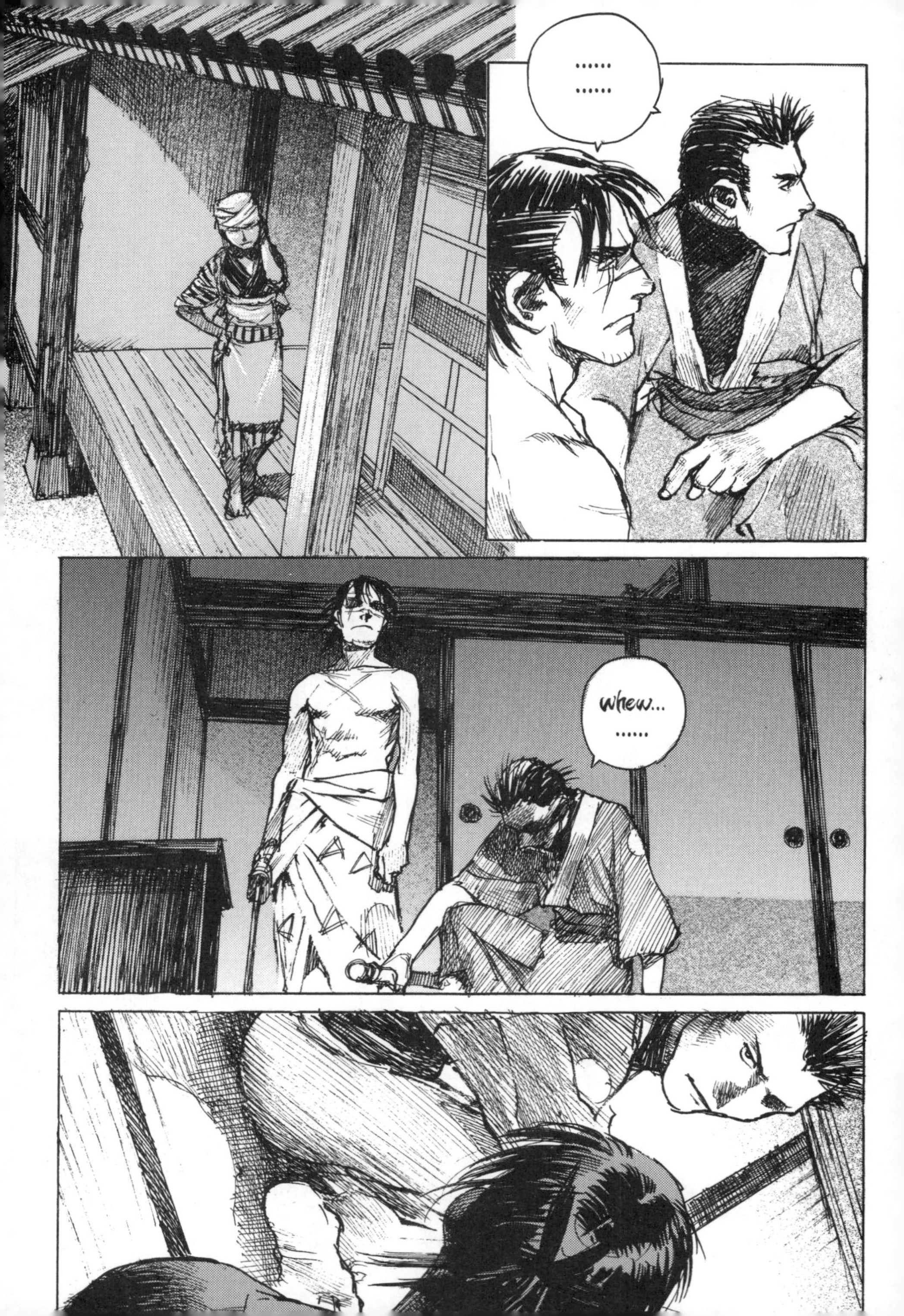
......
......
whew...
......

GO AHEAD. *YOU* SIT, TOO.

IF YOU'RE WORRIED ABOUT THE *ITTŌ-RYŪ*... FORGET IT.

I WALKED. A LONG TIME AGO.

...I JUST DON'T *FEEL* LIKE IT ANY-MORE.

AND REALLY...

NO REASON TO CUT YOU UP.

......
......

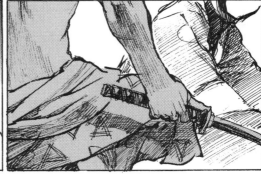

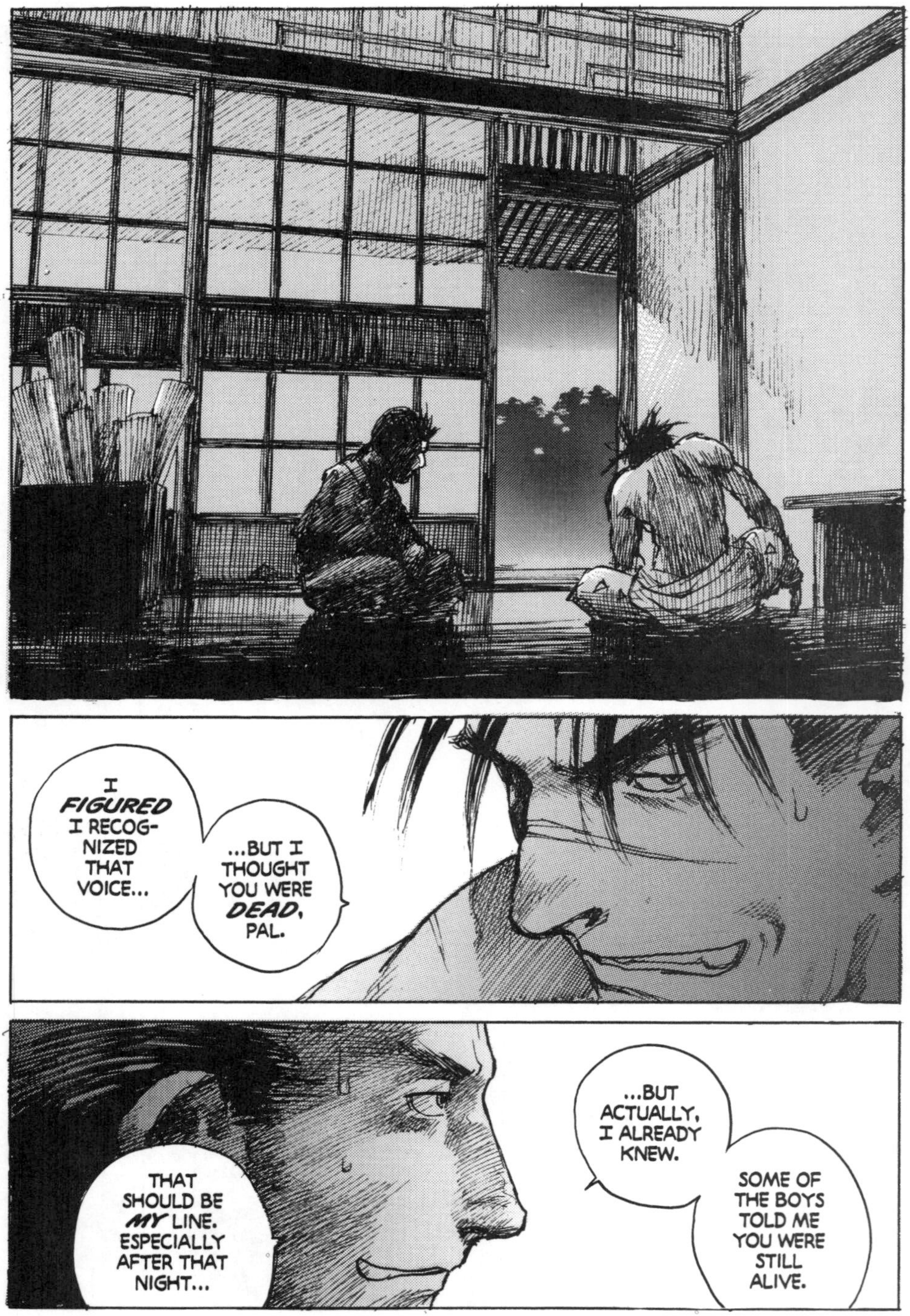
I FIGURED I RECOGNIZED THAT VOICE...
...BUT I THOUGHT YOU WERE DEAD, PAL.
THAT SHOULD BE MY LINE. ESPECIALLY AFTER THAT NIGHT...
...BUT ACTUALLY, I ALREADY KNEW.
SOME OF THE BOYS TOLD ME YOU WERE STILL ALIVE.

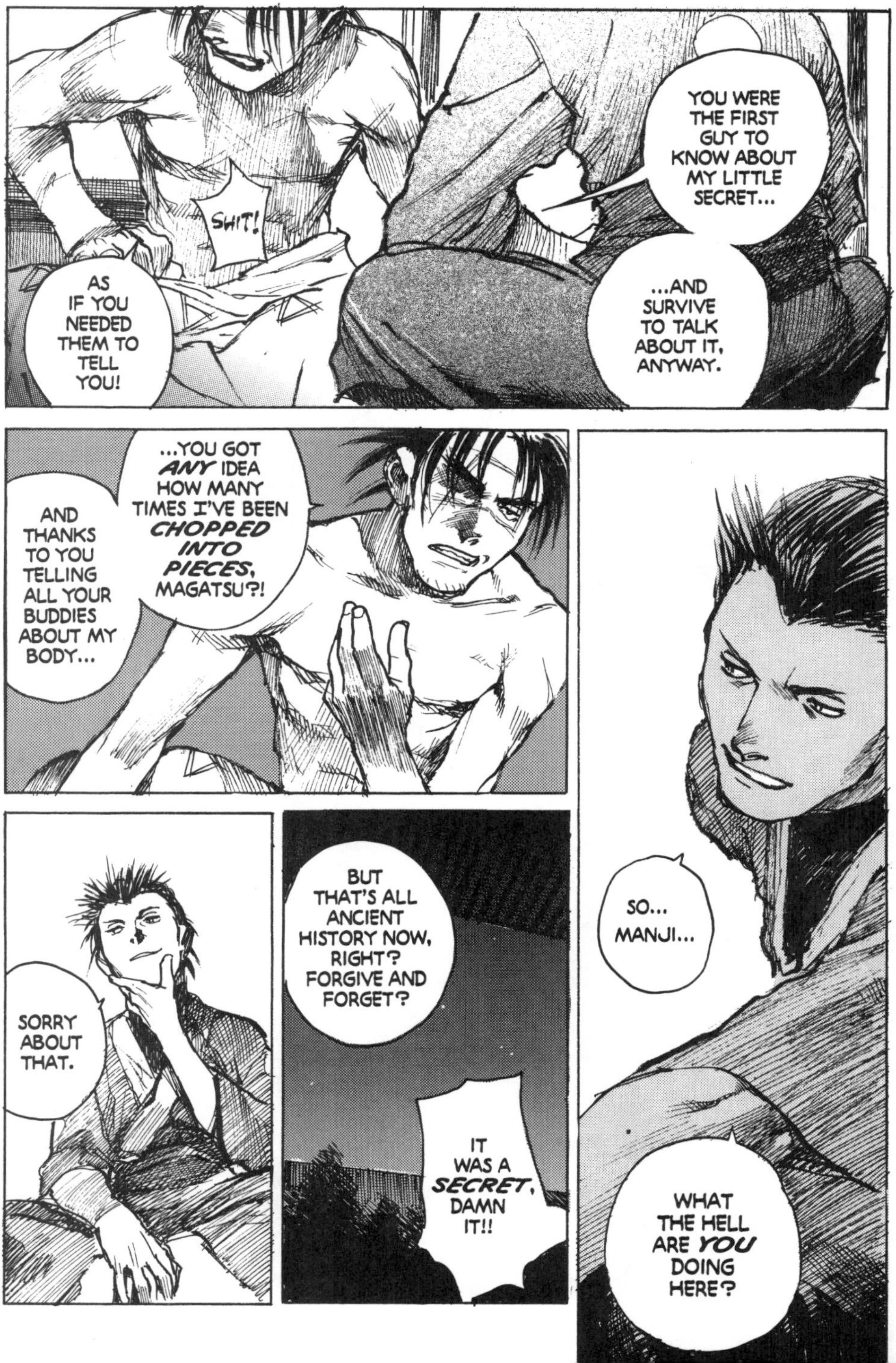
YOU WERE THE FIRST GUY TO KNOW ABOUT MY LITTLE SECRET...
...AND SURVIVE TO TALK ABOUT IT, ANYWAY.
SHIT!
AS IF YOU NEEDED THEM TO TELL YOU!
AND THANKS TO YOU TELLING ALL YOUR BUDDIES ABOUT MY BODY...
...YOU GOT ANY IDEA HOW MANY TIMES I'VE BEEN CHOPPED INTO PIECES, MAGATSU?!
SORRY ABOUT THAT.
BUT THAT'S ALL ANCIENT HISTORY NOW, RIGHT? FORGIVE AND FORGET?
IT WAS A SECRET, DAMN IT!!
SO... MANJI...
WHAT THE HELL ARE YOU DOING HERE?

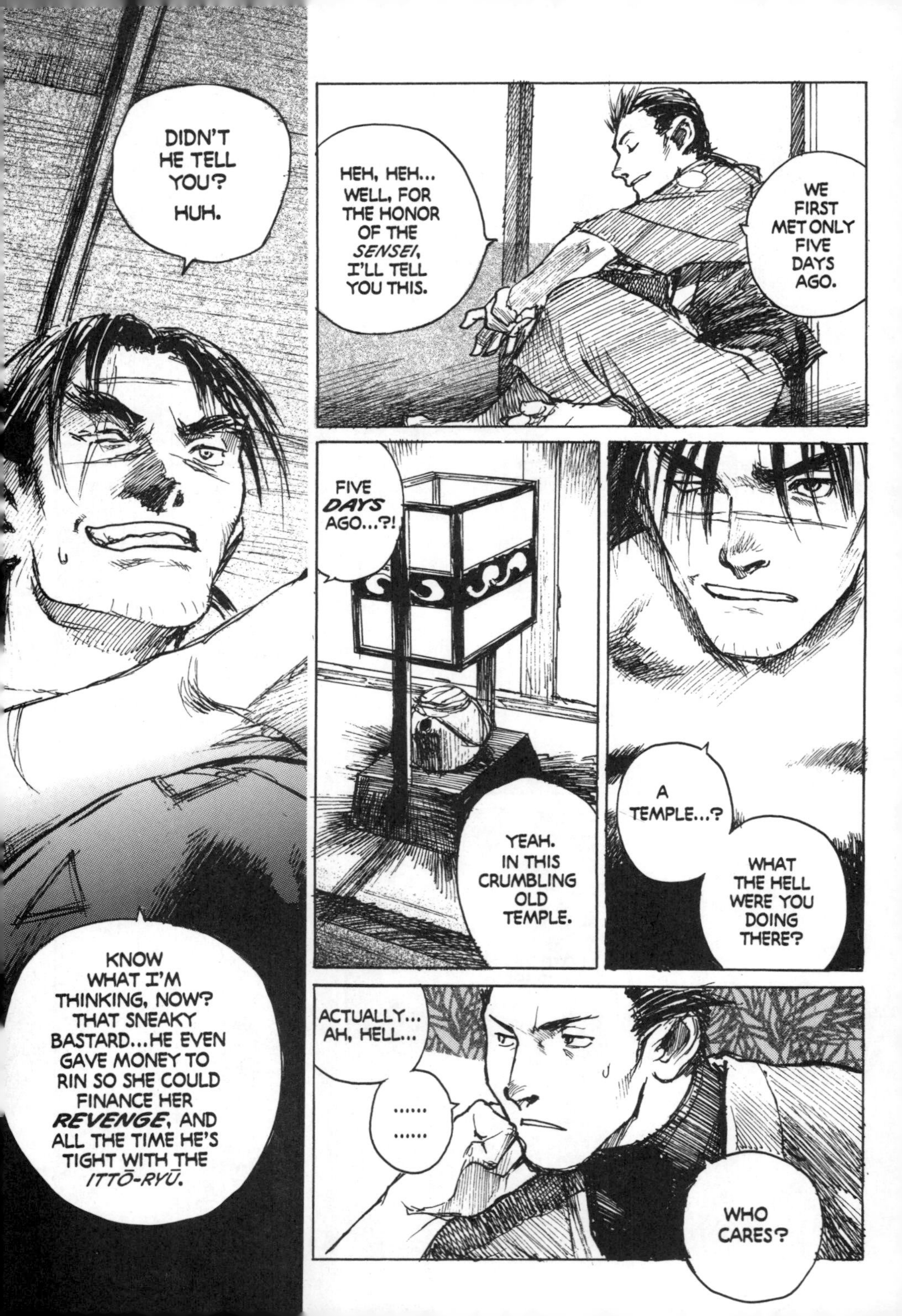
DIDN'T HE TELL YOU?
HUH.
KNOW WHAT I'M THINKING, NOW? THAT SNEAKY BASTARD...HE EVEN GAVE MONEY TO RIN SO SHE COULD FINANCE HER *REVENGE*, AND ALL THE TIME HE'S TIGHT WITH THE *ITTŌ-RYŪ*.
HEH, HEH... WELL, FOR THE HONOR OF THE *SENSEI*, I'LL TELL YOU THIS.
WE FIRST MET ONLY FIVE DAYS AGO.
FIVE *DAYS* AGO...?!
YEAH. IN THIS CRUMBLING OLD TEMPLE.
A TEMPLE...?
WHAT THE HELL WERE YOU DOING THERE?
ACTUALLY... AH, HELL...
....
WHO CARES?

IT DOESN'T REALLY *MATTER*, DOES IT?

IT'S NOT LIKE I'M SOME DAMN *DISCI-PLE!*

WHAT THE HELL'S HE TALKING ABOUT?

LOOK... MANJI.

RIGHT NOW I'M TRACKING THIS... CERTAIN GUY.

SO I CAN *KILL* HIM. IF YOU'RE WONDERING WHY I DON'T EVEN FEEL LIKE HAVING IT OUT WITH *YOU*, WELL...

...THAT'S THE REASON.

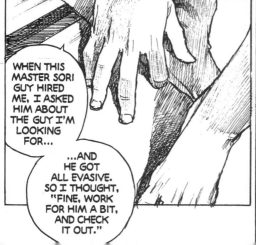

WHEN THIS MASTER SORI GUY HIRED ME, I ASKED HIM ABOUT THE GUY I'M LOOKING FOR...

...AND HE GOT ALL EVASIVE. SO I THOUGHT, "FINE, WORK FOR HIM A BIT, AND CHECK IT OUT."

DON'T KNOW HIS *NAME*, DON'T KNOW HIS *FACE*.

ALL I KNOW IS HE KILLED SOMEONE *IMPORTANT* TO ME.

SO WHO *IS* THE BASTARD?

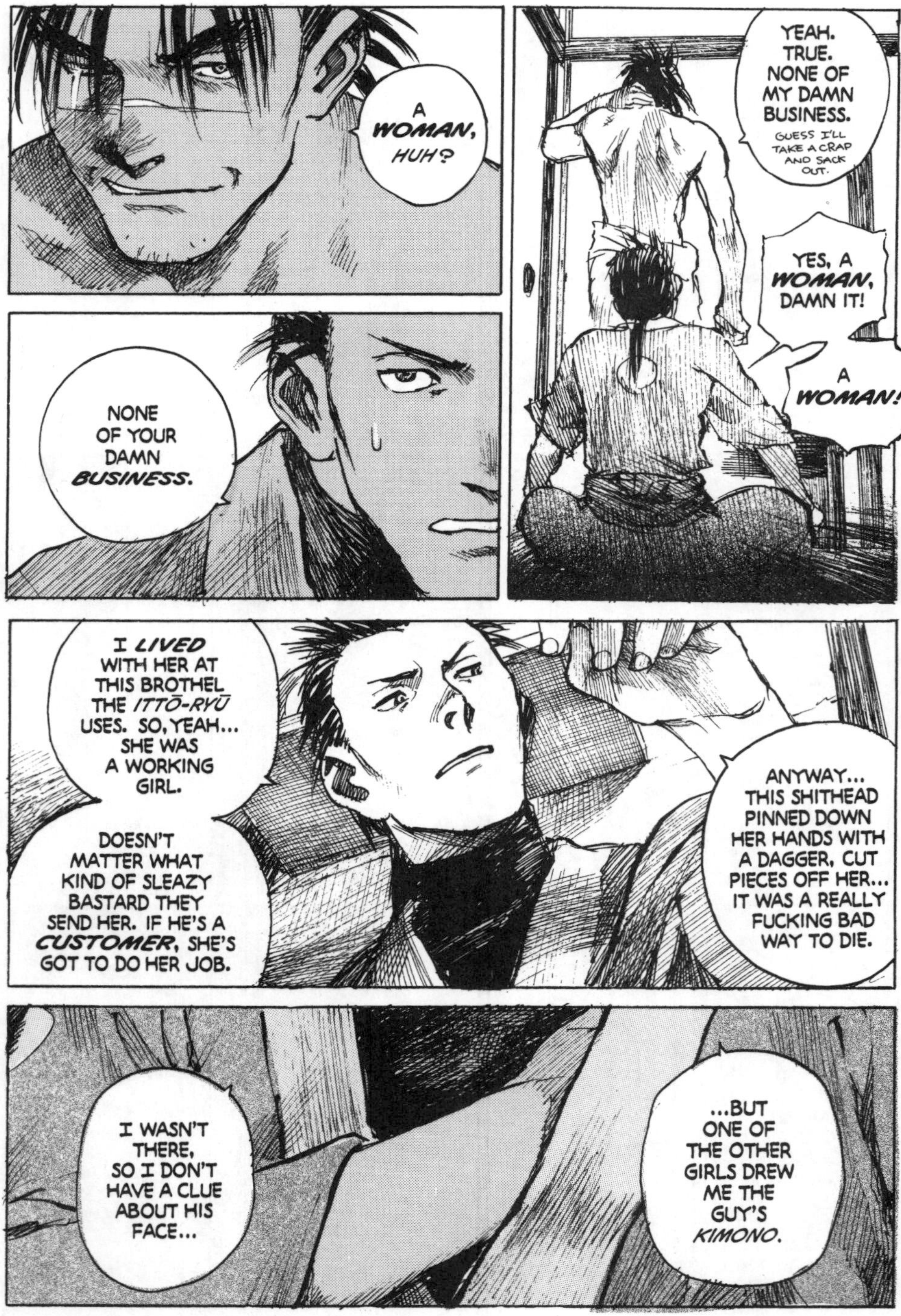
A *WOMAN*, *HUH?*
NONE OF YOUR DAMN *BUSINESS*.
YEAH. TRUE. NONE OF MY DAMN BUSINESS.
GUESS I'LL TAKE A CRAP AND SACK OUT.
YES, A *WOMAN*, DAMN IT!
A *WOMAN!*
I *LIVED* WITH HER AT THIS BROTHEL THE *ITTŌ-RYŪ* USES. SO, YEAH... SHE WAS A WORKING GIRL.
DOESN'T MATTER WHAT KIND OF SLEAZY BASTARD THEY SEND HER. IF HE'S A *CUSTOMER*, SHE'S GOT TO DO HER JOB.
ANYWAY... THIS SHITHEAD PINNED DOWN HER HANDS WITH A DAGGER, CUT PIECES OFF HER... IT WAS A REALLY FUCKING BAD WAY TO DIE.
I WASN'T THERE, SO I DON'T HAVE A CLUE ABOUT HIS FACE...
...BUT ONE OF THE OTHER GIRLS DREW ME THE GUY'S *KIMONO*.

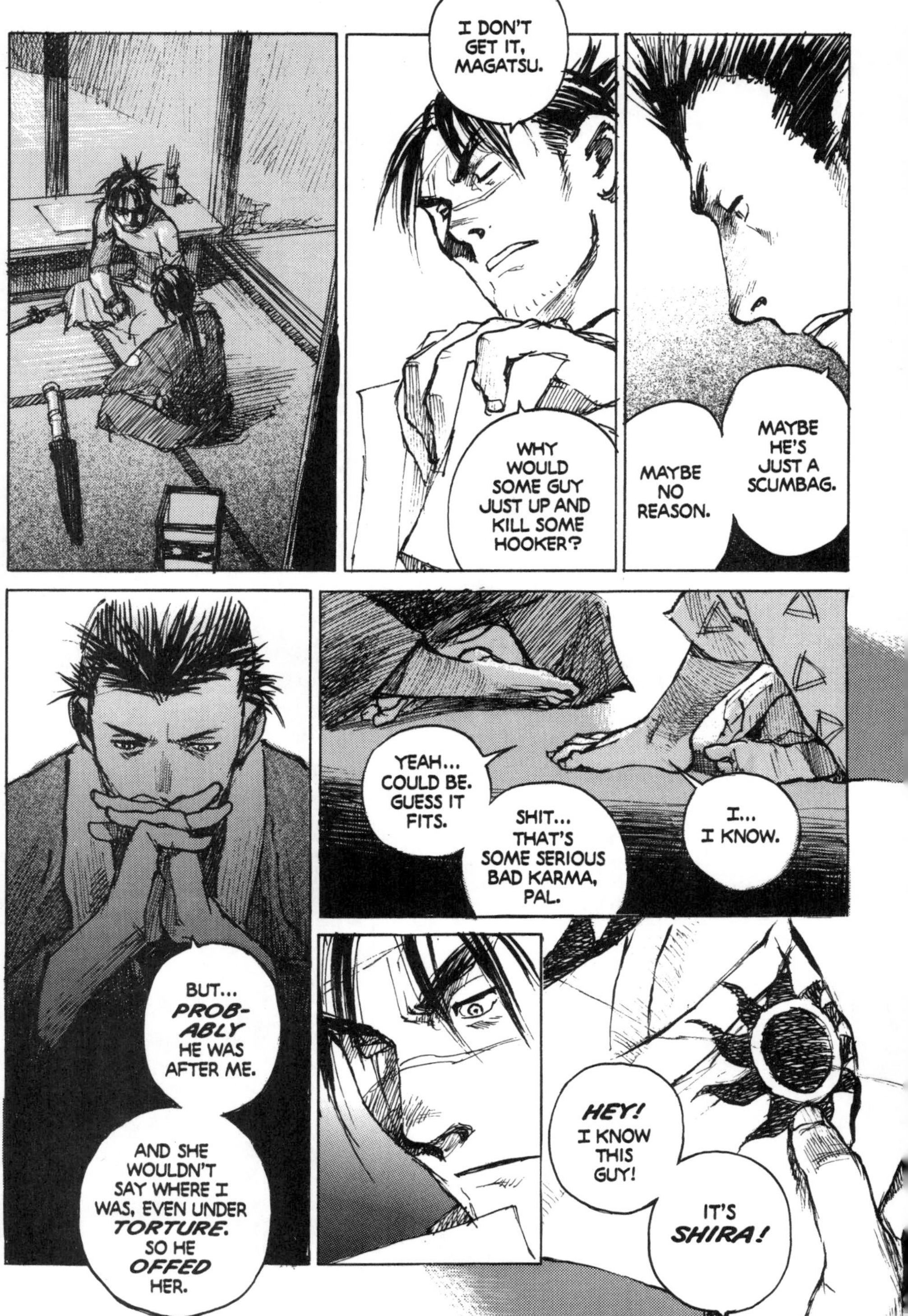
I DON'T GET IT, MAGATSU.
WHY WOULD SOME GUY JUST UP AND KILL SOME HOOKER?
MAYBE NO REASON.
MAYBE HE'S JUST A SCUMBAG.
BUT... PROB-ABLY HE WAS AFTER ME.
AND SHE WOULDN'T SAY WHERE I WAS, EVEN UNDER TORTURE. SO HE OFFED HER.
YEAH... COULD BE. GUESS IT FITS.
SHIT... THAT'S SOME SERIOUS BAD KARMA, PAL.
I... I KNOW.
HEY! I KNOW THIS GUY!
IT'S SHIRA!

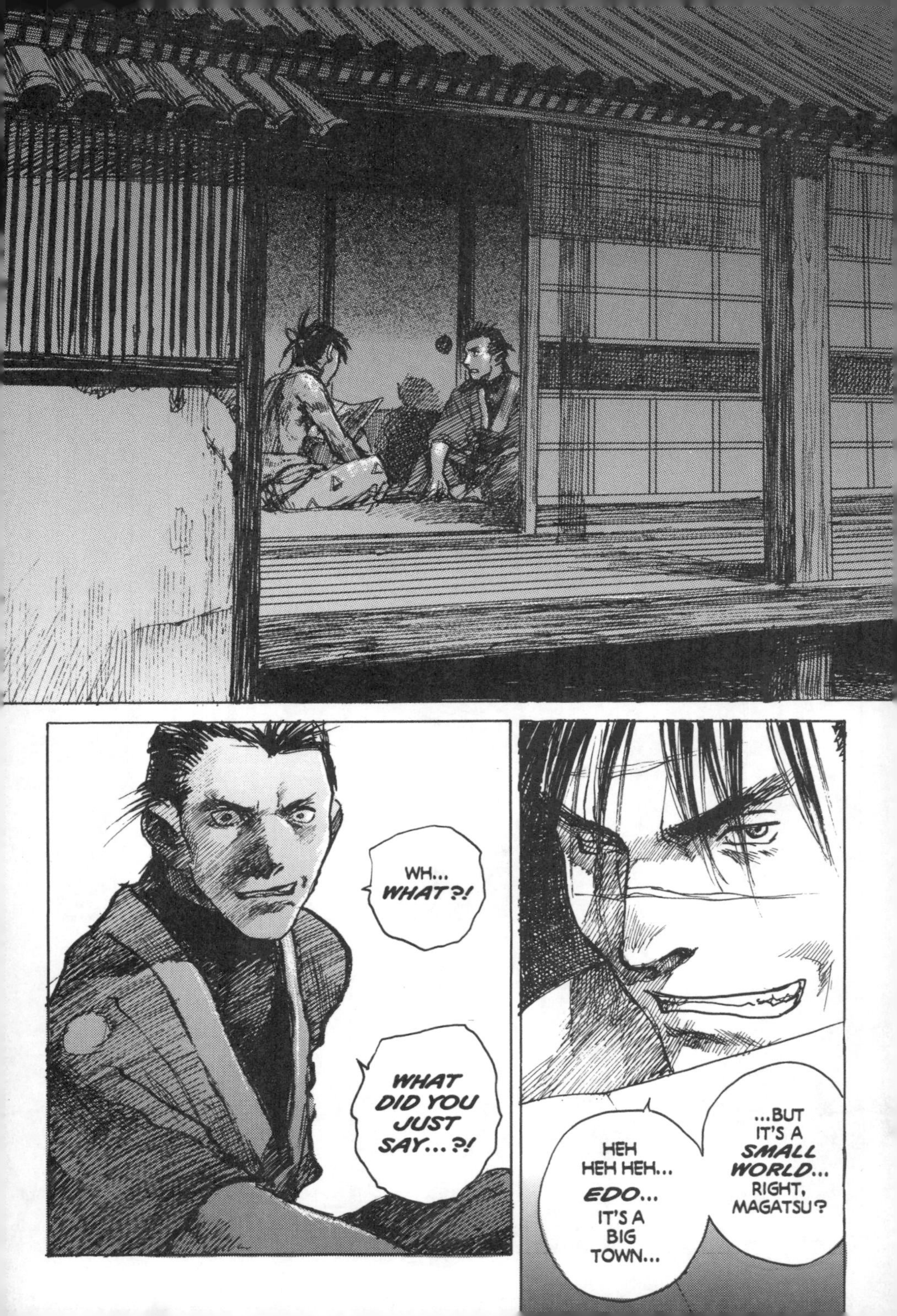
WH... WHAT?!
WHAT DID YOU JUST SAY...?!
HEH HEH HEH... EDO... IT'S A BIG TOWN...
...BUT IT'S A SMALL WORLD... RIGHT, MAGATSU?

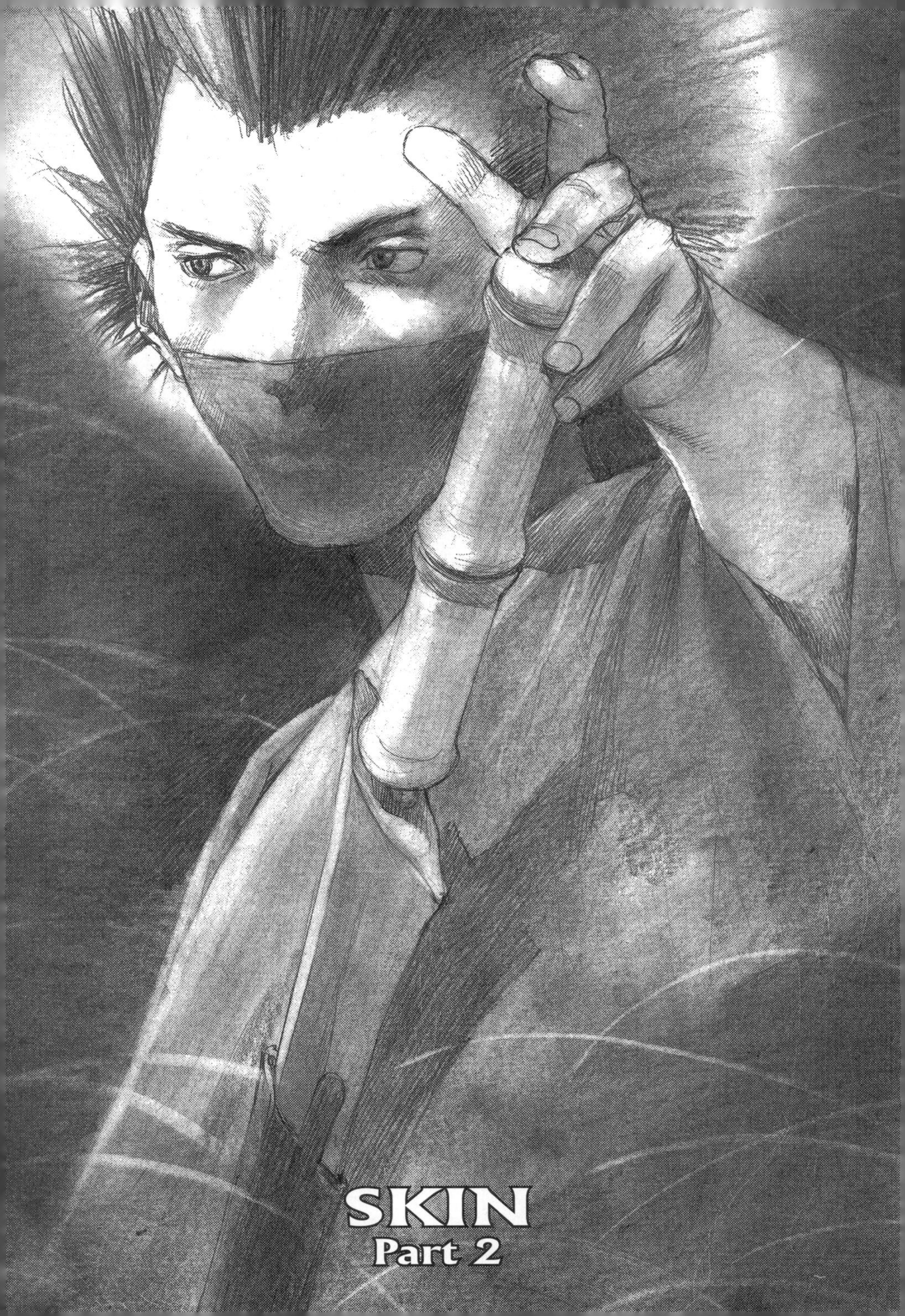
SKIN
Part 2

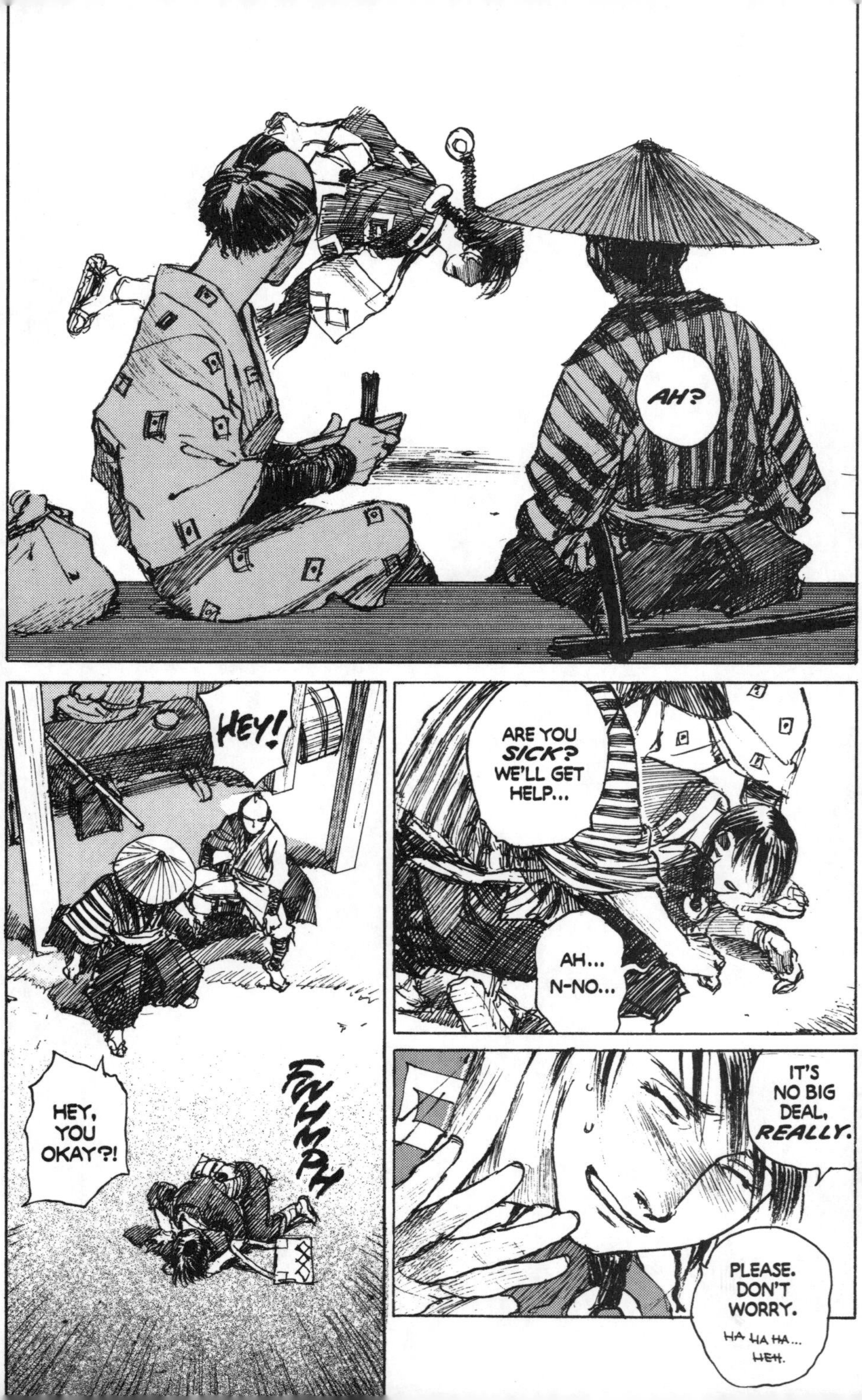

AH?
HEY!
HEY, YOU OKAY?!
FWHMPH
ARE YOU SICK? WE'LL GET HELP...
AH... N-NO...
IT'S NO BIG DEAL, REALLY.
PLEASE. DON'T WORRY.
HA HA HA... HEH.

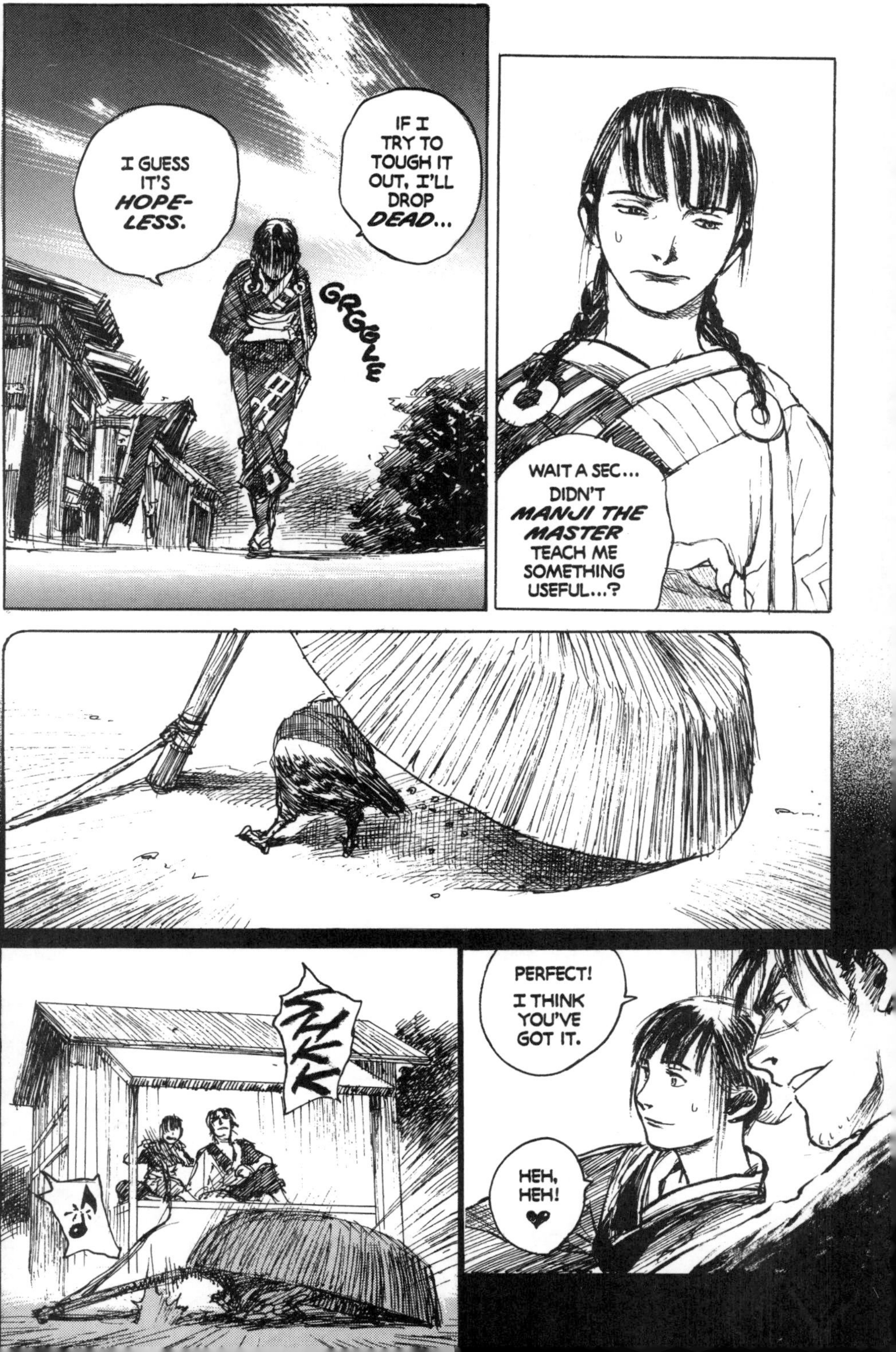
I GUESS IT'S *HOPE-LESS.*
IF I TRY TO TOUGH IT OUT, I'LL DROP *DEAD...*
GRGGLE
WAIT A SEC... DIDN'T *MANJI THE MASTER* TEACH ME SOMETHING USEFUL...?
PERFECT! I THINK YOU'VE GOT IT.
HEH, HEH! ❤

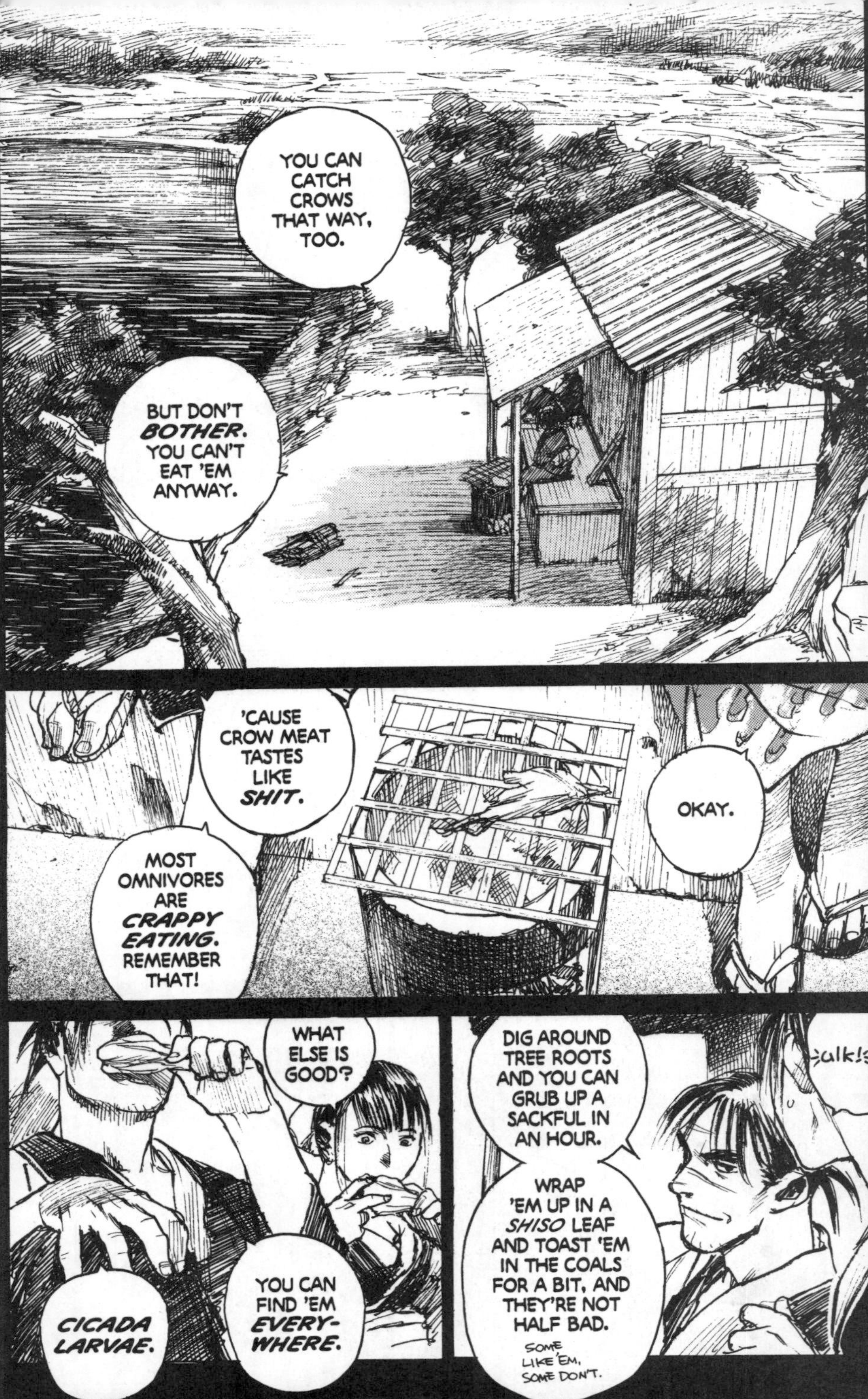
YOU CAN CATCH CROWS THAT WAY, TOO.
BUT DON'T *BOTHER*. YOU CAN'T EAT 'EM ANYWAY.
'CAUSE CROW MEAT TASTES LIKE *SHIT*.
MOST OMNIVORES ARE *CRAPPY EATING*. REMEMBER THAT!
OKAY.
WHAT ELSE IS GOOD?
CICADA LARVAE.
YOU CAN FIND 'EM *EVERY-WHERE*.
DIG AROUND TREE ROOTS AND YOU CAN GRUB UP A SACKFUL IN AN HOUR.
ulk!
WRAP 'EM UP IN A *SHISO* LEAF AND TOAST 'EM IN THE COALS FOR A BIT, AND THEY'RE NOT HALF BAD.
SOME LIKE 'EM, SOME DON'T.

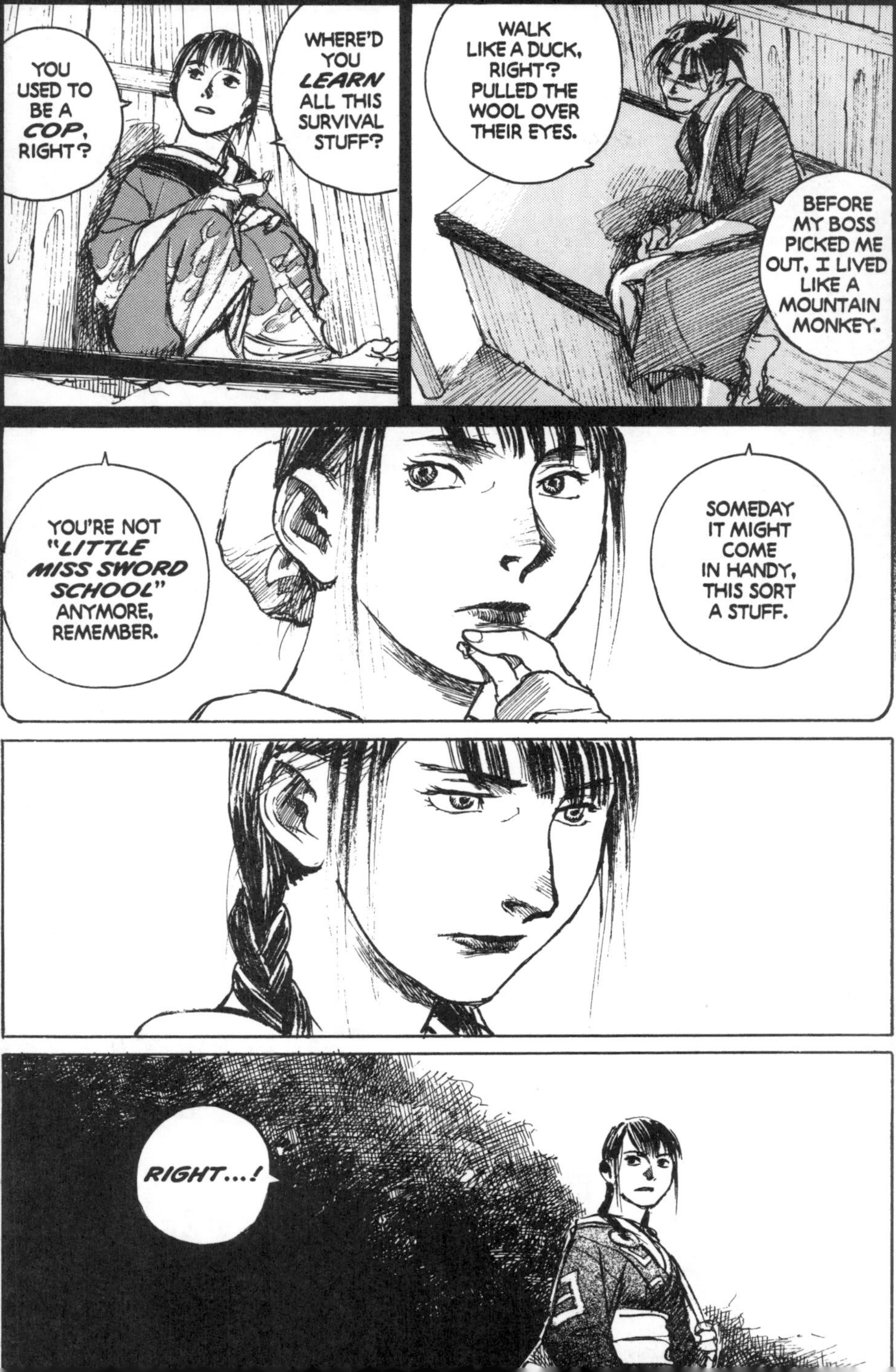
YOU USED TO BE A *COP*, RIGHT?
WHERE'D YOU *LEARN* ALL THIS SURVIVAL STUFF?
WALK LIKE A DUCK, RIGHT? PULLED THE WOOL OVER THEIR EYES.
BEFORE MY BOSS PICKED ME OUT, I LIVED LIKE A MOUNTAIN MONKEY.
YOU'RE NOT "*LITTLE MISS SWORD SCHOOL*" ANYMORE, REMEMBER.
SOMEDAY IT MIGHT COME IN HANDY, THIS SORT A STUFF.
RIGHT...!

NOW...
I'M SURE
MANJI
GAVE
ME A
HOOK...

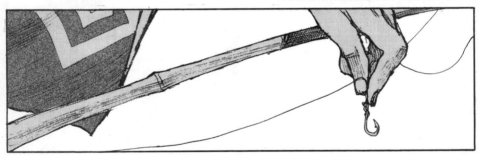

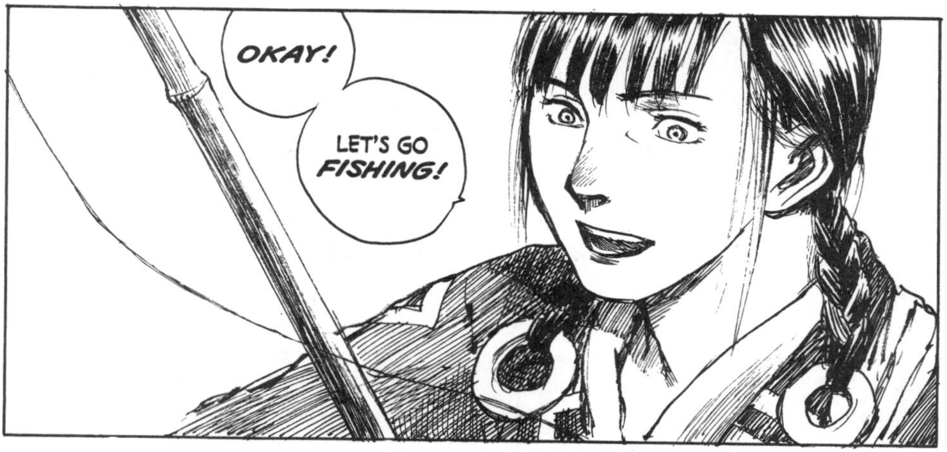
OKAY!
LET'S GO FISHING!
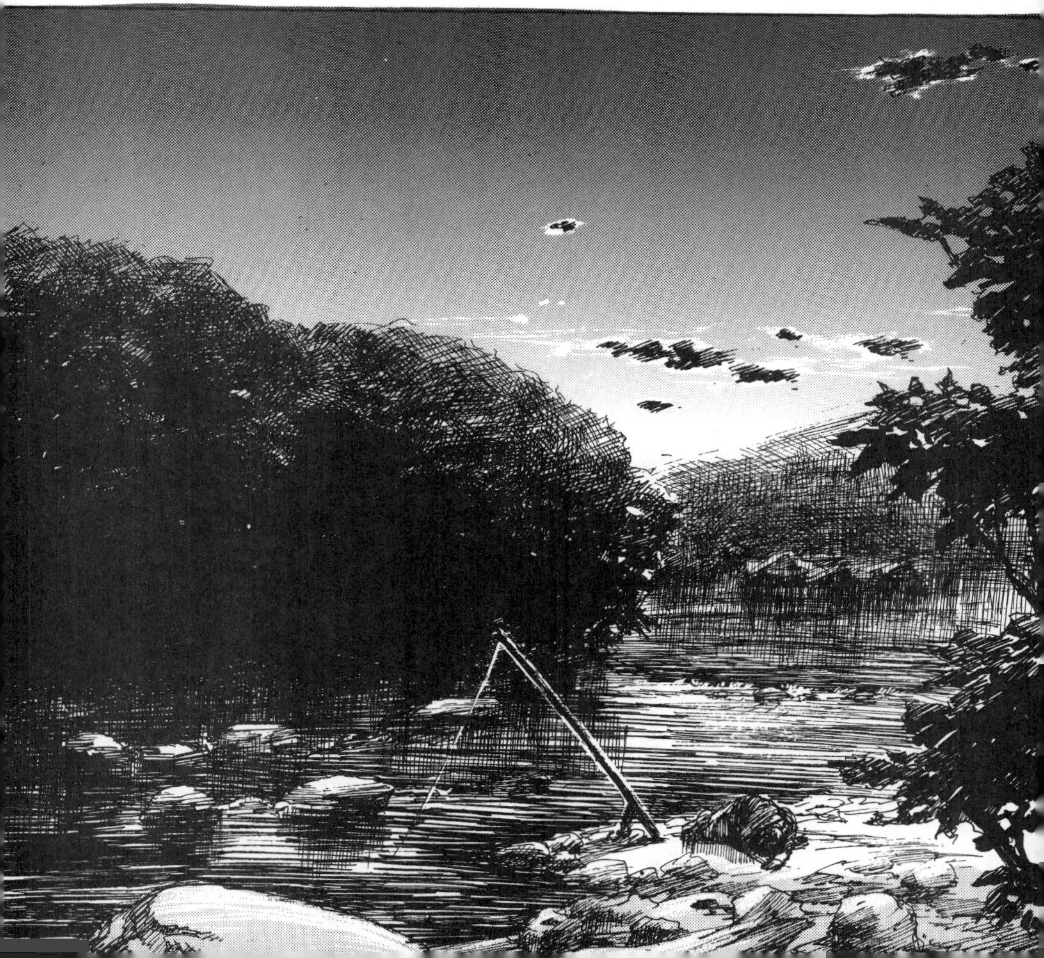

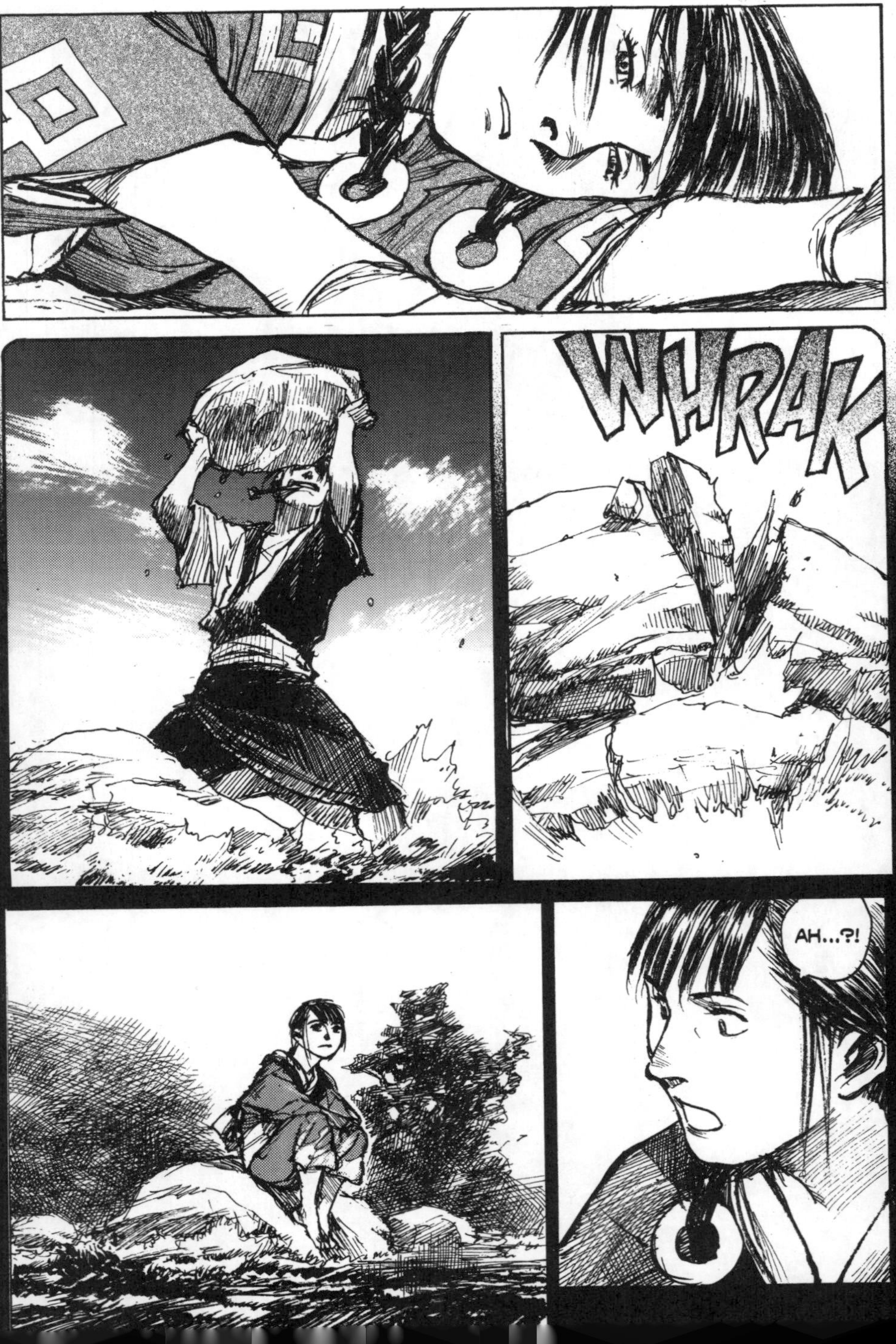
WHRAK
AH...?!

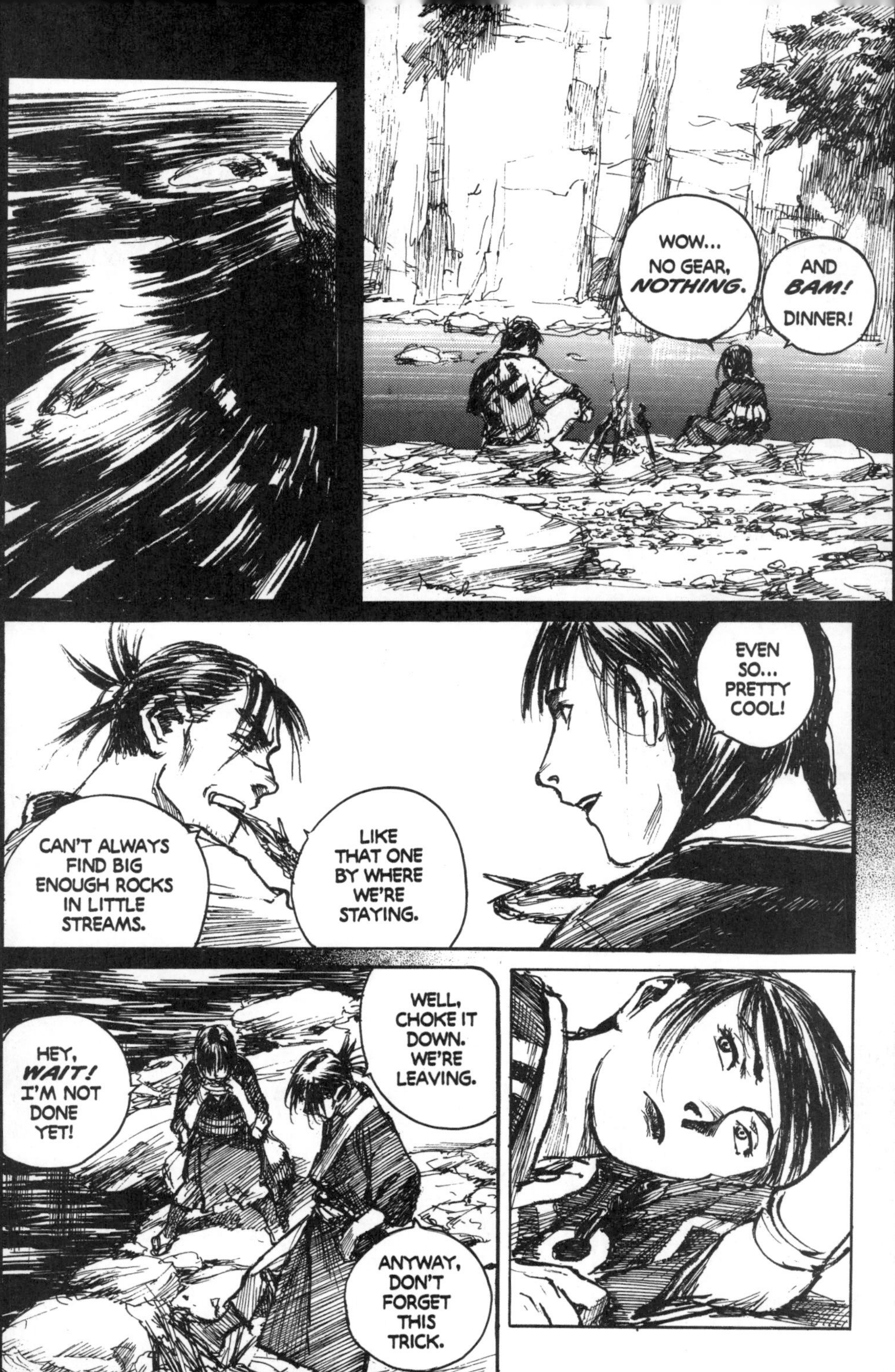
WOW... NO GEAR, NOTHING.
AND BAM! DINNER!
CAN'T ALWAYS FIND BIG ENOUGH ROCKS IN LITTLE STREAMS.
LIKE THAT ONE BY WHERE WE'RE STAYING.
EVEN SO... PRETTY COOL!
HEY, WAIT! I'M NOT DONE YET!
WELL, CHOKE IT DOWN. WE'RE LEAVING.
ANYWAY, DON'T FORGET THIS TRICK.

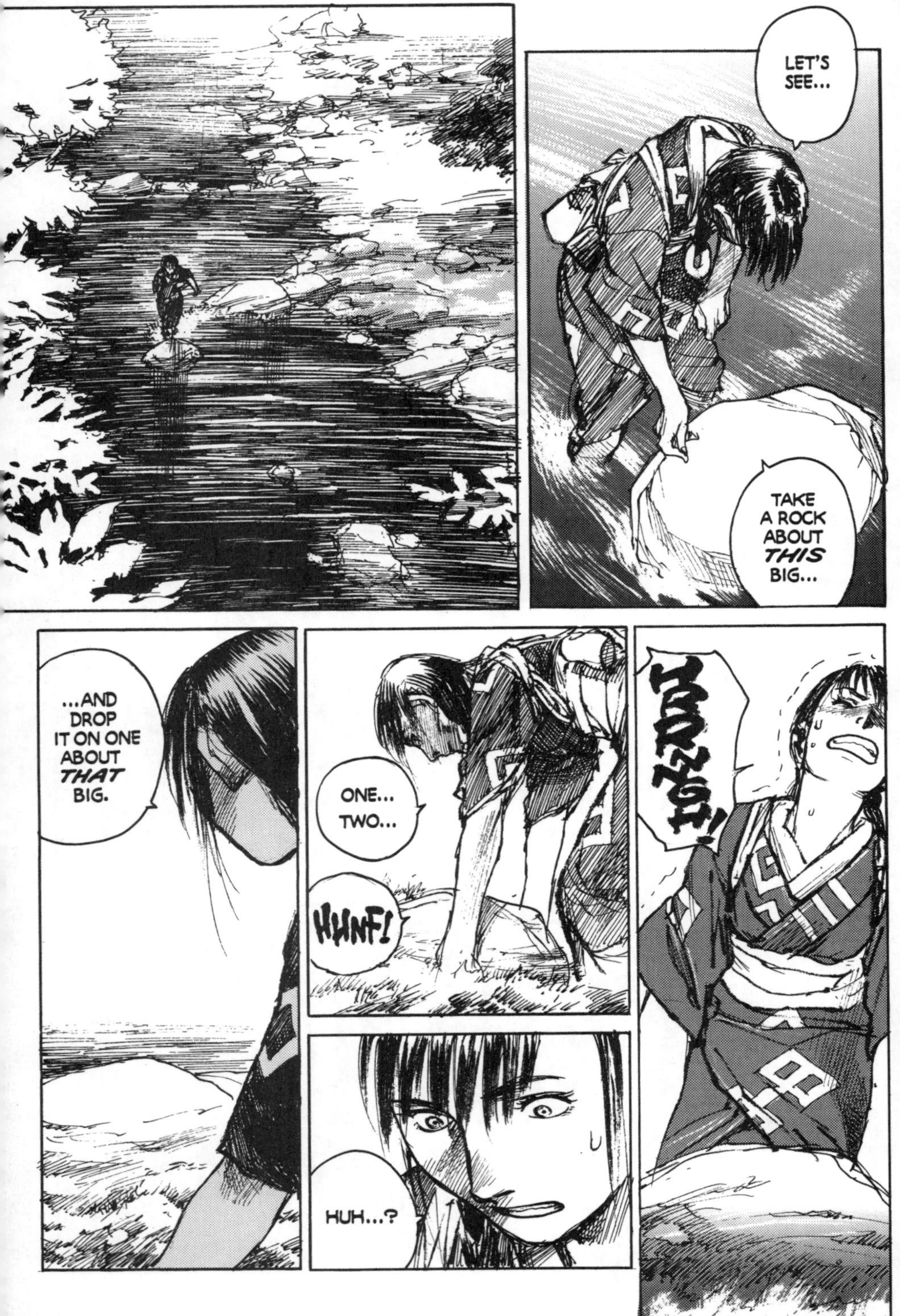
LET'S SEE...
TAKE A ROCK ABOUT *THIS* BIG...
...AND DROP IT ON ONE ABOUT *THAT* BIG.
ONE... TWO...
HHNF!
HRNNGH!
HUH...?

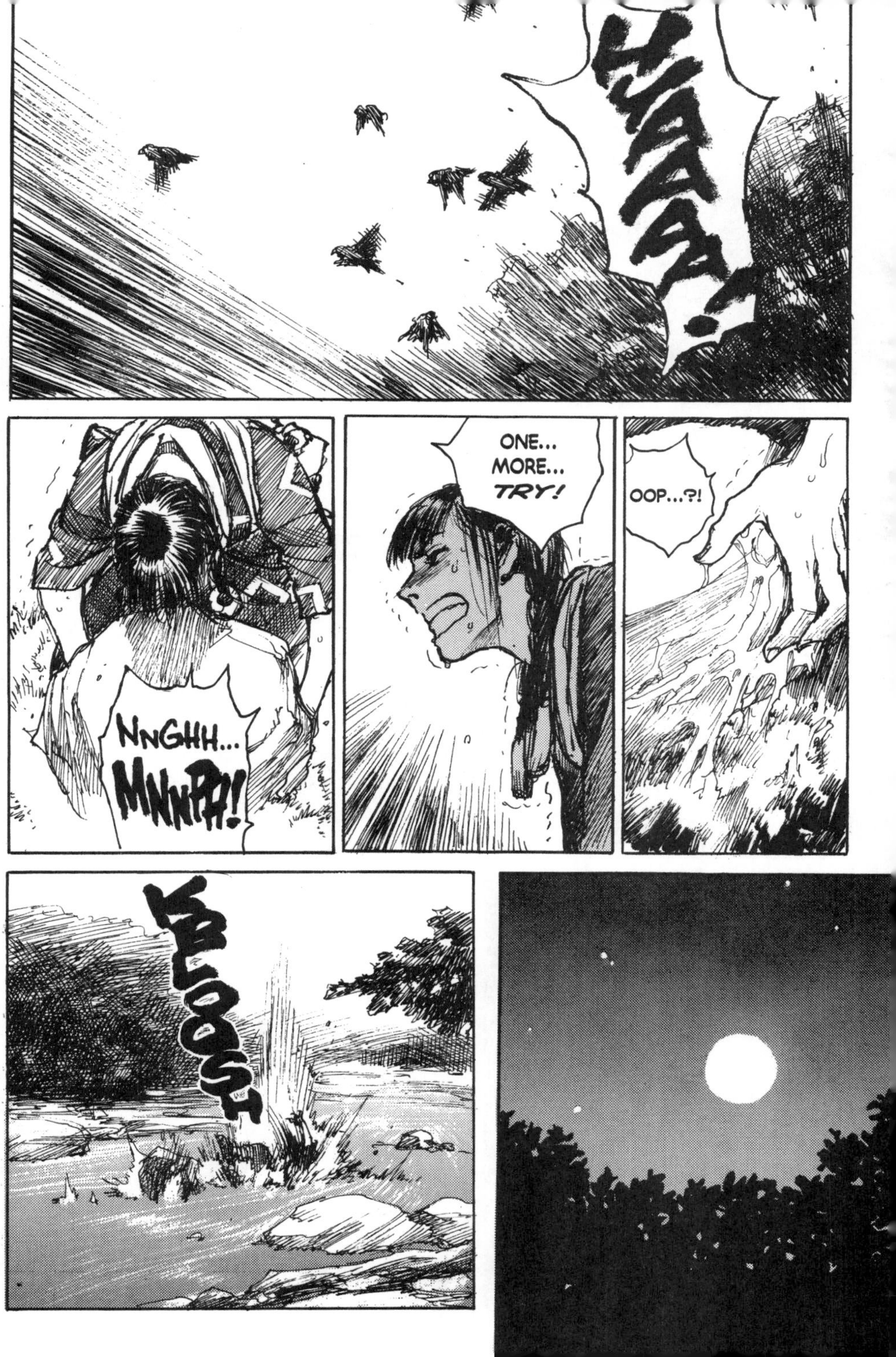
NNGHH...
MNNPH!
ONE... MORE... TRY!
OOP...?!
KBLOOSH

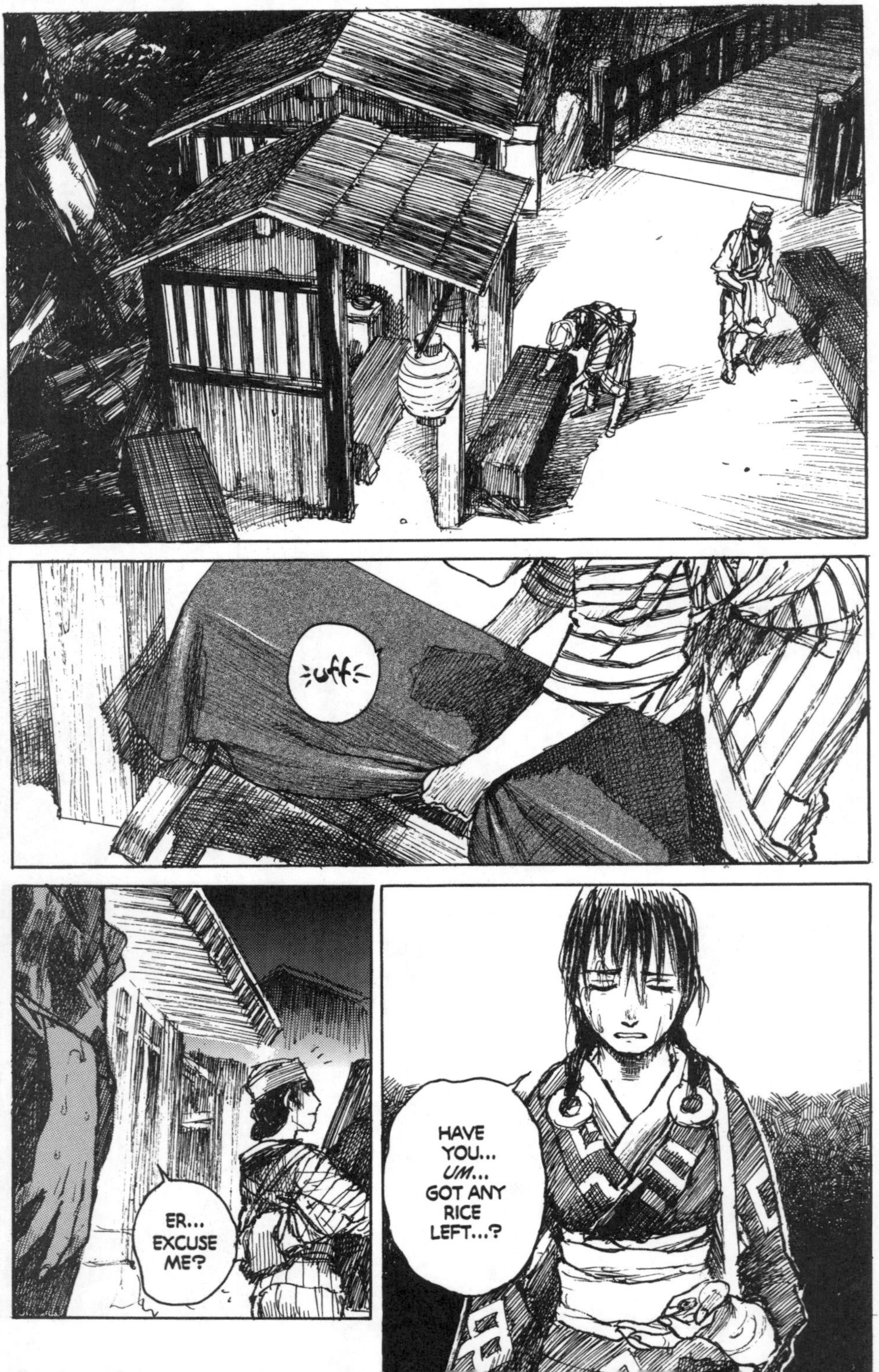
uff
ER... EXCUSE ME?
HAVE YOU... UM... GOT ANY RICE LEFT...?

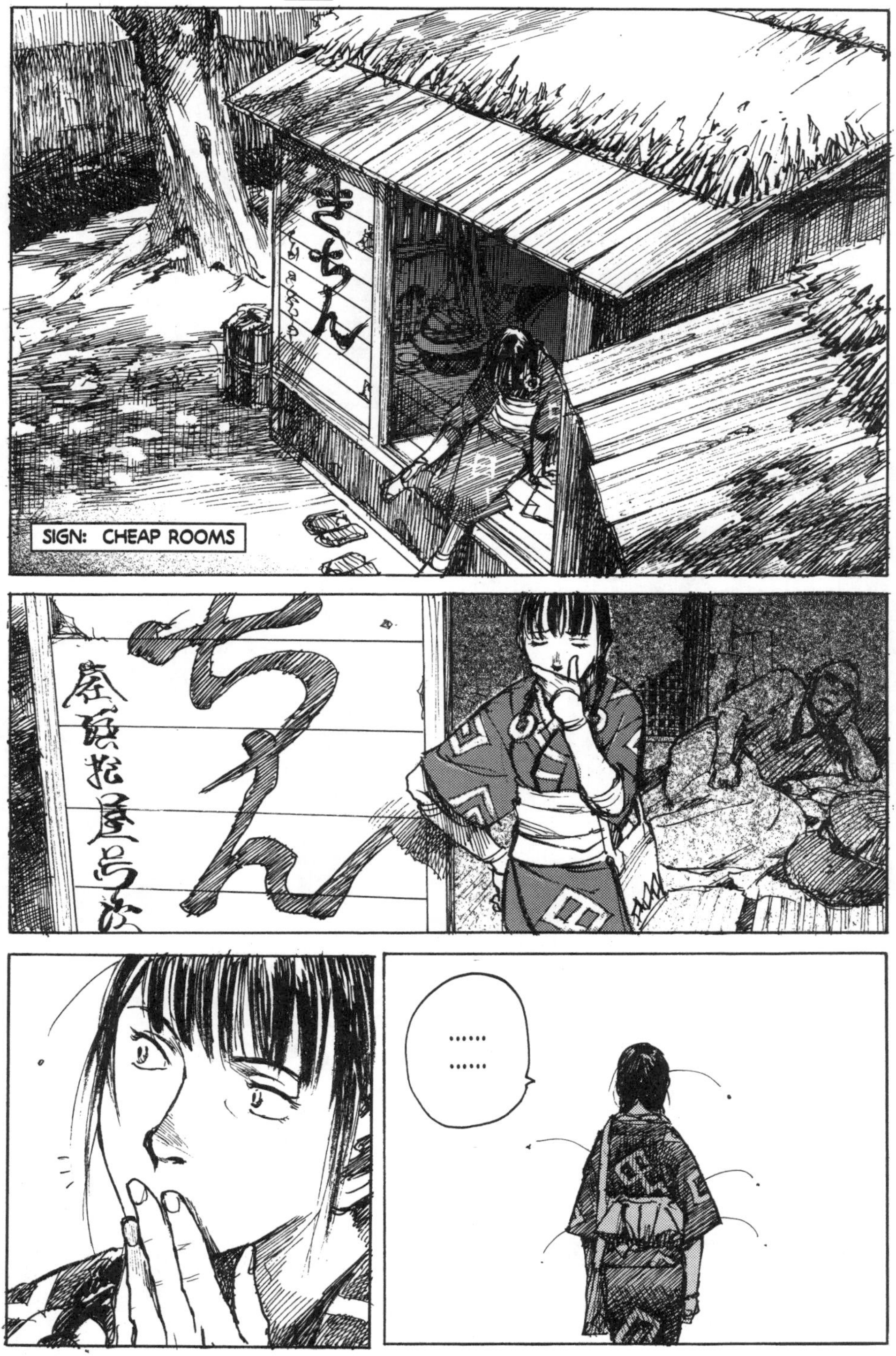
SIGN: CHEAP ROOMS
......
......

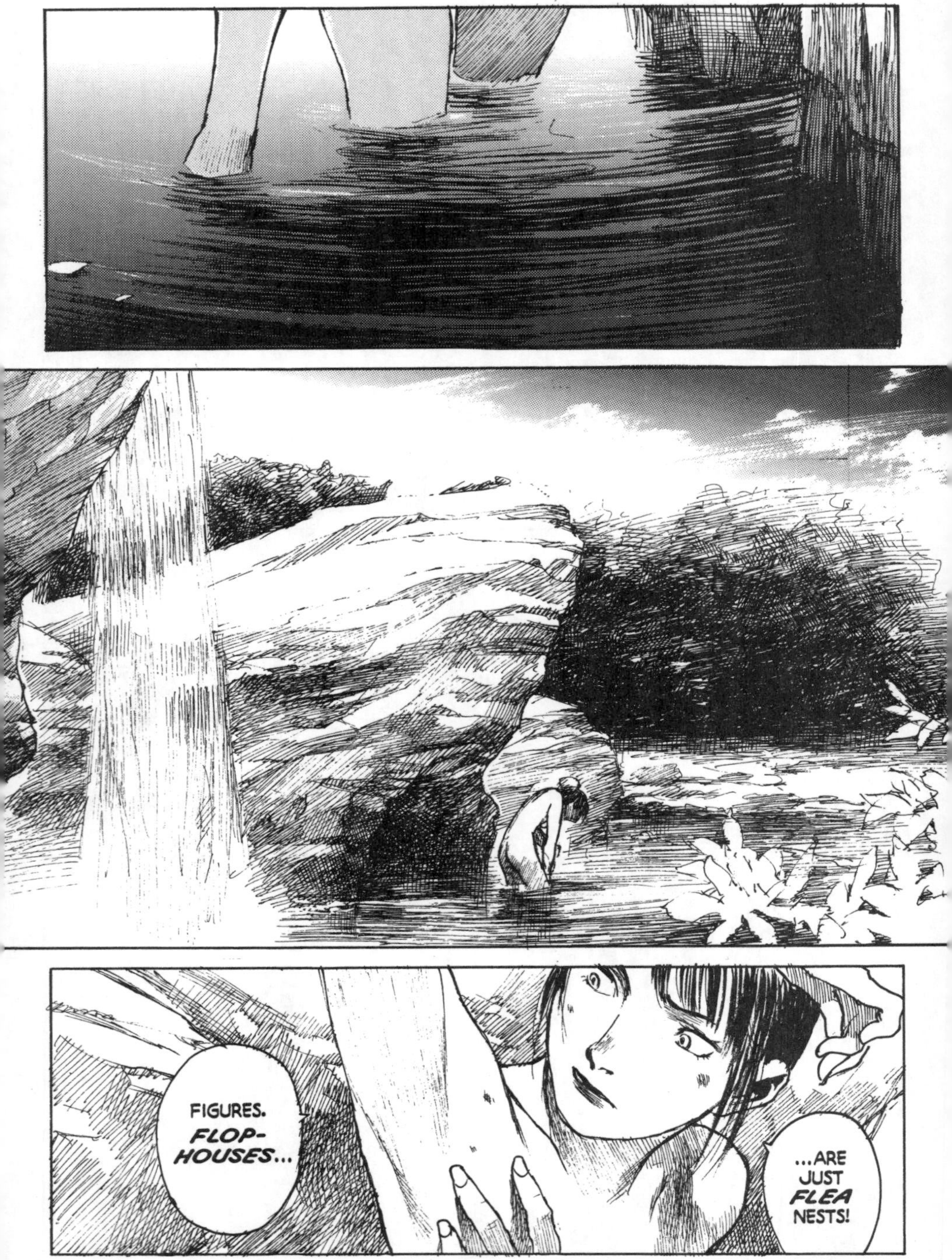
FIGURES. *FLOP-HOUSES*...
...ARE JUST *FLEA* NESTS!

GUESS
I'M JUST...
I DUNNO...
*SHOWING
OFF.*

THAT'S
ALL.

BUT
SOMEHOW
I FEEL
*ASHAM-
ED*...

...TO
WASTE
THE
ELEVEN
RYŌ
SATO LEFT
ME.

BUT...
*FLOP-
HOUSES?*
EATING ON
SIXTEEN
MON
A DAY?

I'VE
TRIED
LOTS
OF
THINGS...

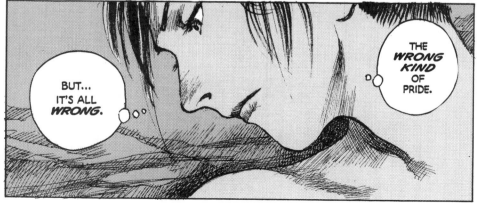

BUT...
IT'S ALL
WRONG.

THE
*WRONG
KIND*
OF
PRIDE.

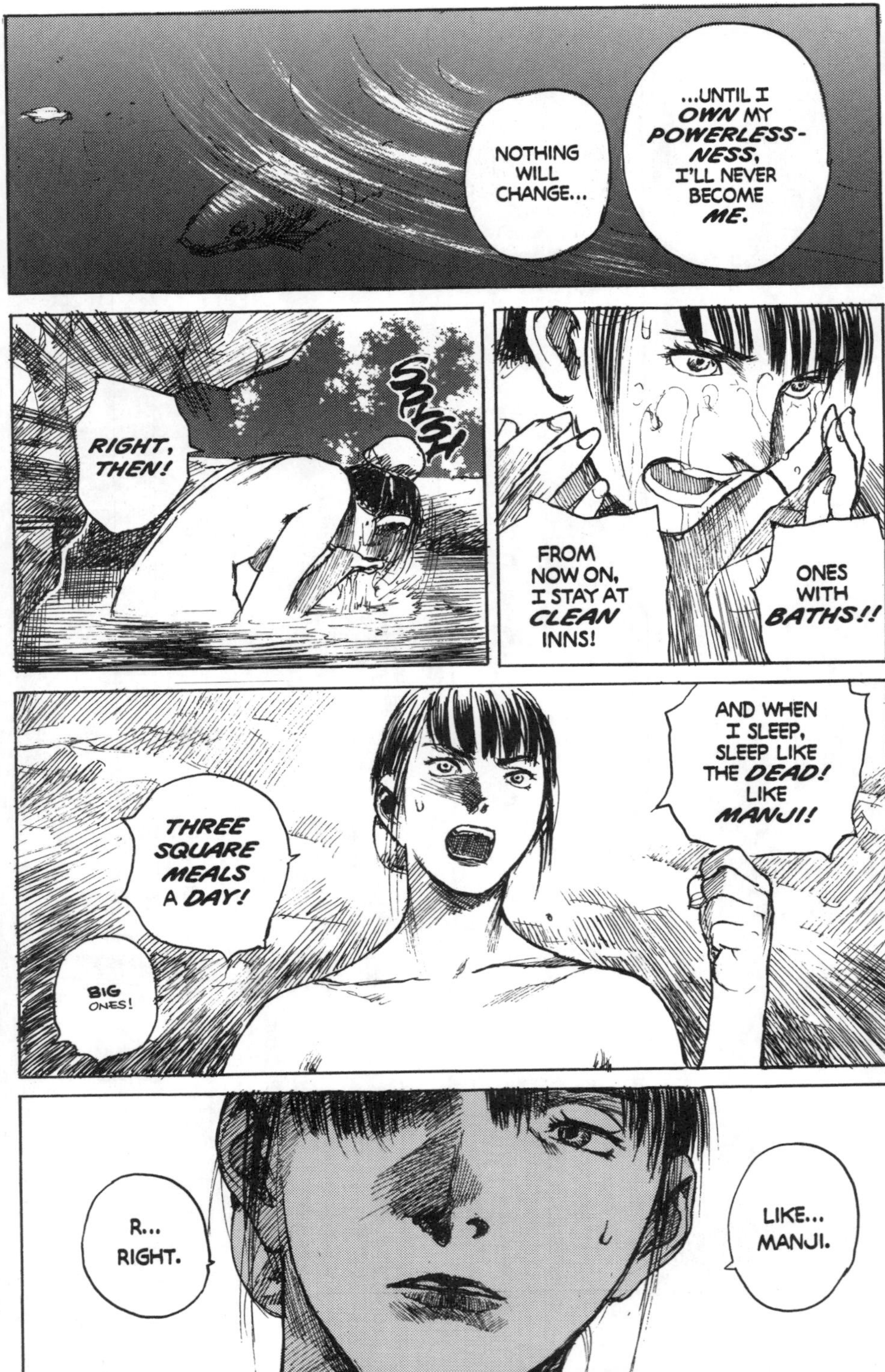
NOTHING WILL CHANGE...
...UNTIL I OWN MY POWERLESS-NESS, I'LL NEVER BECOME ME.
RIGHT, THEN!
SPLOSH
FROM NOW ON, I STAY AT CLEAN INNS!
ONES WITH BATHS!!
THREE SQUARE MEALS A DAY!
BIG ONES!
AND WHEN I SLEEP, SLEEP LIKE THE DEAD! LIKE MANJI!
R... RIGHT.
LIKE... MANJI.

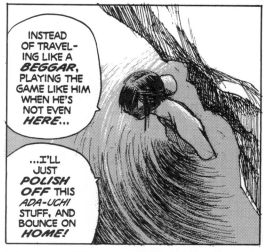

INSTEAD OF TRAVELING LIKE A **BEGGAR**, PLAYING THE GAME LIKE HIM WHEN HE'S NOT EVEN **HERE**...

...I'LL JUST **POLISH OFF** THIS ADA-UCHI STUFF, AND BOUNCE ON **HOME!**

THAT'S MORE LIKE IT, AND A...

AH...

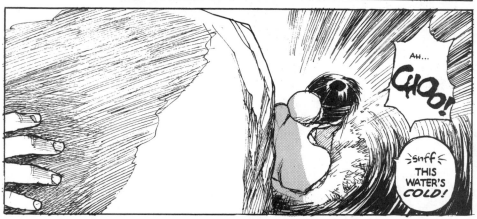

AH...

CHOO!

≈snff≈ THIS WATER'S **COLD!**

SPLASH

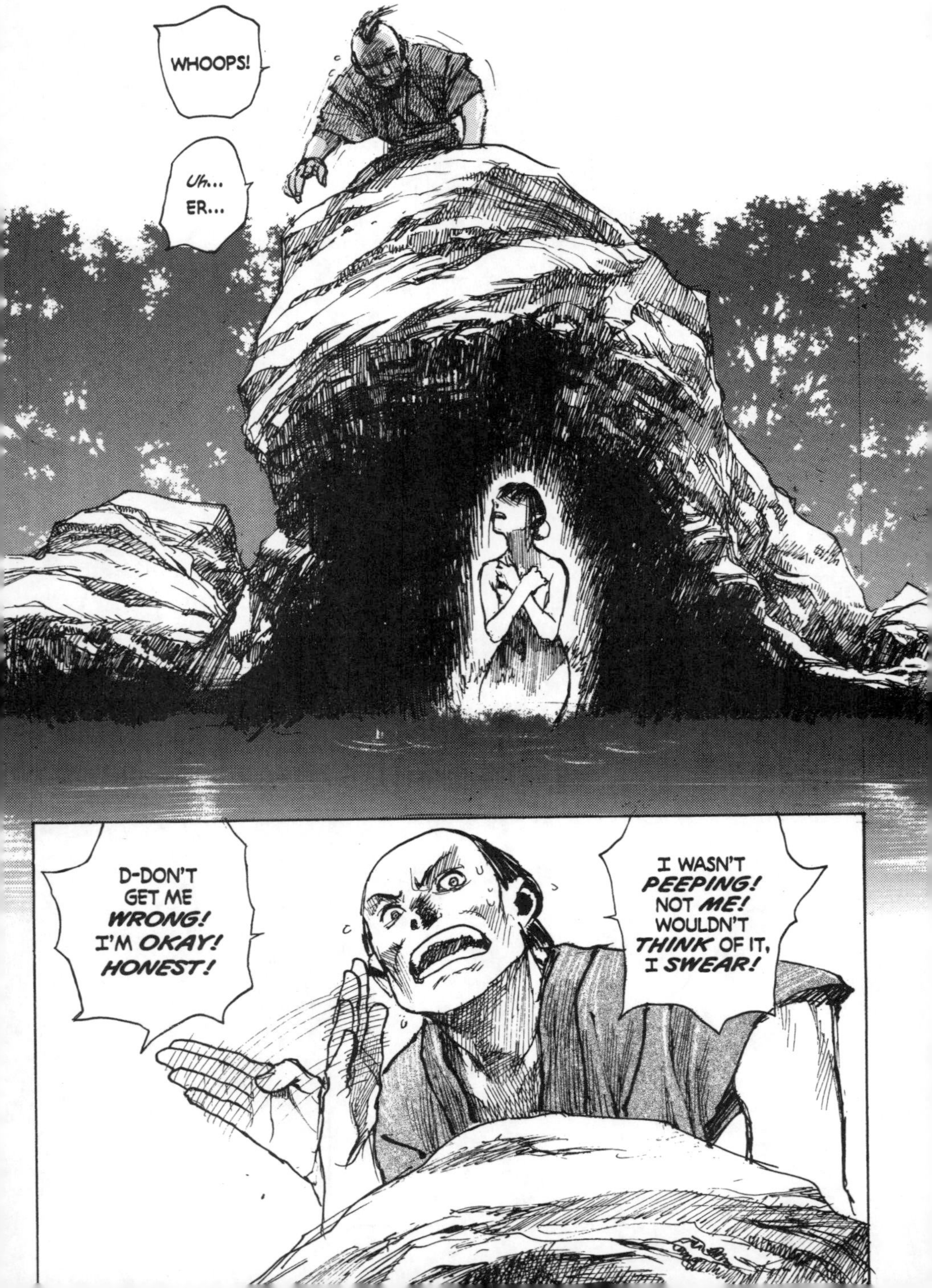
WHOOPS!
Uh... ER...
D-DON'T GET ME WRONG! I'M OKAY! HONEST!
I WASN'T PEEPING! NOT ME! WOULDN'T THINK OF IT, I SWEAR!

SO, Uh... DON'T BE *AFRAID.*

I JUST... LIVE AROUND HERE.

WAS OUT IN THE WOODS, HEARD A *WOMAN'S VOICE,* AND... Y'KNOW...

SHEESH... I, I'M *SORRY.* I'LL JUST *DISAP-PEAR.*

ENJOY YOUR *BATH!*

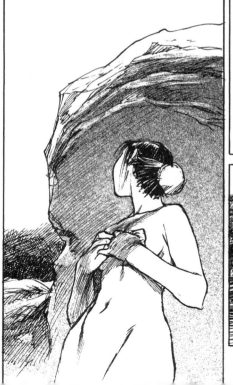

......
......

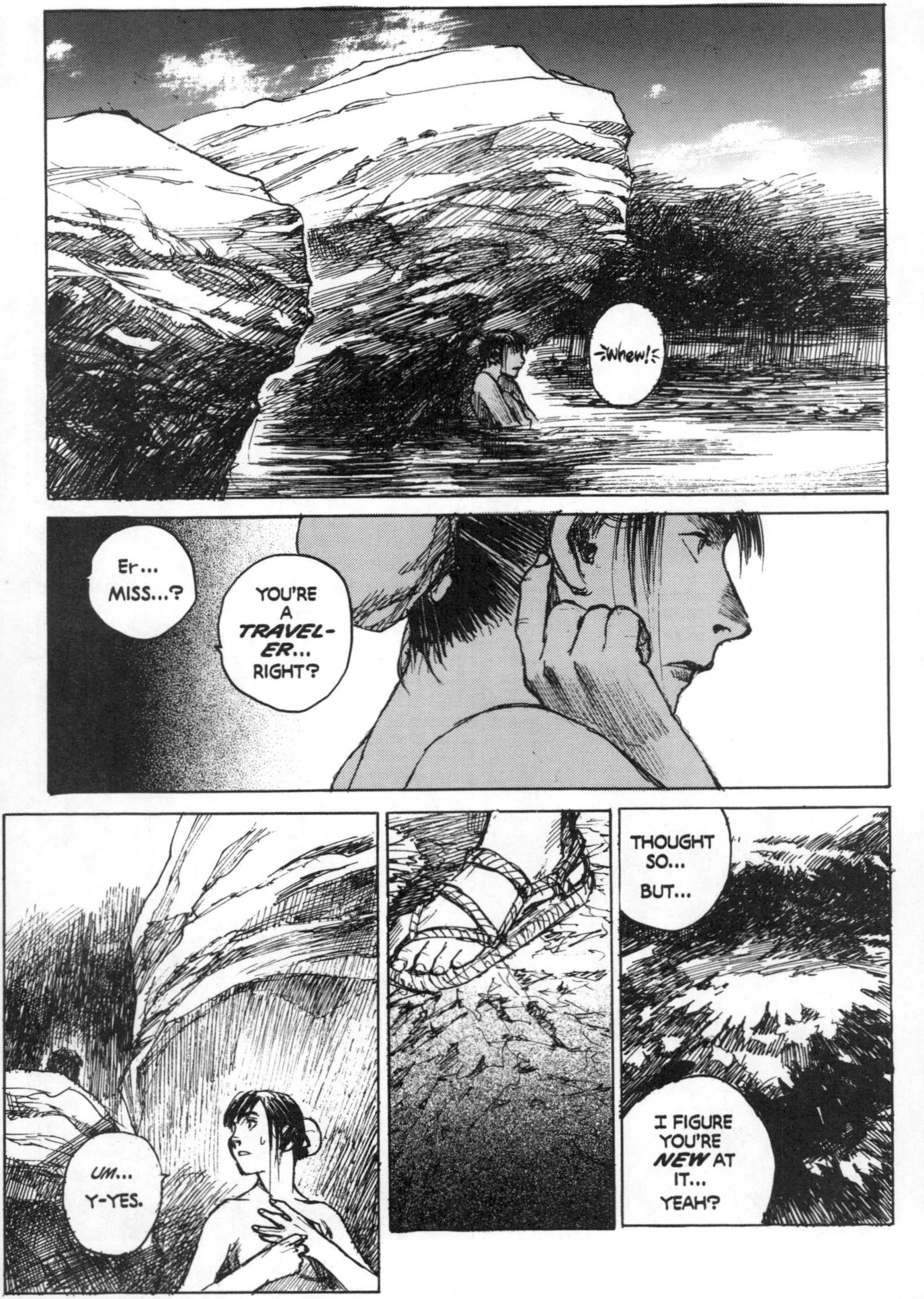
Whew!
Er... MISS...?
YOU'RE A TRAVELER... RIGHT?
UM... Y-YES.
THOUGHT SO... BUT...
I FIGURE YOU'RE NEW AT IT... YEAH?

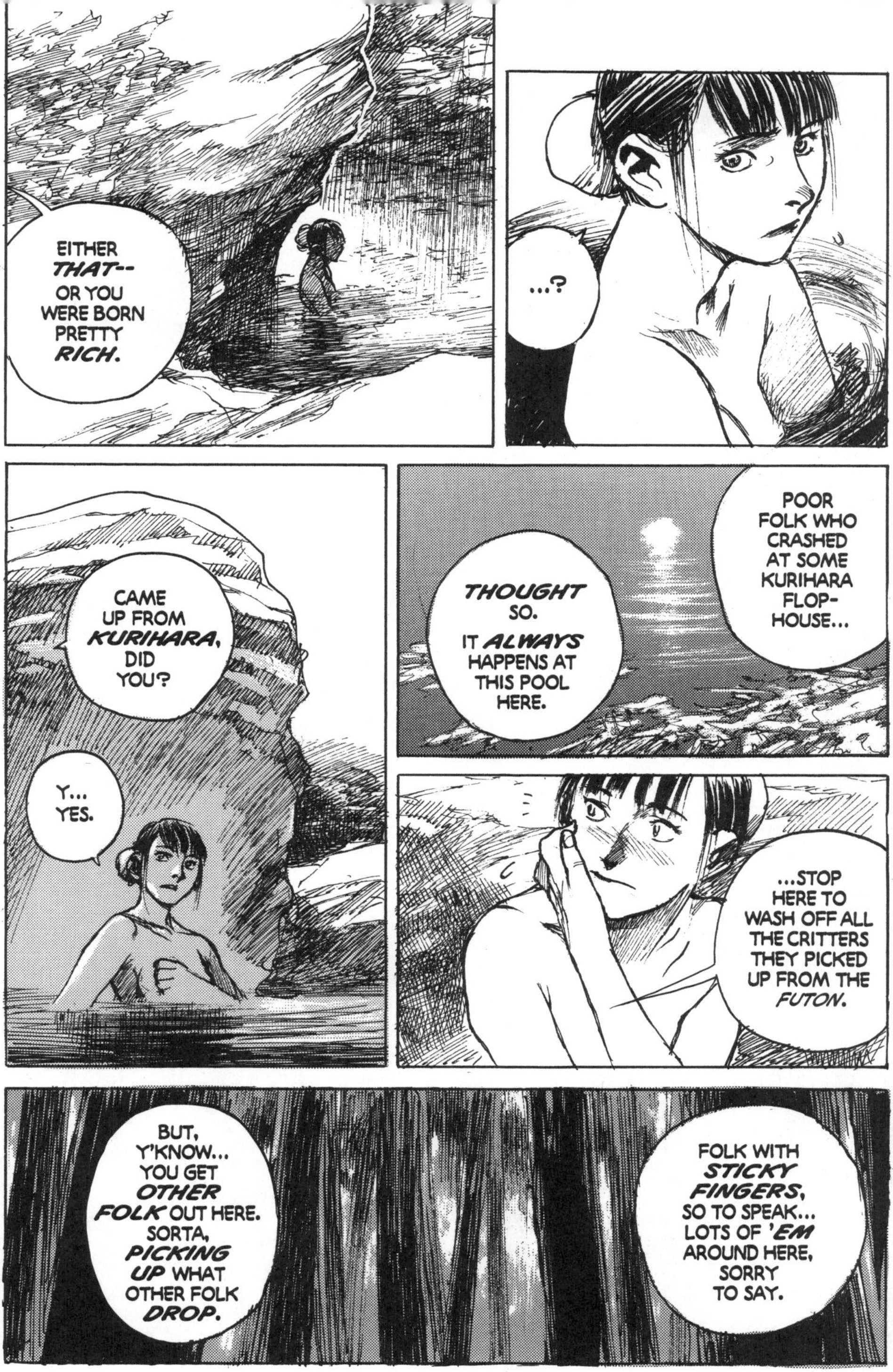
EITHER THAT-- OR YOU WERE BORN PRETTY RICH.
...?
CAME UP FROM KURIHARA, DID YOU?
Y... YES.
THOUGHT SO.
IT ALWAYS HAPPENS AT THIS POOL HERE.
POOR FOLK WHO CRASHED AT SOME KURIHARA FLOP-HOUSE...
...STOP HERE TO WASH OFF ALL THE CRITTERS THEY PICKED UP FROM THE FUTON.
BUT, Y'KNOW... YOU GET OTHER FOLK OUT HERE. SORTA, PICKING UP WHAT OTHER FOLK DROP.
FOLK WITH STICKY FINGERS, SO TO SPEAK... LOTS OF 'EM AROUND HERE, SORRY TO SAY.

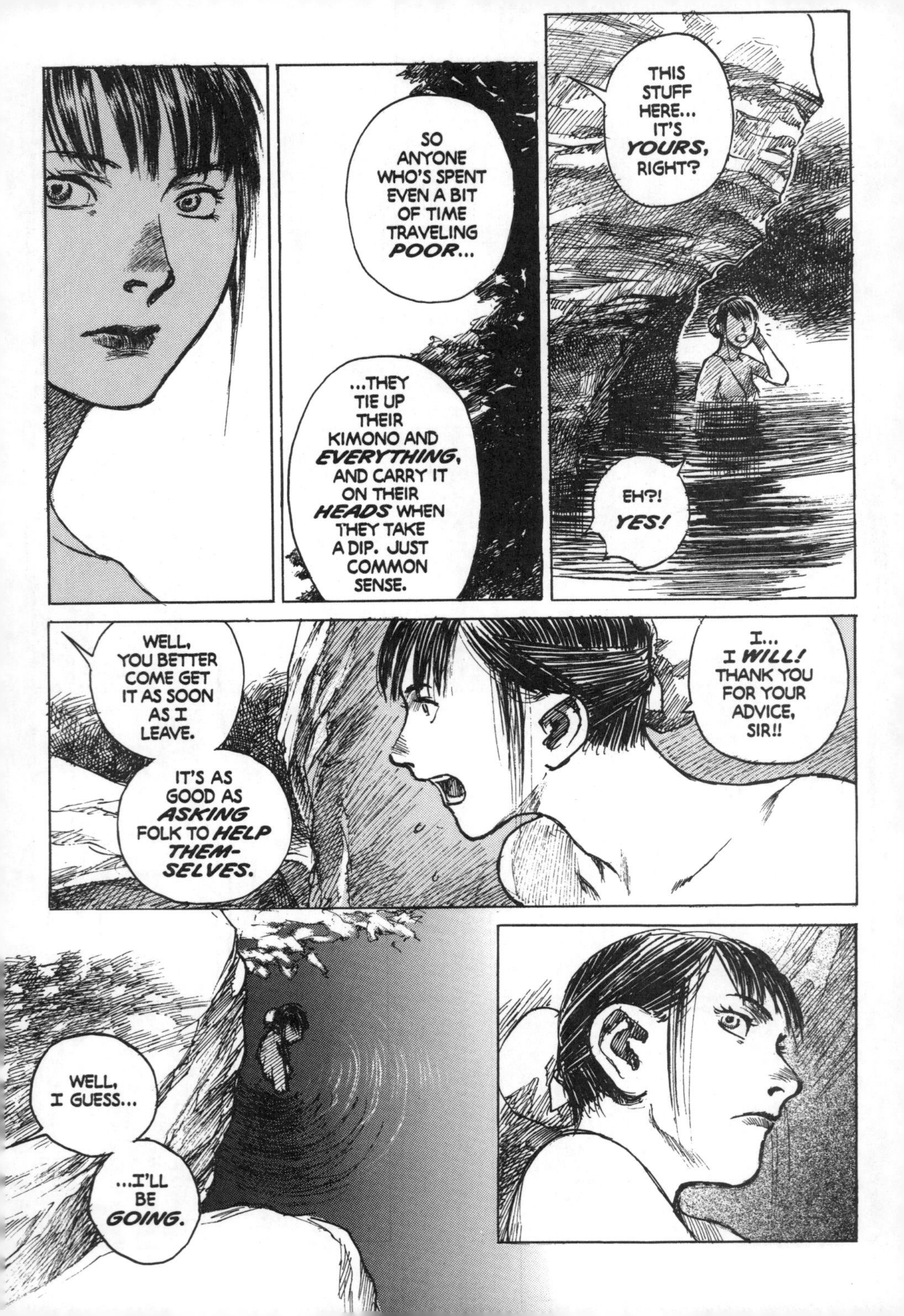
SO ANYONE WHO'S SPENT EVEN A BIT OF TIME TRAVELING *POOR*...
...THEY TIE UP THEIR KIMONO AND *EVERYTHING*, AND CARRY IT ON THEIR *HEADS* WHEN THEY TAKE A DIP. JUST COMMON SENSE.
THIS STUFF HERE... IT'S *YOURS*, RIGHT?
EH?! *YES!*
WELL, YOU BETTER COME GET IT AS SOON AS I LEAVE.
IT'S AS GOOD AS *ASKING* FOLK TO *HELP THEM-SELVES*.
I... I *WILL!* THANK YOU FOR YOUR ADVICE, SIR!!
WELL, I GUESS...
...I'LL BE *GOING*.

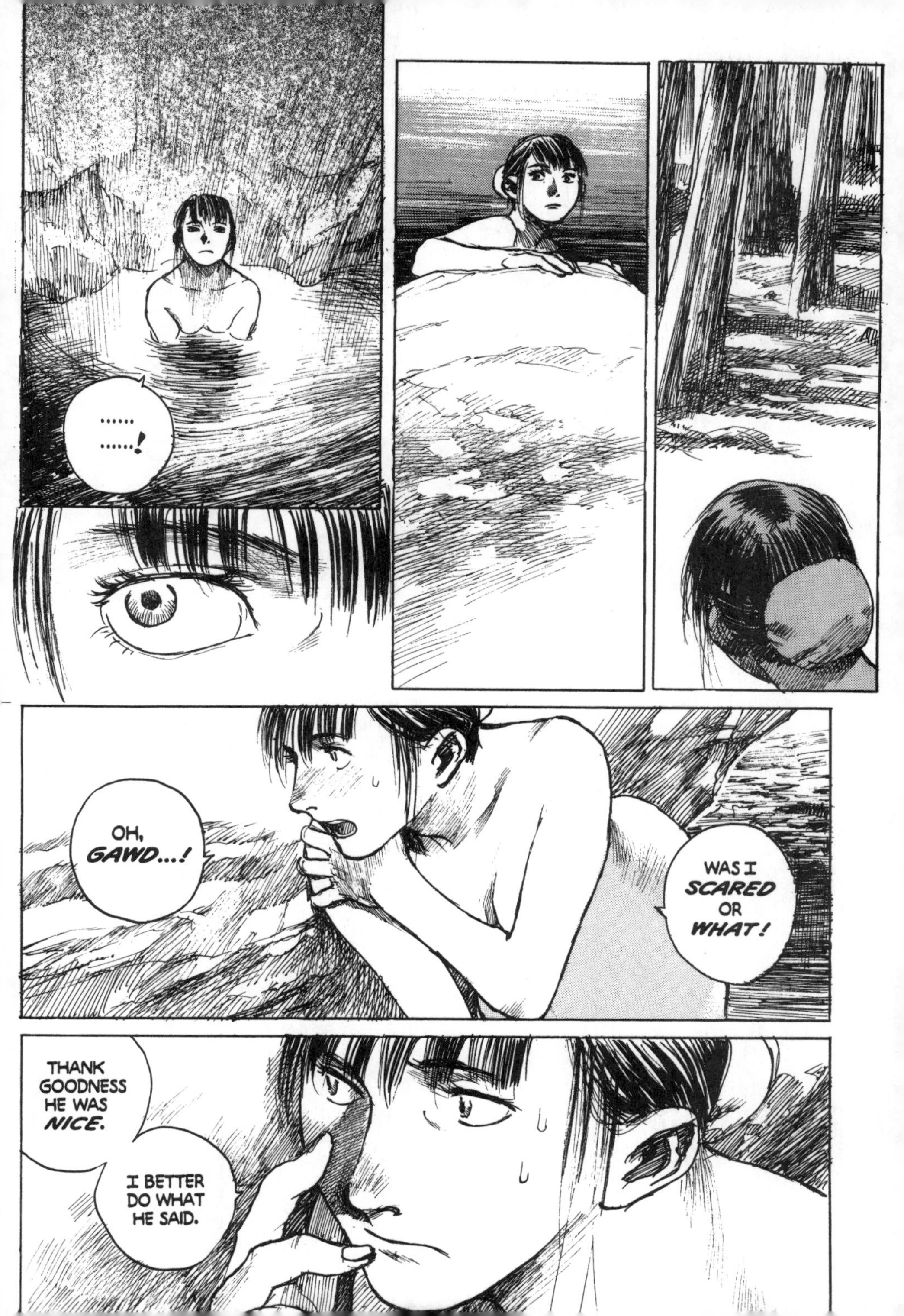

....!
OH, GAWD...!
WAS I SCARED OR WHAT!
THANK GOODNESS HE WAS NICE.
I BETTER DO WHAT HE SAID.

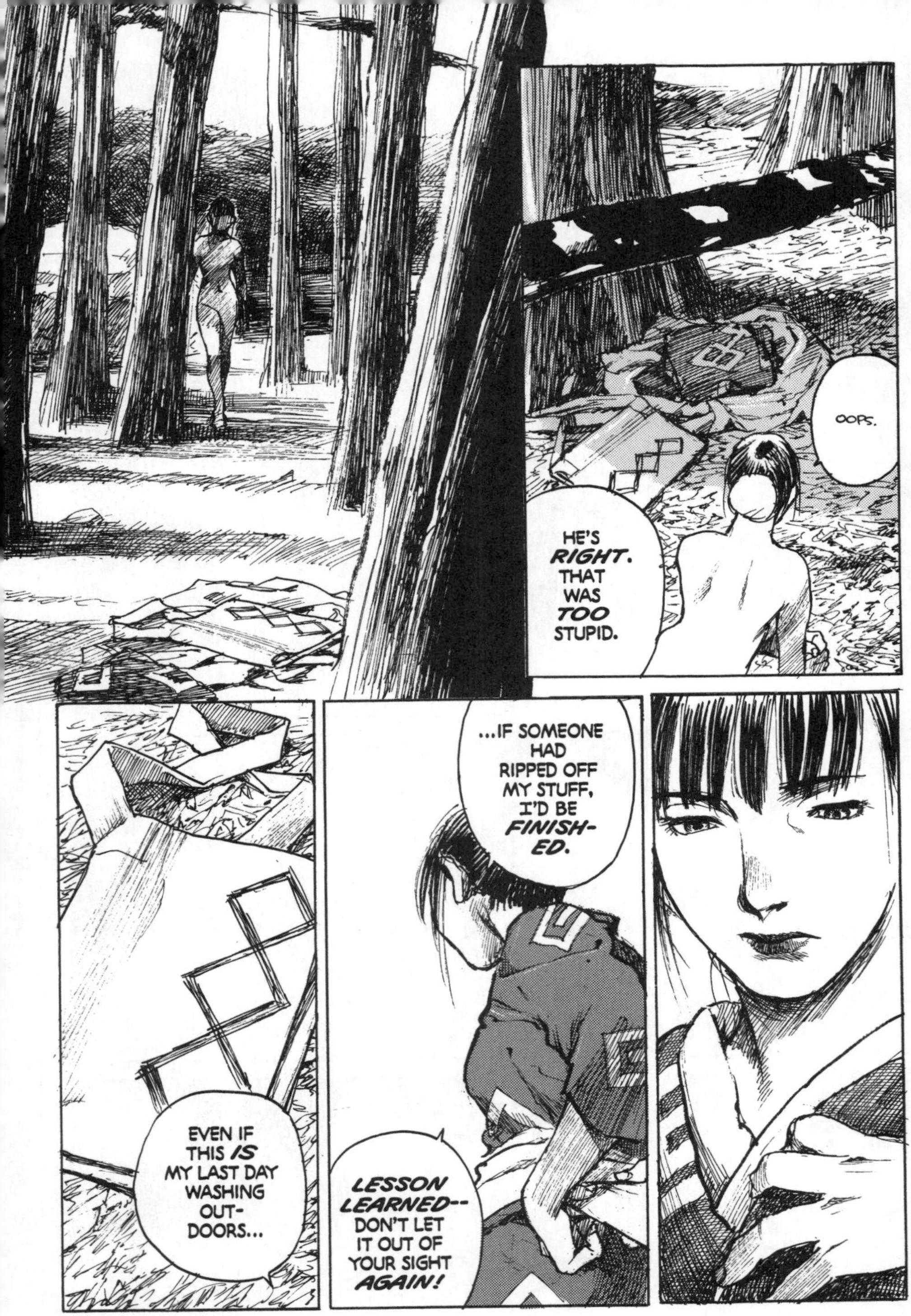
OOPS.
HE'S RIGHT. THAT WAS TOO STUPID.
EVEN IF THIS IS MY LAST DAY WASHING OUT-DOORS...
...IF SOMEONE HAD RIPPED OFF MY STUFF, I'D BE FINISH-ED.
LESSON LEARNED-- DON'T LET IT OUT OF YOUR SIGHT AGAIN!

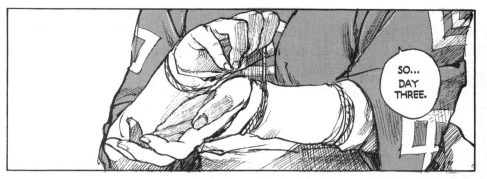

SO...
DAY
THREE.

I ALREADY BOUGHT LUNCH.

I CAN MAKE TEN *RI* BEFORE SUNDOWN.

AND *THEN*...

!?!

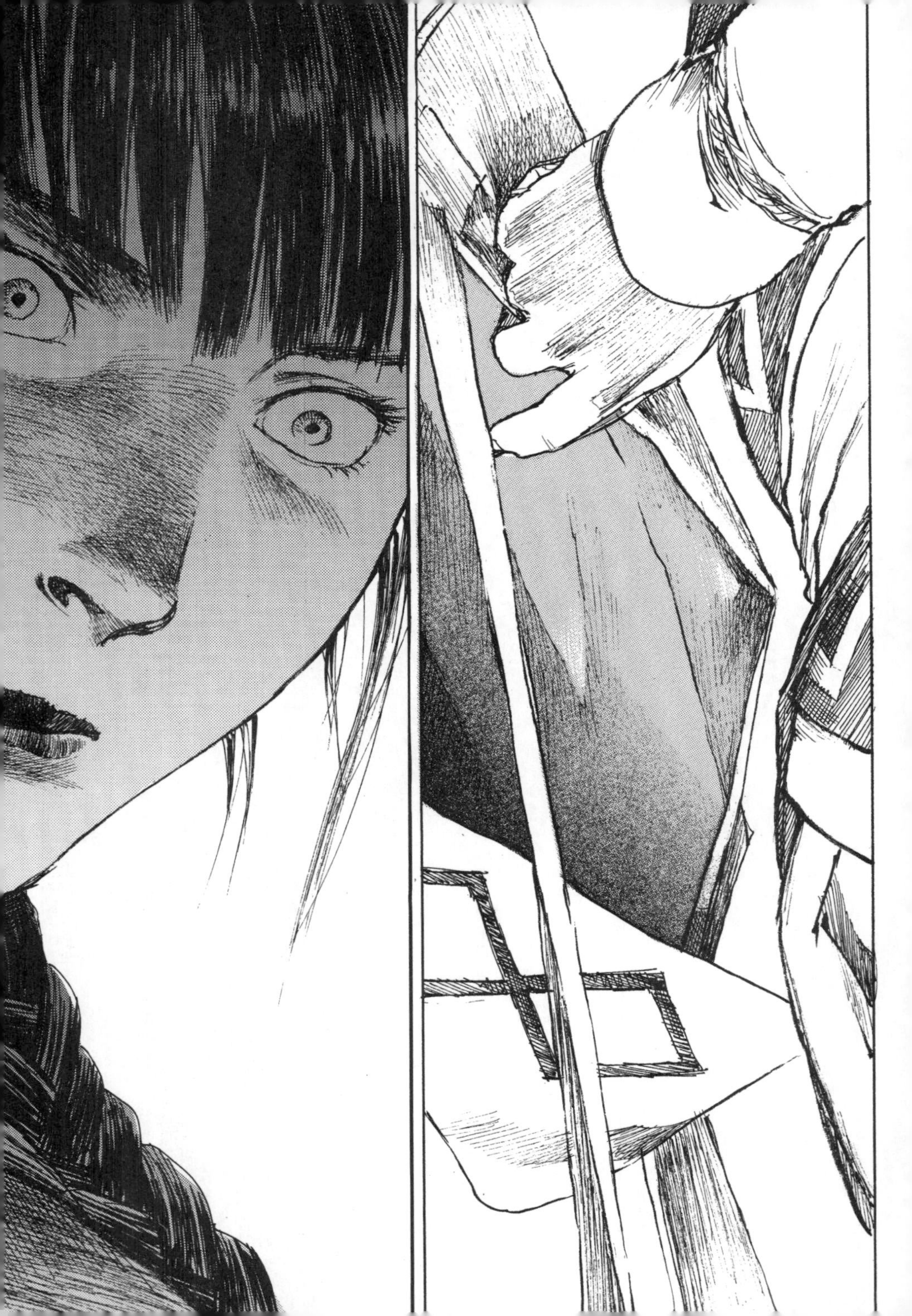

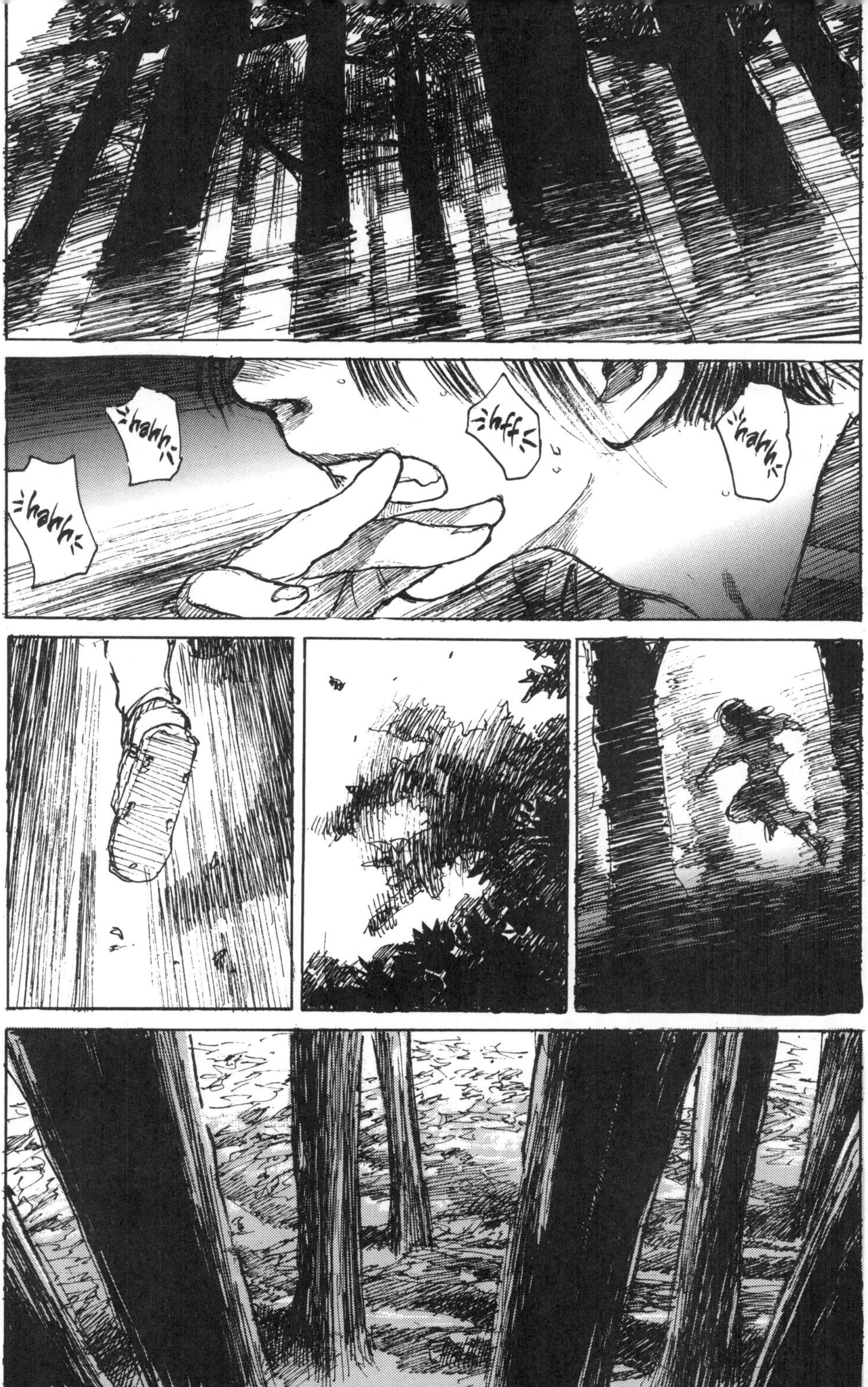
hahh
hahh
hff
hahh

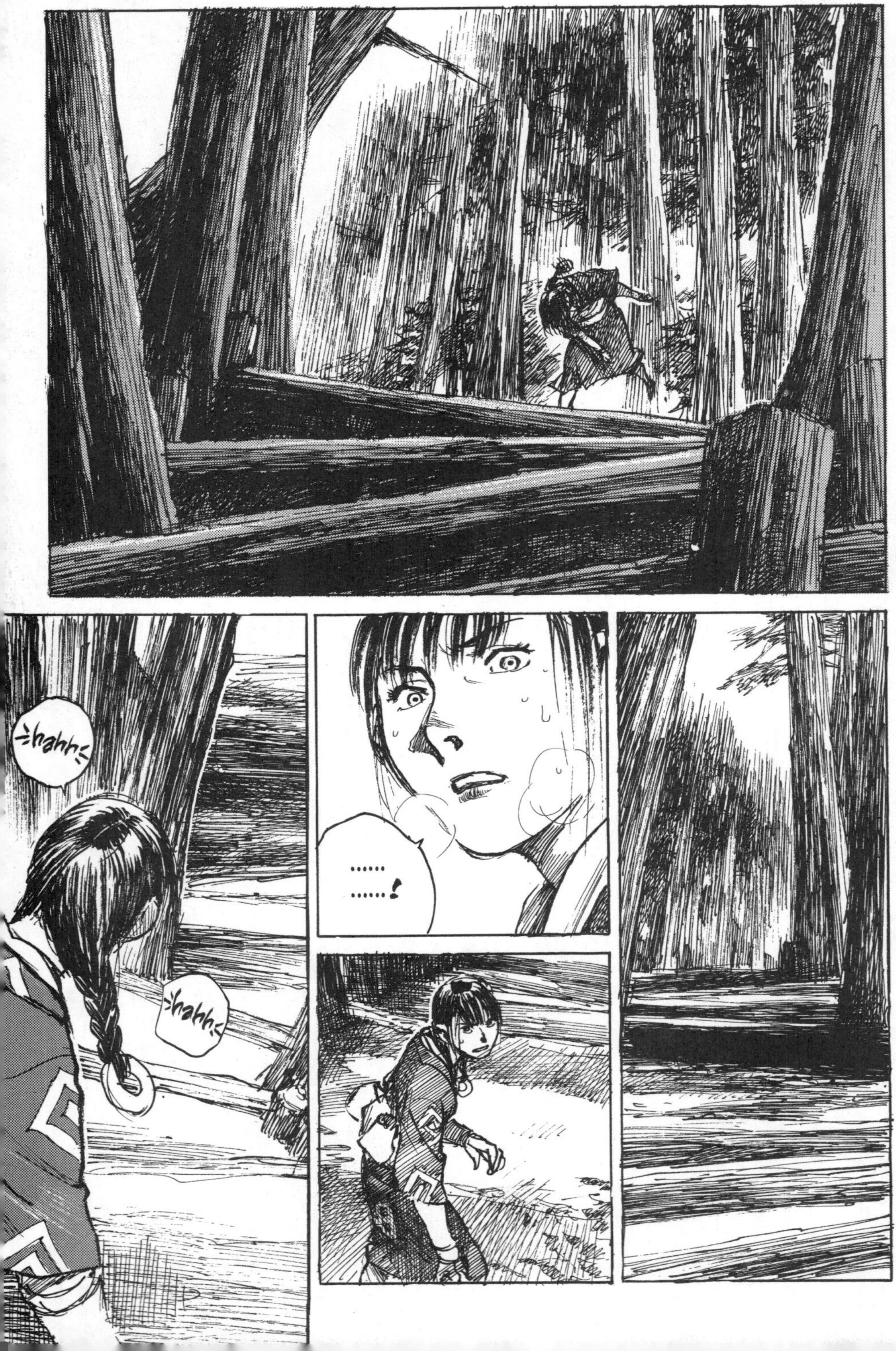
hahh
hahh
......
......!

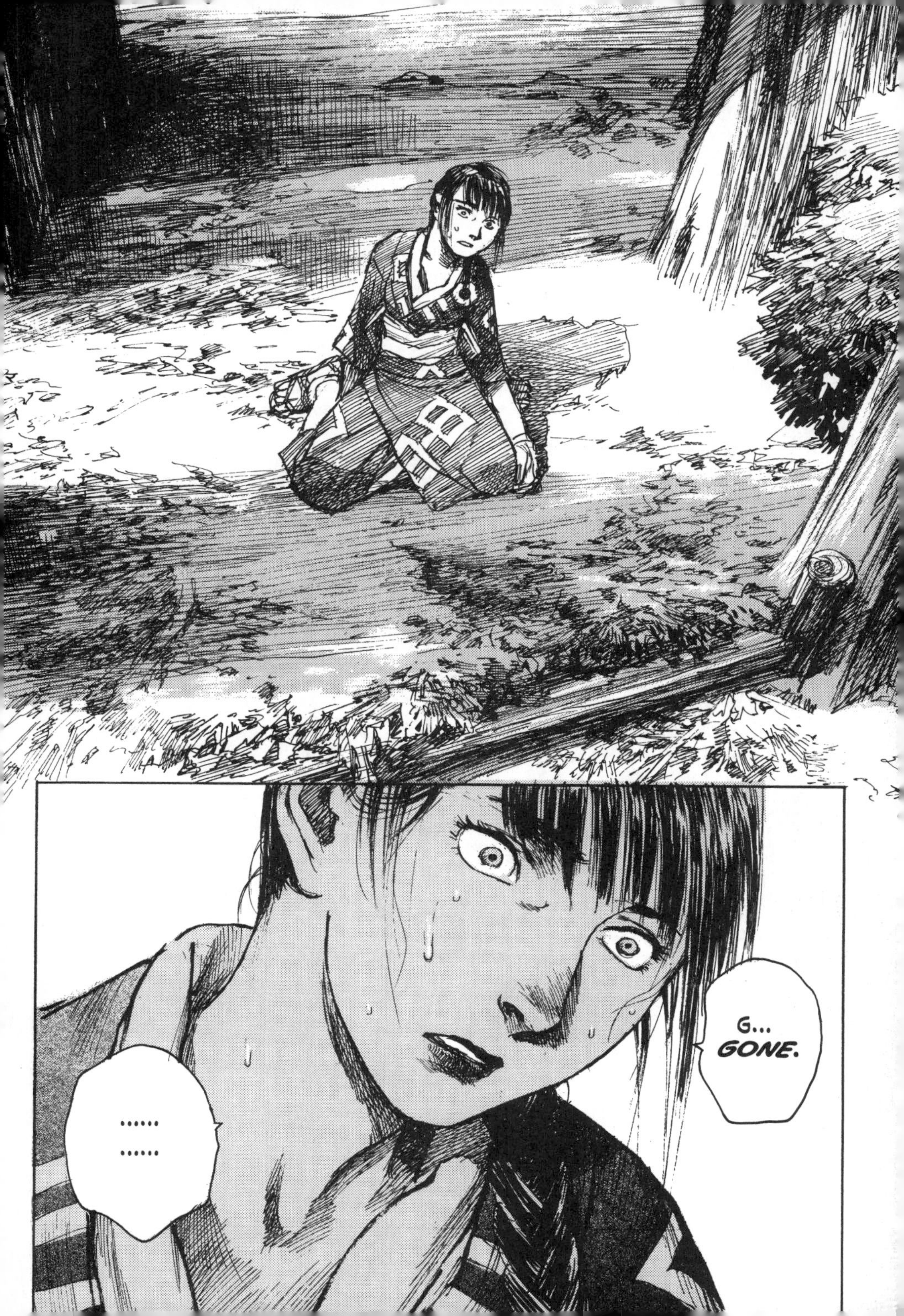
G...
GONE.
......
......

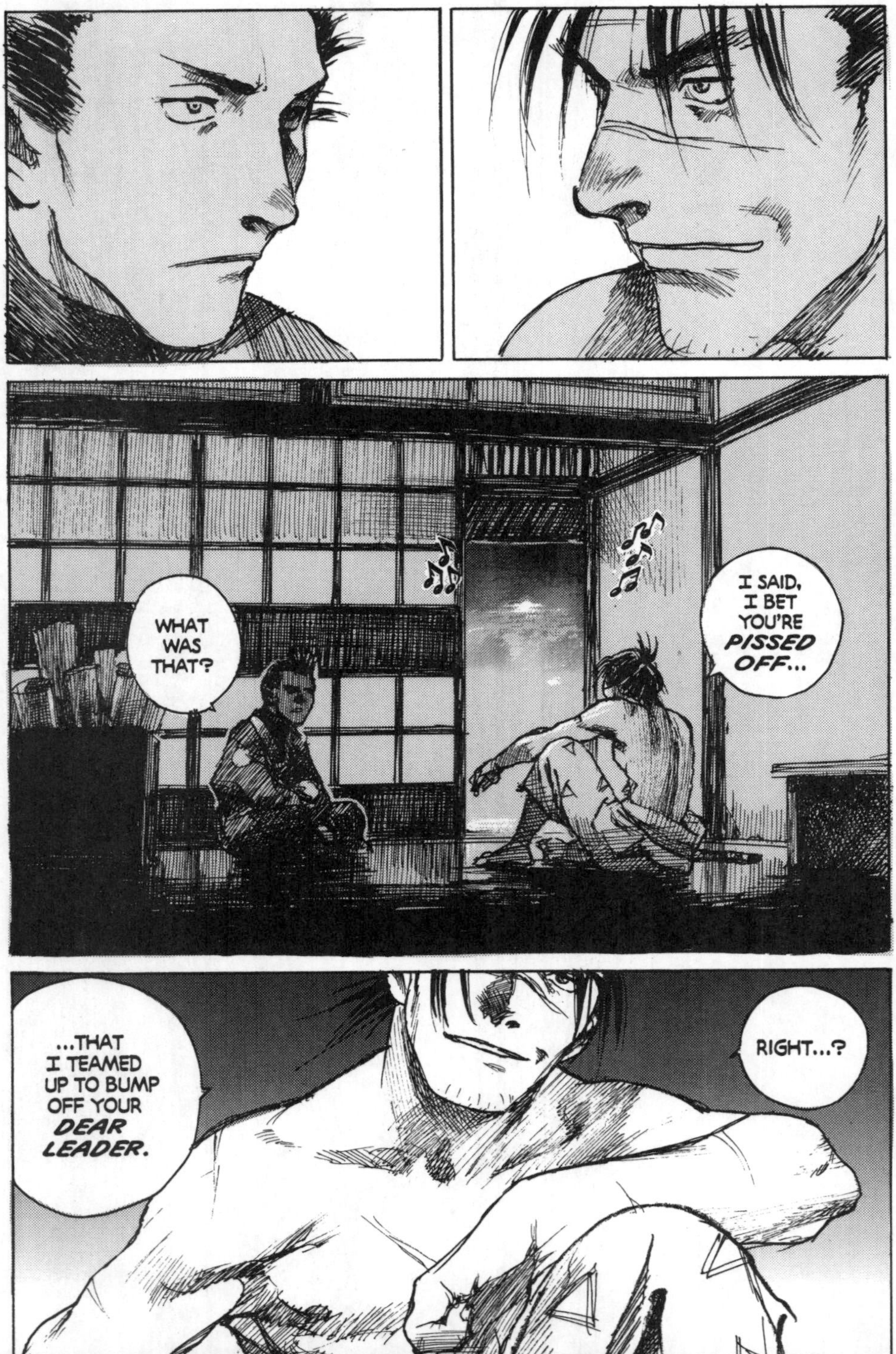
WHAT WAS THAT?
I SAID, I BET YOU'RE *PISSED OFF*...
...THAT I TEAMED UP TO BUMP OFF YOUR *DEAR LEADER*.
RIGHT...?

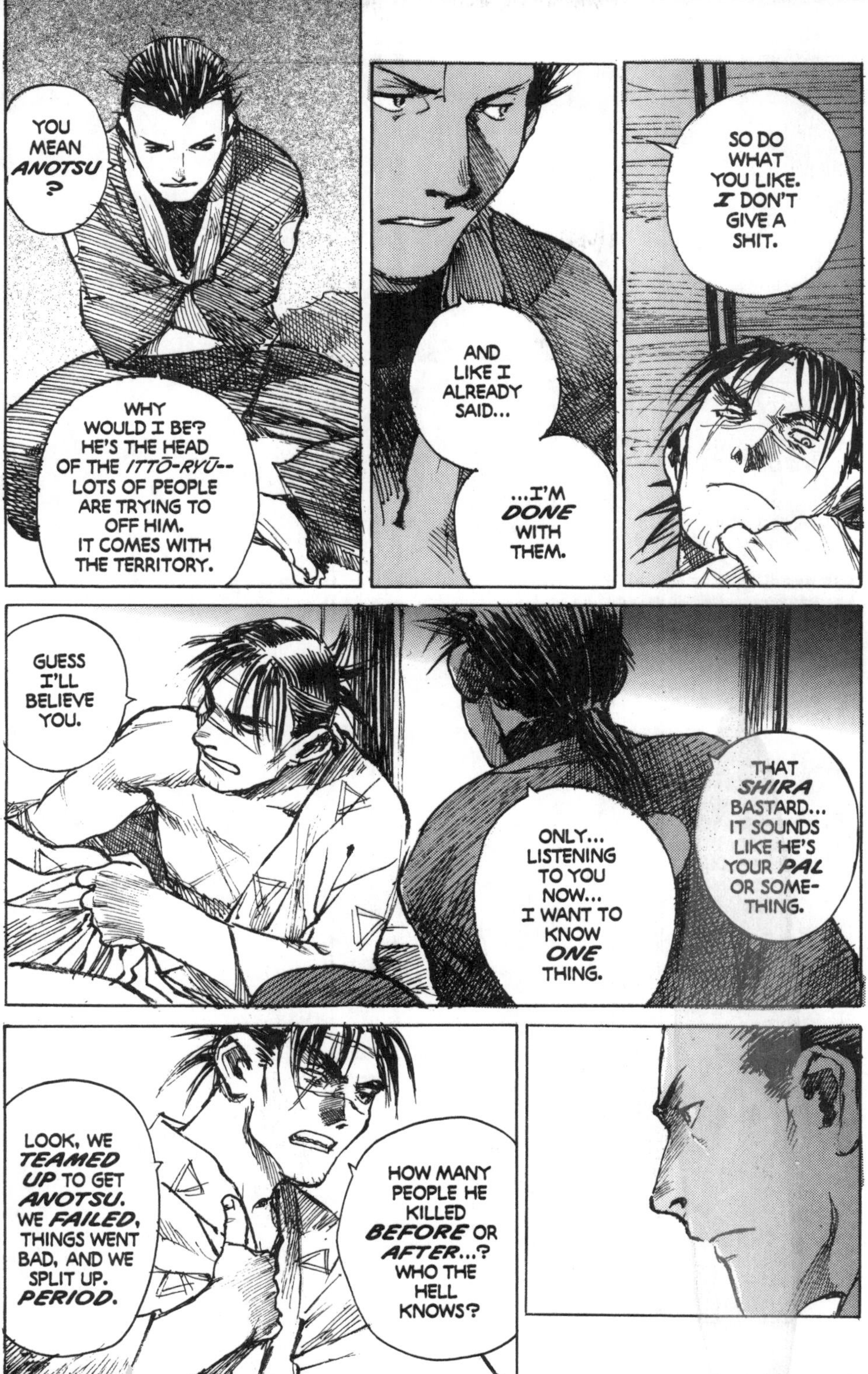

YOU MEAN ANOTSU?
WHY WOULD I BE? HE'S THE HEAD OF THE ITTŌ-RYŪ-- LOTS OF PEOPLE ARE TRYING TO OFF HIM. IT COMES WITH THE TERRITORY.
AND LIKE I ALREADY SAID...
...I'M DONE WITH THEM.
SO DO WHAT YOU LIKE. I DON'T GIVE A SHIT.
GUESS I'LL BELIEVE YOU.
ONLY... LISTENING TO YOU NOW... I WANT TO KNOW ONE THING.
THAT SHIRA BASTARD... IT SOUNDS LIKE HE'S YOUR PAL OR SOME-THING.
LOOK, WE TEAMED UP TO GET ANOTSU. WE FAILED, THINGS WENT BAD, AND WE SPLIT UP. PERIOD.
HOW MANY PEOPLE HE KILLED BEFORE OR AFTER...? WHO THE HELL KNOWS?

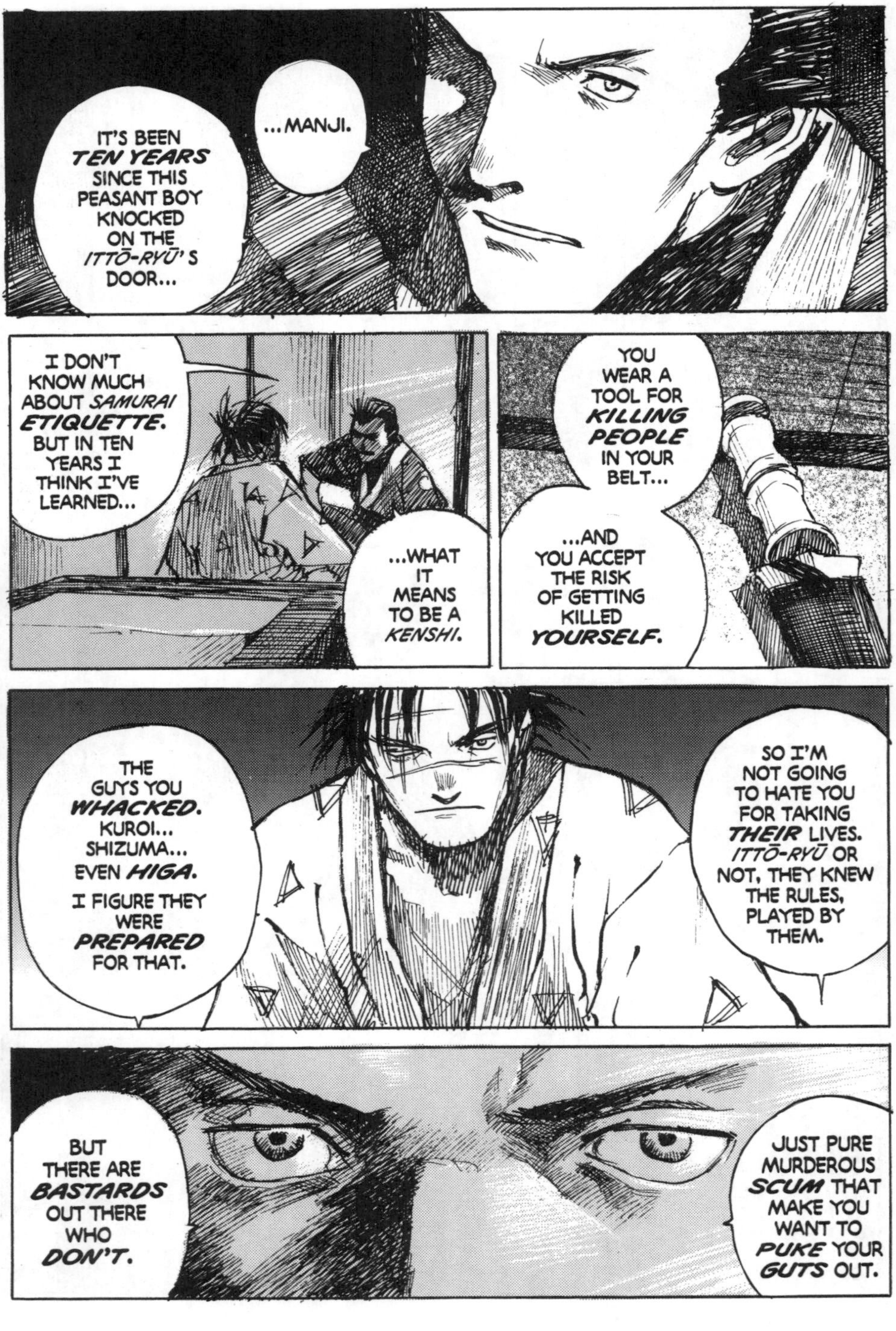
IT'S BEEN TEN YEARS SINCE THIS PEASANT BOY KNOCKED ON THE ITTŌ-RYŪ'S DOOR...
...MANJI.
I DON'T KNOW MUCH ABOUT SAMURAI ETIQUETTE. BUT IN TEN YEARS I THINK I'VE LEARNED...
...WHAT IT MEANS TO BE A KENSHI.
YOU WEAR A TOOL FOR KILLING PEOPLE IN YOUR BELT...
...AND YOU ACCEPT THE RISK OF GETTING KILLED YOURSELF.
THE GUYS YOU WHACKED. KUROI... SHIZUMA... EVEN HIGA. I FIGURE THEY WERE PREPARED FOR THAT.
SO I'M NOT GOING TO HATE YOU FOR TAKING THEIR LIVES. ITTŌ-RYŪ OR NOT, THEY KNEW THE RULES, PLAYED BY THEM.
BUT THERE ARE BASTARDS OUT THERE WHO DON'T.
JUST PURE MURDEROUS SCUM THAT MAKE YOU WANT TO PUKE YOUR GUTS OUT.

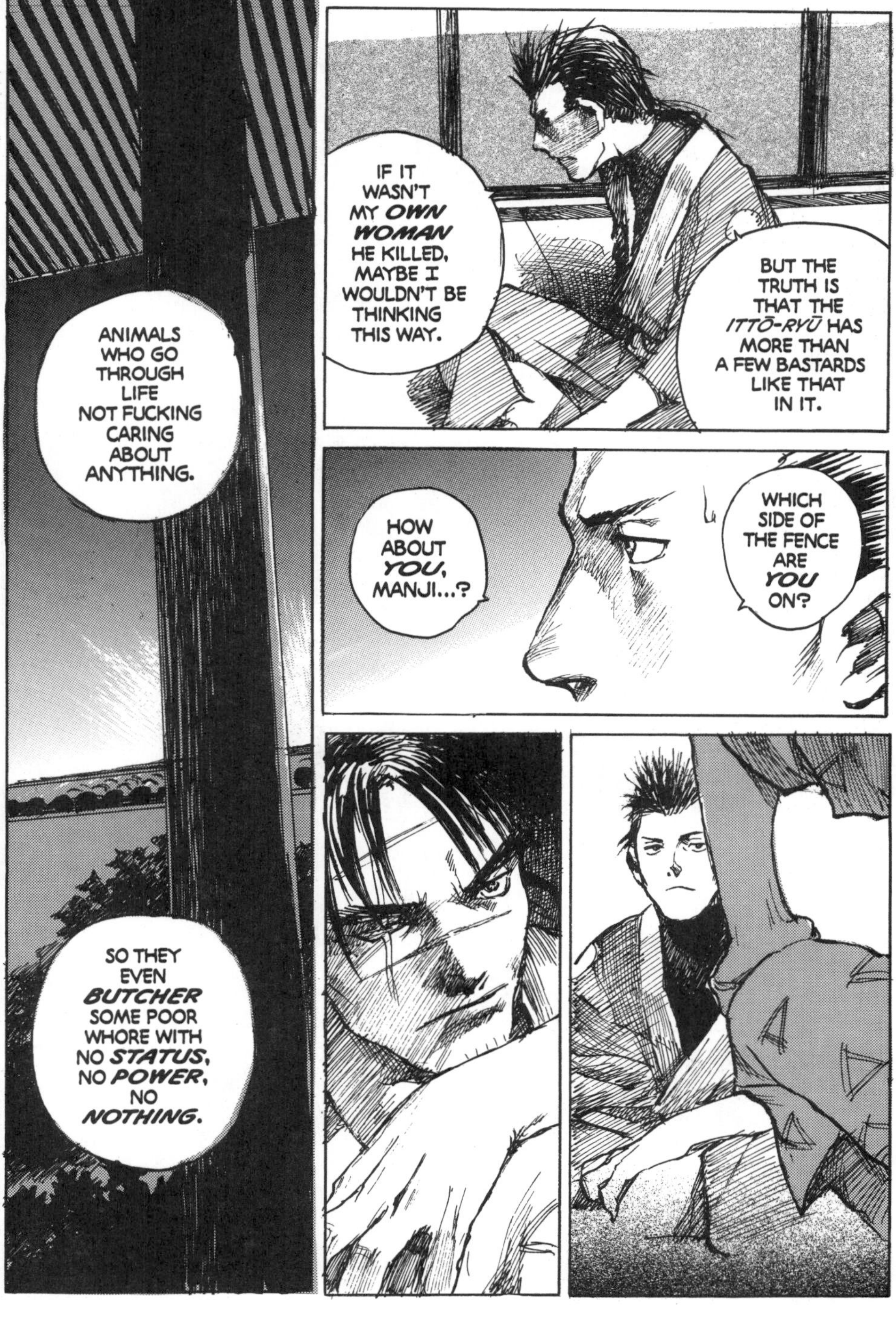
ANIMALS WHO GO THROUGH LIFE NOT FUCKING CARING ABOUT ANYTHING.
SO THEY EVEN *BUTCHER* SOME POOR WHORE WITH NO *STATUS*, NO *POWER*, NO *NOTHING*.
IF IT WASN'T MY *OWN WOMAN* HE KILLED, MAYBE I WOULDN'T BE THINKING THIS WAY.
BUT THE TRUTH IS THAT THE *ITTŌ-RYŪ* HAS MORE THAN A FEW BASTARDS LIKE THAT IN IT.
HOW ABOUT *YOU*, MANJI...?
WHICH SIDE OF THE FENCE ARE *YOU* ON?

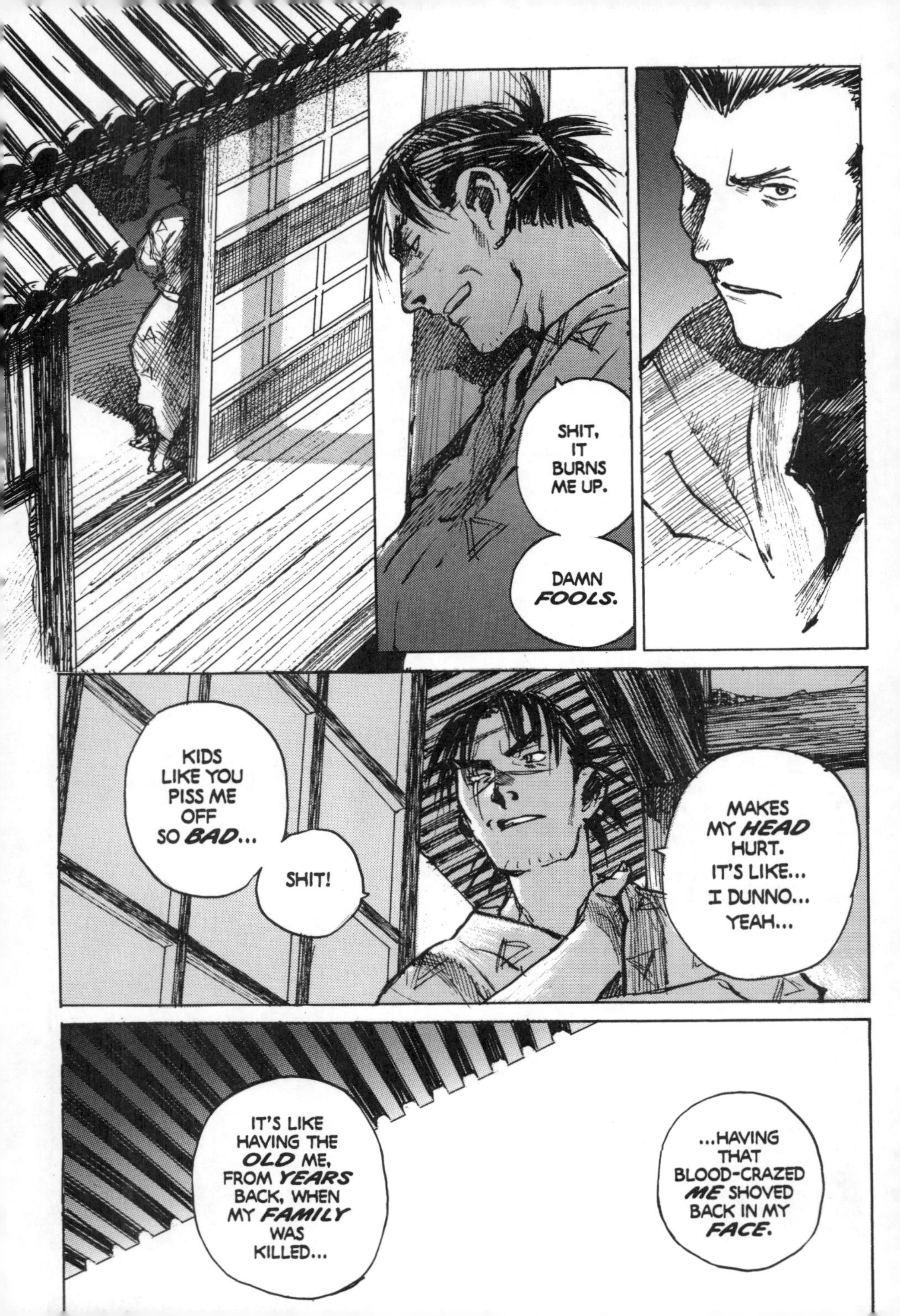
SHIT, IT BURNS ME UP.
DAMN FOOLS.
KIDS LIKE YOU PISS ME OFF SO BAD...
SHIT!
MAKES MY HEAD HURT. IT'S LIKE... I DUNNO... YEAH...
IT'S LIKE HAVING THE OLD ME, FROM YEARS BACK, WHEN MY FAMILY WAS KILLED...
...HAVING THAT BLOOD-CRAZED ME SHOVED BACK IN MY FACE.

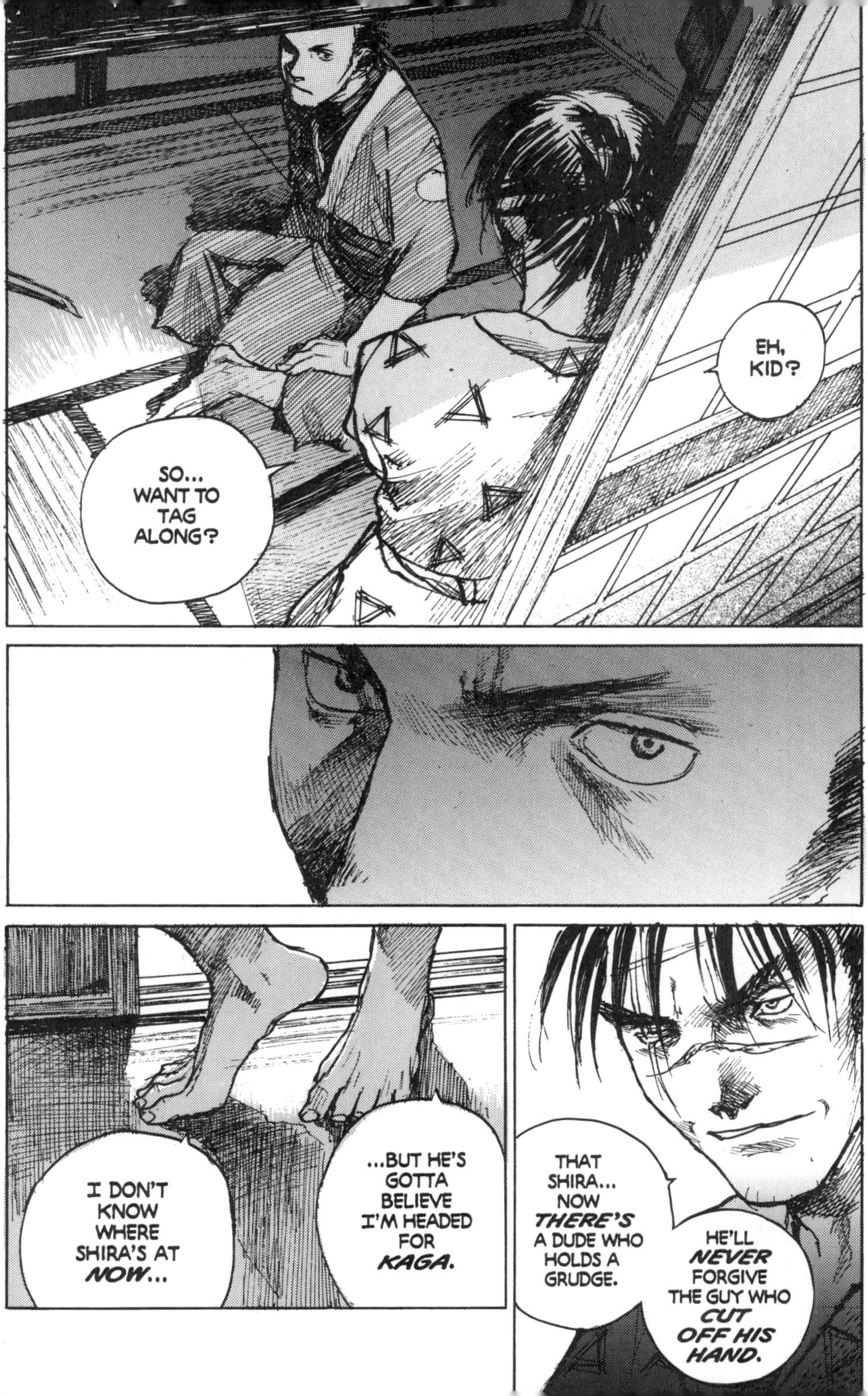
SO... WANT TO TAG ALONG?
EH, KID?
I DON'T KNOW WHERE SHIRA'S AT NOW...
...BUT HE'S GOTTA BELIEVE I'M HEADED FOR KAGA.
THAT SHIRA... NOW THERE'S A DUDE WHO HOLDS A GRUDGE.
HE'LL NEVER FORGIVE THE GUY WHO CUT OFF HIS HAND.

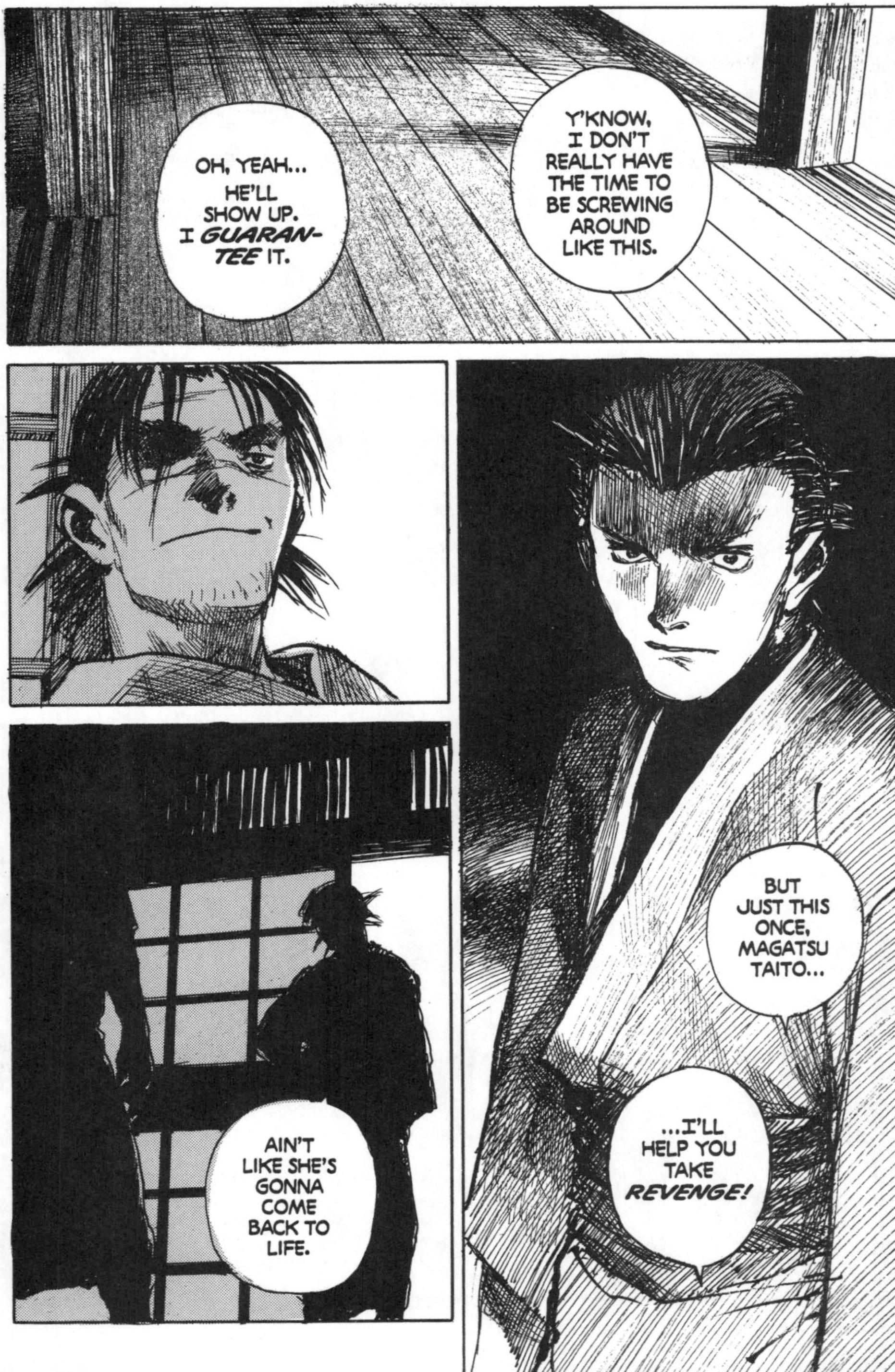
OH, YEAH... HE'LL SHOW UP. I *GUARANTEE* IT.
Y'KNOW, I DON'T REALLY HAVE THE TIME TO BE SCREWING AROUND LIKE THIS.
AIN'T LIKE SHE'S GONNA COME BACK TO LIFE.
BUT JUST THIS ONCE, MAGATSU TAITO...
...I'LL HELP YOU TAKE *REVENGE!*

GLOSSARY

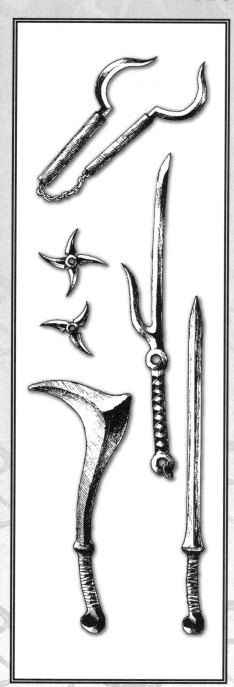

ada-uchi: an act of private vengeance, similar to 19th Century duels of honor. Such revenge was legal if approved by the proper authorities.

banshi: samurai manning a *sekisho* (checkpoint)

bugyō: a high-ranked samurai in charge of keeping the peace, with the help of the men under his command and volunteer "posse" members

dango: small balls of sweet rice paste skewered on a stick, sometimes topped with sweet bean paste or a soy sauce glaze

dōjō: a hall for martial arts training; here centers for swordsmanship

Edo: capital of pre-modern Japan, later renamed Tokyo

han: a feudal domain

Ittō-ryū: the radical sword school of Anotsu Kagehisa

Kaga: a remote feudal domain on the Japan Sea coast southwest of Edo

kenshi: a swordsman (or swordswoman), not necessarily born into the samurai caste

kessen-chu: mystical bloodworms that can heal all wounds and grant their host immortality

mon: a small coin

Mugai-ryū: sword school of the Akagi assassins; literally, "without form"

ri: unit of measurement equivalent to 3.9 kilometers (approximately 2.4 miles)

rōnin: a masterless samurai

ryo: a gold piece

sekisho: checkpoint regulating travel from Edo to other *han* (feudal domains). All travelers had to submit papers at official checkpoints along the main highways into and out of Edo.

sensei: a teacher, a master

Shingyōtō-ryū: a variety of swordsmanship

tatami: a thick, rice straw mat used as flooring in traditional Japanese households, still commonly found in at least one room of a residence even today

tegata (tsūkō tegata): official travel pass for transiting *sekisho*

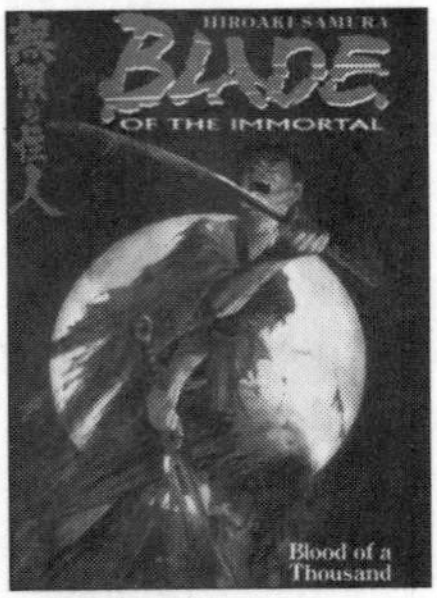
HIROAKI SAMURA
BLADE OF THE IMMORTAL
Blood of a Thousand

BLOOD OF A THOUSAND
ISBN: 1-56971-239-5 $14.95

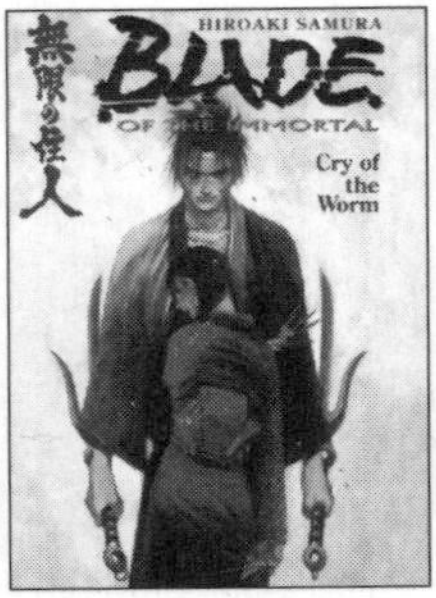
HIROAKI SAMURA
BLADE OF THE IMMORTAL
Cry of the Worm

CRY OF THE WORM
ISBN: 1-56971-300-6 $14.95

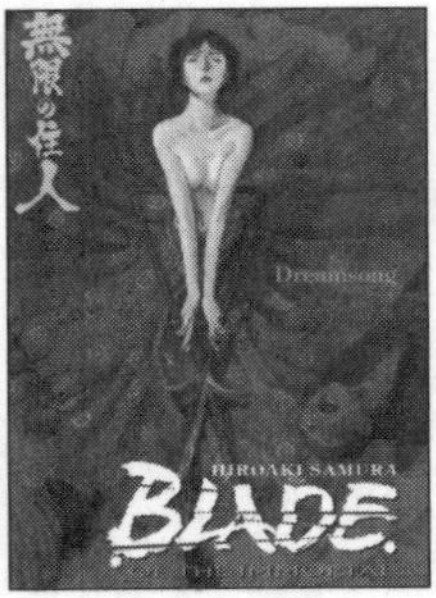
Dreamsong
HIROAKI SAMURA
BLADE

DREAMSONG
ISBN: 1-56971-357-X $14.95

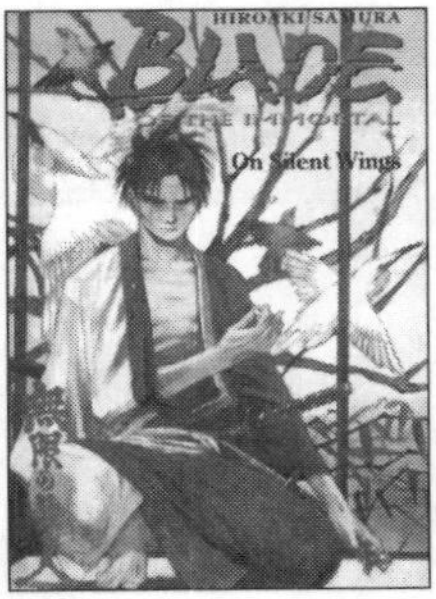
HIROAKI SAMURA
BLADE OF THE IMMORTAL
On Silent Wings

ON SILENT WINGS
ISBN: 1-56971-412-6 $14.95

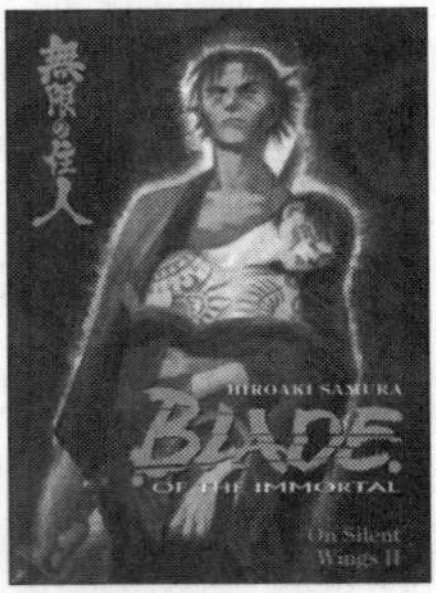
HIROAKI SAMURA
BLADE OF THE IMMORTAL
On Silent Wings II

ON SILENT WINGS II
ISBN: 1-56971-444-4 $14.95

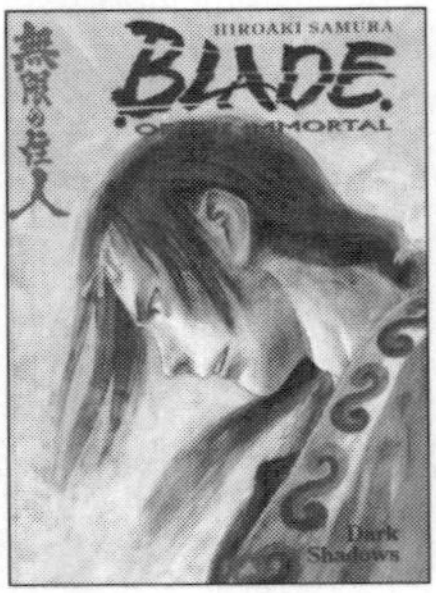
HIROAKI SAMURA
BLADE OF THE IMMORTAL
Dark Shadows

DARK SHADOWS
ISBN: 1-56971-469-X $14.95

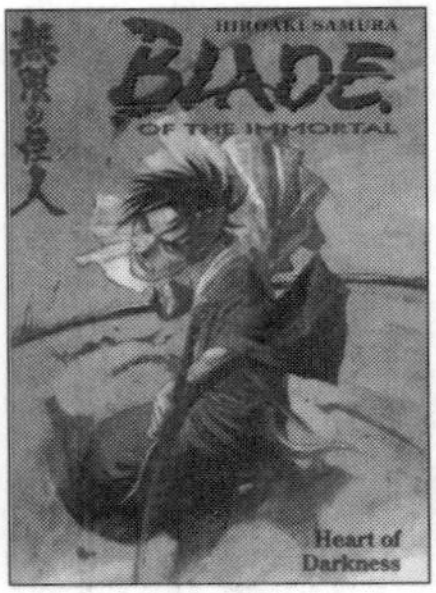
HIROAKI SAMURA
BLADE OF THE IMMORTAL
Heart of Darkness

HEART OF DARKNESS
ISBN: 1-56971-531-9 $16.95

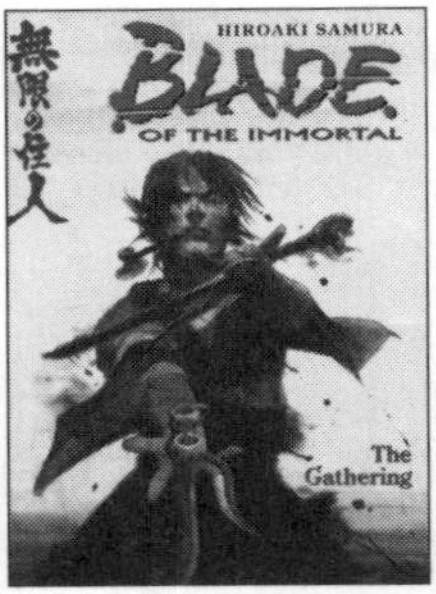
HIROAKI SAMURA
BLADE OF THE IMMORTAL
The Gathering

THE GATHERING
ISBN: 1-56971-546-7 $15.95

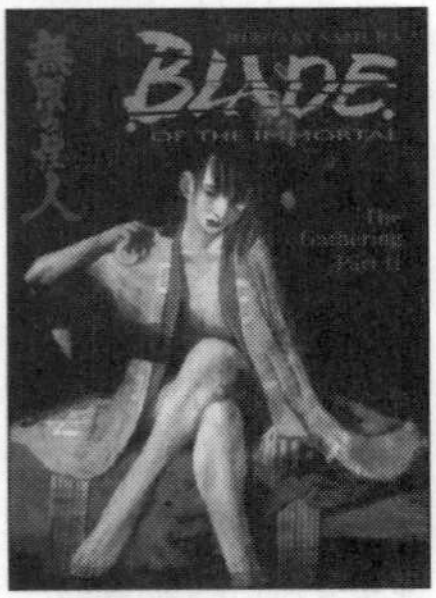
HIROAKI SAMURA
BLADE OF THE IMMORTAL
The Gathering Part II

THE GATHERING II
ISBN: 1-56971-560-2 $15.95

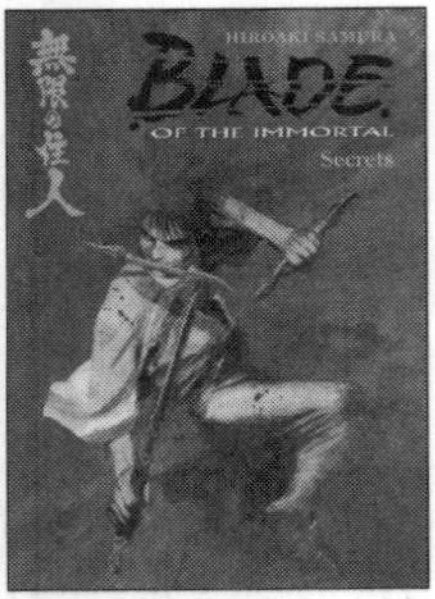
HIROAKI SAMURA
BLADE OF THE IMMORTAL
Secrets

SECRETS
ISBN: 1-56971-746-X $16.95

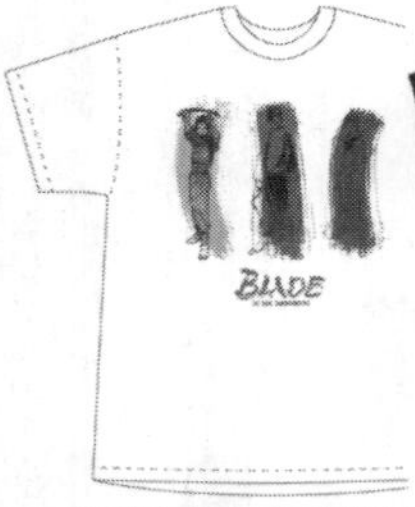
BLADE

T-SHIRT: ANOTSU, MANJI, & RIN
#11-949 $17.99/$19.99

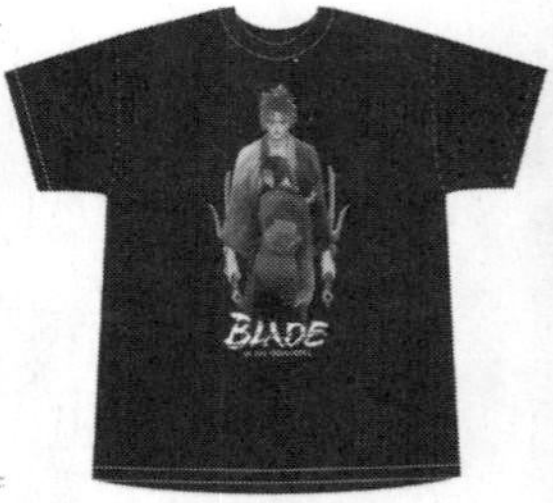
BLADE

T-SHIRT: MANJI & RIN
#11-950 $17.99/$19.99

HIROAKI SAMURA

BLADE OF THE IMMORTAL

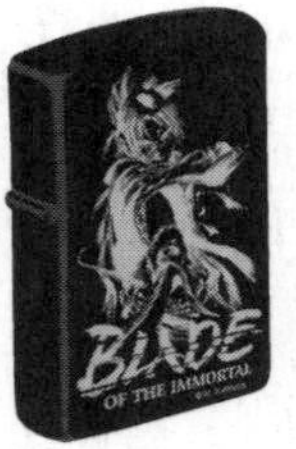
BLADE
OF THE IMMORTAL

ZIPPO® LIGHTER #2 BLACK/BRASS
#19-169 $29.95

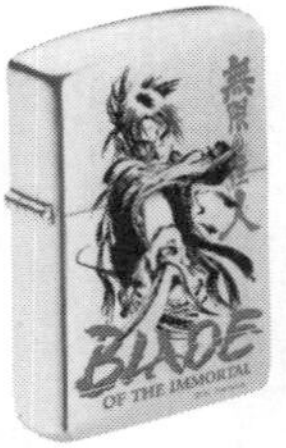
BLADE
OF THE IMMORTAL

ZIPPO® LIGHTER #1 CHROME
#19-063 $29.95

Prices and availability subject to change without notice.

To find a comics shop in your area, call 1-888-266-4226

For more information or to order direct: •On the web: www.darkhorse.com •E-mail: mailorder@darkhorse.com
•Phone: 1-800-862-0052 or (503) 652-9701 Mon.-Sat. 9 A.M. to 5 P.M. Pacific Time